CHILD AND YOUTH CARE IN THE FIELD

CHILD AND YOUTH CARE IN THE FIELD

A Practicum Guidebook

Carys Cragg

CANADIAN
SCHOLARS

Toronto | Vancouver

Child and Youth Care in the Field: A Practicum Guidebook
Carys Cragg

First published in 2020 by
Canadian Scholars, an imprint of CSP Books Inc.
425 Adelaide Street West, Suite 200
Toronto, Ontario
M5V 3C1

www.canadianscholars.ca

Library and Archives Canada Cataloguing in Publication

Title: Child and youth care in the field : a practicum guidebook / Carys Cragg.
Names: Cragg, Carys, author.
Description: Includes bibliographical references.
Identifiers: Canadiana (print) 20200221248 | Canadiana (ebook) 2020022137X |
    ISBN 9781773381787 (softcover) | ISBN 9781773381800 (PDF) |
    ISBN 9781773381794 (EPUB)
Subjects: LCSH: Social work with children—Canada—Textbooks. |
    LCSH: Social work with youth—Canada—
    Textbooks. | LCSH: Practicums—Canada—Textbooks. | LCGFT: Textbooks.
Classification: LCC HV745.A6 C73 2020 | DDC 362.70971—dc23

Page layout: S4Carlisle Publishing Services
Cover design: Liz Harasymczuk

Printed and bound in Ontario, Canada

Canadä

For Greg Saunders

CONTENTS

ACKNOWLEDGEMENTS

Many ideas, people, processes, and approvals needed to come together in order for this guidebook to emerge as it does, at this time, in this space, and in this way.

Greg Saunders: thank you for bringing forth my theoretical orientation to practice. I'm so lucky to have been taught practicum by you. Jennifer White and Daniel Scott: thank you for supporting my development as an academic, professional, and creative writer in this field. Jonny Morris and Kristy Dellebuur O'Connor: thank you for walking alongside and having faith in all of my bold projects. Julie Tilsen: thank you for your passion, mentorship, and prolific writing abilities. Amanda LaVallee: thank you for your review of Chapter 6's content and, more importantly, its intentions.

For my generous mother, Marion, who offered care for my little one while I desperately caught up to deadlines, and for my son's babysitter, Jeove, and child care centre's teachers (and for that matter, the BC NDP's child care benefits): without trust and peace of mind, I wouldn't have been able to continuously focus on such a project. And to my little one: thank you for being patient and independent while Mama wrote and edited on the couch, but most of all for showing me all my dreams can come true. Thank you to Shannon and Joanne for celebrating all the steps along the way.

Thank you Emma Melnyk and Carli Hansen at Canadian Scholars' Press for identifying a gap in the market and wanting to fill it with more Canadian-based CYC voices and educational resources. To Nick Hilton and later Jordan Ryder and Ashley Rayner: thank you for your guidance, direction, and patient response to my overly detailed lists of questions! To my peer-reviewers—both for the book proposal and full manuscript—thank you for your attention, consideration, and time.

All of the CYC student, supervisor, and faculty-instructor consultants: thank you for taking the time to so brilliantly respond to my questions! Your voices threaded throughout this guidebook make it all the more meaningful. To the scholars, professors, practice and organizational leaders who offered the insights that now open each chapter, thank you for your considered words.

At Douglas College, thank you to my CYC, YJ, and Aboriginal Stream colleagues, my CFCS administration, Elizabeth and Karla, Gretchen's support in the library, and college leadership: what a great privilege it is to be at this institution at this time and place, to be co-creating student learning experiences together. Specifically, thank you to the Educational Leave Committee: your gift of time made this book move from an idea to a manuscript.

Finally, thank you to my practicum students, past, present, and future—this book is grounded in our conversations over the years. Your openness to learn, connect theory with practice, and challenge yourselves to find a place in CYC where you wish to contribute your wonderful ways of being was this book's inspiration.

This book was written on Kwikwetlem, Sto:lo, and Katzie First Nations land, the unceded and ancestral territories of the Coast Salish Peoples. I am grateful to live and work here and vow to pay this hospitality forward by using my many locations of privilege to make more space for marginalized voices and concerns. All my relations.

PREFACE

Practicum is central to Child and Youth Care (CYC) postsecondary education. Early in their credentials, thousands of students across Canadian CYC programs go out on practicum to practise, learn, and contribute to their communities. How we facilitate that process is important. This CYC practicum guidebook is born from a place of critical reflection—assessing contexts, noticing needs, and providing options—to support students through that process. It is inspired by a number of intersecting factors.

Over the past decade or so, many aligned fields and their academic programs have adopted practicum guidebooks to support student learning. The CYC field has, for the most part, relied solely on program manuals and field guides; borrowed guidebooks from aligned fields including counselling, early childhood, social work, or general human services; translated US-based content to a Canadian context; or simply gone without.

Reflecting on my instructional practice, I noticed a gap that I desperately wished was addressed. Teaching practicum to hundreds of students in Child, Family and Community Studies (CYC, Youth Justice, and Aboriginal Stream) practicum courses since 2011, I wished for something to build upon students' learning opportunities at their site, with their supervisor, and in seminar with their peers and me. Much of CYC literature is focused on reflecting on practice; however, I wanted something tailored entirely to the practicum student's experience.

I also thought back to my experience in three CYC practicum placements at the undergraduate (2003–2004, 2004–2005) and graduate level (2007) to ground myself in the student experience, while also accumulating and examining current students' and recent graduates' voices: their experiences, their questions, their needs, their hopes, their processes, and their struggles. While each student will ultimately have a unique practicum experience—due to the thousands of intersecting factors, across contexts, roles, and communities—students also have common and anticipated experiences in practicum, ones we expect them to move through.

Meanwhile, at the 2018 20th Canadian and 12th Triennial International Child and Youth Care Conference, held in Richmond, British Columbia, attendees discussed many manifestations of its theme: Transitions and Transformations. Present at this gathering to discuss the current state of practicum in CYC were representatives from the University of Victoria, Ryerson University, Mount Royal University, Douglas College, George Brown College, University of the Fraser Valley, Durham College, Red River College, St. Clair College, MacEwan University, Lethbridge College, and more. The Practicum Panel—comprised of many of the members of the CYC Educational Accreditation Board's Research Committee—posed many questions for discussion, which inspired more questions than answers (Snell, Magnuson, McGrath, & Pauls, 2018).

- How do we keep the diversity of practicum structures built across each community while also looking for standardized language and outcomes across CYC programs?

- How do we operationalize the meaning of foundational concepts for learning, skill development, and assessment?
- How do we assess learners across contexts, who come to practicum with a spectrum of personal and professional lived experiences?
- How do we communicate expected outcomes to stakeholders (students, employers, the profession, the public)?

Further, many CYC scholars, practitioners, and governing bodies in Canada are asking and exploring pointed questions about practicum, encouraging the discussion to move forward (Ainsworth, 2016; Child and Youth Care Educational Accreditation Board of Canada Research Committee, 2016; Keough, 2016; Snell, McGrath, Pauls, & Magnuson, forthcoming).

All in all, CYC practicum is being discussed in most, perhaps all, CYC contexts: the student required to take it; the faculty-instructor who teaches it; the supervisor who generously offers their time and wisdom to mentor it; the ministries and governmental bodies setting vocational standards for it; and the researchers, boards, and associations looking into it. Practicum is everywhere. As it should be.

With the support from Douglas College's Educational Leave Committee as well as Canadian Scholars' Press's vision for more CYC educational resources in the field, informed by my educational and professional experiences in the field, I was able to write this guidebook. What follows is a resource meant to support and enhance (but not override nor subvert) the wisdom of the instructional and learning-centred pedagogy offered across Canadian CYC programs. It is an offering to the field, an educational resource to consider and blend among the many existing learning opportunities our students experience in practicum.

This guidebook's purpose and design is meant to follow the student-learner alongside their first or second practicum experience in a CYC program, applying and building upon the theory and skills accumulated thus far in typical first-year CYC courses. It is also an invitation for students to influence the field as it collectively grows, expands, and critically reflects on its presence in the lives of young people and families across all communities. Grounded with the voices of CYC students, supervisors, and faculty-instructors, this practicum guidebook offers support—support for the anxiously excited student embarking on what will likely be one of their most memorable CYC experiences, one they'll carry with them through their participation in the CYC field.

Thank you for reading.

INTRODUCTION

Welcome. Here you are, in one of your first practicum courses. You are joining thousands of students across Canada in one of Child and Youth Care (CYC) programs' core course requirements: practicum. No matter if you're arriving to this place with just the few hours of volunteer experience it took to apply to your CYC program or coming back to school to obtain your degree after 25 years of practice or anywhere in between, practicum is a place to apply, focus upon, and personalize your learning.

Each person reading this guidebook will arrive to practicum from a different position and leave in a different direction. One thing will remain central: our early practicum experiences stick with us over the years, throughout our experiences contributing to the CYC field. Why? Perhaps it's because of the intensely focused learning; perhaps because of the spectrum of emotions we experience; or perhaps because it's where we are first challenged to connect theory with practice, practice with theory.

There will be differences that are unique to you in this space, at this time, in this location. What remains the same across all Canadian CYC educational programs is that "the most important aspect of practicum learning is learning to build relationships and, in the first placement, experience the integration of classroom learning as it applies to relationships" (Ostinelli, 2015, pp. 37–38)—relationships with young people, your professional peers, your supervisor, your faculty-instructor, and yourself.

Overall, CYC practicum aims to help students learn to:

- ✓ Practice and develop skills
- ✓ Process challenges
- ✓ Receive and integrate feedback
- ✓ Connect theory with practice
- ✓ Reflect on their professional identity
- ✓ Prepare and socialize into the profession
- ✓ Struggle through complexity
- ✓ Practice and refine reflective practices
- ✓ Observe practitioners' styles
- ✓ Reflect on self and others
- ✓ Work through learning goals
- ✓ Practice skills supporting young people in their life space
- ✓ All through a supervised learning environment (Ainsworth, 2016, p. 9)

In the 35+ CYC programs, specialties, majors, and concentrations at postsecondary institutions across Canada there are common elements to practicum course descriptions, objectives, and desired outcomes. Whether you're enrolled at Red River College, Selkirk College, Fleming College, Concordia University, Mohawk College, Saskatchewan

Polytechnic, Mount Royal University, Humber College, University of Victoria, Medicine Hat College, or another program, your practicum experience will centre on the following goals:

- ✓ Develop, maintain, and strengthen relationships with children, youth, and families
- ✓ Demonstrate professional behaviour, including work habits, professional judgement, ethical decision-making, developing a professional network, and taking safety precautions to protect young people
- ✓ Develop, facilitate, and evaluate therapeutic activities and interventions, including fostering therapeutic environments
- ✓ Work effectively and collaboratively on multidisciplinary teams
- ✓ Celebrate and promote diversity, developing cultural competence, humility, and responsiveness
- ✓ Understand systems, reduce barriers, and advocate for the rights of young people across diverse sociocultural contexts
- ✓ Seek, receive, and integrate feedback and supervision to advance one's learning
- ✓ Demonstrate self-awareness, including values, biases, and an understanding of one's social location, as well as awareness of strengths and areas for improvement
- ✓ Engage in self-care and wellness strategies
- ✓ Conduct and record formal and informal observations; document and write reports
- ✓ Communicate effectively, both orally and in written formats
- ✓ Engage in reflective practice
- ✓ Integrate theoretical knowledge into practice
- ✓ Develop a professional development plan

How we accomplish these objectives will look different across roles, communities, and contexts. But we will all strive for these common goals on our journey as emerging CYC practitioners.

The purpose of this introduction—rather than jumping into Chapter 1—is to orient you, the reader, to the guidebook's purpose, pedagogical approach, structure and features, common terms, suggestions for use, and voices that inform and shape its content. Yes, you could skip this part and immerse yourself in the guidebook's main content chapters. However, orienting yourself to these foundational concepts will allow you to best understand and engage with the material that follows. Not doing so will not cause you hardship, but doing so will certainly help your learning process.

PURPOSE

The purpose of this guidebook is to offer a learning resource to accompany practicum students on the journey through their first or second practicum and its anticipated learning needs. It is similar to a textbook in the sense that it is material meant to prepare you, the student, for the course content (your practicum experience). It is dissimilar to a textbook in the sense that it is meant to be engaged as a workbook. It will guide you through a learning process. It will ask you to actively participate (reflect, respond, seek out, be challenged by) more than most textbooks will. It will build upon concepts you've recently been introduced to in your coursework (or that are soon to come).

CYC practicum has many components: prerequisite and concurrent courses, faculty-instructor guidance, experience at the practicum site, supervisor mentorship, seminar and classmate support, course syllabus and manual directions, and assignment expectations. All these components are designed to facilitate your learning in practicum.

This guidebook is here to support, enhance, and expand upon each of those learning components, especially in the times when you may not have immediate access to your faculty-instructor, supervisor, or classmates. This guidebook is here to walk alongside you and to hopefully remotely connect you to the thousands of other students in practicum right now, in spirit.

PEDAGOGICAL APPROACH

All educational resources have an implicit or explicitly stated pedagogical approach. In informal terms, this guidebook takes a no-pressure, hands-on, encouraging approach to your individual learning experience. Take what resonates with you; discard the rest. Use the activities, reflective questions, stories, consultant quotes, and practice scenarios to help your learning process. In very few future contexts will you have such focused attention on your learning and practice. Ultimately, this guidebook is an offering: a curated process of learning opportunities for students. More formally, there are a handful of guiding perspectives that frame and inform the content and structure of this guidebook's pedagogical approach.

Because of the applied nature of the practicum course, this guidebook's learning opportunities will build upon students' knowledge gained in the classroom. Following the hierarchy of Bloom's (revised) taxonomy of cognitive learning, students will be encouraged to move from *remembering* and *understanding* concepts they learned in class toward *applying*, *analyzing*, *evaluating*, and *creating*, using the concepts in class and their collective personal and professional experiences to date (Anderson & Krathwohl, 2001). Meanwhile, the continuously evolving framework for CYC praxis frames the rationale for the questions, activities, stories, and practice scenarios in this guidebook. That is, all the learning opportunities will focus on one or more aspects of *knowing* (what theories, perspectives, and lived experiences inform our practice), *doing* (how we demonstrate that practice in the life-space of young people and families), and *being* (who we are and how we show up to our practice; White, 2007).

Further, taking a less hierarchical and nonlinear approach to learning, this guidebook hopes to align with the Indigenous orientation and values described in the First Peoples Principles of Learning (First Nations Education Steering Committee, 2008). That is, it intends to support experiential and holistic learning opportunities, where learning supports the community, focuses on relationships and connectedness, recognizes the impact of one's actions, is embedded in story, takes time, and explores identity (First Nations Education Steering Committee, 2008, p. 1). At the same time, this guidebook is introduced at a time where all practitioners, students, instructors, scholars, and institutions are being invited into a process of reconciliation and decolonization. As such, we may ask ourselves: how has CYC participated in the harms of Canada's treatment of Indigenous Peoples? How has CYC participated in and maintained colonialist structures and forces? How do we resist them? How will we not replicate harm? How do we move forward in a good way?

Lastly, this guidebook takes an *integrative approach* to student learning. That is, its learning strategies are "process-oriented, experientially-based methodology which focuses on the individual learner and the needs of the learning group" (Hills, 1989, p. 23). In this approach, the group is a resource, educators are facilitators of learning opportunities, and learners are aided in their "discovery of meaning" through experience and reflection (p. 24).

All students beginning practicum will have completed or are concurrently enrolled in a few common courses. Namely, these will likely include Introduction to CYC Practice and Lifespan Development and may also include Interpersonal Communication/Helping Skills, Activity Facilitation, and Behavioural Change. Students will soon or concurrently be enrolled in courses that build upon their learning thus far, which may include Working with Families, Facilitating Groups, Indigenous Perspectives, Mental Health Practice, and more specialized courses on CYC therapeutic interventions. This guidebook intends to review and apply these prerequisite and concurrent courses, rather than introduce entirely new content. Further, the engagement in one's practicum experience, including deliberate reflection, will help prepare students for these future courses in the sense that they will bring experience, previous reflection, and critical thought. However, due to the variability of CYC programs, there will likely be gaps, repetition, or irrelevant information. It is important for you to keep this in mind, and always prioritize your faculty-instructor's guidance and your program's course content.

Since this guidebook is speaking to you, its reader, and because of the centrality of self-in-practice that grounds the CYC field, an emphasis threaded through all learning opportunities in this text will invite readers to focus on oneself and one's learning, so as to benefit the young people and families we work alongside.

But above all, this guidebook is about practicum.

STRUCTURE AND FEATURES

This guidebook is organized into three overarching sections. Setting the Stage—Chapters 1 through 5—focuses on the information, concepts, and materials students need to review in order to best prepare for and begin practicum. We will review foundational perspectives in CYC, prepare for the practicum placement process, review professional practice standards, plan to make the most of your learning opportunities, and strengthen your ability to be a reflective practitioner. In the Midst—Chapters 6 through 10—focuses on the development and application of skills, knowledge, and ways of being in CYC practice across settings. First, we will discuss diversity—the diversity of people, of our practices, and of the possibilities of CYC work. We'll review how we can facilitate therapeutic change across systems. We'll review common challenges in the practicum experience. We'll also focus on observation and report writing. The final section, Ending and Moving Forward—Chapters 11 through 13—focuses on students' closing process at the practicum site as well as with the practicum course itself. We'll reflect on wellness, attend to the ending of relationships, and encourage students to reflect on the practicum journey, while anticipating next steps: back to the classroom and working in the field. The last section of the guidebook includes a learning journal.

Within each chapter, readers can expect to see:

- ✓ CYC Competencies that each chapter's content focuses upon
- ✓ Illustrative figures and tables adapted for the practicum context, some covered in previous coursework
- ✓ Reflective questions and brainstorming activities to prompt learning, apply concepts, and encourage critical thought
- ✓ Numerous lists, Dos and Don'ts charts, and other At-a-Glance summaries
- ✓ Excerpted quotes from CYC student, supervisor, and faculty-instructor consultants
- ✓ Stories from CYC practicum students, past and present
- ✓ Discussion Questions for Practicum Seminar or Community of Practice groups
- ✓ Practice Scenarios, with practicum students at the centre

COMMON TERMS

As you will observe, the following choices have been made in terms of CYC terminology, which may or may not be familiar to you. While our programs have many names—Child and Youth Care, Child and Youth Work, Youth Worker, Child and Youth Studies, Child and Youth Care Counselling, and so on—this guidebook will use *Child and Youth Care*, abbreviated as *CYC* throughout. Similarly, we refer to ourselves in many ways—Child Care Counsellor, Youth Worker, Child and Youth Care Worker, Youth and Family Worker, and so on. This guidebook will use the term *CYC practitioner* to allow for the diversity of roles we occupy. Further, we work with young people (and their families) from early childhood through early adulthood. We use terms such as infants and toddlers, children, youth, adolescents, teens, young adults, and more. To be inclusive, for the most part, we'll use the term *young people*. Across postsecondary institutions, CYC programs name each of the three main roles in practicum slightly differently. First, there is the student, who completes practicum. Second, there is the faculty-instructor, who is the postsecondary CYC program representative, who may or may not be in charge of placing a student at a practicum site, visits the student at the practicum site, facilitates seminars at the postsecondary institution, and evaluates the student and assigns their academic grade (sometimes referred to as the faculty-supervisor or faculty-advisor). Third, there is the supervisor at the practicum site, who guides and observes the practicum student, provides formal and informal supervision, and completes performance evaluations (sometimes referred to as a mentor). In this guidebook, we will refer to these roles as *student*, *faculty-instructor*, and *supervisor*. Lastly, across Canadian CYC programs the practicum experience is referred to as practicum, internship, fieldwork, and, occasionally, service-learning or a capstone project. Here, it will be referred to as *practicum*, as, above all, practicum is about the application of what a student has been, is, and will be learning in their studies.

SUGGESTIONS FOR READERS

This guidebook's intended reader is the first- or second-year CYC student embarking on their first or second practicum experience. Faculty-instructors will also use this book to support students' learning. So too may supervisors be accessing this guidebook to guide their students through the practicum experience. As such, the following suggestions are recommended for each group.

Suggestions for Students

- Take this guidebook around with you—to seminar, to practicum, and to and from your practicum sites.
- Use this guidebook as it is intended: as a guidebook. Break it in, mark it up, take notes, flag items for later, and tear out appendices. Make it well-used.
- Do some activities, but not all of them. There are many. Flag activities and questions that you wish to come back to.
- Use what you believe will be useful for you, in your context, at this time, in this space.
- If you come across a theory, perspective, or approach you're unfamiliar with, research it. Be aware that some programs will cover some perspectives in-depth, whereas other programs will focus on other perspectives. Replace whatever theory is presented here with the relevant theory you're learning in class to ensure the learning is relevant to you.
- Keep this guidebook as you would syllabi and your favourite texts. Looking back after two or four years can show you just how much you've continued to grow.

Suggestions for Faculty-Instructors

- This guidebook attempts to speak to a typical first- or second-year practicum student in a CYC program in Canada. This is an impossible task, of course. CYC programs, course content, order, and delivery differ. Alter the expectations of this guidebook to suit your expectations of your students.

- Each practicum course will have different pre- and co-requisite courses. This will influence what student-readers of this guidebook will already know and be prepared to explore in more depth.
- Depending on your program's requirements, you may have a practicum preparation seminar, a co-occurring integration seminar, and/or post-practicum seminar. Use this guidebook's chapters to fit your program's design.
- As you assign chapters to your practicum students—individually or as a seminar group cohort—re-order chapters as they fit with your instructional design. For example, you may wish to assign Chapter 11: Wellness and Self-Care in CYC earlier in the term.
- Use, alter, or discard the seminar discussion questions as per your preference.
- Encourage your student groups to develop communities of practice apart from seminar groups and to use discussion questions there too.

Suggestions for Supervisors

- This guidebook may be helpful for the newly assigned supervisor or a supervisor who does not have a CYC credential.
- The practicum experience can vary widely, but there are foundational CYC concepts that educational institutions expect first- and second-year practicum students to learn and practise. Use this guidebook to understand what a practicum student may want to learn at your site.
- Supporting and mentoring students is your expertise. Use the features in this text—on feedback, on supervision, on facilitating change, and so on—to assist you to do what you already know how to do so well.
- While coursework and assignments are typically left to the student and faculty-instructor, your support to identify opportunities for student learning is appreciated. This guidebook may help you identify more learning opportunities, beyond students' individual goals.

VOICES THAT INFORM THIS GUIDEBOOK

There are four main sources of voices that inform this guidebook, blended to create a meaningful learning experience for the reader. These voices include: 1) typical CYC curriculum and the aligned CYC literature base; 2) CYC student, supervisor, and faculty consultants; 3) myself, a CYC practitioner, faculty-instructor, program coordinator, and author; and 4) you, the reader.

CYC Literature

As I reviewed the literature to inform each chapter of this guidebook, as well as its overall structure, I have attempted to ground its knowledge base in CYC curriculum guidelines, scholarship, research, social service delivery, and so on, within a Canadian context. To direct my review of the literature, I began with current Canadian CYC postsecondary program practicum courses: practicum curriculum guidelines, course descriptions, course syllabi, and in some cases vocational standards. As much as possible given the diversity of course delivery, this guidebook attempts to address and speak to each component of these practicum courses.

I concurrently explored CYC literature, prioritizing CYC-based resources and authors writing about practicum and/or its typical subject matter. With respect to CYC resources, I attempted to prioritize CYC-led publications, such as *Relational Child and Youth Care Practice*, the *International Journal of Child, Youth, and Family Studies*, *CYC-Net*, the *Journal of Child and Youth Care Work*, and so on. With respect to CYC authors, I attempted to prioritize stories and research written from the perspective of CYC writers: scholars and researchers, faculty, practitioners, and students. In all cases, I attempted to prioritize stories and information within a Canadian context—research conducted in Canada, description of practice or practicum stories based in Canada, content derived from Canadian CYC educational and social service programs, and so on and so forth. Because there is little primary research available on CYC practicum in Canada (or elsewhere), I tried to balance CYC practicum stories with research on practicum from other aligned human service fields, including education, counselling, social work, and psychology. I also use North American CYC initiatives (see Appendices), in part because many Canadian provinces have adopted them and/or our CYC leaders were a part of their creation.

CYC Consultants

As a way to 1) ground the material I present throughout this guidebook, 2) connect its ideas immediately to the practicum experience, and 3) help the reader to attach to voices other than my own and other authors' summarized work, I offer student, supervisor, and faculty-instructor consultant quotes sprinkled throughout the text. I have followed the model Tilsen (2013, 2018) used for her youth work practice texts—*Therapeutic Conversations with Queer Youth* and *Narrative Approaches to Youth Work*—where she integrated her youth work consultants into the content of her texts. All consultants were asked questions about their first and second practicum placement in their CYC program, or were asked about supporting students through that experience.

These consultants include 12 current students and recent graduates of CYC diploma and degree programs, 8 practitioners supervising CYC students in practicum, and 7 faculty-instructors teaching and coordinating practicum across Canada. Most, but not all, are currently located in Metro Vancouver's lower mainland. Across all consultants, representation attempts to be as diverse as the field in terms of age, gender, ethnicity and cultural heritage, citizenship, years practising in CYC, and spectrum of experience across CYC settings and service-delivery, along with professional and personal lived experiences. Their profiles are described in Appendix A: Guidebook Consultants, where they were asked to share their name, gender, ethnic and cultural background, location, relevant CYC practicum experience, and what inspires them about their work. Flip now to Appendix A to become acquainted with them.

Myself

Finally, there is me, the author of this guidebook. If someone else wrote this text, it would look different: concepts would be described differently, chapters would be emphasized differently, different questions and activities would be offered, and different people and literature would be consulted. As any text is as unique as its creator, understanding that creator at the outset is important.

I am faculty in Child and Youth Care at Douglas College, based in Coquitlam, British Columbia. I am co-coordinator of the CYC degree program; past coordinator of the Aboriginal Child, Family and Community Studies Stream; and have been teaching practicum in CYC, Youth Justice, and the Aboriginal Stream since 2011. It is my most favourite course to teach. As a faculty-instructor, I prefer that my role be understood as curating meaningful learning experiences, rather than being an expert at the front of the class. I hold a BA (2005) and MA (2008) in CYC from the University of Victoria (completing three practicum placements, mainly in educational settings), as well as a number of post-graduate clinical counselling certificates. Since 2002, I've worked in educational, residential, and community-based settings in child and youth mental health, outreach counselling, child welfare, crisis response, school consultation, student advising, program coordination, and quality assurance roles. I'm a Registered Clinical Counsellor, a member of the CYC Association of British Columbia, and a recent volunteer with the Downtown Eastside Writers' Collective and Roots of Empathy programs.

My professional essays, book reviews, and research articles have appeared in *Canadian School Counsellor*, *Insights into Clinical Counselling*, *Relational CYC Practice*, and the *International Journal of Children's Spirituality*. I've written about theories of change, translating theory into practice, closing practices, journal writing, grief and loss, higher education, and improving practice. My first book, *Dead Reckoning*, tells the story of my experience of surviving violent crime and years later engaging in a restorative justice program. I speak to postsecondary and non-profit agencies on its themes. I like to read, and I love to write.

My cultural heritage descends primarily from Scotland and England, with familial threads arriving to Canada a number of generations ago from Scotland, England, Germany, and Algeria, settling on the traditional and unceded territory of the Coast Salish Peoples. I've been raised, educated, and have practised CYC in Western Canada, and I currently live with my young son along the river in Port Coquitlam, British Columbia, on Katzie, Kwikwetlem, and Sto:lo First Nations' land.

I hope that these biographical details help inform you as to who is communicating to you throughout this guidebook.

You

Each reader of a text will make meaning of it in their own way. Depending on thousands of factors—social location, life experiences, time, and so on—you will arrive at this information differently. You will take it forward differently. Take these chapters, ideas, activities, and stories into your own context and bring them forward in some way that makes sense to you, at this time, and in this place. It is only an offering. It is up to you what you do with the information.

Point of View

Lastly, you will notice that, throughout this guidebook's pages, I use a number of pronouns. In first person, I will use *we* and *us* when referring to you (that is, you, the individual student or collective group of CYC students) and me (practitioner/faculty/author) within the CYC profession. In second person, I will use *you* when referring directly to you (the individual student or group of students). In third person, I will use *he*, *she*, and *they* when I am telling stories of practicum students from CYC literature or my instructional experience.

Most frequently, I write as *we*, as in, we in Child and Youth Care, the collective group of students, practitioners, supervisors, scholars, researchers, and leaders that form this group. I do not intend to speak *for* other people in this diverse group; rather, I intend to speak as *part of* the group. While this choice of pronoun is uncommon, I uphold its importance for this context: welcoming emerging practitioners into the CYC field. In this way, I hope that, as a reader, you may be able to imagine us as a community of practice, encouraging each other to reflect on our practice. Why? Because we're all in this together.

Welcome.

FEEDBACK AND IMPROVEMENT

The context of CYC practicum is continually changing, along with its structure, defined outcomes, assessments, and expectations. Future editions of this guidebook will reflect those changes. Feedback is welcomed and encouraged. It can be sent to: craggc@douglascollege.ca.

PART I
Setting the Stage

CHAPTER 1

Your Theoretical Orientation to CYC Practice

Competencies for Professional Child and Youth Work Practitioners				
Professionalism	Cultural and Human Diversity	Applied Human Development	Relationship and Communication	Developmental Practice Methods
Awareness of the Profession Professional Development and Behaviour Personal Development and Self Care		Practice Methods Sensitive to Development and Context	Characteristics of Helping Relationships Relationship Development	

Good theories help us to think and act in ways that go beyond superficial or taken-for-granted understandings about the world and help us to imagine new ways of going on together. To me, this is the hallmark of a CYC professional—someone who can draw on ideas and frameworks of meaning to help make sense of things in thoughtful, useful, and culturally relevant ways. Good theories help us to see anew. They open up space for new possibilities. They introduce a useful pause or stutter in our habitual ways of thinking, and expose the ways that history has shaped us, and in some cases, erased us. Theories serve as little reminders that things might be thought otherwise.

    —Jennifer White, Professor and former Director,
    School of Child and Youth Care, University of Victoria

Everything you see unfolding in front of you is connected to what happened behind you and all around you at that moment and for years prior. Whatever you see in front of you is already connected to theory; you can find that connection if you make sure you look behind yourself and all around yourself;

both in space and in time, whenever something you see in front of yourself tries to pretend to be the only game in town.

> —Kiaras Gharabaghi, Associate Professor and Director,
> School of Child and Youth Care, Ryerson University

Call it a theoretical orientation to Child and Youth Care (CYC) practice. A framework for practice. A practice philosophy. A worldview that guides our understanding of and relation to young people and the work we do alongside and in collaboration with them. As students in CYC programs, you've been introduced to new language, ideas, and examples of practice that have common philosophical underpinnings, a foundation of values and assumptions that guide our work. As you complete your credential, you will layer this orientation with experiences, theories, conversations, reflections, and more. In practicum, you have an opportunity to intentionally engage in a learning environment where you can explore the synthesis of these theories, observe them in a practice environment, and come to a greater depth of awareness as to what CYC practitioners do and what informs their practice. This synthesis—of theory and practice—guides our first chapter as you enter into your practicum experience. After all, we need to remind ourselves of why we're here and set the stage for what will come. It will be your challenge to attempt to articulate your own theoretical orientation to your practice, knowing that you will continue to do so long after this course has concluded.

WHAT IS CHILD AND YOUTH CARE

What is CYC? What is a CYC practitioner? A simple, yet complex question. Consider these responses:

- Responding to the needs of young people in their environment…
- Facilitating therapeutic change alongside young people in their context…
- Caring for children and youth…
- Promoting the optimal development of young people throughout our communities…

Child and Youth Care has and will continue to be informed by an interdisciplinary tradition. We meet young people "where they're at," and so it should not be surprising that we draw upon multiple fields of professional practice and scholarship to describe and define who we are and what we do. The Council of Canadian Child and Youth Care Associations (n.d.) states,

> Child and youth care practitioners work with children, youth and families with complex needs. They can be found in a variety of settings such as group homes and residential treatment centres, hospitals and community mental health clinics, community-based outreach and school-based programs, as well as in private practice and juvenile justice

programs. Child and youth care workers specialize in the development and implementation of therapeutic programs and planned environments and the utilization of daily life events to facilitate change. At the core of all effective child and youth care practice is a focus on the therapeutic relationship; the application of theory and research about human growth and development to promote the optimal physical, psycho-social, spiritual, cognitive, and emotional development of young people toward a healthy and productive adulthood; and a focus on strengths and assets rather than pathology. (para. 2)

Many scholars add to this description. White (2011) states, "child and youth care has evolved into a unique field of practice that promotes young people's flourishing by engaging with children and youth in their social contexts. It emphasizes strengths-based, relational, collaborative, socially just, and empowering practices" (p. 33). Anglin (2001) characterizes CYC as focused on young people's growth and development, their competence (not pathology), and the totality of their functioning, where CYC practice occurs within young people's life-space and involves "the development of therapeutic relationships" (para. 8). Garfat (2012) describes relational Child and Youth Care practice as the "joining together that creates the in-between between us," where we see engagement, connection, and being together that is "co-created and mutually formed" and "we find the context for healing" (pp. 11–12). Meanwhile, Burns (2006) reminds us of Child and Youth Care's interest in the therapeutic milieu, calling attention to the therapeutic environments where we intentionally facilitate change. In these spaces, we create relationships and respond relationally to develop opportunities for growth, learning, change, and healing to occur.

Take a moment and recall your Introduction to Professional Child and Youth Care (or similarly titled) course. Recall being presented with numerous ideas, practices, theories, and approaches. Remember what resonated. What spoke to you? What made you feel proud and excited to be part of this field? Now ask yourself: what does Child and Youth Care mean to you?

_____

_____

Now, think of your upcoming practicum placement (or a recent volunteer or work agency, if your placement has not yet been confirmed). Consider the population it serves, the programs it offers, its mandate, its multidisciplinary teams. Ask yourself: what do you think Child and Youth Care means to your upcoming practicum agency?

> You think you're not going to remember everything that you've learned, but then once you're in the actual situation, it all comes back.
> —Trina, CYC Student

_____

_____

In understanding how the present moment has come to be—that is, your practicum placement, this practicum course—it is important to be reminded of where we've come from. Let's turn our attention to a brief history of CYC to connect that history to the current environment that we find ourselves in and are learning about in practicum.

A BRIEF HISTORY OF CYC

As you have learned directly in your professional practice courses or indirectly in your lifespan development, activities, interpersonal communication, and other courses, CYC has a long history of engaging with young people in their life-spaces to promote optimal development. As the field has evolved to meet young people where they're at and respond to the social conditions around them, our theories and approaches to those circumstances have changed. What we now consider to be fundamental to CYC scholarship and practice is continually changing, just as it always has and will continue to do. What we consider and describe as essential to our CYC identity is up for debate, and we encourage you, during your early practicum experiences, to critically approach, evaluate, and determine whether or not that description is satisfactory to you, through your experience of your work with young people. Then, take that hard work and compel the field to move forward. It is through you, in this practicum, combined with all other CYC scholars and practitioners doing their good work right now, in these spaces and communities that the field will shift, morph, and move forward. What sits with you as reflective of our field of practice? What doesn't? What will you do to contribute to the field? This practicum experience you are preparing for (or just beginning) is part of that work. We look forward to where you take it.

While adults, mentors, healers, Elders, and so on have supported young people as long as people have existed, it's important to consider how our field has formally developed. This includes the educational programs, scholarship, and practice settings that have defined, supported, and informed CYC practice. Supporting young people in their life-spaces—on the street, in and outside of educational settings, in residential homes, and elsewhere—has been influenced by socioeconomic conditions, cultural shifts, technologies, local and world events over time, just as all professions have and will be.

We can look to long-time practitioners, scholars, and faculty in the CYC field to learn its history and how that relates to the present. Charles and Garfat (2009), for example, summarize a number of concurrent movements over the past few hundred years, including the "orphanages, industrial and training schools, residential schools, and community based recreational services, [and residential youth homes and shelters]... in North America," where practitioners needed to respond to the needs of the young people in those environments (p. 19). Freeman (2013) similarly reviewed "the roots of child and youth care work as a distinct field in North America... traced through the development of institutional homes of the 1700s, camps and clubs of the early 1900s following the industrial revolution and growing immigration, and contexts of residential care, hospitals, and juvenile justice programs... [that were] focused on the unique needs of young people and shared the common factor of promoting their optimal development" (pp. 101–102). Charles and Garfat (2009) also highlight that many of these programs were developed to respond to shifting conditions and demographics—such as poverty and immigration—along with colonialist and deficit-based worldviews; they underscore "the roots of the profession were very ethnocentric, in that the organizations from which it grew tended to reflect the values and beliefs of the Anglo-Saxon elites of North America," where many organizations were "often oppressive in their application of a 'right' way to help children and families" (p. 19). Likewise, many other aligned professions have also developed in these contexts.

Let's consider the practicum placement that you are about to begin or have just begun. (If you're not in a practicum placement yet, consider your current CYC workplace or most recent volunteer experience.) Where are you placed? A school, a group home, a day treatment program, a temporary shelter, a drop-in youth centre? What is the history of the program, service, organization, and role of which you are now a part? Try to trace its history through time. Ask questions, make some educated guesses, and think about not just the past few years a specific program has existed but also the influencing systems, institutions, and organizations that have shaped it into what it is today. It did not appear from nowhere.

- You may be a practicum student shadowing a youth worker at a residential group home for adolescent girls. Ask yourself, how did it come to be that children were cared for in this way: in a home, away from their families, in this arrangement? What organizations have provided this care over time?

- You may be a practicum student supervised by a recreational youth program manager at a youth drop-in centre, co-located at a municipality's recreational community centre. Or you may be a mentor at a Big Brothers and Big Sisters, or a child care worker at a Boys' and Girls' Club or YM/WCA program centre. Why does this specialized programming exist? What is the history of this organization?

- You may be a practicum student working alongside a neighbourhood house assistant, child and family counsellor, or other support worker at an elementary school. Or you may be a practicum student supervised by a number of youth workers at an alternative school program. How did these roles come to be? How have elementary and secondary educational institutions been organized over time? Whose needs do they meet and for what purpose?

Sometimes we can go straight to our agency or organization's website to find out the history of the program and service. Sometimes we have to do some more digging. Sometimes we can ask our supervisors, community Elders, or other leaders and keepers of historical knowledge. Do this, then explore some more. However you go about finding this information—through people or documents—it is important to know the history of where you are practising, in part to understand how that impacts the present environment.

CYC GUIDING EDUCATIONAL AND PRACTICE FRAMEWORKS

CYC programs are guided by overarching educational and practice frameworks that evolve over time and will continue to do so. As a field, we have always been concerned not only with the knowledge we have and the skills we practise, but also who we are: the unique

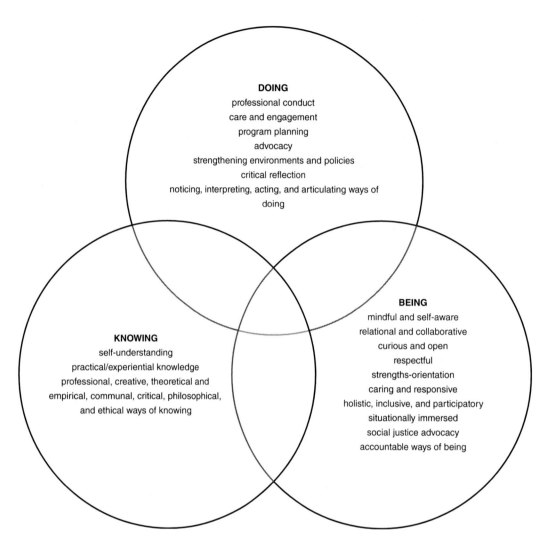

Figure 1.1: CYC Praxis: Knowing, Doing, and Being

Adapted from White, J. (2007). "Knowing, doing and being in context: A praxis-oriented approach to child and youth care." *Child and Youth Care Forum, 36*, p. 231.

selves we bring to our work in relationship with young people, their families, in the communities we find ourselves in. Figure 1.1: CYC Praxis: Knowing, Doing, and Being, and Figure 1.2: CYC Praxis: Web of Influences illustrate one such framework that allows us to see the interconnected, interwoven, and interdependent nature of our complex practice.

Notice, in Figure 1.1, the various ways we can embody knowing, doing, and being. Notice, in Figure 1.2, the complex and continually changing contexts we operate within. White (2007) introduced the concept of praxis to Child and Youth Care in this way, as a way of understanding CYC practice, where she defines "praxis as ethical, self-aware, responsive and accountable action" (p. 226), which is "seen as the active integration of knowing, doing and being" (p. 231). Practicum focuses on this active integration. Notably, the praxis model expands our conceptualization of practice toward a more "social, moral and political" space and understanding necessary for our times, one that is a "more contextually rich, theoretically informed, explicitly moral, and dynamic view of CYC practice" (White,

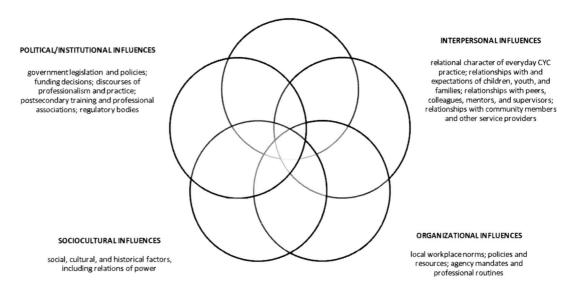

COMMUNITY INFLUENCES

local knowledge; understandings and expectations; local service delivery context; media influences

POLITICAL/INSTITUTIONAL INFLUENCES

government legislation and policies; funding decisions; discourses of professionalism and practice; postsecondary training and professional associations; regulatory bodies

INTERPERSONAL INFLUENCES

relational character of everyday CYC practice; relationships with and expectations of children, youth, and families; relationships with peers, colleagues, mentors, and supervisors; relationships with community members and other service providers

SOCIOCULTURAL INFLUENCES

social, cultural, and historical factors, including relations of power

ORGANIZATIONAL INFLUENCES

local workplace norms; policies and resources; agency mandates and professional routines

Figure 1.2: CYC Praxis: Web of Influences

Adapted from White, J. (2007). "Knowing, doing and being in context: A praxis-oriented approach to child and youth care." *Child and Youth Care Forum, 36*, p. 242.

2007, pp. 230–231). Let's focus in on ourselves (Figure 1.1) and the context (Figure 1.2) to understand how this can help us think about our practicum experience. Practicum is often where we witness how this all comes together.

As you anticipate your practicum placement, consider the questions in Figure 1.3. In or around the circles, jot down your first thoughts. If you have not been placed just yet, think about a recent CYC work or volunteer experience or an agency/program where you'd like to complete a practicum. If you're struggling to respond to any of these questions, that's okay; they're here to generate conversation and reflection. Keep moving, and in no time you will have some responses. Remaining in a state of curiosity, complexity, and uncertainty are good CYC skills to master.

Central to our understanding of CYC praxis are our guiding theories, perspectives, and approaches; the characteristics of CYC practitioners; and how we understand ourselves in CYC practice. We use all these factors to develop our own theoretical orientation to practice. These are the next focus of this chapter.

CYC GUIDING THEORIES, PERSPECTIVES, AND APPROACHES TO PRACTICE

As this field has developed, we have come to know our practice and our approach to it through a number of common perspectives, which include relational, developmental,

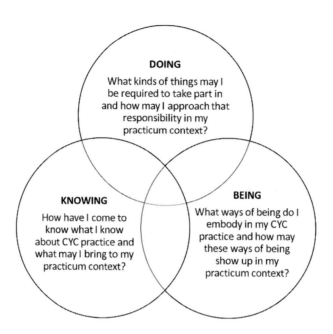

Figure 1.3: CYC Praxis: Applying Knowing, Doing, and Being

Adapted from White, J. (2007). "Knowing, doing and being in context: A praxis-oriented approach to child and youth care." *Child and Youth Care Forum, 36,* p. 231.

> Relating stories and experiences to underline the theories is important as it helps the theory come alive.
> —Rose, CYC Practicum Supervisor

strengths-based, contextual, and social justice practice in the life-spaces of young people, their families, and communities. These terms should not be new to you, and they certainly do not encapsulate nor represent the entirety of the current discussion(s) on CYC practice. In fact, part of why you're in practicum is to observe and interact with these perspectives in CYC and do your part to determine, alter, add, remove, and make meaning of what has and will guide our collective practice forward.

Here, we will review each common theory, perspective, and approach to CYC practice and encourage you to reflect on your understanding of these ideas as well as how you may anticipate experiencing these ideas come into being at your upcoming practicum setting. If you have not been assigned a practicum setting, consider a past CYC experience. If you have not yet begun your practicum placement but know where you will be placed, acknowledge that you will not know for certain. These activities are designed to initiate this reflection, not for finding a "correct" answer.

Relational Practice

CYC *relational practice* focuses not only on the relationship developed between the practitioner and young person—which takes into consideration connection and disconnection; beginning and ending; and the activities, conversations, and challenges that make up that relationship—but also the ways in which we relate relationally—generating and making meaning of moments together. We do things in collaboration with and alongside young people, as opposed to "to" and "for" them. We consider young people and the relationships in their lives, both in their immediate environments and across environments and systems, including relationships with land, culture, and over time.

Think back to the classes in which you directly and indirectly learned about relational practice. Or consider going to your notes, readings, assignments, or texts from that classwork. Ask: what does relational practice mean to you? How may you see relational practice occurring at your practicum setting?

<hr>

<hr>

Holistic Development

CYC practice focuses on the *holistic development* of the young person. Attuned to the physical, social, emotional, cognitive, sexual, identity, vocational, moral, cultural, spiritual (and more) development of the young person, CYC practitioners utilize developmental theory to help understand, plan for, intervene, and reflect on young people and our work with

> We use recreation to build relationships, skills, and empowerment.
> —Chris, CYC Practicum Supervisor

them. Concurrently, CYC attempts to resist normative language and the rigid boxes that developmental theories have created and currently create. If a developmental theory and/or its effects are not helpful nor ethical and do not reflect the reality of how young people make sense of their world, we discard it and look for something that is.

Think back to the classes in which you directly and indirectly learned about developmental theory. Or consider going to your notes, readings, assignments, or texts from that classwork. Ask: what does developmental practice mean to you? How may you see developmental practice occurring at your practicum setting?

<hr>

<hr>

Strengths-Based Perspective

CYC practitioners work from a *strengths-based perspective*, which honours, acknowledges, and holds up young people's lived experiences as central, significant, and worthy of attention. First and foremost, we view young people through a lens of capacity, competence, ability, resilience, courage, interest, skills, connection, survival, agency, and strength. A strengths-based perspective, as opposed to deficits, abnormality, less-than, pathology, and risk, reframes the questions we ask about young people, the ways in which we understand them, and the work we do with them and on their behalf. Through a strengths-based perspective, we see every opportunity and interaction with young people as a chance to develop strength, working from a place of strength. Where there is conflict, we focus on repair. Where there is disconnection, we focus on connection. Where there is loss, we focus on restoration. Where there is adversity, we focus on agency. Where there is oppression, we focus on resistance. Where there is despair, we focus on hope. We do this intentionally, not to ignore or be naive to challenge but to see strengths that survive alongside, emerge from, and exist despite difficulty.

> Look at the strengths behind it. I would go in and think these parents are here to see their kids and that's already something. Try to find those things when it seems negative.
>
> —Heather, CYC Student

Think back to the classes in which you directly and indirectly learned about strengths-based perspectives. Or consider going to your notes, readings, assignments, or texts from that classwork. Ask: what does a strengths-based perspective mean to you? How may you see strengths-based practice occurring at your practicum setting?

Contextual and Systems Theory

Often, one of our first introductions to *contextual and systems theory* and practice begins by drawing upon ecological systems theory, developed by Bronfenbrenner (1979), to understand the young person situated in environments, relationships, and systems that influence their development and lived experience over their lifetime. Where the individual young person is at the centre—with their individual demographics and social location, knowledge, attitude, disposition, characteristics, health status, and ways of being centered—we then move to a series of concentric circles. We then understand that young person in their immediate environments (microsystem)—family, school, neighbourhood, home, shelter, community centre, place of worship, and so on—which is often where we find CYC practitioners. We then notice the relationships between and across the young person's immediate environments (mesosystem), allowing us to focus on, for example, interactions between family and school. Next, we have the contexts that the child is not part of physically, but which nonetheless influence their lives (exosystem) and through which we can see how, for example, a parent's workplace rules and regulations impact a young person, or how legal policy, social services, mass media, and local industry affect them too. The outermost circle includes the social and cultural values, attitudes and ideologies, economic and political systems, social conditions and movements, and so on (macrosystem). Meanwhile, we understand all these layered and interconnected systems over time (chronosystem), the life events that occur for individuals over time as well as the sociohistorical conditions that occur over time. The existence of or change in one area (e.g., war, job loss, birth of a sibling, illness, change in political party, and so on) impacts all others, no matter how big or small that influence may be. That impact will be experienced differently, depending on when these events or conditions occur during a young person's life.

As CYC practitioners, we see the limitless spaces, factors, and systems in which we may practise to create therapeutic change for a young person. Contextual and systems theories can help us link development to context, the relationships among contexts, the strengths and challenges within contexts, and the injustices embedded within the systems and structures that young people are influenced by and how we may go about changing that. While CYC practice occurs directly with young people and their families in their communities, contextual and systems theory and practice also helps us see that CYC practice can occur in program design, evaluation, policy development and analysis, and institutional change.

> Bronfenbrenner's systems theory has a lot of intricate details that go into it but when you see the microsystem and what kind of policies and programs are affecting the child's life—when you see that happen in front of you it makes a lot of sense.
> —Margaret, CYC Student

Think back to the classes in which you directly and indirectly learned about contexts and systems. Or consider going to your notes, readings, assignments, or texts from that classwork. Ask: what does contextual and systems theory mean to you? How may you understand the contextual and systems influences occurring at your practicum setting?

Social Justice

CYC practitioners are committed to *social justice*, changing the unjust systems, processes, and environments that young people and practitioners find themselves in. We advocate alongside young people and empower them to do so themselves. We encourage young people to fully participate in decisions that affect them and the programs in which they are involved. We consider the rights of young people and the responsibilities we have for their care. We facilitate and appreciate diversity, and consider young people experts of their lived experience in the world. We work with anti-oppressive approaches so that we may shift the very institutions and practices we are part of. We commit to our own self- and collective-awareness regarding the historical and current institutions and structures that have and continue to advance colonialist, neoliberal, Euro-Western ideologies, which privilege some people and oppress others. We view care as justice and justice as care.

> We just went to pick up a youth who was getting kicked out of their house and things were kind of in crisis mode. We just took him out for sushi and I feel like it was an aha moment. I realized that the work is complicated but it really is simple moments like these that are the work. It's the conduit for them to get the support that they need.
> —Jenn, CYC Student

Think back to the classes in which you directly and indirectly learned about social justice. Or consider going to your notes, readings, assignments, or texts from that classwork. Ask: what does social justice mean to you? How may you see social justice occurring at your practicum setting?

Life-Space

All of CYC practice occurs in the *life-space* of young people, which acknowledges that we meet young people and their families in their communities "where they are at"—developmentally, physically, relationally, geographically, spiritually, and so on. We work within the daily goings-on—rituals, routines, activities, interactions, conflicts, and challenges—that occur where young people are experiencing their lives. This could be in their home, on the street, at school, at a program they attend, or going to and from these environments. We do not expect them to speak our professional language. We speak theirs. We do not artificially require them to leave environments in which they exist. We go to them. We meet them where they are.

Think back to the classes in which you directly and indirectly learned about how and why CYC practice occurs in the life-spaces of young people. Or consider going to your notes, readings, assignments, or texts from that classwork. Ask: what does life-space practice mean to you? How may you see practice occurring in the life-spaces of young people at your practicum setting?

It is not enough to simply adopt the taken-for-granted theories, perspectives, and approaches of our profession; we must critically evaluate the theories that we work with to guide our practice. There is no better place to deconstruct theory than in practicum. In fact, White (2011) asks, "who, for example, can argue against strengths-based practices, inclusion, best interests of the child, collaboration, or social justice?" She writes, "where agreement breaks down and cracks start to show is when we try to decide on the meanings of these abstract principles and attempt to figure out what enacting and embodying them might look like within actual, local contexts" (p. 37). Tilsen (2018) offers a list of questions that can help us identify assumptions, gaps, and effectiveness behind each theory (and approach) we work with, where we can ask:

> How does this model or theory explain young people? How does it expect you to act in your work? How does it expect young people to act with you? Who is considered to have knowledge and expertise? What are the effects of this practice on youth? What is valued in this model or theory? What is devalued or disvalued? (p. 42)

> We can use theory to understand his past trauma history, and put his behaviour into context using a trauma-informed approach.
> —Farah, CYC Practicum Supervisor

These questions may also lead us to consider: how are our common CYC perspectives not enough? Not enough to describe our work? Not enough to capture young people's experience of the world? Not enough of a vision to move forward? Not enough to create radical change? What else may you include as essential to our work?

In the space here, list some of the theories, perspectives, and approaches you have been introduced to in your course work and other learning experiences that you believe are essential to your understanding of CYC practice. What do these perspectives mean to you? How may you see this perspective embodied in your practicum setting?

_____

_____

TRANSTHEORETICAL PERSPECTIVES AND A CRITICAL APPROACH

In acknowledging the transtheoretical nature of our practice, we must continually evaluate, critique, expand, and change how we collectively describe how we practise and from what frameworks. Ainsworth (2016) recalls that "CYC emerges from a diversity of interdisciplinary traditions and theoretical perspectives," arguing against binary views of what is or is not CYC so as to enrich "dialogue about practice, theorizing, and ethical decision-making, and introduce… a host of potentialities of seeing the world of children, youth, families and communities" (p. 6). Likewise, in de Finney, Little, Skott-Myhre, and Gharabaghi's (2012) discussion, they invite "conversations that are not interested in distilling an essence of CYC but those that focus on the possibility of the field… [believing] we need to contribute, alongside other helping professionals, to the overall project of social justice. How does one's work, whether individually, collectively, in a kitchen or an office, contribute to dismantling social norms that actually get in the way of healthy pursuits?" (p. 133). Meanwhile, Loiselle, de Finney, Khanna, and Corcoran (2012) remind us that "dominant Eurowestern psychological models, with their focus on relational, developmental, individualizing practice, are too apolitical, not critical enough, and therefore inadequate to address deep-seated structural inequities" (p. 201). Little (2011) is resolved when she writes that "the story of what constitutes a 'strong CYC philosophy,' then, is open to editing and rewriting… to move beyond the relational and into the political" (p. 11). How may you edit and rewrite our CYC philosophy?

> I invite students to think more about what they are learning in their theory courses that fits and often more importantly doesn't fit with what they are experiencing/ noticing in their first placement. These moments of confusion/ discord can provide us an entry point into important discussions.
> —Kristy, CYC Practicum Faculty-Instructor

Theory is here for us to frame, inform, utilize, make sense of, critique, and hopefully advance our practice into more responsive, caring, and just spaces that reflect the lived experiences of young people and practitioners. Likewise, practice should be an opportunity to inform, critically evaluate, alter, and generate new and more responsive theory. Theory and practice intersect at every moment. They are in relationship together. They should move us forward in creating better relationships with and environments for young people. By connecting theory to practice, and practice with theory, we can become more articulate practitioners, understand what we do, why we do it, and what impact it has, and by extension improve our practice to benefit the young people we serve. Skott-Myhre and Skott-Myhre (2011) call attention to this: "we do not only theorize and reflect, but that our theories allow us new avenues of action that have the capacity to change the world" where "hopeful practice requires radical, critical action—otherwise it reproduces the very things we hope to change" (as cited in Loiselle et al., 2012, p. 201). How do you identify as a change-maker?

These guiding theories, perspectives, and approaches to our practice collectively set us apart from aligned and overlapping professions and schools of thought, offering us a generative space in which to integrate, grapple with, add to, extend, and critically question the ways in which these theories, perspectives, and approaches are enacted. Your practicum experience will help you to continue to define your understanding and application of these ideas. Call upon your past learnings—in classrooms, in conversations, while reading, and elsewhere in life—to help you see and make those connections. We hope you ground yourself in these foundational and transtheoretical ideas as a way of moving forward, to enter your practicum setting with these ideas at the forefront of your mind.

THE CYC PRACTITIONER

When we think about ourselves in practice, what is expected of us, how we work alongside young people, and what connects CYC practitioners across contexts, we can look to a number of descriptions that may help us enliven and embody these ways of being as we determine our own individualized approach that we bring to our work.

Denholm (1989) references the "European Educator" as one of the influences on our field, where, in a post-war response to young people at risk, organizations sought educators who had "skills of the teacher, psychologist, and recreational worker" to respond to young people's needs across a number of environments (Hobbs, 1967, as cited in Denholm, 1989, p. 3). More recently, we can look to CYC practitioners, scholars, and faculty to understand how the CYC practitioner may embody CYC practice with young people, irrespective of and across contexts. Garfat, Freeman, Gharabaghi, and Fulcher (2018) remind us of the 25 Characteristics of a CYC Practitioner (see Figure 1.4). They offer us language as to how we may *be* with young people.

Notice how the characteristics' verbs—interpreting, being, and doing—align well with the praxis model described earlier in the chapter—knowing, being, and doing. Freeman and Garfat (2014) suggest we ask a number of questions of the 25 characteristics as a whole, and you may wish to mark up (e.g., check, cross out, circle, highlight) each characteristic listed in Figure 1.4.

- Which category or characteristic(s) seem [to] come more naturally to you? Why do you think that might be?

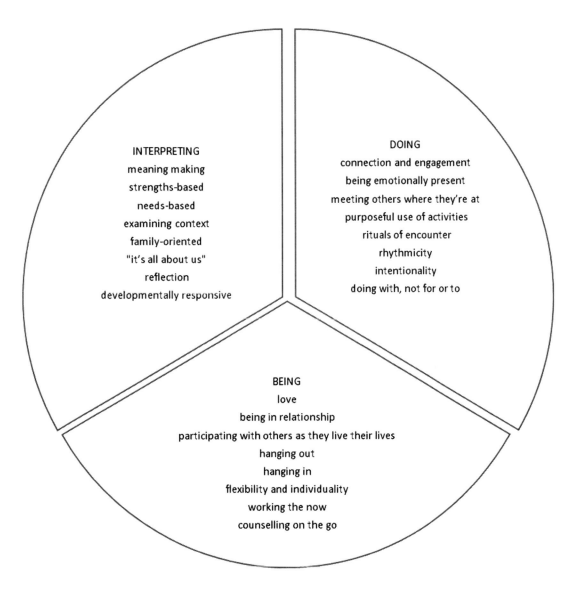

Figure 1.4: The 25 Characteristics of a CYC Practitioner

Adapted from Garfat, T., Freeman, J., Gharabaghi, K., & Fulcher, L. (2018). "Characteristics of a relational child and youth care approach revisited." *CYC-Online: E-Journal of the International Child and Youth Care Network,* 236, 13.

- Which ones would you like to grow or improve? What's your plan to do so?
- Which characteristics do you admire in others? Why? (p. 27)

It is through these ways of knowing, doing, and being that we create space for therapeutic relationships to thrive. As we approach and begin the practicum experience, it is worth considering how we may embody each characteristic, how each characteristic has developed for us, which characteristics we're unsure about or may wish to describe in another way, and how others may perceive and experience our embodiment of these characteristics in practice. (Don't feel bad if these concepts stay abstract until you're doing the work in practicum.)

THE SELF

When we think about what CYC practice is, what perspectives we hold, what approaches we take, and what ways of being we embody, we cannot *not* discuss how *we—ourselves—* play a central role in formulating, interpreting, understanding, and implementing these practices. Central to CYC's roots are the acknowledgement, incorporation, and understanding of ourselves and the use of self in relationship with young people. It is through the self that we engage relationally, understand the environments and people we work with and alongside, practise intentionally, reflect, and continually improve.

In each course you take in your CYC certificate, diploma, or degree you will be invited to understand yourself in a number of ways. Practicum is but one invitation in which to intentionally focus on a number of things, including yourself:

- How do you enter your practicum setting's space?
- What do you consider important? What are you compelled to care about? What do you notice or not notice?
- How do you understand what is going on around you?
- How do you engage with young people and colleagues?
- Which parts of yourself do you bring to the foreground? Which parts move to the background?
- What past experiences inform your present self's interpretation of a situation?
- What is it you hope to learn? What is it that you actually learn?
- What do you learn about yourself? About young people? About practice?
- What meaning does this learning have for you? Where will this meaning take you?

> How does my education, experience, and who I am influence how I experience the world? What was my own experience of school, recreation, and/or residential care? What is the perception of the youth and staff I will be learning from? How do they see me? What are their ideas?
>
> —Yvonne, CYC Practicum Faculty-Instructor

The questions are endless, and that is a good thing. We are always the moderator, reconciler, and negotiator of the situation, the information before us, and the very lens that we look through and upon. We cannot remove ourselves, nor would we want to. Given this acknowledgement, we must explore how we show up to this practice.

Self-Awareness

Ricks (1989) introduced a self-awareness model to the CYC field, the Being Aware Model, a useful starting point to thinking about how we as CYC practitioners arrive, occupy space, and are in our work, where "to know about the client requires being aware of self since the client only exists out of one's self experience of the other person" (p. 35). Meanwhile, Burns (2012) reminds us that "the self is the interpreter of reality, and you, like the rest of us, interpret reality differently," including "our personal experiences, our physical and intellectual limitations and potentialities, and our state of mind in the moment," where "there is no such thing as an impartial, unbiased, or neutral observer; our individual realities depend on our interpretation of the experience" (p. 9). Put another way, our understanding of young people requires us to be aware of ourselves, since our understanding and experience of the young person only exists from our understanding of ourselves. How you experience and interpret a young person will be different than the person sitting next to you, the next person, and the next, and so on. That matters. We do not explore ourselves for navel-gazing, self-involved, narcissistic reasons. We explore ourselves because it directly affects the young person we work alongside. With such power comes great responsibility.

To get there, Ricks and Griffin (1995) advise we begin by exploring our belief systems—our beliefs, values, and ethics—the "things we hold to be true, important, and guide how we operate" and how this system shifts over time and presents itself in the world (p. 35). Ricks (2011) invites us to ask ourselves "how am I presenting right now, how do I feel, what am I thinking, what am I doing?" (p. 10). To this end, Charles and Garfat (2013) include a number of factors that influence our way of perceiving the world: values and beliefs, previous experiences, knowledge, cultural experiences, gender and age, upbringing, needs in the present moment, and our interactions with other people and systems over time.

But it is not enough to understand the thousands of characteristics that make up ourselves. Just what exactly do we mean when we talk about the self?

Kouri's (2015) exploration of the self in CYC illuminates how the conceptualization of the self can be viewed in different ways. It can be viewed as 1) something practitioners possess (e.g., values, beliefs, and assumptions), 2) the "use of self as a mediator of knowledge and skills" (p. 599), and 3) a self that is "situational, complex, and dynamic" (p. 613). White (2007) shifts our thinking in that direction too when she focuses on *being*, where the "ways of being are the expression of specific moral values, ethical commitments, and orientations to the world" (p. 238). Here, we are invited not to know the self for its own sake, but to know how we show up in our practice. We move from a static understanding of self to a dynamic understanding of self: one that is active, always becoming, and always in relationship with another, in space, time, and position in the world.

> Understand yourself in relation to your context. Be open to the development of yourself in relationship to an ever-changing context.
>
> —John, CYC Student

Implicit in discussions of the self is a need to engage in self-awareness, that is, efforts to become continually more aware of how we show up in our practice and what impact that has. Advising human service practitioners, Shebib (2013) contrasts new counsellors with and without self-awareness (see Table 1.1).

Looking at this list hopefully inspires rationale for us to become more self-aware. Our lack of self-awareness has real consequences for the young people we work with. Each chapter in this guidebook will explore the self and self-awareness in different ways. Chapter 5, Reflective CYC Practice, and Chapter 6, Diverse People, Diverse Practices, and Diverse Possibilities, explore self-reflection in much more depth. You're encouraged to visit them to explore more. We caution you, though, that there is no end-point to

Table 1.1: Human Service Practitioners' Self-Awareness

Human Service Practitioners' Self-Awareness	
With Self-Awareness	**Without Self-Awareness**
• Recognize and understand their emotional reactions • Know where their feelings end and those of their clients begin • Recognize and accept areas of vulnerability and unresolved issues • Understand personal values and their influence on the counselling relationship • Recognize and manage internal dialogue • Understand and control personal defence mechanisms • Know how they influence clients and counselling outcomes • Modify behaviour based on reactions of clients • Set professional goals based on knowledge of skill and personal strengths and limitations • Accurately identify and appraise counselling skill competence • Know those areas that are likely to trigger unhelpful feelings or responses	• Avoid or are unaware of their feelings • Project personal feelings onto clients • Respond inappropriately because unresolved problems interfere with their capacity to be objective • React emotionally to their clients but don't understand why or how • Unconsciously use clients to work out their own personal difficulties • Remain blind to defensive reactions • Remain unaware of how their behaviour influences others • Behave based on personal needs and style rather than in response to the needs and reactions of clients • Avoid or limit goal setting because they are unaware of personal and professional needs • Overestimate or underestimate counselling skill competence • Are reactive without insight

Adapted from Shebib, B. (2013). *Choices: Interviewing and counselling skills for Canadians* (p. 25). Toronto, ON: Pearson.

achieve. It is an ongoing process, constantly in flux. After her graduate practicum placement in CYC, Newbury (2007) repositions self-awareness: "whereas I may have once thought that to be self-aware means to understand myself, I now believe it means to admit that I will never fully understand myself, but to try to anyway, while knowing that is what I am doing" (p. 55). It is the attempting to… the seeking… the exploration… the reflective way of being that we emphasize in CYC, as opposed to some place of being "fully self-aware" which, we hope you agree, is impossible.

Now that we've explored a number of topics central to our practice, let's move forward with this foundational knowledge toward how we put all of this together to form our theoretical orientation to practice.

YOUR THEORETICAL ORIENTATION TO PRACTICE

Given these factors—history, frameworks, theories and approaches, characteristics, and consideration of self—we attempt to develop our own theoretical orientation to practice, one that we acknowledge continually evolves and responds to environments, conditions, and experiences over time. This theoretical orientation can offer us a purpose, a guiding way of being, a contribution, and a reminder of what we do, why we do it, and what effect our practice has on young people.

> I see theories as more of a lens you're looking through than something you're using.
> —Cody, CYC Student

Practicum carves out space and time to intentionally reflect, practise, and reflect again. Only through active engagement, continually reflecting on our practice, will you move beyond the rigid boundaries of completing the requirements of a practicum course and into the realm of becoming an "ethical, self-aware, responsive and accountable" practitioner in the field (White, 2007, p. 226). It is in this space that learning occurs.

With that said, what is your theoretical orientation to CYC practice? Let's begin with a reflective activity to help you articulate yours, in your own words.

1. I believe Child and Youth Care practice is…

    _____

2. As a Child and Youth Care practitioner, I support young people by…

    _____

3. I believe essential Child and Youth Care perspectives and approaches include…

    _____

4. I am here, doing the work I do, because…

    _____

5. I believe young people change when…

    _____

6. The experiences that guide my practice include…

    _____

7. Young people…

    _____

8. Young people who are struggling need…

    _____

9. Young people's families who are struggling need…

    _____

10. Caring means to…

    _____

Look at the reflections you've written above. Notice what you wrote. Notice any themes or trends across your responses. If you were asked to complete this activity five years ago, what do you think would be different? What would be the same? What if you were to complete this list on behalf of the agency where you are going to do your practicum? Would there be similar responses? Differences? How might you make sense of that?

Now share your responses (where comfortable) with a classmate and notice their descriptions, purpose, intentions, and reflections. What do you observe? What similarities and differences do you notice? Does listening to someone else share their thoughts, reflections, and experiences help you to extend, expand, or redefine your own? We hope it does. That is in part why we are here learning together.

In this chapter, we've used prompts to explore some of the underlying beliefs we have about our practice. Just above, we've considered a list of questions that may prove helpful in a group setting too. We'll keep doing these activities and guided questions throughout this guidebook—some individually and some in groups—to make the most of the learning opportunities that come your way.

In the remaining portion of this chapter, we focus on learning activities that will conclude each chapter in this guidebook: Learning Journals, Practice Scenarios, and Communities of Practice. Here, we introduce the concepts and provide a rationale for them, in part to convince you to incorporate them into your practicum experience.

YOUR LEARNING JOURNAL

The learning journal that accompanies this guidebook will provide additional reflection time to describe, integrate, challenge, critique, and strengthen your practice. This learning journal is not meant to replace nor contradict any learning journal that may be a required component of your practicum course. However, it is suggested that you use this learning journal throughout your practicum experience, and if need be, alter it based on your course's requirements. Meanwhile, also consider your preferred method of communication, expression, and processing. Do you prefer writing or speaking? A learning journal doesn't need to be recorded on paper. Think about voice or video-recordings or even illustration too.

"But I haven't begun my practicum yet; what would I write about?" you may be asking. Even better. Utilizing your learning journal before, during, and after your practicum experience provides the opportunity to track your process over time, which is beneficial in a number of ways. First, learning journals are proven ways to create space and time to process your thoughts, feelings, actions, learning, dilemmas, confusions, challenges, and successes in a safe and confidential space for you to make sense of them and the complex practice that we do. They also provide a great source of data when it comes time to preparing for your seminar discussions, supervision meetings, performance evaluations, and course assignments. They are a great reminder of the tasks and responsibilities we were given throughout our practicum. They are a good source of description to help us prepare for job applications. We are so often prone to forgetting details. Learning journals are a place to notice and track your own development, make shifts in the moment where needed, to direct your learning so that it is more impactful and meaningful to you. Finally, through observation and recording, discovery, as well as the development of awareness and critical self-reflection, learning journals help us become more attuned to the young people we work alongside. Here, we can notice connection and disconnection, the effects of our daily interactions and interventions, and relationship rupture and repair. In this sense, our attention to learning has a direct benefit to their lives.

> I always recommend journaling but journaling can look different. I am used to a book and a pen. But what I've suggested to my students is doing their own personal online journal or creating a folder on their phone with their notes.
> —Saira, CYC Practicum Faculty-Instructor

Student Learning Journal

Let's look at an example of a CYC practicum student's learning journal to guide us. Liptak (2009) shares excerpts from her learning journal to show her day-to-day feelings, observations, challenges, and successes while on practicum at a school setting. Like so many students, she begins with a spectrum of emotions, including difficult ones: uncertainty, awkwardness, and discomfort. Later, she shifts to pride, excitement, and fun, despite complexity. She traces the relationships she forms, the interactions and interpersonal dynamics she notices, and challenging tasks she's asked to perform. She makes sure to end her short entries with something important she's noticed, learned, realized, and the self-awareness she's developed. As she moves through her practicum placement, we witness how she forms her own theoretical orientation to practice with young people: situated in context and centred around the value of dignity and respect. She also challenges herself to develop a working definition of what it means to be a CYC practitioner. It is a valuable window into a fellow student's experience, even if written a while ago. Here is one brief entry:

September 20, 1996

I started my practicum today and experienced a mixture of emotions. I felt nervous because I am not really sure what I will be doing and what is expected of me. I also felt quite excited because I am finally working in the field... I did a lot of observing today and I found it most difficult to tune out the teacher and observe the students. I also found it difficult to try and watch everything at once. I have been noticing that I do a lot of assuming while I observe the kids. I think that I might be doing this because I want there to be some hidden meaning behind the observed behaviour... So far, the learnings from school that I am able to apply to my placement are observational skills and attentive listening. I am also building relationships... (Liptak, 2009, paras. 1–3)

Consider the following questions: What do you notice about what she shares? Do you share any common feelings with her as you anticipate your practicum placement? How do you notice she is attempting to connect theory with practice?

Learning Journal Recommendations

When it comes time to using a learning journal, there are some recommended Dos and Don'ts:

- ✓ DO set a regular time to write—e.g., before or after seminar, before a day off, or at the end of a shift. You can even write at the end of the week or before or after practicum seminar. Make it a ritual, an expected part of your routine.
- ✗ DON'T force it—if at first the writing process seems artificial, let the prompts guide you, to help you generate descriptions, ideas, and reflections.
- ✓ DO check in with a classmate at some point after—if you know you prefer to debrief through dialogue, use the journal pages as notes for these purposeful conversations.
- ✗ DON'T evaluate or edit your writing as you write it—this is not an assignment to submit, and perfection is not helpful nor the goal of the activity.
- ✓ DO focus on what comes up through the writing—trust that your thoughts and reflections know where they want to go, as opposed to something you think you "should" be reflecting on.
- ✗ DON'T forget to use generic terms instead of identifying anyone.
- ✓ DO use the reflections in your journal as sources of data and inspiration for your other required work: assignments, supervision meetings, evaluation reviews, etc.
- ✗ DON'T spend too little or too much time with the learning journal—decide what will be meaningful for you. Five minutes won't allow you to enter into a reflective space. An hour may become too ruminative where you've exited a learning zone. Twenty minutes is a good place to start.
- ✓ DO use the learning journal as a ritual to "end" and "close" your day—attend to what you need to in the journal, close its pages, and move on to the other activities and responsibilities in your day, trusting that you tended to what you needed to.

Flip to the learning journal located in the last section of this guidebook. Notice that there are 26 journal pages. They are formatted to be completed weekly (based on the average 13-week academic term). Use them more or less frequently, based on your academic term and the duration of your placement. This learning journal is both structured (walking you through a series of guided questions to help explore various aspects of your practicum experience) and unstructured (more open-ended, where you have more freedom to explore, generate, and direct your own reflections). It may be worth trying out both types before you settle on one, or you may wish to continue both throughout your practicum course.

When writing, be sure to remove all identifying information—about the site/location, names of staff and young people, and so on. Use generic names—"my site" or "the agency" in lieu of your site name, "the kids" or "Student A" or "M," and "teacher" or "counsellor" or "supervisor" instead of staff and supervisor names. Not only will this be a chance to practise confidentiality and anonymity through writing, it also will be necessary in the unfortunate occurrence that you misplace your guidebook or it is stolen. You, your supervisors, faculty-instructors, and more importantly the young people and families will appreciate that you tended to this professional practice by keeping their names and identifying features out.

> Try arts-based practices, such as photography, poetry, drawing/painting, song-writing, comic-book storyboarding. Journalling works well for some students, but can also feel arduous when they have a host of other written assignments.
> —Kristy, CYC Practicum Faculty-Instructor

PRACTICE SCENARIOS

While it is important for CYC practitioners to learn from established practitioners in the field, including supervisors and faculty-instructors, it is also helpful to consider experiences of those learners who are in the midst of the complexity of practicum. Many applied textbooks in CYC will use practice scenarios (also called case scenarios), applying the chapter content to real-life situations. Each chapter of this guidebook includes two practice scenarios inspired by actual events. Each scenario gives an example of a student (or students) grappling with a challenge in their practicum, as they are immersed in new and uncertain contexts.

Try not to skim by them as you finish each chapter. As you read, it may be helpful to jot down notes about what each scenario reminds you of in your own placement. You may have advice for the student in the scenario. Perhaps your mind begins to think of a recent or past encounter with a young person or family. Maybe you'll be inspired to reflect on the encounter and ask yourself similar (or different) questions, such as these students do of themselves. All this is important learning.

Take a look at the Practice Scenarios that conclude this chapter: "Akiko's Welcome" and "Amanda's Sunny Day." Each scenario focuses on a practicum student working through a challenge in their practicum placement. Use the content in this chapter to inspire your thinking about the scenario. Notice how the scenario may relate to your own situation at your current practicum placement, even if it is not exactly what you are experiencing. Consider the questions posed at the end of each scenario to help you expand and apply the concepts presented in this chapter.

SEMINAR GROUP AND COMMUNITY OF PRACTICE DISCUSSION QUESTIONS

Throughout your practicum experience, you will be part of many groups focused on your learning experience. Seminar is a purposeful environment where, facilitated by your faculty-instructor, you and your classmates can check in with each other, process your learning together, and debrief difficulties, confusions, and successes with people who are experiencing similar learning challenges and questions. It is a place to integrate your learning. Likewise, practicum is an opportune time to extend your learning through the creation of *communities of practice*, particularly if you find that you learn best through dialogue with people.

Communities of practice are purposeful groups focused on discussing and reviewing practice. In her review of CYC practicum models, Ainsworth (2016) describes Wenger's (1998) Communities of Practice model, where "learning [is] a lived and social activity that is constantly being negotiated" and that ultimately "learning comes from constructed identities—who we are, how we interpret meaning, and how we participate" (pp. 46–47). Consider forming a group. The composition of a community of practice group can look different. They can include:

> It was our little cohort within a cohort.
> —Heather, CYC Student

- Fellow practicum seminar students who are able to and interested in meeting together (i.e., a smaller group than the seminar group, perhaps 3–5 students)

> Having different perspectives that are polar opposite as to what you believe really helped open my mind. Having that interaction with another person to see what they think from that perspective helps you realize there are other lenses out there.
> —Margaret, CYC Student

- Fellow practicum seminar students at similar sites (e.g., group homes, schools, hospitals, etc.) or across similar demographics (e.g., adolescent girls, Indigenous youth, etc.) or social conditions (e.g., supporting young people experiencing poverty, immigrant or refugee youth) or in similar locations (e.g., rural/remote, a specific municipality, etc.) so as to share experiences, resources, and so on that could prove helpful in your process of developing your professional practice
- Practicum students at the same site (where students could be across different levels of practicum study, types of programs, or postsecondary institutions)

Each chapter of this guidebook will close with a series of focused questions for communities of practice. These can be used with whichever group that forms—organically or as a required component of your course. You may be required to prepare a response to the list of questions, you may wish to bring the question to your community of practice, or you may wish to reflect individually. Use all of them, some of them, or none of them and create your own. The purpose of the questions is to begin a generative conversation, then let the group take any direction it deems to be useful.

Review the following questions in your seminar group or community of practice:

1. In the activities earlier in the chapter, we defined common CYC theories, perspectives, and approaches in CYC practice and imagined possible ways in which we may be witness to these perspectives in action at practicum. Share these in-progress definitions and examples with your classmates. (Notice how they make meaning of each perspective, the examples they give, and notice how this helps your own expanding understanding of these perspectives.)

2. What CYC characteristics do you feel comfortable, skilled, or familiar with? What characteristics do you feel uncomfortable, unskilled, or unfamiliar with?

3. What aspects of yourself do you think would be useful for you to reflect upon as you enter your practicum experience? How will you go about doing this?

4. What is your theoretical orientation to practice? What knowledge and experience informs your theoretical orientation to practice?

IN CLOSING

In this chapter, we have focused on developing our theoretical orientation to practice, by way of reviewing our guiding practice frameworks, perspectives, and approaches, understanding ourselves in our work, while also encouraging you to critically evaluate the very foundations we stand upon. Through these topics, you've been encouraged to apply this knowledge to your current (or upcoming) practicum placement in order to fully immerse yourself in it, and to begin using your learning journal as but one way to process what you are learning. We hope that this discussion of theory grounds your entry into practice. Practicum can be one of the first professional experiences CYC practitioners undertake in their practice journey and is an essential component to your academic learning and professional development. You may be surprised to learn that it is often quoted as one of the most memorable experiences professionals have during their education. We appreciate you rising to the challenge.

I encourage students to share an interaction with a youth, and their reflection process. From there we consider what skills and knowledge was used within this interaction, and what might have been possible. We talk about CYC principles of practice, as well as different theoretical approaches that may have been evident or could have been employed. We also talk about what fits with theory or challenges what theory tells us.
—Deb, CYC Practicum Faculty-Instructor

PRACTICE SCENARIOS

Akiko's Welcome

Akiko's practicum is at an elementary school. Its student population is primarily Indigenous. In the centre of the entrance area sit four couches in a circle. Each morning, families are welcomed to stay, have tea, and connect. Her practicum supervisor has asked Akiko to "hang out" each morning to welcome children, meet families, listen to stories, and offer tea and snacks.

What CYC perspectives does this morning welcoming practice embody? What interpersonal, organizational, community, sociocultural, and political or institutional influences do you imagine must be in place for this morning welcoming practice to exist at this school?

_____

_____

_____

Amanda's Sunny Day

One week into her practicum at the group home, Amanda was shocked when the youth workers put a movie on for the kids; she thought they could go enjoy the sunny spring day. She wasn't sure if she should say anything. The following weekend, it happened again. Amanda thought it was a beautiful day and that they could all do something outside, but the youth workers put a movie on the television. She was not sure what to do.

What can Amanda's shock and frustration reveal to her about her developing theoretical orientation to practice? How could she be proactive in this situation, while respecting everyone's role at the house? Is there anything that you're surprised about at your practicum, in terms of practices, procedures, schedules, or activities? What does this surprise reveal to you about your developing theoretical orientation to practice?

_____

_____

_____

CHAPTER 2

Finding and Preparing for Your CYC Practicum Placement

Competencies for Professional Child and Youth Work Practitioners				
Professionalism	Cultural and Human Diversity	Applied Human Development	Relationship and Communication	Developmental Practice Methods
Awareness of the Profession Professional Development and Behaviour Personal Development and Self-Care Awareness of Law and Regulations			Teamwork and Professional Communication	

Practicum students contribute new, current theories and perspectives to our practices. They contribute energy and excitement to our program activities and to the children in our space.

—Jessica Forster Broomfield, Manager of Children's Programs, DIVERSEcity Community Resources Society

As each of you start the practicum placement process, confirm a practicum site and supervisor, and begin orienting yourself to the practicum setting, there are a number of items to attend to. This part of the process is replete with questions, curiosities, uncertainty, and sometimes angst. Across all Child and Youth Care (CYC) programs in Canada, each student will undertake multiple practicum placements. Our first practicum placement is the one where we learn our program's expectations and rules and where we are oriented to the process. However, knowing the uncertainty that comes along with new learning, it is helpful to review some typical processes practicum students will experience, in order to help this stage be as smooth as possible. No placement process is perfectly straightforward, nor should it be. In fact, how we respond to the anticipated challenges, helpful reflections, and required details of the placement process relates to how we function as emerging professional practitioners and is a part of the learning process in and of itself.

CYC SETTINGS

Child and Youth Care settings transcend boundaries. After all, we meet young people in their life-space; thus we can work virtually anywhere (even in virtual spaces). Most CYC settings—and therefore practicum placements—can be categorized into three types of environments: community-based, school-based, and residential-based settings. However, these categories are diverse and overlap, especially when we move from more generalist to specialist types of settings. Some programs may cross all three boundaries. Take, for example, a family development centre partnership between a school board, health authority, and social services ministry that delivers education, family support, and outreach programming to meet the needs of the young people they serve. Or think of a co-located hub of program delivery, a one-stop shop for youth to attend alternate school programming, employment support, youth clinic, and so on. Practicum students are placed with one main supervisor, but by the very nature of the site, the students are exposed to a variety of programming and people. In this sense, these three categories are arbitrary; however, they give you a sense of the vast number of placements students attend, what your practicum coordinators review when making a match, as well as what your practicum cohort will likely represent in terms of types of CYC settings. Take a look at the list of typical CYC practicum settings in Figure 2.1.

Notice programs that you've worked in, volunteered for, or heard of through colleagues and friends. When you look at each of these settings, ask yourself the following:

- Which settings are you drawn to? Curious about? Why do you think that is?
- Which settings do you approach with apprehension? Why do you think that is?

Within each setting, there will be many professional practitioners supporting young people. Each practitioner will have their own purpose—teachers, social workers, nurses, counsellors, and so on—including Child and Youth Care practitioners. However, because we perform so many roles and because the need for our presence has developed within the context of each site and community, the names of the positions we hold will be different: Child and Youth Care Practitioner, Child Care Counsellor, Youth and Family Counsellor, Neighbourhood House Assistant, Youth Activity Worker, Outreach Worker... the list goes on and on.

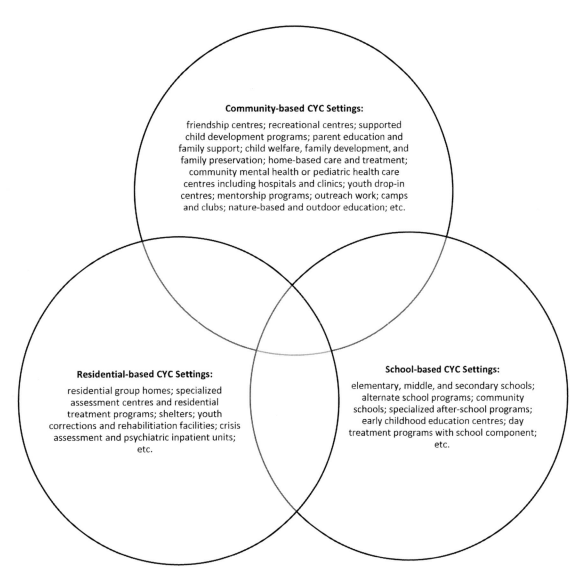

Figure 2.1: Typical CYC Practicum Settings

THE PLACEMENT PROCESS

Across Canadian CYC programs, the approach to placement will vary. At one end of the spectrum, students will be required to find their own practicum placements, with some advising from their program. On the other end of the spectrum, practicum coordinators/faculty-instructors will place the student with minimal input from the student. Usually, it's somewhere in the middle. Your program has final approval, as it is their responsibility to keep the entire picture in mind. The placement process can begin as early as you are accepted into your program, but typically, the action happens in the academic term before you begin practicum. That said, some CYC programs have a pre-internship placement seminar or workshops. Some programs integrate planning and preparation into prerequisite courses. You will be oriented to that process as part of your enrollment with the program, and it's important to complete all required information beforehand. Not sure? Ask your program's student advisor, practicum coordinator, chair, or practicum instructors, and they'll direct you to the right spot.

There are common considerations that placement coordinators (faculty-instructors or coordinators) keep in mind when matching students to sites including site, student, and program factors (see Figure 2.2). Keep these factors in mind, or at least appreciate the complexity that goes into determining and confirming your placement.

As you can see, there are many factors in this decision-making process. A change of one factor can change the entire plan. Some factors will be prioritized over others, depending on the context. Meanwhile, time will influence this equation, as the term approaches and students need to begin.

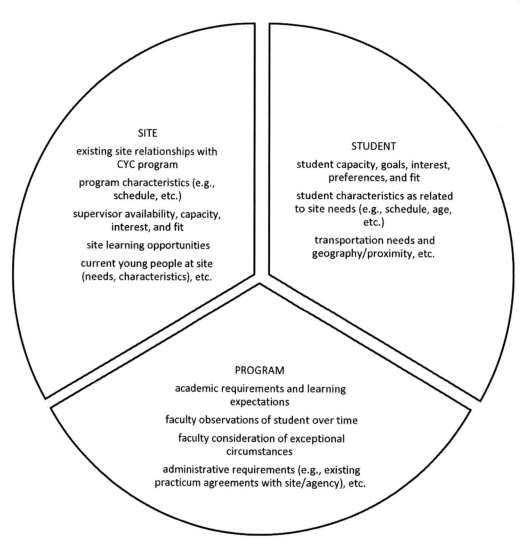

SITE

existing site relationships with CYC program

program characteristics (e.g., schedule, etc.)

supervisor availability, capacity, interest, and fit

site learning opportunities

current young people at site (needs, characteristics), etc.

STUDENT

student capacity, goals, interest, preferences, and fit

student characteristics as related to site needs (e.g., schedule, age, etc.)

transportation needs and geography/proximity, etc.

PROGRAM

academic requirements and learning expectations

faculty observations of student over time

faculty consideration of exceptional circumstances

administrative requirements (e.g., existing practicum agreements with site/agency), etc.

Figure 2.2: Practicum Placement Considerations

Further, CYCs are known for their ability to work across settings and across ages. Throughout your practicum experiences (all programs will have more than one practicum placement), we want you to challenge yourself. Let's say you're very interested in working in school settings. That's great—but we'll want you to gain experience across school settings and ages. If you have volunteer experience in an elementary school, we may get you to do a practicum placement in a secondary school. If you have experience in a secondary school and really want to stay working with youth, we may want to place you in an alternative school program or other specialized program. Or let's say you're very interested in working with youth but have limited experience. Across your multiple practicum placements, we'll want you to work in a variety of settings: a youth drop-in centre, a high school or alternative program, and a youth shelter, for example. Keep this in mind as you experience the practicum placement process, as it's helpful to know what your faculty-instructors are thinking. Or let's say you're interested in working with young people with common characteristics: kids in government care, kids who experience developmental disabilities, newcomers to Canada. Considering this interest, think about the diversity of settings in which you could support these young people and start your exploration from there.

Preparation Brainstorming

Before you go ahead and get too attached to a particular setting, it is helpful to do some preparatory work, some exploration and reflection to assist advising your practicum coordinator/faculty-instructor in their determination of suitability and fit for your placement. It's likely that you will be invited to complete a preference form to inform them of your past experiences, interests and goals, where you live, your access to transportation, schedule/availability, and so on (see Appendix B for an example). Even before you complete and submit that (or a similar) form, it's advisable that you do some "vocational reflection" so as to best articulate your preferences and interests (acknowledging that they will always be in development).

Brainstorm your responses to the following activity, adapted from Ryerson University's School of Child and Youth Care (n.d.) Pre-Internship Handbook. Even if you've already confirmed a practicum placement, you may identify additional goals, strengths, and needs, so it is worthwhile to complete the activity anyway.

Activity 2.1: Pre-Placement Self-Assessment and Reflection

Where Have I Been

What environments have I worked in with young people?

_____

What are the main activities I have engaged in with children and youth?

_____

What populations and cultures do I have experience working with?

_____

What skills am I confident in my ability to perform?

_____

What experience or situation have I had that I am really proud of and would like to build upon?

_____

Examine Gaps and Uncertainties

What environments or settings would I like the opportunity to explore?

_____

What skills am I unsure of and would like the opportunity to practise in a guided and safe atmosphere?

_____

What populations, groups, or cultures would I like to learn about and gain experience in working with?

_____

What subject areas and issues interest me?

_____

Looking Ahead

What specializations am I interested in completing in my CYC program, if available?

_____

What types of CYC jobs or graduate school programs do I envision myself applying for upon graduating?

_____

What am I passionate about and how can I incorporate this into my work?

_____

What hobbies, extracurricular activities, and interests that bring me joy and foster creativity do I engage in, and how may these be incorporated into my work?

_____

Adapted from Ryerson University School of Child and Youth Care. (n.d.). *Pre-internship hand-book* (pp. 15–16). Toronto, ON: Author.

Working backward from a future goal is a helpful way to think through your preferences. Consider the following examples. A first-year CYC student has a goal of working in child welfare and wishes to do the child protection specialty within their degree program, including a child protection practicum. Knowing this goal (even if it changes over time), the student may consider what skills, settings, and knowledge would be ideal for a graduating student to have when applying for a child welfare position. At this point, the student speaks to a friend of a friend who is a child welfare practitioner and an instructor of the child protection specialty courses, and asks, "What skills, settings, knowledge would be helpful to gain at this point in my development?" Many child welfare practitioners would advise that students learn about alternative school programs, street outreach and youth shelter programs, family support, residential treatment centres, and residential group homes. Why? Because we need to learn how to support young people in these settings, understand young people's lived experience of these programs, as well as the specialized knowledge and skills that occur in these settings where young people in government care may receive services (e.g., crisis response, reporting, mental health, relationships between systems of care, etc.).

With future goals in mind, we can think through the functions, knowledge, populations, systems, and relationships we could develop during our practicum placements, slowly building our capacity to support young people in a diversity of settings. What if we change our minds halfway through our degree and no longer have the same long-term goal? No problem! Since we have multiple practicum placements across a diversity of sites, we develop many, many transferable skills suitable for many, many future jobs. All is certainly not lost. Rerouting is part of the process. With that in mind, complete Activity 2.2 to attend to your own situation.

Activity 2.2: Looking Ahead to Inform the Present

Look ahead to inform your present decisions. Work through the questions in Figure 2.3 on the left, from top to bottom. Use the example in the centre for direction. Ask for help if and when you need it. Let this brainstorming help inform your conversations in the placement process.

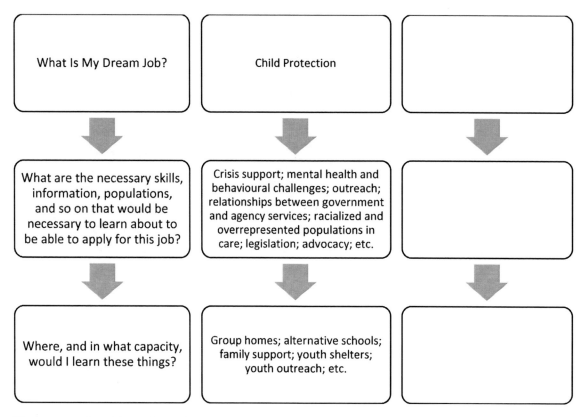

Figure 2.3: Looking Ahead

Meeting with Your Faculty-Instructor

You will receive word from your assigned faculty-instructor or practicum coordinator of the steps you are required to complete to initiate the practicum process. Some will be administrative, and some will be more process-oriented.

Administrative Items
- Confirm criminal record check
- Register for practicum course
- Update required immunizations
- Update resume and cover letter
- Other: _____
_____
- Other: _____
_____

Process-Oriented Items
- Complete and submit practicum preference form
- Meet with practicum faculty-instructor (or practicum coordinator)
- Obtain and read practicum manual, field guide, and/or other orientation materials
- Other: _____
_____
- Other: _____
_____

Across Canada, practicum is often team-taught by several (or even all) faculty-instructors. Each faculty-instructor will have a group of practicum students they follow from beginning to end, and it is common practice for multiple groups to meet together for seminar and break off into smaller discussion groups. In this way, you are exposed to many faculty-instructors' teachings and learning methods and groups of other students at numerous sites so as to add layers of diverse learning. Today, practicum seminar can also occur online, where the same groups are represented in digital space. Learning is intentionally structured this way so that you—as one individual, at one site, with one supervisor, with one approach to CYC practice—are actually learning from multiple students, at multiple sites, with multiple supervisors, with multiple approaches to CYC practice. In this sense, learning is exponential. We hope you realize and take advantage of that opportunity.

Your faculty-instructor may send you messages orienting you to their practicum teaching philosophy, requesting information, asking for your preferences and availability, and giving you recommendations for beginning the placement process in a good way. Read them! Feel free to ask them questions too. Bring a list of questions for them during your meeting or in your correspondence:

- What's their teaching and learning approach to the practicum course?
- How can students successfully demonstrate their knowledge, skills, and ways of being through the practicum course?
- What should a student do if there's a problem?
- What do you know about the program and supervisor you're sending me to?
- Could I be connected with a student who did a practicum placement at this site before?

At this point in time, what questions do you have?

_____

_____

Try to identify what you're curious about. (In this case, we can often reframe our worries and apprehensions into questions of curiosity.) This is particularly helpful if you have not been taught by your faculty-instructor in a course thus far. Get to know them as they get to know you.

CYC faculty-instructors have extensive experience working in the field and will focus on the application of what you're learning in your CYC courses with what you're going to observe, learn, and contribute at the practicum placement. They'll also be mindful of what you will soon be learning in concurrent and future courses. Faculty-instructors will want to see you make these connections and will provide opportunities for you to do so in a number of ways: through seminar, one-on-one discussions, and check-ins, through a variety of assignments, and through your performance evaluations. A common approach to practicum learning is not that faculty-instructors expect you to perfectly develop a skill over the duration of the practicum course; rather, they'll focus on your learning and where that takes you. In other words, faculty-instructors will not be concerned whether you developed a perfect group activity, if it went smoothly, if loads of kids participated, and if it had significant benefits to the young people at your site. If that's the case, great! But if it's the exact opposite—a group activity that wasn't well-attended, that had lots of glitches, and that wasn't very useful to young people—faculty-instructors will want to see what you learned from the experience, how you will change or continue for next time, and how that informs your approach to CYC practice. Both scenarios and every situation in between will provide learning opportunities. That is why you're here.

What to Expect

It is important to outline the expectations of the main roles and processes in practicum, including expectations of students, supervisors and supervision, and faculty and seminar. Why? So we can understand what is expected of us and others as we approach the practicum experience, so we can follow through with what is expected of us, so we can check in when something isn't going smoothly, and so we know where we can receive support when we need it. The following three lists outline expectations that we generally assume across all CYC programs, but it's important to check in with your faculty-instructor. They're here to develop a relationship with and guide you, including being transparent with expectations. You're here to ask, find out, and follow through with those expectations too.

Meanwhile, as you read the following expectations, notice how this relates to Child and Youth Care practice. How do we begin relationships and programs with young people? Do they come into programs wondering the same things as us? How can they learn what is expected of them and of their relationship with you, as they participate in the services your program delivers? Reflect on this topic as you begin your time at your practicum and how you may also be transparent with expectations.

Students
- Complete any practicum placement forms (identifying preferences, availability, etc.) and accompanying material (i.e., resume) for your practicum coordinator or faculty-instructor
- Familiarize self with academic requirements (i.e., course syllabus and/or manual, including evaluation processes)
- Obtain a supervision manual and provide a copy (paper and electronic) to your supervisor before your practicum placement begins
- Consider providing your supervisor a copy (paper or electronic) of your assignment outlines, so they can help you meet those requirements (but clarify that assignments are submitted to your faculty-instructor only, to protect the integrity of the learning process)
- Before your placement begins or within the first week of starting practicum, establish a schedule in collaboration with your supervisor; provide that schedule

to your supervisor and faculty-instructor. Ensure the schedule will allow you to complete the predetermined number of hours required by your practicum course
- Clarify your role and responsibilities at practicum
- Participate in practicum orientation activities facilitated by your supervisor and designated staff
- Engage professionally and relationally with young people at the practicum site
- Actively pursue the objectives of the practicum course, as outlined at your institution (in your syllabus, practicum manual, and/or curriculum guideline), as tailored to the specific context of your practicum site and role, and involve yourself in all learning opportunities at the site
- Meet with your supervisor on a regular basis for formal and informal supervision to invite, identify, understand, and integrate feedback, including strengths and ideas for improvement
- Prepare for, participate, and assist in organizing beginning, mid-point, and final performance evaluation meetings with you, your supervisor(s), and faculty-instructor, as well as any additional meetings as required
- Attend and actively participate in your practicum seminar (and/or online discussion boards), respecting classmates' learning process and confidentiality
- Seek support from your faculty-instructor when and as needed
- If ill during practicum, inform your supervisor and faculty-instructor as soon as possible
- Complete and submit required assignments, as per assignment due dates
- Follow personnel policies including punctuality, illness, absence, use of vehicles, etc.
- Contact your supervisor and faculty-instructor when issues arise and where necessary

Supervisors and Supervision
- Provide and ensure an environment that facilitates and welcomes learning
- Meet with student to establish agreed-upon learning opportunities, goals, schedule, and set number of hours
- Use relevant academic, work experience, and professional expertise working with children and youth, as well as knowledge of adult learning and supervisory strategies (including providing strengths-based, constructive feedback) to facilitate student learning
- Provide student with orientation to agency, program, and team including reviewing relevant policy and procedure manuals, protocols, and rules
- Identify learning opportunities through practicum site, as well as any related and relevant interagency training opportunities that may arise
- Prioritize the needs of the young people at the site above the learning opportunities of the student, and intervene where necessary
- Make oneself available to directly observe and supervise practicum student, and identify other staff to do so in one's absence, via an alternate supervisor
- Notify faculty-instructor concerning any issues that may arise regarding professional practice (e.g., tardiness, absences, professional judgement)

- Provide verbal and written evaluations to faculty-instructor, while gathering and representing information from other staff who have observed the student
- Where necessary, and in collaboration with faculty-instructor, remove student if professional issues arise, where it is inappropriate for the student to continue

Faculty-Instructors and Seminar

- Orient students to practicum course including objectives, desired outcomes, content, structure, evaluation, and expectations for conduct and successful completion of the course
- Secure placement for practicum students (or in conjunction with practicum placement coordinator)
- Inform students and supervisors of any relevant policies, including criminal record checks, vehicle insurance limitations, and so on, from the educational institution's point of view
- Teach, supervise, and support students through regular contact, as established in formal meetings (seminar and performance evaluations) and as needed (office hours, etc.)
- Liaise, support, and maintain connection with site supervisor
- Facilitate integrative seminar to connect classroom experiences with practicum experiences
- Visit practicum site for beginning, mid-point, and final performance evaluation meetings to clarify roles, requirements, and timelines; advise and consult on learning opportunities; contribute to feedback discussions; and assess progress and intervene where necessary
- Assess and evaluate students—taking into consideration self-assessments, written and verbal supervisor evaluations, assignments, and seminar participation—to determine, in consultation with the student and supervisor, a final grade
- Where necessary, and in conjunction with site supervisor, remove student where professional issues arise, where it is inappropriate for the student to continue

Along the lines of being clear and transparent with our expectations, it is also important to outline some roadblocks to beginning well in practicum. What may get in the way?

Students can struggle with a number of things: thinking they can only work with a certain age group. Being concerned that they will make a mistake. Being asked to do something they are not ready to do. Being afraid to ask for what they need. Taking initiative to suggest activities.
—Deb, CYC Practicum Faculty-Instructor

DEALING WITH MYTHS, BARRIERS, AND PRECONCEIVED NOTIONS

The time before and as practicum begins is replete with myths about, barriers to, and preconceived notions of what practicum is all about. We can experience these tensions internally as individuals, as well as externally as a group. After all, you're beginning one of your first practicum experiences. Naturally, there will be questions, concerns, and differing perceptions as you approach this experience. In times like these, our brains like to fill in those gaps with assumptions, assurances, expectations, comparisons, and worries that try to attend to that uncertain space. Let's try to halt those tendencies in their tracks and begin to practise our ability to deal with uncertainty and difference.

Kalau (2018) asks practicum students to ask themselves: "What are the attitudes, beliefs and expectations they bring to practicum? ... What barriers are in the way of forming accurate perceptions that may influence the meaning a student makes of their experience resulting in them limiting their opportunities to learn?" (p. 22). Let's deconstruct some common statements that occur at the beginning of practicum.

> A student can struggle with a number of things: Should I believe what my instructors say? If I just pass the theory, then I'll be fine. Surely the systems actually work together! The red carpet will be rolled out when I arrive on practicum.
> —Andrew, CYC Practicum Faculty-Instructor

1. *"I haven't been placed yet, which means I'm not going to get a good placement."*

By the very fact that practicum coordinators and faculty-instructors are working on a timeline, some students will be placed first, some later, and some last. Making associations between being placed first with the quality of a placement, at the very least, is incorrect and, at the very worst, starts you off on the wrong foot in practicum. As reviewed earlier in the chapter, there are many factors that go into the placement process, and all of them need to be attended to before confirming a placement. In fact, when a student is placed early in the process, it often just means that the site supervisor and student had an opening in their schedule that aligned, which allowed them to confirm the process. No correlation exists between an early placement confirmation and a successful practicum. There are, however, active steps students can take to put their best foot forward to ensure they are placed in a practicum, which is the focus of this chapter. Take the tips and tricks, dos and don'ts lists, and reflections into consideration as to how you want to approach this journey.

2. *"Why did that person get their first choice and I didn't get mine?"*

We often approach the practicum experience with particular preferences in mind. This is helpful to get a sense of what we want to learn, focus on, and so on. However, it's important to not get too attached to a particular vision, despite all the hard work you're doing to brainstorm and explore what you'd like to learn.

Let's hover on the topic of good and bad placements. They don't exist. Learning can happen at any site. Any CYC practicum placement can transfer foundational, core learning to another role and setting. We are learning transferable knowledge, skills, and ways of being. Faculty-instructors and practicum coordinators are ethically bound to create partnerships with agencies and supervisors who have student learning as central to their intentions, as well as providing the best care to the young people at their site. You can learn anywhere.

> Take out of it as much as you can, even if you don't like your placement.
> —Margaret, CYC Student

Common to many experienced CYC practitioners' hard-won wisdom is the following paradox.

What a student learned at the site that they didn't want to be at, in the job that they didn't like, with a program they had problems with, with the supervisor they didn't mesh the best with, and so on, was a more profound learning experience compared to the site that they dreamed of, that they adored being a part of, where they meshed fantastically with their supervisor, where they didn't have many problems and connected well with the young people.

Why? It is often true that when we are placed in a setting that rubs us the wrong way, that doesn't jive with our values and ways we want to practise CYC, or that we just plain-old didn't like, it actually helps us define who we are, how we want to be, what we want to be doing, and where we want to be spending our time. When we're placed in a "perfect" practicum setting, in a perfect role, with a perfect supervisory relationship, we have a more difficult time understanding and learning why it's a good fit. In either situation and every situation in between, however, it is your responsibility as a practicum student—and the supervisors and faculty-instructors who help facilitate your learning—to figure out why. How does this difficult scenario help define how you want to respond to young people's needs? How does this program delivery fit with what you believe, have learned, and know to be true as to how to respond to young people's needs? How does this relationship reflect how you want to be in your CYC practice? These are the questions of utmost importance as you are on this learning journey.

> Try not to compare yourself to other people in your class.
> —Sam, CYC Student

3. *"Because I'm not paid, like staff or a co-op placement, I think I am more of a volunteer."* It's difficult to understand our role as a practicum student. We can find ourselves comparing it to other established roles. You may find it more helpful to frame your role as an emerging practitioner or emerging professional. Why? In this sense, we acknowledge the developmental nature of *becoming* a professional practitioner. We are not employees, bound by that relationship agreement at the site. We are students, learning to practise well. In that comparison, we can see that where a staff person does something "wrong," a supervisor may reprimand them in some way. In practicum, a supervisor would treat the situation as a learning experience with the student. You are not a co-op student, earning an income and there for the sole purpose of gaining work experience related to your degree, where supervisors commonly treat co-op students more akin to employees. We're here to learn and to practise. In that sense, the supervisor and site are contributing a great amount of labour to that development. Likewise, we're not a volunteer, where we are solely contributing our time to the space and tasks that need to be done. Volunteers are not expected to connect what they observe to what they're learning in class. Further, volunteers (in typical CYC settings) are often not expected to bring a level of professionalism that students are. We expect much more from the emerging practitioner than the volunteer—more time, more contribution, more learning, and application of skills, knowledge, and ways of being.

4. "*Practicum is all about* doing, *so it'll be a nice break from my typical class homework and assignments.*"

Ah, if this were only the case. Is it not enough that we're opening up our schedules to be able to complete the 150–300 hours of time at the practicum site above what we typically do for class? Is it not enough that we're paying for sometimes double the amount of credit as a typical classroom-based course? Why do we even have to read this guidebook?! You may or may not be thinking these things. And when you open your course syllabus or practicum manual, you may be shocked to learn that yes, you have a number of formal assessments that will represent part of your official course grade. Why? As mentioned, a practicum is not solely a set number of hours nor is it a checklist of items to complete. It is an experience, focused almost entirely on your learning, development, and growth as an individual practitioner and as part of a collective CYC practice. In order to demonstrate and assess that learning, we need to use a variety of methods to check in on that process.

5. "*I'm just a practicum student*" or "*I'm just shadowing, not really doing anything.*"

Whether you are at your practicum placement for six weeks or eight months, you will make an impact. Your presence is welcomed by the supervisor's refrain: practicum students bring energy, ideas, and reflection to the space that enlivens their commitment to practice and offers more possibilities for connection with the young people. By the very fact you are present, embodying CYC perspectives and approaches, you will offer much more than you will ever know.

But it is also a common refrain that students feel they're not participating as much as they'd like, because they must first complete the phase where we're primarily focused on observation. Sometimes this is referred to as shadowing, where we shadow our supervisors to get a sense of their daily tasks, activities, responsibilities, and relationships. It is important to remind ourselves that observation is a necessary part of the learning process, and if we attend to observation intentionally, we can set ourselves up for even more success when the time comes to shift to more "doing." Hillman (2018) reminds CYC practicum students that when we are new to a practice setting, observational learning is key and that students can and "should engage in active observation at their placements" (pp. 70–71). This *active* observation can happen a number of ways: taking the required time, intention, and energy to focus on "[engaging] deeply in observing one's surroundings" and observing the agency's spatial set up, its "interface with the public," "employees' body language and use of space," verbal communication observations (i.e., tone, language, content), and more (p. 71). What else would you include in active observation of the practicum setting, especially in those first few weeks?

> Practicum is what you make it. You can either coast and sit back and be told what to do and do it. Or you can ask questions, give opinions, and really try and do the good work you're there to do.
> —Jasmine, CYC Student

6. "*Why do I have so many supervisors? Who will be evaluating me?*" or "*My supervisor and I aren't getting along, therefore I'm going to get a bad grade.*"

It's often the case that practicum students have more than one supervisor. Sometimes there will be a point-person, a main supervisor responsible for curating a practicum student's learning experience, but that person may not be present at all times. At those times, they will assign their staff with supervisory responsibilities and instruct them to report back on those experiences so the main supervisor can have a fulsome picture of the practicum student's activities and functions. At a community recreation youth drop-in centre, for example, you may have a program manager as your main supervisor, and you may have multiple youth activity facilitators and youth outreach workers with whom you're paired for various tasks. At an elementary school, you may be placed primarily with a child care counsellor in a specialized support room, but you also rotate across classrooms and before/after school programs with many staff helping orient you to these contexts. Sometimes this can be confusing: knowing who is supervising you, getting to know each supervisor's approach, understanding where the sources of evaluation will come from, among other concerns.

What is helpful at this point, as you prepare for and begin your practicum placement, is to ask! Sometimes supervisors will immediately be clear about their expectations, but sometimes not. Asking what supervision looks like—who will supervise your work, in what way will you check in, how will people report back—are all things you can inquire about.

When it comes time to evaluate, if you have had multiple people supervising your work, you will have multiple sources of feedback. Having multiple people supervising your work gives you the opportunity to see how different styles of practice can look, to have access to more resources and connections, and to be able to check in with people who connect in different ways. When it comes time for supervisory check-ins or more formal performance evaluations, be sure these voices—especially the people who have supervised the work you're most proud of contributing or showed the most growth in a challenging environment—are represented. Sometimes more than one supervisor comes to a performance evaluation meeting. In all cases, the main supervisor should and will check in with those people they've tasked with observing your work. Your evaluation will be a more layered, reflective, and accurate result.

Across many, if not most, CYC programs, it is ultimately the faculty-instructor who assigns you a grade. You can take solace in this knowledge if you are at all concerned about the quality of your relationship with your supervisor having an impact on your grade. Your faculty-instructor will seek your supervisor's consultation through discussion at performance evaluations and through written feedback including assessment on a variety of scales, for example. Your faculty-instructor is there to assess your learning. One aspect of your learning is your ability to develop a relationship with your supervisor, seek and integrate feedback, and journey through conflict and challenge if and when that occurs. As long as you can communicate and represent that *learning*, your faculty-instructor will be able to see the big picture, the wide scope of the purpose of practicum.

7. *"Why do I have to do so much reading? I want to begin!"*
We can appreciate one's enthusiasm in this statement. You're keen on beginning your practicum experience, and you feel bogged down by the fact your supervisor has assigned you loads of reading to do before you are out there, connecting with young people at the site: policies and procedures, emergency situations, accreditation manuals, agency reports, program descriptions, organizational structures and staffing, agency forms, client files, and so on. You're bored, sifting through loads of information that don't seem to stick in

your mind, when all you want to do is meet the young people and staff at the program. So why would a supervisor begin this way? There are many possible reasons:

- You need to know the rules and procedures so as to know the limits of your practice, the site's service provision, etc.
- The agency's accreditation process and insurance it requires
- You need to know what to do in a "what-if" scenario
- You're waiting for your criminal record check to be processed
- Other: _____

Your patience will pay off in the long run. As a way to actively engage with these materials, go one step beyond just reading. Ask various staff how these policies and procedures come into practice. For example, do you feel inundated with the forms and reports that are required as a part of a young person's care in a group home? Ask your supervisor to show you these reports on a timeline—from intake and assessment, through incidents, activities, and interventions, all the way to planning to leave the program. Get a sense of how it all looks through the experience of the young person. Do you know what to do in case of an emergency (fire, allergic reaction, lock down, etc.)? What if you were with a young person outside, what would you do then? What about in the gymnasium? Do you know who to connect with if a young person discloses abuse or neglect in your care? What about if you were on an outing and a youth runs away from the activity? Which people do you need to make sure you have access to? Run through the hypothetical scenarios with your supervisor or a staff person you've just met. Otherwise the materials will continue to be dry. At the very least, make note of where you need to return to when you are no longer in the hypothetical situation, but rather are out there in your practicum setting.

8. "I'm not a cook, so why am I stuck in the kitchen?"

Often as a part of orientation, practicum students are encouraged to rotate across various locations and with various staff at the setting, either at the beginning of or some point during the practicum experience. Sometimes this can mean our practicum experience is filled with activities that we were not expecting. Take for example, a practicum student tasked with cleaning up after the lunch activity in the school's kitchen, frustrated that she's having to clean up the kitchen mess with a kid in the program. Take a practicum student in a teacher's classroom, who feels as though all they're doing is helping kids out with their homework.

At first, instead of saying that CYC is "this" and not "that," or assuming that these activities will be the entirety of one's practicum experience (all 150–300 hours of it), let's open ourselves to consider what else the opportunity has for us. We could ask ourselves: what opportunities exist in this space, in terms of connection and engagement with young people? Think of the various spaces in your upcoming practicum placement and the possibilities for engagement.

Students can quickly become disappointed because they are not conducting counselling sessions, or family meetings because of confidentiality, and also their skills are not fully developed yet.
—Saira, CYC Practicum Faculty-Instructor

9. *"I'm only a year older than the youth at this site, people are confusing me for the youth here" or "I'm not a parent; the parents are going to judge me when I talk to them about their kids."*

I'm kind of more of a quieter person. I made connections with those quieter youth, who maybe wouldn't have adjusted to the other styles of workers there. All personalities have value in the field. Don't think you don't have anything to offer. You always have something to offer.

—Trina, CYC Student

One skill I pulled from practicum was taking the parts of me and using them to my full advantage. I'm kind of weird and goofy and I used that to my advantage. Build relationships and show them it's okay to be silly and that you don't have to be a perfect adult to do what you want to do.

—Margaret, CYC Student

When students are young and don't have children often the reaction from families is 'What do you know? You don't have kids yourself.' It can be a struggle. I encourage students to agree with families. I say, 'You're right, I don't have children. I'm trying to learn from you so I'm hoping we can talk about this because I'm totally new to this.' That will also help create a trusting relationship because they're being honest and open.

—Mindi, CYC Practicum Supervisor

We come to practicum with certain characteristics that, at least for the duration of the practicum experience, we cannot change. We cannot change our parental status, our age, or personality. Nor should we want to. Rather, we can take the opportunity to explore and deconstruct why we're worried about these factors. It all seems to come down to the central desire and purpose of our work: connection. It is only natural and expected that we worry about our ability to connect. Any factors that we, or others, perceive as a potential barrier to connection can be cause for concern, but we must be authentic about where we come from.

If you are or look to be a similar age of the youth at your site, that's what you're dealing with. Use it to connect with the youth and use the challenges as a learning opportunity. What strengths come from this position? What potential challenges may arise? Let's say, upon reflection, you are worried the young people may take advantage of you or not treat you like a professional. What ways of being will you then need to practise when you're there? Perhaps you'll experiment with different attire, language choice, and more transparent relationship boundaries (such as how you introduce yourself and your role, how you negotiate expectations of the space, and how you deliver feedback when challenged).

Wanting to work with families, supporting, facilitating, and advocating for their development and wellness is an important part of CYC practice. You may be at an elementary school where you interact with parents on a daily basis at drop-off and pick-up times. You may be working with families in a family preservation, support, and outreach role. Whatever your contact with families, as a student who is not a parent, you still have much to bring to the relationship. Remember, you are a CYC practitioner and have a passion for supporting young people, focusing on their strengths, development, and relationships. All caregivers want this too! Parents' and caregivers' perception and anticipation of judgement only occurs when judgement has happened in the present or past. Curiosity, connection through shared interest, bringing our authentic selves to the relationship, and empathizing with their experience is the place we begin all relationships. Begin there. Begin where you are.

10. "How will I know what to do?" or "I've only taken a few courses. Am I ready?"
You have waited a long time to begin practicum. You've taken courses focusing on child and youth development, activity facilitation, ethics, interpersonal communication, working in communities, among others. But then it hits you: a seemingly never-ending list of worries. How will I know what to do? What if the kids don't like me? What if I don't know what to say? How will I know how to respond? What if this, that, or some other thing happens? These questions can be overwhelming and often override the excitement you experience as you approach the beginning of your practicum. It can be helpful to reframe these unhelpful worries into an opportunity. Remember these mantras as you begin this new journey:

1. I'm not supposed to know what to do all the time—I'm here to learn.
2. There will be people around me who I can actively observe.
3. There are people who trust that I'll be okay; otherwise, they wouldn't allow me to register.
4. I was accepted into the CYC program; I've learned some skills, knowledge, and ways of being in my classes; and I have a life of experience interacting with people, including being a young person myself, so I know I'll be just fine starting out.
5. I can trust myself—that my curiosity and excitement to learn about skills, the site, and people will show me the way.

Try to acknowledge the worries, then focus on the excitement and curiosity in its shadow. "I can't wait to meet the young people at the site!" "What will they be like?" "I wonder what will come up in conversation." "I'm looking forward to participating in the activities." "I am looking forward to shadowing my supervisor to see how they do their job." "I'm excited to see what I will learn!" Acknowledging and then replacing worry with curiosity and excitement can go a long way.

On Perfection

Central to many of the myths about, barriers to, and preconceived notions when beginning practicum is the common fear of making a mistake, and we can blame this on our collective culture of perfection and certainty. Milne (2018) echoes this message in her advice to practicum students: "the biggest mistake we are inclined to make is to approach practicum in fear of making a mistake... The student who plays it safe has the misconception that they are protecting themselves, when in reality they are putting up barriers to achieving their own potential. Now is the time to make mistakes" (p. 28). Meanwhile, Hillman (2018) advises CYC practicum students that "one of the most important feelings to become familiar with is being in the tension of not knowing" (p. 69). Think about these messages and how they land for you.

> Many students believe they need to have the answers and/or need to present as overly competent. I remind them their practicum is a place to learn, to ask questions and explore; to be curious; and it's okay, and even expected, to make mistakes.
> —Rhonda, CYC Practicum Faculty-Instructor

What is, and has been, your relationship with perfection and certainty? With your experience of making mistakes? With needing to know? With believing we should know? What memories and experiences come up for you? How have you carried these experiences forward? Are they generative and helpful? Are they limiting and unhelpful? Do they encourage fear? Do they encourage learning? Let's try to approach this experience differently than we may have been supported to do so in the past.

> Anxiety is such an interesting thing because it shows you that you're actually caring and wanting to do something. Try to recognize where the anxiety is coming from.
> —Sam, CYC Student

Practicum is a time where we intentionally open up space for a new experience. We are opening our minds to consider new knowledge, skills, and ways of being. We are opening up ourselves for connection with young people. We are opening up our lives for new experiences. We are open. Let us stay open as we notice fear, worry, and apprehension pass by. All those feelings are doing is attempting to keep us safe. For that, we can thank them. But they do not allow us to learn, change, be creative, nor be effective. Let's acknowledge perfection, know where it comes from, recognize how it manifests in our lives, and attempt to encourage ourselves to be open in the presence of it, in the face of it attempting to close our experiences down to something superficial. Let's stay open.

STARTING WELL

At this point in time, your practicum coordinator or faculty-instructor will likely tell you that they're going to introduce you to a potential practicum site supervisor, and the following section will attend to this stage.

Meeting with Your Potential Practicum Site Supervisor

Hamlet (2017) suggests that practicum students act as though the practicum is an extended interview, where you put your best foot forward at all times. In fact, if there's a job opening, a practicum placement is a fantastic way to get hired at an agency. When faculty-instructors send students out to meet with a potential practicum site supervisor, it is often for an informal interview. That is to say, both student and site supervisor meet each other to determine if this will be a good fit, with a general assumption that a lot of gatekeeping work has been completed by the faculty-instructor or practicum placement coordinator. That is not to say, however, it should be treated informally; a student should approach this interview professionally. Know that you are not in competition with hundreds of other applicants. The site supervisor is looking forward to meeting you, curious to know what you want to learn, and they want to bring you on as a practicum student. Don't give them reasons not to.

> I had a student send me an email. She had me at hello. She described herself, her previous experience, and her areas of interest. She described her framework and what she hoped to get out of the placement. I was like: Yah, when can you start.
> —Sonja, CYC Practicum Supervisor

First and foremost, we should show up with an engaged attitude to all of our time at the practicum site. This includes the entirety of the practicum experience, but it also includes the interview (even during the correspondence that confirms the interview itself), as this is a time we begin establishing relationships and enter into the potential practicum space. Consider McGrath's (2018) suggestions about how CYC practicum students can show up with a positive attitude, to remain "positive, even when things are challenging" (p. 124), detailed in Table 2.1.

> Come in knowing that our kids are spectacular human beings, resilient, creative, compassionate individuals, not 'kids in care.'
> —Farah, CYC Practicum Supervisor

Table 2.1: McGrath's All about Attitude

McGrath's All about Attitude	
Much to Learn	• Go with fresh eyes and open ears • Notice what is happening around you • Try to recognize what resonates with you • Recognize what makes you uncomfortable
Reflect	• Process what you are thinking, feeling, and doing • Be open and honest • Select something that works for you: journalling, music, art, etc. • What excites you? What are you afraid of? What confuses you? What do you still want to learn? • Begin individually, then discuss with others
Be Curious	• Talk to your supervisor, staff, other students, and faculty • Ask about roles, education, prior work experience • Ask about programming, policies, emergency procedures • Understand the agency and staff team • Be clear on expectations with your supervisor and know that this will change. Do you want direct feedback on how you can improve? Do you need your strengths identified too? • Be curious with young people. Learn about them • Find commonalities and interests to create meaningful activities and interventions • Share some of yourself and your story
Make Mistakes	• Accept that you will make mistakes • Fear of doing things "right" can stop you from doing anything • Don't just sit back and watch. Do things Show initiative and take action • Ask • When you make a mistake, acknowledge it, and ask for feedback • Try not to make the same mistake again • This is the most useful learning

(continued)

Table 2.1: Continued

McGrath's All about Attitude	
Share	• Share what you're learning from classes • Bring readings and resources that resonate with you • Offer to speak about a new theory or intervention in a staff meeting, share an activity, or bake your favourite cookies • Present information to be helpful and supportive, not challenging and unsupportive of people at your practicum
You Are Not the Only Priority	• The young people at your practicum site deserve your best self • Supporting your learning is important, but not staff's first priority • Reflection, debriefing, and taking care of yourself supports others • There will be times when you're stressed, frustrated, or insecure; learn how to work through these emotions and don't be too hard on yourself • Think about why you're there • Acknowledge the complex history and present challenges experienced by the people with whom you are working
Be Yourself	• This is the most important thing you'll learn and can be the most challenging • Don't try to be someone you're not; don't prioritize impressing people over being genuine • You are enough!

Adapted from Kostouros, P., & Briegel, M. (Eds.). (2018). *Child and youth care practice: Collected wisdom for new practitioners* (pp. 124–126). Cape Town, South Africa: CYC-Net Press.

Interview Recommendations

When preparing for and participating in a practicum site interview, listening to site supervisors' and past students' wisdom is best. Consider the following wisdom. Remember, supervisors look forward to meeting you and seeing how you may contribute to their site.

Words of Wisdom from CYC Practicum Supervisors and Students

Arrive on time. Dress appropriately for the setting. Think about the reasons why they want this practicum. Come prepared to ask the questions they need to, to ensure they can achieve these goals. Learn a bit about the organization ahead of time.
   —Annie, CYC Practicum Supervisor

Search the place you're going to be. Try your best to understand what the expectations are in this environment. How long am I going to be there? Am I to have a lunch break? Understand the philosophy. Even just, what do I wear? There's different expectations at different workplaces.
   —Jenn, CYC Student

Look at our website. Have some knowledge around our values and mission statement, what our agency does, who we service as a whole, and our overarching goals with our families. Having all of that tells me students are invested and interested in what they want to do and really want to be a part of this shift and moving children out of care.
  —Mindi, CYC Practicum Supervisor

Read up and learn as much as you possibly can about their service, what they provide, what their philosophy is, what their motivations are, what they're hoping to achieve with the population they're working with. I'd also ask the supervisor more about their role and learn what a day-in-the-life in the role looks like. Be able to anticipate what you might be engaging in as a student.
  —Jasmine, CYC Student

Go on our website. Read about our organization. Bring a cover letter, a resume, and dress professionally. Come as a learner, not an expert.
  —Farah, CYC Practicum Supervisor

Start open.
  —Harman, CYC Student

I want to find out their passions and their goals so that I can build their practicum around what they want.
  —Chris, CYC Practicum Supervisor

Before your interview, you should spend some time exploring the agency's website (mandate, programs, etc.) and physical surroundings (location, structures, program areas) and attend to administrative items (confirming attendance, arriving early, and bringing a copy of your resume). During your interview, you should be prepared to respond to the following questions:

1. Why are you interested in doing your practicum at this site?
2. What volunteer, work, and educational experience is relevant to preparing you for this practicum experience?
3. What strengths do you bring to your role as a CYC practitioner?
4. What areas do you want to improve and skills you want to build?
5. What are you hoping to learn?
6. Where do you see yourself after you complete your credential?

Finally, it is helpful to develop a few questions to ask the practicum site supervisor. Consider this time an opportunity

Why do you want to come here? What will you bring? What do you want to learn? How do you think you'll engage the young people here? What interests do you have that may interest the young people? What do you know about the community? What do you need to complete academically while you're here? What's your availability? What do you want to contribute? Why are you in the CYC program? What experience do you have already?
  —Tom, CYC Practicum Supervisor

to learn more about the agency and about your potential contribution and learning experience. These questions could include:

- Could you tell me about your program and how it fits within the wider organization?
- What does a day-in-the-life of a CYC practitioner look like here?
- What are some of the biggest challenges facing the young people/families here?
- How is wellness supported at this agency?
- When will I hear back about if I will be a good fit for the placement?
- If I were to get this placement, who would my supervisor be? What hours would I be working? Where would I be located? What should I wear?

Be sure to let your faculty-instructor or practicum coordinator know when the interview is scheduled, so that they're aware of this meeting and so they can support you and the supervisor with any information you may need. Be sure to let your faculty-instructor or practicum coordinator know the interview occurred. You will know this, because you participated in it. But how will your instructor or coordinator know? Meanwhile, some supervisors will confirm that they'll want to take you aboard in the interview. Be sure to inform your faculty-instructor of this determination as soon as you can. Other supervisors want to confirm or consult with the faculty-instructor or practicum coordinator before confirming with a student. This is why it's helpful to correspond with your faculty-instructor or coordinator, so that they can contact the potential site supervisor and inform you both of the next steps.

Before You Begin

After confirming your placement, practicum students can begin to prepare. To assist not only in beginning well but also to start the process of goal setting and establishing relationships with people at your site, consider following questions. Also consider recording your responses in your learning journal.

- What do you know so far about the program of which you'll be a part? What overarching organization or agency is it a part of? What do you know about it?
- What do you know about the role you'll be performing at practicum?
- What was it like visiting your practicum site for the first time during the interview? What did you notice about its space, the young people there, the activities happening, and so on?
- What are you looking forward to? What are you apprehensive about?
- What do you hope to learn in this practicum setting? (Recognize that you have not yet begun and that you can, should, and will evolve these goals.)
- You'll likely be hearing from your classmates about their placements, as they are confirmed. What are you looking forward to learning about their experiences?

Get to Know Your Practicum Site

Your placement has been confirmed. You have a start date. You're about to begin. You are anxiously awaiting to start. Something you could be doing to begin immersing yourself at the site is to explore the site and community at arm's length. Follow through with any of the suggested activities below and you'll be ahead of the game. These orientation activities will be particularly helpful for those of you placed in communities where you haven't worked, lived, or studied before. Even if you don't end up working in the community where you're completing your practicum, you will nevertheless transfer what you learn to the next community you work within and do the same there.

Orientation Activities

Note your reflections for the following activities.

- ☑ Explore the agency on the internet—read their website, look for reports, pamphlets/program descriptions, news articles, or other documents on the Web that expand your knowledge about the programs and wider organization.
- ☑ Explore other services and institutions in the area and take the time to wonder about the connections they may have (e.g., school, library, advisory committees, recreation centres, neighbourhood houses, health clinics, etc.).
- ☑ If appropriate, visit your agency (or your agency's overarching organization) and try to take the perspective of a young person or family coming there for the first time. What do you notice? Who welcomes you into the space? Are there informal and formal gathering spots? How is it designed/decorated? Who is/seems to be welcome? Not welcome? Is it child/youth/family friendly?
- ☑ Reflect on your visit to your agency during your practicum interview (or your agency's overarching organization). Who welcomed you into the space? How do people move through the space? Are there gathering spots (inside/outside)? Who is welcome? Not welcome?
- ☑ Walk around the agency's community—reflect on what this walk tells you about the agency and community. Notice where young people hang out: the proximity to transportation, services, parks, etc.
- ☑ Start to learn about the Indigenous land that the agency occupies. What is the history of this land? What relationship exists between the agency and the Indigenous people of the community.
- ☑ Visit the community's government representative offices (municipal, provincial, federal). Introduce yourself as a practicum student, and ask if there are any resources and issues you should know about in this community. Ask how the representatives serve the young people in the community.
- ☑ Review the community's local newspaper and other news media for articles about the community—issues, services, upcoming events, etc.

☑ Visit the local library in your community. Explain your upcoming role and ask the librarian to help link you to relevant resources that will help you understand the community.

(adapted from Szewello Allen, 2012, p. 29)

> Come in with questions. After our walkabout, I hope they'll have honest questions for me.
> —Donna, CYC Practicum Supervisor

This is purposeful work, intended to benefit your contribution to the practicum site. Don't forget to include some of these hours as part of your practicum preparation, if you are permitted to do so.

Your First Week

You've just begun. You may be overwhelmed with observations, new names, policy and procedural information, and so on. You may be thrilled to dive into the action and connect with the young people at the site. During this time, your supervisor will walk you through an orientation to the site, specific to its programs and your upcoming role. As you are oriented, consider the checklist for your first week at practicum.

Checklist for Your First Week at Practicum

✓ Be keen, interested, and proactive. Above all, be yourself!
✓ Bring a notebook to note things you wish to remember—questions, names, acronyms, and jargon you don't yet understand
✓ Learn the flow of the space—who and what exists where
✓ Learn basic office routines (e.g., entry/exit sign in and out, phone use, door locks, etc.)
✓ Learn who will be your primary (and secondary) supervisor, including their contact information
✓ Meet the staff. Where relevant, ask to shadow and observe multiple staff in various roles
✓ Begin a list that includes resources you notice staff talk about and use most frequently
✓ Ask your supervisor if, over the duration of your practicum, you can visit those resources to learn more
✓ Review policy, manuals, procedures, relevant agency reports, staff flow charts, and so on, and ask for and review related legislation
✓ Ask specifically about the site's policies around confidentiality, disclosures of abuse and neglect, and emergency procedures
✓ Review client files, if permitted and encouraged, with purpose, respect, and attention to confidentiality

✓ Show your supervisor your assignment descriptions, so they can be aware of learning opportunities for you to successfully complete them

✓ Ask to attend meetings, activities, and upcoming community events

✓ Try to remember the names of young people and something positive you've learned about them in your first interactions with them

✓ Plan for reflective practice at the end of the day/week to establish a regular routine

✓ Be patient with yourself as you are on a learning curve

Adapted from Drolet, J., Clark, N., & Allen, H. (2012). *Shifting sites of practice: Field education in Canada* (pp. 30–31). Toronto, ON: Pearson.

Meanwhile, like many new jobs, placements, or educational programs, some necessary paperwork will need to be completed. It's suggested you review some of the templates in the Appendices section of this guidebook, and use them or seek out similar forms required through your agency or school (summarized in Table 2.2). Some of these forms will be required before practicum begins, as it begins, throughout your placement, and afterward. Review what is required of you.

While some of this information seems obvious and repetitive, it's helpful to have copies of some of these forms for each person: student, supervisor, and faculty-instructor. Why? So you know who to contact and how to contact them in the case of emergency, illness, or change of plan. You never know when you'll need this information, and you'll thank yourself when you don't have to go back into email archives or day planners for it.

Combined, the preparatory work listed in the chapter thus far should provide a foundation as to what we expect as we begin practicum. Further, it should give us a sense of what is necessary for us to show up to and begin well in a new practice space. Doing the tasks above is part of our professional work. Put another way, attending to those pieces is part of being professional. In Chapter 3, Professional CYC Practice, we will review professionalism in more depth and detail. We'll focus the remainder of this chapter on aspects of professionalism that relate to showing up to practicum well and what happens when we do not do so.

DEMONSTRATING PROFESSIONALISM AND PROFESSIONAL JUDGEMENT

At a very basic level, professionalism includes being mindful of appropriate dress/attire, sticking to a planned schedule, being respectful of and pleasant with everyone we meet, acting ethically, displaying competence, being prepared, seeking and integrating supervision and feedback, and communicating well (including being aware of technology use, such as smart phones, etc.). This also means we arrive on time, dress and groom ourselves

Table 2.2: Practicum Appendix Forms

Appendix Form	What Does It Include?	How Is This Form Used and by Whom?	When Is the Form Completed?
Appendix B Student Preferences Form	Indicates helpful student information to assist faculty/coordinator in the placement process	Completed by student Reviewed by faculty/coordinator	Before practicum begins
Appendix C Placement Information Form	An at-a-glance description of the basic information about your practicum site and practicum requirements	Completed by student, supervisor, and faculty-instructor Copy given to each person	As practicum begins
Appendix D Emergency Contact Form	Best way to reach each person in practicum in the case of emergency (illness, crisis response, etc.)	Completed by student in consultation with supervisor and faculty-instructor Copy given to each person	As practicum begins
Appendix E Timesheet and Activities Form	A running record. A summary of activities and tasks completed each day of practicum, along with a calculation of hours	Completed by student Signed by supervisor Reviewed by faculty	Throughout practicum
Appendix F Recommendation for Practice Form	A summary of placement information, student strengths and areas for improvement, and overall recommendation for the field	Completed by supervisor Used by student	End of practicum

appropriately for the site and role, show consistent effort, and are tactful, patient, and proactive. We are aware of and maintain safety standards, promote a positive atmosphere, and work collaboratively with young people and staff. Meanwhile, we display sound professional judgement.

On professional judgement specifically, we acknowledge that we are always learning, but that we attempt to perform a number of professional actions that centre the needs of young people before our own. Consider the University of the Fraser Valley's (2017)

Table 2.3: UFV's Professional Judgement in CYC

UFV's Professional Judgement in CYC			
Regarding the welfare of the child, youth, family, and/or community as the primary obligation	Respecting confidentiality and exceptions	Understanding roles and responsibilities of self and others	Developing effective working relationships
Being mindful of actions and their impact on others	Maintaining appropriate self-care and self-regulation	Respond thoughtfully, rather than reacting to situations	Knowing when personal biases or circumstances are impacting practice, and taking actions to minimize their impact
Seeking supervision and consultation when necessary	Being trauma-informed, including recognizing the impact of vicarious trauma and taking steps to manage it	Maintaining a focus on strengths and needs, rather than behaviour	Observing/asking questions to learn from others before acting independently
Taking steps to improve effectiveness	Producing clear and logically organized work	Using discretion in use of all electronic communication, both professional (e.g., email) and personal (public social networking)	Other

Adapted from University of the Fraser Valley. (2017). *CYC 410: Comprehensive field guide for students and field supervisors* (p. 15). Abbotsford, BC: Author.

degree-level CYC practicum program's professional judgement expectations of practicum students, listed in Table 2.3.

Ultimately, we are learning to practise good professional judgement. We observe others acting with professional judgement, we reflect on how we've experienced professional judgement, and we see the impacts of the presence or absence of professional judgement on the young people looking to us for support and guidance. Practicum is a time to learn what professional judgement looks like, in the context of each of our practicum placements.

Not the Right Time

Unfortunately, it is often the absence of these basic professional expectations and professional judgement that is cause for students' removal from their practicum site. This is an undesired outcome from all positions, and only very occasionally required. Usually these observations are made early and frequently enough to cause concern.

You may have read the list in Table 2.3 and thought to yourself: "Of course this should happen!" We hope you feel that way. Now read back through the list again and imagine if any item, or all of them, were to not occur. Put yourself in the shoes of the young people and staff at the site and imagine how they would experience that behaviour.

The following situations are examples where a supervisor and faculty-instructor have questioned a student's readiness to complete practicum.

- A practicum student informs their faculty-instructor or practicum coordinator that they must be placed in a school-based setting but is only available in the evening and on weekends, or a student declares interest in completing the practicum course but does not or is unable to make space in their schedule to complete the required number of hours
- A practicum student fails to show up for a confirmed pre-placement interview, with no follow-up with their potential site supervisor or faculty-instructor
- A practicum student frequently arrives late to practicum shifts, disregarding feedback from their supervisor and faculty-instructor
- A practicum student acts inappropriately toward young people/families: for example, they disclose confidential information to a third party; they post a photo of a young person on a social media site without permission; they share inappropriate personal information with young people; or they disrespect a young person or family in some way, where the student disregards feedback or guidance, or does not comprehend the significance of their behaviour
- A practicum student engages in dangerous activity without regard for young people's or their own safety
- A practicum student experiences health issues that cause them to not be present, responsive, and able to participate during shifts, and has not sought out and made suitable plans to accommodate that health issue
- A practicum student misses too many shifts so as to disrupt the relationships built at the site, so much so that it is inappropriate for them to return
- A practicum student continually refuses to integrate or is unable to recognize constructive feedback regarding their actions

Central to many removal decisions is the absence of self-awareness of the issue at hand and the disregard for the perspective, perceptions, and experiences of young people, families, and colleagues at the practicum setting. In the rare but necessary case where it is not the right time for a student to continue, alternate plans must and will be made by and in collaboration with the faculty-instructor and practicum supervisor. When this happens, this will also be treated as a learning opportunity for the student. What is it about this time, the conditions in a student's life, the context of which a student is unable or unwilling to participate professionally in practicum? That is the learning opportunity a student will need to move through in order to re-assess readiness when planning to begin practicum again.

You may have noticed, by the very fact of attending to each topic, activity, list, question, and reflection in the guidebook thus far, that practicum is a lot more than just showing up for X number of hours. You are being introduced to a set of expectations that go beyond what a classroom-based course or introductory work experience may have asked of you. It is important to attend to how that added responsibility and change impacts our lives.

LEARNING JOURNAL

Using your learning journal, complete the structured and/or unstructured question prompts. If you are in the beginning of the placement process—that is, not yet placed, only have just gone to the interview—just be where you are. Think of the relationships you are forming in this context (e.g., your collaborative learning and seminar group members, your supervisor, and your faculty-instructor), the theories and perspectives you're incorporating into this stage of the process (e.g., the coursework you're reminding yourself of, the ideas presented in this book, etc.), and so on. You may not yet be placed or even have an idea as to where you'll be placed, whereas many of your classmates are going to interviews, researching their sites, and so on. This can cause significant anxiety, especially as time passes. Again, be where you are—what is coming up for you? What are you apprehensive about? At the very worst, some students are placed later, but students are always placed in a practicum placement. Knowing this, how could you best be spending your time? How could you initiate a reflective practice that will help you once you begin?

PRACTICE SCENARIOS

Take a look at the Practice Scenarios that conclude this chapter: "Tala's Worry" and "Students' Concerns." Use the content that you've read in this chapter to inspire your thinking about each scenario. Notice how the scenarios may relate to your own situation at your current practicum placement, even if they are not exactly what you are experiencing. Consider the questions posed at the end of each scenario to help you expand and apply the concepts presented in this chapter.

SEMINAR GROUP AND COMMUNITY OF PRACTICE DISCUSSION QUESTIONS

As you begin your practicum seminar and are oriented to your practicum classmates, consider developing a community of practice, following the guidelines in Chapter 1, Your Theoretical Orientation to CYC Practice. Many of the questions listed in this guidebook would fill up a seminar discussion in no time. Further, your faculty-instructor will tailor your seminar, facilitating the topics and questions based on your group and community context. Using a community of practice as a discussion group will take your learning to an additionally helpful space; not only will you discuss relevant and timely topics, facilitated by the structure of this guidebook (and everyone's contributions), but by the very fact that you'll be together, you'll help support each other through this process, from beginning to end.

1. What and where is your practicum placement (agency, program)? What is your role (as best as you know it at this point)?
2. What are you looking forward to? What are you apprehensive about?
3. What are some assumptions you are making as you begin your practicum placement?
4. What are your post-graduation goals and how do you think your upcoming practicum connects to those goals?

Look for ways to shine, to go beyond what is expected, and to think critically about the work of the wider agency to find ways to contribute to the health and functioning of the agency. Human kindness and genuine curiosity about the people they work with will carry them far. Show up early and say hello. Eat lunch with folks who work in different programs and ask them about their roles. Be a good guest.
—Kristy, CYC Practicum Faculty-Instructor

IN CLOSING

As you begin your practicum placement, there are many checks and balances to attend to, which can be overwhelming, exciting, and a lot to take in. Beyond the necessary, required, and helpful administrative items is the focus on process. How can we begin well in new places? How can we be intentional about engaging in new relationships? How can we set the stage for good learning to happen? These are all the things we devote an incredible amount of time and attention to, but in the end, it benefits us all through our strengthened relationships, developing ourselves as practitioners, and our overall practicum experience.

PRACTICE SCENARIOS

Tala's Worry

Tala is a practicum student just starting at a family development centre, placed alongside the outreach workers who conduct visits in the home to support families' goals with their children. Her supervisor describes their day-to-day work as never the same: they cook and share meals, play games together, focus on positive discipline strategies, go on outings to parks, as well as do errands and household chores. Tala thinks she'll enjoy the home and community-based nature of the experience. However, she's worried about one thing: she doesn't have children. She has experience working with young children as a nanny for a few summers, and she's taken care of her younger cousins all her life. However, she believes that the families may judge her or not want to work with her because she isn't a parent.

How should Tala approach this situation? How would you suggest she introduce herself to the parents? Is there any area in your upcoming practicum experience where you think you may lack "credibility"? Is there something about your identity that you think may be judged at your practicum placement?

_____

_____

_____

Students' Concerns

Sonya was chatting with a classmate about their upcoming placements, each at an elementary school, and comparing notes about what they'll each be doing—one placed in a classroom with a teacher and the other given a caseload of students to support throughout the school, Sonya now fears that she got a placement that'll be too challenging. Meanwhile, Ari is thrilled to learn he got what others are saying is a "perfect" practicum placement, at a hospital's child psychiatric unit. Rumi doesn't understand how she'll complete all of her required hours when the youth drop-in centre isn't open enough during the week; yet another student in her cohort has already set a schedule at the family centre and will complete her hours early. Meanwhile, Linds hasn't confirmed her practicum placement yet, and the rest of her cohort is about to begin.

What is happening for each student before their practicum placement begins? How is comparison not helping each student? What would you suggest that each student do to start off well at their practicum placement, despite all these different beginnings?

_____

_____

_____

CHAPTER 3

Professional CYC Practice

Competencies for Professional Child and Youth Work Practitioners				
Professionalism	Cultural and Human Diversity	Applied Human Development	Relationship and Communication	Developmental Practice Methods
Awareness of the Profession Professional Development and Behaviour Professional Boundaries Professional Ethics			Teamwork and Professional Communication	Health and Safety

As a CYC student, there is a focus on defining your own sense of self-awareness and professionalism in context to working with others and as a part of a multi-disciplinary team. The first year is full of exploration both personally and professionally and I would encourage students to take the time to look at what professional resources exist and are available to offer further support, learning and mentoring, such as their provincial Association for CYC and the CYC Certification Board. Often additional training opportunities and other learning are available through these resources.

—Julia Margetiak, Chair, Certification Process Committee, CYC Certification Board

When we discuss professional practice in Child and Youth Care (CYC), we mean a number of things, including, but not limited to, the development of our field over time and the professional standards that we expect of ourselves and what other people can hold us accountable to. Practicum is a time when we observe other professionals practise their work and when we, sometimes for the first time, begin to see ourselves as emerging professionals: out in the field, contributing our perspectives, approaches, and selves for the benefit of young people.

Many of us were introduced to Child and Youth Care as a profession through our Introductory to Professional Practice (or similarly titled) course in our first term of our educational program. There, we likely studied many of the topics we reviewed in Chapter 1, as well as some that come up in this chapter, where we'll focus on professional practice in more detail and depth. We may have also been introduced and welcomed into the discussions, debates, and critiques regarding the professionalization of our field. Either way, by enrolling in a CYC program and immersing oneself in a practicum experience, we have the chance to enact these professional values, standards, and aspirations by intentionally contributing to the field. As one of the thousands of CYC students across Canada, you get to define what the profession is and what it will become. You get to bring the great work of leaders in the CYC field forward to respond to the social conditions of our time in the way you collectively determine. There is great responsibility in that awareness and invitation. As well, there is great opportunity for you—yes, you—to expand, promote, call into question, advance, discard, and redefine what it is we do.

LOOKING TO THE PAST

Before we look to the future, let's look to the past. What does professionalism mean?

Hills (1989) states the hallmark of a professional is skillfulness, which involves four elements:

1. Contextual Awareness, which allows you to "recognize the salient features in a given situation"
2. Discretionary Decision-Making, which requires you to "make qualitative distinctions or judgments about how to respond effectively"
3. Performance, which is the ability to "demonstrate specific behaviours and techniques"
4. Confidence, which is defined as "trust in [your] ability… and to perform effectively" (pp. 17–18)

Moving from the individual (professional) to the collective (profession), Curry, Schneider-Munoz, and Carpenter-Williams (2012) comment on the roots of the word *profession*, which is "to proclaim publicly—a commitment to an ideal" (p. 7), whereby they identify eight common elements that comprise a profession:

1. Commitment to a higher calling or service
2. Altruistic purpose
3. Public profession
4. Rigorous and extensive training, primarily intellectual in nature

5. Systematic body of knowledge
6. Ethical code
7. Professional culture or association
8. Professional autonomy and self-regulation over work recognized by a society (pp. 7–8)

Keeping in mind that CYC is developing as a profession—unlike already well-established professions such as engineers, physicians, nurses, teachers, psychologists, and social workers, for example—how do you align with and pursue each of the elements above? Much of your practicum experience will do so.

Sercombe (2010) suggests a profession is a *relationship*. In this relationship of service, "the professional is there to service the client, not the other way around," and a CYC practitioner creates "spaces within which that can happen well, and walks with young people through the process" (p. 18). Moving from abstract to concrete, he also refers to the professional as the facilitator and protector of a "sacred circle," which includes trust, confidentiality, vulnerability, risk, transformation, healing, and alternative ways of being, as well as codes of ethics, professional associations, and "strategies designed to protect the inner and outer integrity of that circle" (p. 18). Let's look at this concept visually to understand it further, in Figure 3.1: Sercombe's Sacred Circle.

> Every single experience that you have, you are always building your professional character. There is always something you can take away.
> —Trina, CYC Student

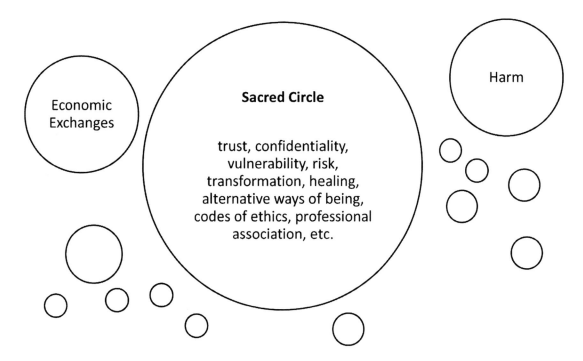

Figure 3.1: Sercombe's Sacred Circle

Adapted from Sercombe, H. (2010). *Youth work ethics* (p. 18). London, UK: SAGE.

Looking at this Sacred Circle, notice what is included and excluded. What else would you include? Exclude? Sercombe suggests that we have "strategies designed to protect the inner and outer integrity of that circle," which is an essential responsibility of professional practice (p. 18). What strategies do we have to protect the inner and outer integrity of this circle? There are many. Think of some yourself: what ways of knowing, doing, and being protect the integrity of the circle? For example, how do you imagine that self-awareness, critical reflection, commitment to ethical practice, establishing boundaries within relationships, and so on are ways we protect the integrity of the professional relationship and of our professional practice? For the remainder of the chapter (as well as other parts of this guidebook, including Chapter 9, Challenging and Challenges in CYC Practice), we will focus on how professional CYC practice serves to support the therapeutic relationship we create with young people, and how we can learn more about professionalism in our current practicum placement.

TOWARD PROFESSIONALIZATION

With our roots always responding to the social conditions of our time, CYC has created educational and academic institutions to support and lead our practice: we've gathered together to form associations and networks; we've formalized processes of accreditation and certification; and we've worked toward the professionalization of our field. Professionalization is the culmination and progression of all these movements. These processes are happening on a local, national, and global scale. It is important to recognize that you are not only a student, enrolled in a CYC program, taking a practicum course. You are also entering the profession, becoming a professional practitioner. We can see this movement over time in Figure 3.2. You are encouraged to participate in these ongoing discussions and debates.

As our field has evolved, it has defined, adapted, and adopted common descriptions of our scope of practice and the standards of practice we hold ourselves to, including competencies and ethics. In Chapter 1, we explored CYC from a theoretical orientation point of view. Here, we will explore CYC from a professional point of view.

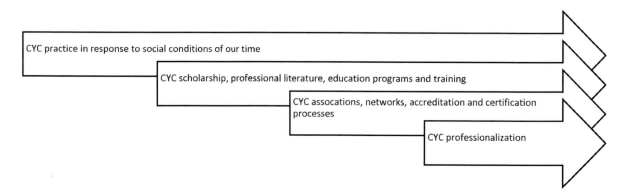

Figure 3.2: CYC Professionalism over Time

CYC Scope of Practice

As our field develops, many practitioners, scholars, activists, organizations, and associations have attempted to outline what Child and Youth Care is. Consider the following sources.

As quoted in Chapter 1, the Council of Canadian Child and Youth Care Associations (n.d.) defines the scope—population, setting, purpose, interventions, goals, and focus—of CYC practice:

> Child and youth care practitioners work with children, youth and families with complex needs. They can be found in a variety of settings such as group homes and residential treatment centres, hospitals and community mental health clinics, community-based outreach and school-based programs, as well as in private practice and juvenile justice programs. Child and youth care workers specialize in the development and implementation of therapeutic programs and planned environments and the utilization of daily life events to facilitate change. At the core of all effective child and youth care practice is a focus on the therapeutic relationship; the application of theory and research about human growth and development to promote the optimal physical, psycho-social, spiritual, cognitive, and emotional development of young people toward a healthy and productive adulthood; and a focus on strengths and assets rather than pathology. (para. 2)

Meanwhile, Stuart (2013) collects the voices of students, practitioners, and scholars, including multiple definitions, scopes of practice, and descriptions of what Child and Youth Care is. She noticed six themes through which CYC has been described: passion, caring, the milieu, social competence, space and time, and experientially. She reminds us that our descriptions are contingent on the audience with whom we're communicating. How we describe our work to other professionals is different than how we describe our work to our friends and family, which is different to how we describe our work for our field. How would you describe our practice for young people and their families? Consider that for a moment.

From a post-structural, critical theory standpoint (ideas you may learn later in your credential), Skott-Myhre (2008) challenges us to think about our work in less rigid and predetermined ways, referring to a radical youth work:

> As a liberatory praxis… where adults are able to forget for a moment that they "know" young people… join youth and adults in creative hazardous performances that escape full definition by dominant cultural standards… a relation of force interested in what has not happened yet… that which has not yet been… an encounter that involves youth and adults… an encounter of potential. (pp. 176–184)

As we move through this chapter, which will focus on specific standards of practice, keep this view of our practice in mind: we create space for potential to emerge.

> The moments I began to consider myself a professional happened when I was given specific responsibilities: Deescalate a situation. Plan a group. Research the needs of a client. Propose something. Actually facilitating something.
> —John, CYC Student

CYC STANDARDS OF PRACTICE

In practicum, we will focus on a number of skills, knowledges, and ways of being. These pieces depend on our own learning goals and what learning opportunities are available at our practicum sites. Due to the expansive nature of what is included in the scope of Child and Youth Care practice, there is ample room to develop many competencies. Competency is central to what a professional practitioner contributes to the therapeutic relationship. For the most part, North American CYC practitioners, Canadian Associations, and educational institutions look to the Association for Child and Youth Care Practice and the Child and Youth Care Certification Board (2010) for its Standards of Practice developed by long-standing practitioners, scholars, and educators in our field.

CYC Competencies

The Association for Child and Youth Care Practice and the Child and Youth Care Certification Board (2010) outline five domains of competencies central to all CYC practice, across all CYC settings, including the foundational knowledge that informs each competency and an outline of the professional competency itself. These competencies are:

1. Professionalism
2. Cultural and Human Diversity
3. Applied Human Development
4. Relationship and Communication
5. Developmental Practice Methods

A copy of this document is included in this guidebook as Appendix G: Competencies for Professional Child and Youth Work Practitioners. As you have noticed thus far, each chapter of this guidebook begins by highlighting the competency subsections that the content reviews. Meanwhile, many of our educational programs are indirectly or directly designed to meet these competencies through content, pedagogical processes and assessments, and practicum experiences and desired outcomes. While your practicum may be assessed through various assessment categories of its own, there will no doubt be overlap between each individual CYC program and these competencies. So, it is worth focusing on these competencies as a short-term goal (i.e., preparatory work toward meeting your practicum requirements) and a longer-term goal (i.e., preparatory work toward becoming a professional practitioner as you complete your educational requirements and move into the field).

Let's turn our attention to the first competency—professionalism. Professionalism and other competency domains will also be explored in other chapters. First, go to Appendix G and review the document in full. While reading the first domain, think about how it applies in your current practicum context. Then complete Activity 3.1.

Activity 3.1: Professionalism in My Practicum

In this activity, we will:

1. Review the competencies and sub-competencies listed under Professionalism in the Competencies for Professional Child and Youth Work Practitioners,
2. Consider how these sub-competencies can directly apply to your practicum placement, and
3. Brainstorm responses to the questions in Table 3.1.

We've reviewed some of the prompts in the chapters thus far; others won't be covered in detail until later chapters. For others, you may need to consult with your supervisor, colleagues, classmates, or policy and procedure manual.

Table 3.1: Professional Competencies in CYC Practicum

Professionalism			
Professional Competencies	**Example of Sub-competency**	**Application to Your Practicum—Questions**	**My Notes**
1. Awareness of the Profession	(a) Access the professional literature	What professional literature do I need to consult to inform my work at practicum? What coursework do I need to review? What evidence-based practice and practice-based evidence research (residential care, educational program, community youth development programming) do I need to review, relevant to my practicum setting? What could my supervisor connect me to, helping me access this literature?	
2. Professional Development and Behaviour	(a) Value orientation (2) State a philosophy of practice that provides guiding principles for the design, delivery, and management of services	What is my philosophy of practice? What is my philosophy of practice that guides my specific roles and responsibilities at my current practicum setting (relationships, activities, ethics, etc.)? What is my supervisor's (and/or colleagues') philosophy of practice? How do I "see" these philosophies of practice in action?	

(continued)

Table 3.1: Continued

Professionalism			
Professional Competencies	**Example of Sub-competency**	**Application to Your Practicum—Questions**	**My Notes**
3. Personal Development and Self-Care	(b) Self-Care (1) Incorporate "wellness" practices into own lifestyle	How am I planning on incorporating wellness practices into my lifestyle? How does my agency support wellness practices?	
4. Professional Ethics	(b) Apply the process of ethical decision-making in a proactive manner	What are some typical ethical situations and/or dilemmas that occur at my practicum setting? What processes do my supervisors and colleagues engage in to make ethical decisions? What process am I encouraged to take if I am confronted with an ethical dilemma? How can I be proactive, rather than reactive, to ethical situations and dilemmas?	
5. Awareness of Law and Regulations	(b) Describe the legal responsibility for reporting child abuse and neglect and the consequences of failure to report	What is the process for reporting abuse/neglect at my practicum site? What are some examples of how my supervisor and/or colleagues responded to a young person's disclosure of abuse/neglect? What were some of the tensions and unease my supervisor/colleagues experienced during this process?	
6. Advocacy	(c) Describe the rights of children and youth and families in relevant settings and systems	What are some relevant rights of young people and families at my practicum setting?	

Adapted from Association for Child and Youth Care Practice and Child and Youth Care Certification Board. (2010). *Competencies for Professional Child and Youth Work Practitioners* (pp. 10–12).

With 5 competency domains, 28 sub-competencies, and 154 items under those sub-competencies, that's a lot of skill, knowledge, and ways of being. Do not fear, however. You won't be asked to focus on all those items; neither will all be entirely relevant to your site and role. But you will be asked to focus on a variety of areas (across competencies) as they relate to your own development as a practitioner, your interests, and the availability of learning opportunities at the site. Trust that by the very fact that you're in a CYC setting, in a CYC role, doing CYC practice, you will be directly or indirectly working on these competencies. You may be surprised at the breadth of competencies you are developing when you check this document and think through each item as it relates to your site. Yes, you'll be developing these competencies at an emerging level, but you must begin somewhere. Keep in mind that the courses you've taken thus far (and the courses you may be taking concurrently with practicum) contain many of the foundational knowledges listed within each competency domain.

In the following chapter, Making the Most of Your Learning and Supervision, you will have the opportunity to develop a learning plan, whereby you will outline specific goals you'd like to work on throughout your practicum experience. No doubt you've already identified a few. Keep these competencies in mind as you move forward. They will offer helpful language and direction.

Underlying all the child and youth work competencies, as they have been defined thus far, with the acknowledgement that our field is continually evolving and redefining itself, the Association for Child and Youth Care Practice and Child and Youth Care Certification Board (2010) lists a number of foundational attitudes. These include:

> Staff aren't expecting perfection right away, but they are expecting students to be in charge of their own learning. Own up to mistakes and search out best practice.
> —Andrew, CYC Practicum Faculty-Instructor

- Accepts the moral and ethical responsibility inherent in practice
- Promotes the well-being of children, youth, and families in a context of respect and collaboration
- Values care as essential for emotional growth, social competence, rehabilitation, and treatment
- Celebrates the strengths generated from cultural and human diversity
- Values individual uniqueness
- Values family, community, culture and human diversity as integral to the developmental and interventive process
- Believes in the potential and empowerment of children, youth, family, and community
- Advocates for the rights of children, youth, and families
- Promotes the contribution of professional child and youth care to society (p. 9)

As you read through the list of foundational attitudes, ask yourself: what is the history of this attitude in your life and how do you imagine it showing up in your practicum experience? How have you observed this attitude in your practicum experience thus far? How have you seen behaviour, conversations, decisions, and other practices that contradict this attitude in your practicum thus far? What meaning do you make of this contradiction?

CYC Ethics

Throughout any description of CYC practice, it will attend to ethical practice. As soon as we read or hear the words *respect*, *best practice*, *well-being*, *responsibility*, or *care* we are entering into the zone of ethical practice. All of our work has an ethical dimension, and some of our work will crystallize into ethical conduct and violations or ethical dilemmas. Whether the situation we find ourselves in is clear-cut or blurry, we engage in ethical work each moment of our day. How we show up to the role, why we are here in the first place, what we believe our purpose and role should be, how we conduct ourselves, what outcomes we promote, and so on are first and foremost a question of ethics.

Before we look at CYC's Code of Ethics in more detail, let's remind ourselves how we've come to position ourselves in relationship with ethics. Consider the following reflective questions, inspired by youth worker Tilsen (2018) in her work with marginalized communities:

How would you describe your relationship to CYC ethics?

_____

_____

What shapes, influences, and informs your relationship to CYC ethics?

_____

_____

When we say a CYC practitioner is acting ethically, what does this mean?

_____

_____

When we say a CYC practitioner is not acting ethically, what does this mean?

_____

_____

CYC Code of Ethics

All codes of ethics for professionals are intended to be guides and foundations upon which we determine directions and make decisions and are not prescriptive in nature for every single situation we will encounter. They are guide posts and collective agreements that our profession has made over time, which help distinguish our role and responsibilities. They also hold us accountable to a heightened standard of practice. All current codes of ethics are based in thousands of years-long discussions on what we as societies believe is good and right, how we should and should not behave, how we will and will not treat one another. Professional codes elevate and expand those discussions, based on the vulnerable nature and power differential between the professional practitioner and the people they serve.

Our most current North American CYC Code of Ethics, widely adopted by many CYC Associations in Canada, is included in this guidebook as Appendix H. The Association for Child and Youth Care Practice (2017) prefaces our code of ethics by stating, "Child and Youth Care Professionals encounter many situations which have ethical dimensions and implications" (p. 3). This guiding document includes five responsibilities:

1. Responsibility for self
2. Responsibility to children, youth, and families
3. Responsibility to the employer and/or employing organization
4. Responsibility to the profession
5. Responsibility to the community

You've hopefully been introduced to this code of ethics, but likely in more of a hypothetical manner, not situated in an actual workplace you are part of. Now you have the opportunity to read through the code with the specific purpose of applying the concepts to your practicum site. We suggest you read through Appendix H with this new purpose. For each line, stop and consider: how may this value statement, example, or direction apply to your practicum site? For example, when you read "reports ethical violations to appropriate individuals," consider who that "appropriate individual" may actually be (The Association for Child and Youth Care Practice, 2017, p. 5). Be aware: it may take some time to answer this question.

Working on Collaborative and Multidisciplinary Teams
In practicum, you will be involved in several types of teams—whether it be your immediate program team, an agency team, or interagency team, and more. Likely, these teams will be multidisciplinary in nature, that is, where each helping professional may have a different role; different professional education, training, and expertise; a different way of communicating; and different factors influencing their presence and purpose. It is important to remember the connective goal of any multidisciplinary team: to provide the best, integrated care to young people and their families.

As you prepare to start or have just started your practicum placement, ask yourself: what teams exist at your site? What is each team's purpose? Who are the practitioners on each team? What professions are represented at your site?

Working on collaborative teams requires us to establish shared meaning, to develop a regular process, to be aware of responsibilities, to be connected and cooperative, to explore and try things out, to expect change and commitment, and to experience bonds and personal change, where we "put aside cherished perspectives in the spirit of discovering new 'truths'" (O'Hara, Weber, & Levine, 2010, pp. 258–261). As you move through your practicum experience and have the opportunity to participate in and contribute to many teams, consider whether you experience them as collaborative. Ask yourself: whose needs are at the centre of this team? What is influencing this team's functioning? What is helpful and unhelpful to its process?

> I recommend students go meet other practitioners from different disciplines. Not understanding and respecting other people's mandates and getting mad at other workers can be a barrier to learning.
> —Sonja, CYC Practicum Supervisor

One way to further understand the perspectives of the practitioners and professions that surround you at your practicum site is to explore their standards of practice—competencies and ethics—too. While we do not necessarily need to know the specific details of the history of their professions, it is helpful to know some of their standards of practice, to understand how these standards guide and influence their work with young people. Complete Activity 3.3 to explore their standards further.

Activity 3.3: Standards of Practice on Interdisciplinary Teams

We work on multi- and interdisciplinary teams. Make a list of the professions that compromise your team (or the collective staff team at your agency). They may include teachers, nurses, psychologists, educational assistants, therapeutic recreation workers, occupational therapists, counsellors, social workers, and others.

_____

_____

_____

What standards of practice (competencies and codes of ethics) govern their practice?

Select one of these documents, one that you haven't previously reviewed in another class. Review it while asking yourself the following questions. Make some notes for reference in the open space below.

- How does their code of ethics position practitioners in relation to young people?
- What points of intersection and overlap do you notice with the CYC standards of practice? What points conflict with or contradict each other?

- How may being aware of these standards help you in your practicum experience with other professionals? With young people?

_____

_____

_____

_____

_____

_____

Understanding the purpose, role, scope of practice, and standards of practice of other professionals you work alongside helps us build the ability to work well on teams with them. Not only is this helpful when it comes to decision-making, integrating services, and so on, it is also helpful during points of misunderstanding, conflict, or disagreement. We need to understand other professionals' language, orientation to practice, and so on, just as they need to understand ours. We need to work together.

Ethical Considerations in CYC Practice

What are some typical or common ethical considerations that cut across all CYC settings and therefore all practicum experiences? Since we are establishing and participating in therapeutic relationships and approaching our work relationally, we can centre the *relationship* in discussions of ethical practice. Introducing this chapter, we discussed the professional relationship, what is included in that Sacred Circle, and what protects its integrity. Sercombe (2010) notes that in our work "the relationship is intentionally limited. These limits are in place in order to create conditions of safety within which a client can make themselves vulnerable" (p. 17). The integrity we are trying to protect and the limits we place on the relationship can also be understood as creating healthy relationship boundaries. We can understand relationship boundaries through our standards for practice.

Professional Relationship Boundaries

When we engage relationally, from a place of respect, we must consider how boundaries— the guidelines we all create that define what we allow and do not allow in a relationship— are established and reinforced with ourselves and young people. What boundaries should we consider when working alongside young people in their life-spaces? Gharabaghi (2010) states that boundaries are "constructed *through* the exploration of self" (p. 22). Further, Phelan (2005) highlights that

> Boundaries in CYC work are much more intimate than in other professions and, because of this, require a rigorous attention to clear and reflective establishing of safe, respectful

personal space. Life-space relationships involve a sharing of experience, a being with the other person that demands an openness to each other that cannot be softened by professional distancing. (p. 351)

Meanwhile, Sapin (2009) offers ways to define professional boundaries in youth work.

Defining Professional Boundaries in Youth Work

The boundaries of youth work practice require a youth worker to:

✓ Be aware of the position of power and responsibility that they have in young people's lives and not abuse it
✓ Steer clear of exploitative or preferential treatment for individual young people
✓ Avoid close, dependent, or emotional relationships with young people
✓ Not engage in work-related activities for personal gain
✓ Understand the difference between an inappropriate gift and a token acknowledgement
✓ Not accept gifts that would lead to preferential treatment or compromise integrity
✓ Take care that behaviour (at and outside of work) does not undermine the confidence of the young people in the profession
✓ Be aware that individuals may wish to discuss personal and private matters they are unable to discuss with others
✓ Recognize the difference between a professional approach based on developing a positive independent relationship and emotional involvement
✓ Take care not to develop close, personal—particularly sexual—relationships with the young people they are working with
✓ Alert a supervisor about any concerns over relationships that may breach professional boundaries

Adapted from Sapin, K. (2009). *Essential skills for youth work practice* (p. 70). London, UK: SAGE.

Establishing boundaries in the life-spaces of young people, their families, and in our communities requires attention to ourselves and our contexts. How another professional responds to this issue is different, because they're considering different factors, coming from a different perspective, and desiring a different outcome. It is important to withhold a need to say there is a right and wrong answer. Rather, our goal within these discussions and topics should be to explore the complexity, context, needs, assumptions, goals, and values behind what we think we should do to promote good relationships with young people in order to support their care. What we believe to be appropriate and inappropriate is a good place to begin. Move through the prompts below to think about a number of ethical considerations related to the practice of healthy relationship boundaries.

Each of the examples asks you to reflect on common issues related to professional boundaries, all topics that you've likely explored in your Introduction to Professional Practice, Interpersonal Communications, Helping Skills, or other courses. Some of the questions can be reflected upon individually, and you will need to consult your supervisor or a trusted colleague for others. Take some time to wonder: what does this look like at your practicum setting? How may it show up differently across different scenarios? How may it look different at a classmate's practicum setting? Why is this important to notice?

> Know your boundaries. Some students want to be the young person's best friend. Some want to rescue the world. Some want to find ways to connect that are not necessarily the most appropriate way.
> —Tom, CYC Practicum Supervisor

1. Respect and Dignity—What do the terms respect and dignity mean? How do you embody and practice with respect and dignity? How can you see respect and the dignity of young people demonstrated at your practicum setting? What policies, spaces, practices, communication, and treatment occur at your practicum setting that demonstrate respect and dignity? Have you been witness to encounters where respect and dignity was not upheld? What did you witness? How can that teach you what you want to demonstrate in your own practice?

2. Informed Consent—What does informed consent mean and look like at your practicum setting? How is informed consent obtained? How are you supposed to participate in obtaining informed consent? What would you need to consider to do that well?

3. Confidentiality—How is confidentiality interpreted and maintained at your practicum site? What is and isn't appropriate to share about your practicum with family and friends? How should you speak about what you are learning at your practicum setting with your practicum seminar group while respecting confidentiality? Why is this important to consider? What would be the impact on young people? On yourself?

> Understand how important it is to uphold confidentiality, especially because you are interacting with so many individuals on and off site.
> —Farah, CYC Practicum Supervisor

Students are often of a similar age or a little older than the youth we serve and as such can be a positive 'near-peer' role model by creating positive, respectful relationships, showing a good work ethic, and using strengths-based language. Older students can be a safe, non-judgmental and approachable adult.

—Annie, CYC Practicum Supervisor

4. Relationships—Sometimes practicum students attempt to become or describe their relationships with young people as "friends." Others describe their relationship as "friendly." What is the difference between the two—being friends and being friendly? What is the power/authority in each position?

_____

_____

_____

5. Physical Touch—What is the policy on physical touch at your practicum setting? What is an example of appropriate and inappropriate physical touch at your practicum? Does that change, depending on different contexts? Think through a variety of specific prompts including, but not limited to, hugs, protection from harm, games/play. Why is a discussion of physical touch important to consider?

_____

_____

_____

6. Practitioner Competence—What is an example of working outside of one's scope of competence? Why is this important to consider as it relates to relationships? What is the impact on young people? On yourself?

_____

_____

_____

7. Wellness and Self-Care—What does your agency do to support practitioner wellness? What is an example of practitioner wellness getting in the way of providing good care for young people? What would be an example of not tending to self-care during practicum? What would be the effect of that lack of self-care? Why is this important to consider as it relates to relationships? What would be the impact on young people? On yourself?

_____

_____

_____

8. Self-Disclosure—What is something that would not be appropriate to share with young people at your practicum? Why? What would be something that would be appropriate to share at practicum with young people? Why? Why is it important to consider self-disclosure as it relates to relationships? What would be the impact on young people? On yourself?

_____

_____

_____

Note your observations and how you make sense of them. Hover over the issues that cause confusion, contradiction, and uncertainty. Bring these reflections back to your practice seminar or community of practice for discussion, particularly if you learned something you did not expect.

Safety in Professional Practice

If it is not already clear, attention to healthy boundaries when establishing therapeutic relationships and working relationally is, in part, for creating safety within those spaces: emotional safety, spiritual safety, relational safety, physical safety, and so on. Without safety, we cannot engage meaningfully nor create meaningful change.

Let's stay on the topic of safety as it relates to our standards of practice. Keeping young people physically safe while in our care should be our and our agency's number one concern, not to mention our own safety in these spaces. We have many policies and procedures to ensure the safety of our young people, both at the site and while we're offsite. But what does that actually look like in practice? Let's explore the following prompts to observe how each issue relates to our practicum site. Recall reading policy and procedure, your orientation, and specific instructions your supervisor provided to you when you were placed at your practicum site. Think of your practicum site and how it attends to the following features of physical safety:

- In terms of the arrangement of physical space (e.g., accessibility, locked doors, furniture arrangement, etc.), what does your practicum site have in place?

_____

- In terms of nutritional needs (e.g., guidelines, policies, individualized plans, etc.), what does your practicum site have in place?

_____

- In terms of medical needs (e.g., location of first aid kits, prescription medication, etc.), what does your practicum site have in place?

  _____

- In terms of emergency procedures (e.g., earthquake, lockdown, etc.), what does your practicum site have in place?

  _____

- In terms of crisis intervention (e.g., Nonviolent Crisis Intervention, risk and threat assessments, etc.), what does your practicum site have in place?

  _____

Finally, when you see your supervisor next, go through a hypothetical emergency or crisis scenario relevant to your site. Try to make it as realistic as possible, so perhaps ask your supervisor to share a story about a recent situation. Ask about one emergency situation that went well. Then ask about one that didn't go well. Prompt your supervisor by asking them to alter various factors in the situation, and how that would change their response to the scenario. You could alter any of the following factors: location at (or off) the site, time of day, ages of the young people, the presence or absence of someone, eliminating an option. Reflect on what you learn from this conversation and how you can prepare yourself for what may occur at your site.

_____

_____

_____

Inherent in the existence of standards of practice is the expectation that we do not violate these standards, that we act with high ethical standards, and that we make sound ethical decisions. And yet, violations occur. Poor ethical choices are made. Consequences result. In Chapter 9, Challenging and Challenges in CYC Practice, we will review more complex scenarios involving ethical dimensions, including ethical violations and ethical decision-making as applied to our practicum settings. For now, we turn our attention to expanding our view of what we mean by ethics.

Ethically Sensitive Practitioners

Myers-Kiser (2016) asks human service practicum students to develop their "ethical sensitivity—that is, the ability to recognize the ethical, legal, and values issues involved in their day-to-day work," which "goes beyond just knowing the ethical standards or recognizing gross ethical violations and extends into the ability to recognize more subtle

Table 3.2: Ethics in CYC Practicum

A practicum student overhears two staff members gossip about a student in the school's staff lunch room	A practicum student sees a youth outreach worker sharing their home address or personal cellphone number with a young person	A practicum student notices a youth worker share a lot of information about herself and the difficulties she's going through, and the youth are offering empathy and attention
A practicum student observes support workers at a group home show up to work under the influence of illegal substances on a regular basis	A practicum student notices a young person faces multiple barriers in accessing services, but the program doesn't change practices to meet the young person's needs	A practicum student notices that their agency claims to be inclusive, but their practices lead the student to believe otherwise
A practicum student observes that their practicum program's orientation to practice is somewhat dated and doesn't include current research in the social services field	A practicum student notices some staff warmly welcome and invite all children's families into the school space, whereas other staff only engage with families when there is a problem	A practicum student notices staff refer to some young people as "hard to reach" and "resistant to intervention" and wonders why they're locating the problem within a young person rather than with their practices

ethical, legal, and values issues that operate within ordinary, everyday practice situations" (p. 83). Take, for example, the situations in Table 3.2 that include an ethical component. Notice what subtle issues are (or could be) happening in the scenarios.

What professional practice and ethical considerations come up for you? Have you encountered these situations before? These are daily scenarios that we come across in our field to which we must attend. As practicum students, we sometimes don't feel we have the ability to effect long-term change. We may feel we're not in a position of authority so as to speak up. But in any challenging situation, we do have the ability to observe, notice, and learn from it. Paying attention to both subtle and gross ethical violations and practice issues helps us become better practitioners. Why? Because it helps us define who we are, how we want to act in the world, and why we're in this field. Because we're immersed in practice at practicum, with the added expectation of continual learning and reflection, we have the chance to focus on this responsibility.

When following standards of practice in our early development as a practitioner, we can become preoccupied with concrete definitions and guidelines. Regardless of context-specific factors, we seek rigid instructions and rules to respond to common ethical issues such as confidentiality, informed consent, boundaries, and competence. However,

White (2011) offers some big questions to keep at the forefront of our minds to help us stay with the big picture:

> Students can forget that there is an educational piece beyond learning how to be a good worker. This requires asking how and why questions and bringing their critical thinking skills into the doing of CYC.
> —Yvonne, CYC Practicum Faculty-Instructor

- What does it mean to live a worthwhile life? Who gets to decide?
- Whose version of human flourishing should prevail?
- What do we mean by dignity? How can we support its emergence within diverse social, cultural, and historical contexts?
- How do our professional practices, intellectual traditions, and available vocabularies shape our understanding of children, youth, families, and communities?
- What unspoken vision of the ideal or normal or well-adjusted human being are our models of practice predicated on? (pp. 46–47)

These are important questions with ethics at their core. As we work to become more ethically sensitive practitioners, White (2011) offers us an outline. As CYC practitioners, we can:

- Recognize the value-laden quality of CYC
- Discern morally relevant issues
- Critically reflect on [our] own social and cultural situatedness and professional assumptions
- Practice articulating moral positions
- Anticipate and respond to ambiguity and uncertainty
- Engage in critical debate
- Generate creative responses, and
- Recognize that taking ethically responsible action is much more demanding than conforming to standards or consulting a code of ethics. (White, 2011, p. 47)

Through these actions, we can actively and continually engage in the high standard with which we wish to approach our field of CYC practice. Meanwhile, ethics will continue to be explored in more depth in Chapter 9, where we will attend to some challenging ethical encounters.

A NOTE ON WELLNESS AND SELF-CARE

Thus far, we have discussed a number of aspects of professional practice. As we approach the conclusion of this chapter, let's shift to one more aspect of professional practice that is important to focus on throughout practicum: self-care and wellness. Chapter 11 will focus entirely on this topic. It's worth reading ahead if this is either required of you or if you think it would be a good idea at this point in time. For the purposes of attending to wellness and self-care over the next few chapters—as you think about this topic, as you begin your practicum placement, as a part of professional CYC practice, as a part of your learning goals, and as you engage with young people—consider the following list of self-care strategies, excerpted directly from Birkenmaier and Berg-Weger (2011) for practicum students in the social services field:

1. Acknowledge self-care as a priority
2. Consider having self-care as a goal in your learning plan
3. Attend to your physical, emotional, social, spiritual, cultural wellbeing
4. Acknowledge your emotional responses in practicum [and] allow yourself to feel emotional concerning your work, the people you work alongside, and the social issues and systems you work within
5. Stay attuned to yourself, and conduct check ins—body and mind—regularly
6. Identify, develop and utilize your personal and professional support systems
7. Join personal and professional groups that you enjoy and that stimulate you
8. Develop a peer-support group at your site or school
9. Ask for help if you need it
10. Build fun activities and down time into your schedule, amongst your work, school, practicum, and family responsibilities
11. Develop relationships with people who challenge you
12. Know and recognize the signals that tell you that you are becoming stressed
13. Ask others to share their strategies for ensuring health and wellbeing; try some out
14. If one strategy is not or no longer effective, try something else
15. Have attainable goals, monitor your progress [and] re-evaluate them on a regular basis
16. Challenge yourself, but do not push yourself beyond your limits, do not overextend
17. Use caution when resorting to artificial means to maintain energy (i.e. depressants and stimulants)
18. Do not expect others to take care of you
19. Work to your strengths, know your limitations, and change what you can
20. Avoid procrastination
21. Choose your battles carefully (p. 42)

While completing practicum, you are adding an extra layer of complexity to your life, anticipating change, and embarking on a new journey. Whether your practicum is a six-week block placement, an eight-month, part-time placement alongside other courses, or anywhere in between the addition of practicum to one's responsibilities is often just that: an addition. Our day-to-day responsibilities, commitments, and relationships continue despite this added component. We need to be mindful of this change, even if it is only temporary. Caring for ourselves, tending to the people, parts, and processes in our lives is essential in this field, not only for our own benefit but for the young people we work alongside. In practicum, some students choose to focus on wellness and self-care as a part of their formal goals; some students are encouraged to focus on wellness and self-care because of the context of the practicum site; some CYC programs require a self-care plan as a part of their assignment package; and some students will neglect to focus on wellness and self-care until they realize they should and could have during their practicum experience. All of these situations are learning opportunities.

When thinking about adding practicum to our life, it can be helpful to acknowledge that this addition can cause stress, and stress shows up differently for each person. Consider some of the following directions, questions, and examples below to help determine how stress shows up in your life. Try to think of multiple realms in your life: social, emotional, mental, physical, spiritual, cultural…

In the open box below, draw an outline of your body. Next, draw an illustration of your home, your work, your school, other important spaces, and the ways you move to and from these places. Finally, draw an illustration of the important people in your life, who you connect with on a regular basis.

Next, consider the following questions: how does stress express itself in your body? Name or draw what that looks like. How does stress show up in the various spaces in your life? Name or draw how that shows up. How does stress express itself in your relationships? Name or draw how that shows up. Reflect on the indicators that tell you that you are stressed in any of these areas (and more). Illustrate them in some way.

As you ask yourself these questions, you may have considered: is your home a mess? Draw this. Do you experience increased irritability or forgetfulness? Indicate this. Do you miss deadlines or fail to respond to someone's request? Do you become a ghost to those who are close to you? Do you go into fight, flight, or freeze mode? Draw how stress appears in your life.

Then ask yourself: when these indicators of stress show up in my life, what helps me through?

_____

_____

Remember, you are learning about wellness and self-care as you move through practicum, whether it is a main focus for you or not. You are with classmates going through a similar process, and it would be wise to use each other as support—to check in, to care for, to understand. This experience will not only help during practicum, but it will also help prepare you for exiting your educational program and work in the field.

PROFESSIONAL ACTIVITIES

We end this chapter on professional CYC practice by bringing our attention from a wide scope of our field as a profession to ourselves, as individual practitioners. As emerging practitioners, how can we contribute to our profession? How can we take advantage of the applied nature of our practicum course, our practicum setting, and our practicum opportunities, to advance both our profession and ourselves as professionals? Many CYC writers and human services practicum advisors have much to say on this topic (Birkenmaier & Berg-Weger, 2011; Gharabaghi, 2010). Consider the following list of activities and notice what you could be incorporating into your current experience:

- ✓ Join your provincial, national, or international association as a student member
- ✓ Attend your provincial association's workshops, annual general meeting, or volunteer for a conference or board membership
- ✓ Plan on seeking volunteer and/or employment experience in the CYC field while you're attending school
- ✓ Prepare for becoming certified as a CYC-P
- ✓ Plan to seek a variety of practicum placements throughout your certificate, diploma, or degree

✓ Keep a portfolio or career file (see Chapter 13) of your academic, practicum, volunteer, and other professional work and community contributions

✓ Read a wide variety of literature connected to the issues and topics coming up at your practicum—scholarly, literary, pop culture, alternative, and so on.

✓ Create a book (or article) club with your classmates to discuss relevant literature in the field

✓ Follow CYC organizations, agencies, and advocacy groups on social media (including your and your classmates' practicum program's social media pages)

✓ Participate in your and your practicum agency's community

✓ Consider your practicum learning team—your classmates, supervisor(s), faculty-instructor—as your professional team

✓ Ask your supervisor to invite you to professional networking and professional development opportunities—interagency, city planning, and school district meetings and training events

✓ Represent CYC wherever you go

✓ Develop your inner young person! Explore today's youth culture. Expose yourself to literature, sporting, gaming, visual and expressive arts, music, and more

What are you already doing? What are you planning to do in the future? Likely, you're directly and indirectly doing a number of these things, perhaps without even knowing that's what you were doing. Being accepted into your CYC program, you've concurrently been welcomed into our CYC profession, one that is developing, evolving, and making itself known. We look forward to your continued contribution.

LEARNING JOURNAL

As you continue to immerse yourself in practicum, even if you have not yet already begun, experiment with your learning journal. Whether you respond to the structured questions, prefer the more unstructured route, complete both, or use a combination of the two, see how the learning journal may help you recall significant observations, identify important learning, and set specific goals for the following week.

PRACTICE SCENARIOS

Take a look at the Practice Scenarios that conclude this chapter: "CYC Hats" and "Boundary Dilemmas." Use the content in this chapter to inspire your thinking about the scenarios. Notice how each scenario may relate to your own situation at your current practicum placement, even if it is not exactly what you are experiencing. Consider the questions posed at the end of each scenario to help you expand and apply the concepts presented in this chapter.

SEMINAR GROUP AND COMMUNITY OF PRACTICE DISCUSSION QUESTIONS

We hope that you engage with these ideas—of professionalism, of ethics—continually as you move through the various spaces you contribute to, from practicum to beyond. These are never-ending questions and considerations. We must continually challenge ourselves to engage in discussion, expand our viewpoints and perspectives, and articulate where we stand on various issues and how we've come to know what we believe to be true and right. We can also remember that we should never be alone in these questions, challenges, and uncertainties. As such, with your seminar discussion group or community of practice, consider the following questions:

1. What is the history of the role of the CYC practitioner at your site? Does everyone know what a CYC does (and contributes to) at your site? If not, why do you think that is?
2. What does informed consent look like at your site? (Share the site-specific considerations you've learned that you need to pay attention to. Ask your supervisor for support to respond to this question.)
3. Using White's (2011) Big Questions, how would your practicum site respond to these questions: "What does it mean to live a worthwhile life?" "What unspoken vision of the well-adjusted human being is its practices predicated on?" (pp. 46–47)
4. What is one thing you could be doing to attend to your wellness as you begin this new challenge in your life? Who will support this attention to wellness? How will you supportively and encouragingly hold yourself accountable to this commitment?

IN CLOSING

In this chapter, we've focused our attention on a number of professional CYC practice issues including defining the scope of our practice, reviewing our standards of practice, looking at establishing relationship boundaries in practice, and becoming ethically sensitive practitioners in our work. These discussions extend what you've been learning in your other courses before you began practicum or what you are concurrently learning and paying attention to. By no means are they the end. In the following chapters, we will extend many of the topics. The information discussed here will serve as a good foundation for those future discussions on, for example, reflective practice, diversity in practice, facilitating therapeutic change and environments, and, of course, challenging and challenges in practice.

PRACTICE SCENARIOS

CYC Hats

In Sam's first week of her practicum placement, she's been tasked with reading a lot of policy and procedure manuals, in part because her criminal record check hasn't cleared. All she really wants is just to hang out with the kids. Jonah is annoyed that he's been told to help clean the alternate school program's kitchen after lunch all week. Will feels like all he's doing is helping out with kids' homework in the classroom. Lisa feels like she's just hanging around the group home doing nothing while she waits for the youth to arrive back from school.

What is the purpose behind these activities? By spending time doing each of these tasks, how do they benefit young people at the sites? How could each practicum student make the best out of an unanticipated or unwanted task or responsibility?

Boundary Dilemmas

Sylvia notices that a lot of the staff at the residential mental health facility go out drinking and partying with each other on the weekend. She's been invited, but she's not sure if she wants to join. A father has told Luca that his child has been struggling with bed-wetting the past few weeks, likely due to the news that he and the child's mother are separating. A teacher expresses frustration to Luca that the child is quite distant and not doing his homework. Luca wants to encourage the teacher to be patient with the child, since there are things going on in his life that are challenging right now. She also wants to respect the child's privacy and confidentiality, so she's not sure what to do. Alan is told that he should never be alone with a young person in an office or classroom by himself. Rachel is at the same school but is told not to worry about that policy, because "it's just for male practitioners." Mandeep wants to share some of her difficult experiences immigrating to Canada with some of the kids at the school who are newcomers too. She's not sure if she should share.

All of these students are thinking through boundary issues as they relate to policy, personal values, and respect for young people. What could they be considering as they move forward in their actions and responses?

CHAPTER 4

Making the Most of Your Learning and Supervision

Competencies for Professional Child and Youth Work Practitioners				
Professionalism	Cultural and Human Diversity	Applied Human Development	Relationship and Communication	Developmental Practice Methods
Professional Development and Behaviour

Personal Development and Self Care | | | Teamwork and Professional Communication | |

> As a new practitioner, it's important to remember you are a part of a larger community of CYC practitioners. Your education and practicum placement are your first steps into a powerful and wide-reaching field. Be yourself... Stay connected... Endure the challenges... Be in the moment... Be open to change.
> —James Freeman, Editor, International Child and Youth Care Network

Learning. That is what each moment in practicum is about. What do you want to learn? What are you expected to learn? How will you be expected to demonstrate what you've learned? These are the questions that are likely occupying your mind as you immerse yourself in the practicum experience. Taking a growth and development orientation to learning—that learning is about growth and development—this chapter will first focus on being an active learner, experiential and transformational learning, moving from comfort to challenge, and Child and Youth Care (CYC) practitioner development. We will then review learning methods—the ways we can engage in and demonstrate our learning—which include supervision, feedback, goal-setting, learning plans, and the assessment of our learning.

BECOMING AN ACTIVE LEARNER

In practicum, like most meaningful experiences in life, you get out of it what you contribute. You could spend your time completing the required number of hours, performing at

> The practicum should be a reciprocal relationship, and students who realize this get far more out of their practicum than those who do not see themselves as having an active role in their learning.
> —Annie, CYC Practicum Supervisor

a competent level, doing what is asked of you, but no more. Or you could consider your practicum placement as a window into Child and Youth Care, with people, activities, and learning all around you, to take your experience to a new level. Of these scenarios, which would you prefer to embody? Which student would benefit more from their experience, including new challenges, interesting events, and learning to bring forward? On the surface, they'll have both completed a practicum in CYC. We hope you choose the latter.

Particularly in the active observation (sometimes referred to as shadowing) phase of your practicum, we can feel as though we are unable to be as active as we'd like. Making the most of your learning involves active participation in the learning opportunities available to you. Hillman (2018) empathizes with students' early practicum placement reflections, not feeling like they're doing much, but he reminds us that observational learning, where "watching is doing" (p. 70), is essential. Sometimes it takes a gentle nudge to become more aware of the opportunities surrounding you. Consider the following list to help you along:

- As an active observer, pay attention to interactions, strategies and interventions, movement/use of space, dialogue, silence, nonverbal behaviour, decisions, and so on over time.
- Don't limit yourself to contact and observation with your direct supervisor(s). Who else works at your site that you could observe and get to know their program? Notice practitioners' styles.
- Notice how you're responding to the daily goings-on at the site. What are you drawn to? What are you not paying attention to? Who are you spending time with? Who have you not yet connected with? Where are you occupying space? Can you occupy other spaces? When are you there? Can you attend at different times in the day?
- Yes, you're placed in one program. What else is happening at the organization? What else could you connect to, learn about, and perhaps eventually collaborate with?
- What issues are you learning about that are catching your attention? A particular mental health issue? School success? Youth homelessness? Reclaiming culture? Learn more! Talk to someone. Read a newspaper article. Watch a documentary.
- Does your organization have any workshops, events, training, or informal professional development activities happening while you are there? Ask to attend.
- Is your practicum in a different city from where you live? Get to know it. Visit other services. Walk around. Find out where the schools, grocery stores, health clinics, and government offices exist. Don't limit yourself to the site.

- Taking a concurrent elective class? Try to connect what you're learning in practicum to what you're required to complete in class, if the assignment allows for that flexibility.
- What's being discussed among the professionals at your site? Local politics? Labour issues? Poverty and access to services? Learn more about the context of your site and the community.
- What's being discussed among the youth? Think about youth culture, digital trends, clothing and aesthetic trends and choices, books, games, sports, hobbies, and other interests. Learn more. Get that book and read it. Play that video game and ask for tips. Explore that website. Learn the slang. Learn the rules to that game.

By no means is this a complete list of activities to get you more involved. They are a jumping-off point, a place of curiosity, to spark interest in learning more. Actively engage in your practicum experience, and it will benefit you in ways too numerous to list. Not only will you likely improve your grade, your experience will be more meaningful, you will make more connections and links to your profession, you'll have a better idea of where you want to go next, and you'll be a better CYC practitioner for the young people at your site.

> Look at different styles of different workers and how they work and how you may see yourself working in one style and maybe not others. Understand who you're going to be in the field.
> —Trina, CYC Student

LEARNING MODELS

To help us understand our learning, growth, and development (and for that matter, the young people we work with), we can turn our attention to a number of experiential learning models. In practicum, you are not memorizing terms, sitting in a lecture hall absorbing information. You are experiencing it. Your learning will be relational, physical, emotional, cultural, and spiritual. Kolb (1984) presented a cycle of experiential learning that suggests students are in a continuous cycle of experiencing, reflecting, conceptualizing, and experimenting, then repeating that cycle again (see Figure 4.1). In this model, we can see the learning process as circular, even as a spiral, and definitely as a layered process, where we are often learning the same skill, knowledge, and way of being at greater depth and quality. We build upon our experiences moment by moment, week by week, year by year.

Applying this concept to the practicum experience, we may think of an interaction with a young person and how and why it was or wasn't effective, what that means for our toolkit of engagement strategies, and how we may try it out again in an altered version. Alternatively, we may think of a series of courses we've taken in our CYC program, how we understand those ideas and concepts in practice, then practise them at practicum, and then formulate new ideas about those ideas and their meaning and significance. We are in constant movement, constant

> Apply. Repeat.
> —Andrew, CYC Practicum Faculty-Instructor

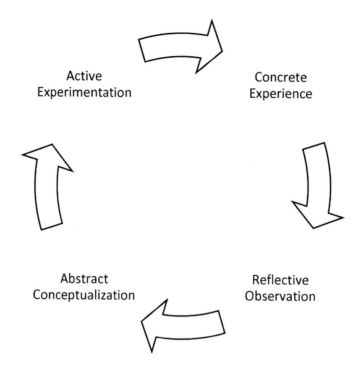

Figure 4.1: Kolb's Experiential Learning

Adapted from O'Hara, A., Weber, Z., & Levine, K. (2010). *Skills for human service practice: Working with individuals, groups, and communities* (pp. 33–35). Don Mills, ON: Oxford University Press.

reflection, constantly reformulating our world based on our ideas and reflections, relational experiences, and the interactions between them.

Note that, in Figure 4.1, what counts as "concrete experience" can be anything: an interaction with a young person or supervisor at practicum, an experience in class, a reflection you have during or after an experience, and so on. Merriam, Caffarella, and Baumgartner (2007) build upon Kolb's (1984) model, telling us that there are four abilities required to learn from one's experience:

1. An openness and willingness to involve oneself in new experiences (concrete experience)
2. Observational and reflective skills so these new experiences can be viewed from a variety of perspectives (reflective observation)
3. Analytical abilities so integrative ideas and concepts can be created from observations (abstract conceptualization)
4. Decision-making and problem-solving skills so these new ideas and concepts can be used in actual practice (active experimentation) (p. 164)

Bogo (2012) extends the experiential learning model to the human service professions' educational programs, using a model she developed to guide practicum students, called the Integration of Theory and Practice Loop Model. It has four phases, and it's suggested you consider using it in practicum to assist in becoming more active in your observations and shadowing, self-supervision (i.e., structured reflection), or even as a format to help structure how you seek feedback and offer discussion in supervision. Practice using the model in Table 4.1, moving through the structured steps and questions, jotting down ideas under the column "My Notes." While it may seem rather arduous going through every step, in no time you'll get the process to the point where you may not even notice you're doing it.

> There are no dumb questions. Every question is pertinent. Being open to their own emotional field and expressing how they are feeling and doing that day. Ask questions as immediately as possible for explanations and feedback.
>
> —Rose, CYC Practicum Supervisor

Transformational Learning

While we focus on skill development, we should also be reminded that the experiential learning process has students' "lived experiences" at the centre and is "an authentic, transformative, active, and holistic process" (Ainsworth, 2016, p. 21). We can then think about practicum as not just a course with a checklist of tasks to complete but a meaningful experience that changes us as people and practitioners. While we have common outcomes that we hope students achieve throughout and by the end of practicum, we also acknowledge that each student comes to practicum with a diverse set of experiences, will make meaning in limitless ways, and will move forward with that learning along unanticipated, generative, and exciting paths.

Transformational learning is closely linked to experiential learning. Shaw, Reid, and Trites (2013) report that "learners in CYC education programs describe their experience as transformational" and, like how many CYC faculty approach practicum instruction, they consider that "transformational theory is grounded in the assumption that the way an individual learner interprets and reinterprets their experience in a culturally and contextually unique way is essential to their meaning making and therefore to their learning" (p. 92). Baldwin, Kelber, Pick, and Wilson (2017) tell us that the transformational learning perspective "views learners as active constructors" as opposed to passive recipients of knowledge, where it "depends on practitioners engaging in internal and very personal reflective analyses," where co-inquiry and collaborative ways of learning are privileged (p. 26). In their application of transformational learning to CYC training, they note that learners engage in a process that "involves discovering one's point of view, examining the basis for those beliefs, and deepening one's understanding of how the view has influenced how one sees and interprets new knowledge and everyday life" (p. 25). *This* is the hard work of practicum.

> Practicum will be what they make it: if they go in and passively wait for people to 'teach' them what to do, they may pass the course, but they won't have developed a sense of themselves as a critically reflective, engaged learner.
>
> —Kristy, CYC Practicum Faculty-Instructor

In this sense, learning becomes holistic and all-encompassing, and it cannot be separated from the self. You come to this space as you are, and you will be changed as a result. While we begin and end at a similar place, in no way do we arrive, experience, and depart in the same way.

Table 4.1: Bogo's Experiential Learning

Bogo's Integration of Theory and Practice Loop Model			
Phase		**Description and Relevant Questions for This Phase**	**My Notes**
One	Retrieve and Recall	Recall a recent practice experience when you felt good about your work. Or recall an experience that is troubling you in some way. What are the relevant facts of the situation?	
Two	Reflect	Identify psychosocial and organizational factors along with societal contexts of the experience. What are your personal reactions to the situation? Recall your thoughts and feelings. What beliefs and attitudes were operating on your part? Did this reflect aspects of your personality, worldview, or particular life experiences? How were these issues apparent in your thoughts, judgements, and behaviour? What effect did your interventions have on the situation? How can you tell?	
Three	Link	Review knowledge and concepts learned in courses (including readings) along with knowledge and concepts in field-setting discussions. Remember that theory guides our awareness of what types of information are important to collect. Ask: why does this problem exist in this situation? How can you explain the situation you observed? What were some of the things you did? Why did you do them? Were your actions based on concepts or ideas from your readings, your classes, or ideas you heard in the setting? Do the explanations you have about this situation come from one or many sources?	
Four	Take Action	New insights and new knowledge are considered. Thought is given to choose next steps. Remember to collaborate with young people as decision-makers in their own care. Plan for the next professional response. Given your reflection, what should happen next? What might you do differently at the next encounter? Do you need more information, knowledge, or advice to make this decision? Where will you find it?	

Adapted from Drolet, J., Clark, N., & Allen, H. (Eds.). (2012). *Shifting sites of practice: Field education in Canada* (pp. 12–14). Toronto, ON: Pearson.

PHASES OF PRACTICUM

Charles and Alexander (2016) describe the practicum place-ment in three phases: Exposure, Immersion, and Mastery—represented visually in Figure 4.2—where each phase focuses on distinct aspects of the practicum learning process.

> Those challenging experiences are often the experiences that you learn the most from and where you experience the most growth.
> —Jasmine, CYC Student

In practicum, students can have the tendency to want to move to mastery quickly. But think of how long it takes to master any skill, let alone the complex ways of being re-quired for CYC practice. When we are in the exposure and immersion phases, the goal is mastery. However, getting there can be filled with angst, discomfort, self-consciousness, and vulnerability. You should know that this is typical. The anticipated feelings of satis-faction, confidence, engagement, and flow will help you move forward. Understanding these phases may help you in a number of ways, including having realistic expectations of yourself and the experience.

How do we move from one phase to the next? The passage of time and passive observation does not automatically move us from one place to another. It is through risk, challenge, and the courage one takes to move from a place of knowing to the unknown.

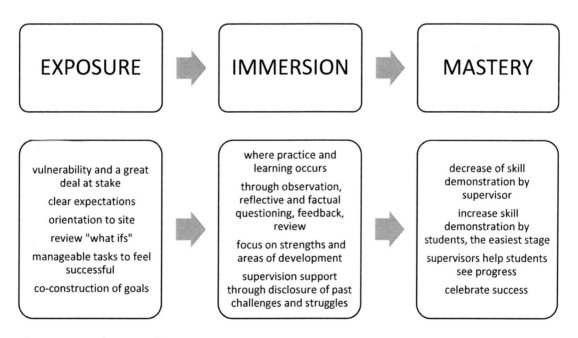

Figure 4.2: Phases of Practicum

Adapted from Charles, G., Freeman, J., & Garfat, T. (Eds.). (2016). *Supervision in child and youth care practice* (pp. 80–87). Cape Town, South Africa: CYC-Net Press.

From Comfort Zone...

- What if it doesn't go as I'd planned?
- What if the young person ignores me?
- What if I mess up?
- What if, what if, what if?

... to Courage Zone

- What if we had a meaningful conversation?
- What if I learn something new about that young person?
- What if I am inspired to do something I cannot yet predict?
- What if I had fun?
- What if, what if, what if?

Figure 4.3: From Comfort to Courage

Adapted from Wright, T. (2018). *How to be a brilliant mentor: Developing outstanding teachers* (p. 95). New York, NY: Routledge.

RISK AND CHALLENGE ZONES

In practicum we often talk about getting out of your comfort zone. We're pretty comfortable there—it doesn't ask much of us, we know the rules, we likely had to learn a lot to get to this space, and we're rewarded with comfort. If we're to leave our comfort zone, where are we going? Lawson and Whitehouse (2018) discuss the meaning of risk-taking and moving into our *courage* zone (see Figure 4.3). They first speak to the fears involved in stepping out of the comfort zone, where they encourage learners to replace the negative "what-if" questions with positive ones, reminding us that "the antidote to fear is action" (p. 95). They share the simple but powerful message when learning to ride a bike: if you always stay in the place of fear or falling over, you'll never have the experience of the wind in your face, exploring the beauty of the outdoors.

CYC STAGES OF PRACTITIONER DEVELOPMENT

We do not only use a developmental lens when understanding the worlds of young people and their families. We also apply this lens to ourselves, as learners and as emerging practitioners in our field. Phelan (2012) reminds us that we are likely to move through three levels of practitioner development: The Capable Caregiver, The Treatment Planner and Change Agent, and The Creative, Free-Thinking Professional. Described in Figure 4.4, practitioners in each level will perform, feel, and need different things, where the practicum student may likely recognize a combination of level 1 and 2, depending on their past experiences. Further, when it comes to supervision strategies—which we'll also address later in this chapter—each level of practitioner development will need a different supervisory approach. As you read through each level, notice what resonates for you.

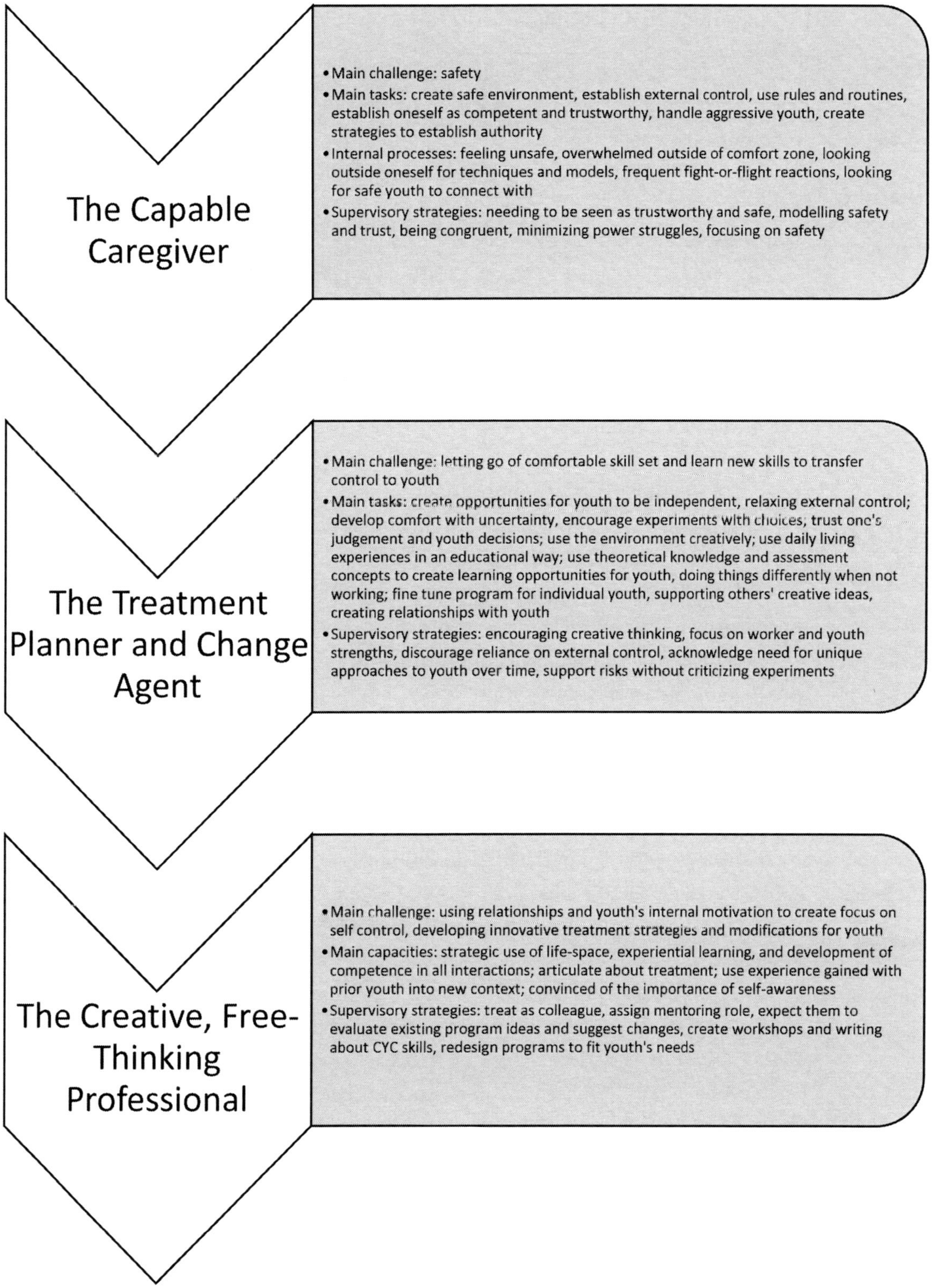

The Capable Caregiver

- Main challenge: safety
- Main tasks: create safe environment, establish external control, use rules and routines, establish oneself as competent and trustworthy, handle aggressive youth, create strategies to establish authority
- Internal processes: feeling unsafe, overwhelmed outside of comfort zone, looking outside oneself for techniques and models, frequent fight-or-flight reactions, looking for safe youth to connect with
- Supervisory strategies: needing to be seen as trustworthy and safe, modelling safety and trust, being congruent, minimizing power struggles, focusing on safety

The Treatment Planner and Change Agent

- Main challenge: letting go of comfortable skill set and learn new skills to transfer control to youth
- Main tasks: create opportunities for youth to be independent, relaxing external control; develop comfort with uncertainty, encourage experiments with choices; trust one's judgement and youth decisions; use the environment creatively; use daily living experiences in an educational way; use theoretical knowledge and assessment concepts to create learning opportunities for youth, doing things differently when not working; fine tune program for individual youth, supporting others' creative ideas, creating relationships with youth
- Supervisory strategies: encouraging creative thinking, focus on worker and youth strengths, discourage reliance on external control, acknowledge need for unique approaches to youth over time, support risks without criticizing experiments

The Creative, Free-Thinking Professional

- Main challenge: using relationships and youth's internal motivation to create focus on self control, developing innovative treatment strategies and modifications for youth
- Main capacities: strategic use of life-space, experiential learning, and development of competence in all interactions; articulate about treatment; use experience gained with prior youth into new context; convinced of the importance of self-awareness
- Supervisory strategies: treat as colleague, assign mentoring role, expect them to evaluate existing program ideas and suggest changes, create workshops and writing about CYC skills, redesign programs to fit youth's needs

Figure 4.4: Phelan's Stages of CYC Practitioner Development

Adapted from Bellefeuille, G., Jamieson, D., & Ricks, F. (Eds.). (2012). *Standing on the precipice: Inquiry into the creative potential of child and youth care practice* (pp. 84–88). Edmonton, AB: MacEwan Press.

LEARNING METHODS

So far, we have reviewed a few models and principles we can bring to our learning experience. There are many methods we can engage to support this learning. In the remaining sections of this chapter, we'll focus on supervision, giving and receiving feedback, goal setting and learning plans, and formal assessments including assignments and performance evaluations. Yes, assignments and performance evaluation—the preparation, articulation, and review of these assessments—are not only a way to demonstrate and articulate learning, they are also designed to produce learning experiences in and of themselves, due to their experiential and reflective nature.

Supervision

One of the most meaningful learning experiences we can have in practicum is through the student-supervisory relationship and supervision process. Phelan (2012) highlights its significance, stating that "good supervision and supportive colleagues help new workers to develop self-awareness and, through this process, to access resiliencies and developmental strengths acquired through life experiences" (p. 88). When it comes to supervision models, CYC has its approach, but given that we work in multidisciplinary settings, alongside supervisors with varied backgrounds, education, and training, the ways supervisors will approach supervision with practicum students will also vary.

Congruent CYC Practice and CYC Supervision

When it comes to supervision—the relationship, where it occurs, and its content—Child and Youth Care aligns its approach to supervision with the practice of CYC itself. Whereas we may spend some time within the four walls of a supervisor's office, we also are going to experience supervision in the life-space of practice: the practicum setting. Meanwhile, we're going to model relational work within the student-supervisor interactions and take a developmental, strengths-based, life-space approach to our understanding of practitioner development.

There is congruency between CYC practice and supervision. Charles (2016) reflects that "if you think about [supervisors'] positive traits, they are closely connected with what we would consider to be characteristics of effective child and youth care practitioners" (p. 10). Batasar-Johnie (2017) connects the experience of being a practicum student to the experience of being a young person: "the feelings of the young people you will work with are quite similar to the feelings of a student practitioner. Feeling lost, trying to establish themselves, figuring out how to communicate... to feel safe, trusted, and validated" (p. 36). Similarly, Kavanagh (2017) discusses the importance of students and new practitioners feeling like they "matter" to their supervisor, where "as CYC practitioners value young people as subjects who have the potential to strive for autonomy and agency, the same can be said for CYC practitioners" (p. 60). In supervision (especially in the beginning of that relationship and at the beginning of our development as practitioners), we are seeking to develop safe spaces, trust, and focus on strengths and interests as a foundation to grow.

How supervision looks and where it happens then becomes much more creative than traditional models. Gharabaghi (2016) describes contrasts in supervision models. We're likely all familiar with the traditional "supervision hour, the office-based session"; he explores "supervision in practice," which moves us "into the realm of everyday practice, experiences, and moments" (p. 99). In this model, supervision occurs during the car ride to the next location, on the sidelines of a soccer game, or while making a meal. It's in the moment, where the focus is on the practice, in or as close to the moment of it happening. Meanwhile, Garfat, Fulcher, and Freeman (2016) outline *the purposeful use of daily life events* as a framework for the supervisory interaction," explaining that "when there is a congruency between our model of supervision and our model of practice there is a higher degree of effective practice and job satisfaction," and "it involves a process of supervision which parallels the form of relational practice in which we wish practitioners to be engaged" (p. 29). As you experience supervision (for the first time for some of you), consider how CYC practice aligns with your experience of CYC supervision.

In the supervisor–practicum student relationship, we focus on how we engage, respond, and focus our time together; we focus on appropriate developmental learning opportunities and understand that we are developing as practitioners; we focus on strengths and support areas of improvement; we recognize our learning occurs within and is influenced by context; we centre young people and our commitment to socially just practices and our learning and development is for their benefit; and that supervision and learning occur in the life-space.

Supervision Is Reciprocal

Agencies generously offer learning experiences for students to benefit in their development as a practitioner. While supervisors devote an incredible amount of time and attention to attend to students' learning, agencies benefit too. Ainsworth (2016) summarizes agency feedback regarding CYC practicum students' contribution to the setting, where supervisors "grow professionally by critically reflecting with students on knowledge and theory" (p. 43). She also notes that CYC supervisors say their students "enliven their settings," bring

> It's empowering when you're a new practicum student. You may not think you have anything to contribute but remember you are new eyes. You can see what they don't always see.
> —Margaret, CYC Student

"creative new ideas," and create a "motivating force" to contribute to a culture of learning at the site (p. 43). You are encouraged to see yourself not solely as a learner nor as a passive recipient of learning opportunities. Rather, you are encouraged to see yourself as an active participant at the site, where you have much to contribute.

Student and Supervisor Qualities

There are many qualities that students and supervisors can bring to the supervision experience. Ainsworth (2016) reports that great CYC supervisors share responsibilities with practicum students, are open to ideas, consult with practicum instructors during challenges, offer a collaborative environment to learn, acknowledge the power dynamic in the relationship, and provide constructive feedback with the student's growth and development in mind. When Deol (2017) was completing a CYC practicum placement at an elementary school with Grade Five and Six students in a behaviour and learning assistance class, he described features of his effective supervision relationship, where his supervisor was available to talk, focused on strengths and areas of improvement, prioritized him, and allowed for autonomy while remaining present and offering guidance. He also noticed organizational factors that influenced this positive relationship, stating that his supervisor had a good working relationship with their supervisor, their previous work experience and education was relevant, and the site had a culture of learning. Meanwhile, Awai (2018) states that *being available* is the most central element of creating a positive supervisory relationship. She summarized five important areas students felt were most important to this relationship: 1) personal connectedness as a foundation, 2) role interpretation as to responsibilities and expectations of students' practice, 3) a developmental approach to students' learning, 4) a collaborative approach to learning and practising skills, and 5) critically examining practice contexts through reflective practice (pp. 24–25). Your supervisors will want to attend to these elements of your relationship and process together. However, knowing that these are elements of what students need, how can you actively show up to this relationship and process knowing what you may need?

Being proactive in your participation in the student–supervisor relationship and process is important. Delano (2010) writes about *owning your own supervision*, supporting students and new practitioners in taking an active role, where students should:

1. Ask questions,
2. Understand supervision as growth not a threat,
3. Seek supervision from anywhere and anyone,
4. Ask yourself, "What information do they have that I don't that will help me to understand this better?" and "What information do I have that they don't that will help them see it my way?"
5. Practice constructive confrontation,
6. Bring an agenda,
7. Seek group supervision,
8. Know what you're being evaluated against,
9. Seek out training opportunities,
10. Figure out how you learn and they teach,
11. Be empathetic, and
12. Create a trusting relationship. (para. 29–41)

To reiterate, as a practicum student, you are not required to experience supervision solely for the purpose of evaluation of your skills. Neither is supervision there solely for you to observe a CYC practitioner and learn new skills, knowledge, and ways of being alongside them. You are also participating in the student-supervisor relationship and supervisory process. How you show up to this relationship, how you engage in observation, discussion, feedback, and challenge, and how you prepare for and develop self-awareness in this relationship is all part of what supervision is about. You will always have a supervisor in your role as a CYC practitioner. How you learn to engage in this relationship now will help develop your skills, knowledge, and ways of being for the future.

Difficulty in Supervision

Where problems emerge, site supervisors and students report conflict and challenge differently but the reports are strongly related. Charles, Freeman, and Garfat (2016) listened to recently graduated CYC students and noted commonly cited characteristics that limited the potential of the supervision process and student–supervisor relationship, including lack of directness, unavailability, power struggles, self-centredness, dependency, sexism, manipulative/defensiveness, lack of self-confidence and/or in staff, and negativity. In response to any of these factors being present, we can experience difficulty. At first, we may emotionally react, perhaps feeling resentful, confused, frustrated, or angry. Let those emotions inform you. If you are angry, what is the source? What is the experience underpinning that emotion? Did your supervisor misunderstand you? Did they not see your actions in a wider context? Did they offend you in some way? Do some reflection first to explore what's happening for you. Resist the urge to fight, flight, or freeze. Gather your reflections and move forward.

> Expressing myself was a big issue. When I was going through hardships with my supervisor, it was hard for me to express to my supervisor. Students may feel hesitant to share what they're going through. My biggest worry was how it would affect my grades and assignments. Having that communication with my instructor helped.
> —Harman, CYC Student

Site supervisors have seen hundreds of students in their time of being a supervisor or working alongside supervisors. They are aware of a wide scope of abilities, stages of development, personalities, and dispositions of students so that they are prepared to work with just about any student. When they experience difficulty and problems, they report that students struggle with the following issues:

- Wellness: wellness and personal issues that distract them from fully participating in the practicum opportunities
- Self-Awareness and Attitude: limited self-awareness regarding the perceptions of youth of practicum student behaviour (e.g., negative attitude)
- Relationship Engagement: struggling with the "being friends" and "being friendly" approach to relationship engagement or waiting for young people to approach them, not the other way around
- Full Participation: availability, presence, and access—to the young people and to the supervisors—where supervisors notice students' inability or unwillingness to participate fully in the practicum site and opportunities

- Interpersonal Communication: lack of communication—as to where students plan on being at practicum or if they need to change schedules, lack of awareness of one's nonverbal behaviour, reluctance to share experiences, and so on
- Supervision and Learning: when students are not open to feedback and learning from others
- Theoretical Orientation: coming into the site with a rigid orientation to how practice should be done

Notice, however, that all of these issues are abilities in development. They become non-issues when a student is open to conversation, improvement, and being active in one's learning. Being open to feedback is key to these scenarios changing. Notice too that both students' and supervisors' main concerns are with availability, positive attitude, and openness to learning. If you can focus on those three elements of success, you're off to a great start. Be proactive in your situation and try to do your part to create the environmental and relational conditions that will help this process. This is not your sole responsibility. However, knowing these characteristics can help you identify what you may need.

Difficulties happen. Sometimes students then worry about the resulting assessment. Sometimes they feel as though they're not getting the fullest, most enjoyable experience, perhaps compared to fellow classmates' reports. While it is difficult to not worry and to not compare, it is helpful to remind ourselves that how we respond to the challenge, barrier, or conflict; what we learn from it; and how it improves our practice—as relational, responsive, and reflective practitioners—should be the focus of our learning experience. How you seek support from your instructor. How you practise your interpersonal communication skills. How you process and reflect on your participation. How you contribute to repair. What you do with this challenge says a lot about your practice.

To best engage in the process and relationship of supervision, complete Activity 4.1, to increase the self-awareness we bring into that interaction.

Activity 4.1: Self-Awareness in Supervision

1. What do you expect from your supervisor in terms of communication style, availability, approach to giving feedback?

   _____

2. What do you expect supervision to look like in terms of space, duration, frequency, topics covered, and recommended preparation?

   _____

3. What do you hope for? What are you apprehensive about?

   _____

4. What experience have you had with supervision in past work, school, or volunteer placements?

   _____

5. What will you bring forward from that experience that may be helpful and/or unhelpful?

   _____

6. How do you prefer to communicate (in person, text/call, email, etc.)?

   _____

Feedback

In supervision, but also through conversations with colleagues, faculty, and classmates, along with interactions with young people and their families, you will have the opportunity to seek out, receive, and integrate feedback. This is a vulnerable state of being, as we open ourselves to constructive critique. It is helpful to remember that in almost all cases, people offer feedback because they value your relationship, believe you will be able and are willing to do something with the feedback, and that they'll benefit from that change. Honour that exchange.

Before we get to some examples and guidelines for giving and receiving feedback, let's take a step back and reflect on our experience with feedback, in Activity 4.2. We can have all sorts of experience with receiving feedback over our lives: at work and in school, in personal and professional relationships, and so on. It can be a loaded experience.

> Students who are open to feedback and are keen to learn from those around them are the most likely to succeed. This can include acknowledging that they may need to reassess what they thought they already knew, or beliefs they previously held.
> —Annie, CYC Practicum Supervisor

Activity 4.2: My Experience Receiving Feedback

Think of a time when you received feedback on something, when it was an unhelpful experience. What was the feedback about? Who was present? What was communicated to you? How was it delivered? What was your internal and external response? What effect did this experience have on your behaviour (or the central aspect of the communicated feedback)? What effect did this experience have on you?

   _____

   _____

   _____

Think of a time when you received feedback on something, when it was a helpful experience. What was the feedback about? Who was present? What was communicated to you? How was it delivered? What was your internal and external response? What effect did this experience have on your behaviour (or the central aspect of the communicated feedback)? What effect did this experience have on you?

_____

_____

_____

Notice your reflections above, and if you feel comfortable, share with a classmate or with your community of practice. Through this experience, brainstorm: what did you learn about yourself and what you need? What barriers may you have to receiving feedback that you need to attend to?

_____

_____

When giving feedback, we should always provide feedback with the intention of wanting the recipient to feel like they can do something with it. In that way, it becomes *constructive*. Hopefully, it should generate discussion rather than halt it in its tracks. "That was great!" or "That was awful!" are equally meaningless and impossible to take forward.

Read the following pieces of feedback and reflect on how they are delivered.

1. "I noticed you remembered Farin's favourite game and how pleased she was to play it with you yesterday." (This feedback will hopefully make you want to keep learning and remembering things about the kids at your site.)

2. "I wonder if you may consider placing yourself in the middle of the room instead of the sides or corners, so the kids may feel you're more approachable." (This feedback will hopefully invite you to consider where you're occupying physical space in each room and how that relates to your approachability and the perceptions of the young people at the site.)

3. "The daily log report you wrote last week for the house seemed to really capture strengths-based language of the youth. Keep it up!" (This feedback will hopefully make you want to review what made that report distinct and how to keep doing that.)

4. "Sometimes, because of our disposition, common interests, and so on, we gravitate to some kids and not others. I notice that you've been spending most of your time with A, B, and C youth. I wonder if for the next while, you could turn your attention to some other kids." (This feedback will hopefully invite a discussion of any internal barriers you may experience that make you hesitant to engage with youth out of your comfort zone.)

For many of us, we have experiences receiving feedback where the delivery of the message was received as judgemental, an attack, or focused on something that is impossible to change. In other words, it was *destructive*. It does not help us move forward. It does not even help us reflect on the feedback in a useful, proactive way. With that in mind, as you enter into multiple feedback discussions throughout your practicum—with your supervisor(s), faculty-instructor, and peers—consider the Dos and Don'ts in Table 4.2.

> You have to step out of your comfort zone.
> —Harman, CYC Student

Table 4.2: Giving and Receiving Feedback

Giving and Receiving Feedback		
	DOs	**DON'Ts**
When Giving Feedback	DO ask if it's an okay time to give feedback DO offer feedback in a tentative way (It seems like…; I wonder if…) DO be aware of the way you're delivering the message (verbal/non-verbal behaviour) DO focus on actions, not the person DO be specific and concrete DO situate feedback in context DO acknowledge progress DO make it relevant to the context DO focus on the benefit of the person receiving feedback or the youth in their care	DON'T minimize or exaggerate DON'T be vague or general DON'T be negative for negativity's sake DON'T offer cheerleading praise or superficial critique DON'T forget to offer tentative suggestions DON'T let too much time pass
When Receiving Feedback	DO be open and listen fully to the feedback DO assume it's coming from a good place DO clarify what you heard DO ask for specifics DO wonder: how could this help me develop? DO ask for follow-up ideas on how you can improve DO acknowledge and appreciate the person giving feedback	DON'T feel judged or become defensive DON'T consider the feedback as the entire truth DON'T assume what they mean DON'T forget: you get to decide what to do with the feedback you receive

Feedback isn't provided or received just for the sake of feedback itself. It is there to improve our practice. It's there for us to mull over, consider, experiment with, practise, and ultimately integrate meaningfully into our growth and development. Consider how you will integrate feedback into not only your performance but also demonstrations of your learning through the methods and assessments below. Remember that in practicum, you are not being evaluated on your pursuit or attainment of perfection; you are being evaluated on your openness to and demonstration of your learning process. Feedback plays a central role.

> Humility is an asset. Know your strengths and weaknesses. Assume. You have a lot of room to grow. Don't take it personally. It's the nature of personal and professional development.
> —Farah, CYC Practicum Supervisor

Learning Goals

As part of your practicum, you will be expected to identify specific goals you'd like to focus on. It should be said that you're going to learn more than just the goals you identify near the beginning of your practicum. However, by focusing your attention on these goals, the hope is that you transfer that ability to all other skills, knowledge, and ways of being you are developing over time. Goals should be a combination of 1) student interest, 2) academic requirements, and 3) site learning opportunities. These goals should be collaboratively developed with your practicum supervisor, as they'll know what opportunities are available and how to access them. Of course, these goals can and should evolve as you spend more time at the site. In your practicum placement interview, you may have been asked what you want to learn. In the first week or two of your placement, you will have identified what opportunities exist. Meanwhile, you've likely oriented yourself to the practicum course expectations of what the program expects you to learn.

Before we explore what goals you could be focusing on, constructing goals and measurable outcomes, and setting that plan into motion, let's review guidance on how to go about the goal-setting process.

SMART Goals

Developing goals using the SMART method is a widely accepted practice across the CYC practicum experience. SMART goals are specific, measurable, attainable, relevant, and time-bound. In order for goals to have meaning, be based in collaboration, and achievable at your site, it is helpful to use the SMART prompts to formulate your goals, particularly if goal setting is a new process to you. Conveniently, we shouldn't just use this goal-setting approach for ourselves and our learning; we can also use goal setting with young people. Practising SMART goal setting for your practicum learning will help you model this process for the young people and families you work alongside. Review SMART goal setting in Activity 4.3 by following the prompts and examples and exploring a goal of your own or just jotting down some notes you have about your own goal brainstorming.

Activity 4.3: SMART Goals at My Practicum

Table 4.3: SMART Goals at My Practicum

SMART Goal	Some Brainstorming Prompts	Practicum Brainstorming Examples	My Notes
Specific	What do I want to learn? What is part of that learning—what are its specific components and steps? Who is part of it? What will happen? What support do I need to achieve it? Where will it be achieved? How will it be achieved? Why do I want to achieve it?	✗ I want to learn about the resources available for youth at the alternative school. ✓ In order to become more knowledgeable about the resources in the community tailored to youth's needs at this alternative school, I will explore three external resources in the community and three internal resources in our agency, focusing on housing, mental health, and employment.	
Measurable	What will I observe when this goal is reached? What will I have created? How will I note progress toward this goal?	✗ I will gain knowledge about resources. ✓ I will ask my supervisors which programs may be relevant to my learning, brainstorm my own, contact the program managers of the resources, visit the programs, and come prepared with relevant questions. ✓ I will present these resources at a staff team meeting, including a map and info sheet.	

SMART Goal	Some Brainstorming Prompts	Practicum Brainstorming Examples	My Notes
		✗ I will incorporate resources into my conversations with youth, if/where relevant. ✓ I will be able to describe these resources—what they're about, how to get there, why they're helpful—in youth-friendly language.	
Attainable	Will it be possible for me to learn at my practicum site? Is it within my range of competency, strengths, and areas for improvement? Will I have the opportunities to do so during the time I am here?	✓ Consider altering the number of resources. ✓ Consider altering the timeline. ✓ Consider altering the subject matter/focus of resources. ✓ Consider altering the range of locations.	
Relevant	Is this goal relevant to my learning? Does it interest me as an emerging CYC practitioner? Does it meet the requirements of my academic program's expectations of me? Is it connected to the site and role?	✓ Is this what I want to learn? ✓ Will this be helpful to the youth/staff/me? ✓ Which CYC competency does it attend to?	
Time-bound	On what timeline can I anticipate this goal to be achieved? Is it possible to complete within the time I have available in my practicum? When will I attend to the various steps of the learning goal's tasks and activities?	✓ By midpoint of my practicum placement I will… ✓ By the end of my practicum placement, I will… ✓ I will explore one resource every two weeks while at my practicum placement…	

Ultimately, students will want to attend to three main questions to guide their brainstorming process:

1. What do you want to develop and focus upon in your practicum placement?
2. What are the observable strategies and learning activities that may achieve this goal?
3. How will you know you've achieved this goal?

Students should begin this process early and with a wide scope in mind. For example, if your CYC program requires you to focus on three goals in your learning process, bring five goals to your supervisor for collaborative review. Your supervisor will help let you know what is possible, the relevant activities you could be a part of, and so on. Your faculty-instructor will help you connect those goals to the assessment categories and assignments that are part of the practicum course. Further, keep in mind that your goals shouldn't be too easy—for example, to show up to work on time—as these are the things that, without question, we already assume you're going to do. In contrast, your goals shouldn't be too complex and out of the scope of your time and ability, such as creating an entirely new, 12-session, evidence-based, social-emotional skills group for the children at an elementary school. It's more realistic in a first or second-year practicum placement to learn the existing social-emotional skills group and assist in facilitating an activity or two, or come up with some new activities to introduce to the existing group. Use the SMART goal method to help you brainstorm. Then, when it comes time to develop a learning plan, you'll have done all the preparatory work necessary to complete it.

> See the smallest one and you feel really good about yourself. And then you develop another one and then build on that. That's the stairway to success.
> —Donna, CYC Practicum Supervisor

Learning Plans

Learning plans represent the main direction you'd like to take at your practicum site. They include the learning goals you will focus on while at practicum. While you'll have many tasks and responsibilities, and a number of assignments to complete, among other things, as part of your practicum, the learning plan will, in essence, guide your time at the site. Learning plans should be thoughtfully constructed and presented professionally to your faculty-instructor. Remember, learning plans are documents that communicate what you want to learn. The way you articulate your plans will help others support you in achieving those goals. Learning plans are often presented formally to your faculty-instructor at the beginning of your practicum placement (after consultation with both supervisor and faculty). They are also presented formally to your faculty-instructor at the end of your practicum placement. In the first submission, the learning plan should present your goals and the rationale behind them. The last submission will likely have a reflective component, including what happened and what changed along the way.

CYC Goals Framework

Let's say you have a blend of goals you'd like to work on: learning about community resources, engaging with young people, attending to self-care, facilitating an activity, and so on. For those of you who are not sure how to approach the stage of narrowing down or focusing your goals within your practicum site, you may wish to use a framework to guide your process. For example, in Chapter 1, we introduced the concept of *praxis*—the practice and educational model CYC often uses to frame its work. Its main concepts—knowing (knowledge), doing (skills), and being (ways of being)—could help you think through your goal setting. Consider Ayna's story below for an example of a more extended learning plan. Keep in mind that your CYC program and faculty-instructor will have a specific process and perhaps even a template they want you to use. In that case, use the examples in this guidebook for inspiration, not direction. Whichever approach you take, you'll want to create a variety of goals to demonstrate your ability to attend to the complexity of our work.

Ayna's Learning Plan

Ayna is a South Asian, female, first-year CYC practicum student placed at a residential group home for adolescent girls in government care. She spends the first week or so actively observing and participating in the goings-on at the site, speaking with her supervisor and new colleagues as to some of the expectations of her in her practicum course, and identifying the things she is interested in learning. She also notices that in the small group home, all three current residents are racialized youth, coming from African-Caribbean and Indigenous (Métis and First Nations) backgrounds. Yet she doesn't notice any culturally specific programming at the site, nor any discussion of culturally diverse resources as a part of their community connections, integrated services, and possible referral resources. Ayna wants to ensure she's diversifying her goals across ways of knowing, doing, and being, to make them more meaningful and complex. She also wants to ensure her goals overlap with some of the required tasks at the practicum site and course assignments. As such, she structures her learning plan as follows:

Knowing

Overall Goal: Become knowledgeable about the culturally responsive recreational, mental health, and employment resources in the community so that I may be able to appropriately refer the youth at the setting to the services, if and when the opportunity arises.

1. Specific Strategies: research and create an eco-map of relevant services (aim for three in each category), checking in with other staff for more ideas,

and asking for recommendations from youth who are already using the services (or used them in the past).

2. Specific Strategies: visit each service to ask further questions, understand the setting and how to get there, assess it for its youth-friendliness, and learn more about its programs.

    • Measurable Outcomes: I will be able to describe each service in youth-friendly language, including how to access the service, a description of its programs, and the benefits it may provide.

    • Measurable Outcomes: I will add the (new and updated) information to the group home's Resource and Referral binder.

Doing

Overall Goal: Throughout my practicum placement, I will develop a therapeutic relationship with at least one resident at the home.

1. Specific Strategies: I will connect and engage the girls at the home by learning about their interests, culture, and background, while connecting through daily life events (e.g., wake up, mealtimes, leisure, transportation to and from school and appointments, etc.). I will be sure to sign up for a range of shifts across the 24-hour day, and both weekday and weekend.

2. Specific Strategies: With their agreement, and where available, I will attend and participate in intake, progress, case planning, and integrated community meetings.

    • Measurable Outcomes: I will collaboratively plan and facilitate three life-skill activities based on our connections, such as, but not limited to, planning and cooking a meal together, creating a resume and searching for jobs, going to a drop-in dance class at the recreation centre, attending a cultural ceremony or exploring cultural roots, and so on.

    • Measurable Outcomes: I will ask my supervisor to observe my application of interpersonal helping skills and give me feedback on areas of strength and improvement, on a weekly basis.

Being

Overall Goal: Throughout my practicum placement, I will develop my reflective practice.

1. Specific Strategies: participate in discussion-based reflection with my class seminar each week, develop a community of practice with my classmates who are also at residential group homes once every two weeks, and work

through reflective question prompts in my meetings with my supervisor and faculty-instructor.

2. Specific Strategies: engage in individual reflection practices, including completing my learning journal at the end of each week and going for nature walks at least twice a week.

   • Measurable Outcomes: I will notice the struggles, "ah-ha"s, discoveries, challenges I experience and address them as they come up by seeking support, asking questions, and following up by processing it.

   • Measurable Outcomes: I will notice and seek feedback on my increased level of self-awareness, benefits to young people, and shifts in my practice.

Brainstorming through each goal in this way helps Ayna to develop the first submission of her learning plan.

> If they're struggling in an area I might ask: What do you think I would need to see in order for me to feel that you've successfully met that competency? What do you think your instructor would need to see?
>
> —Mindi, CYC Practicum Supervisor

Remember that there will be an official way you present your goals, likely through a learning plan. There will also be individual approaches that supervisors may recommend. For example, CYC practicum student McManus (2009) reflects that she was required to write weekly goals that were based on the five competencies from our CYC competency document. She joined that requirement with her longer-term goal of being able to apply for certification at the end of her credential. That, combined with regularly writing in a learning journal, made it easy for her to find evidence of her learning at the end of her practicum when it came time to submit a review of her learning plan and other accompanying assignments.

No matter how you structure your learning plan, be sure to approach the task with thoughtful intention. Consult the CYC competency document, your syllabus, and this guidebook to help you with brainstorming, focus, and language. Use your supervisor, faculty-instructor, and classmates to help you plan. Hold yourself to high standards but do not let perfection and over-extension enter the space. Collaborate with those around you, but make sure your learning plan is meaningful to you.

ASSESSMENTS

Throughout and by the end of your practicum course, you will be assessed via a number of components: a set number of hours at your site + performance evaluations + seminar participation + an assignment package. These components evaluate your learning according to the course's established objectives and outcomes. They are a chance for you to communicate and demonstrate your learning. Meanwhile, remember that assignments and performance evaluations in practicum are designed to be learning opportunities in and of themselves.

Table 4.4: Types of CYC Practicum Assignments

Learning Goals and Learning Plans	Case Plan Reports	Activity Plans and Activity Reports	Exams
Professional Development Plans	Presentations	Skill Demonstration (video, audio, and in-person observations)	Observation and Recording (more on that in Chapter 10)
Reflective Journals	Agency Profiles and Community Maps	Task Checklists	Legacy/Capstone Projects (more on that in Chapter 12)
Reflective Papers (on various subjects: ethical decision-making, abuse and neglect, relationship building, etc.)	Research Papers and Projects (on various agency/population-related topics)	Online or Seminar Discussions	Portfolios (more on that below and in Chapter 13)

Assignments

Assignments look different from one school to the next and will be outlined in your course syllabus. Consider the list in Table 4.4, cross-check your syllabi, and check off what will be required of you. The most important piece across all assignments is your ability to connect what you are learning in class to what you are doing in practicum.

> The reflective assignments help to scaffold my learning, integrating theory with practice.
> —Jenn, CYC Student

Portfolios

Portfolios are a common way of collecting, sorting, and presenting your learning as a whole. Whether a portfolio is required of your practicum experience or not, it is helpful to keep the information for future reference, so as to help you with future practicum placements, assignments, and applying for jobs down the road. Are you required to submit a portfolio? See Chapter 13, Consolidating Your Learning and Working in the CYC Field, where we review typical portfolio components and how you can demonstrate your learning with supporting materials (also called evidence).

Peer Consultation

Whether it be an in-person seminar, online discussion board, or community of practice, consulting with peers is a common thread that holds exponential opportunities for learning. As referred to in Chapter 1, formal and informal communities of practice resonate with the practicum experience in part because of the assumptions these groups have of the learning process: that learning occurs through engagement with the social world, that learning is about making meaning of our shared experiences, and that the focus and goals of our learning are socially constructed and produced (Ainsworth, 2016). The design of practicum seminar, online discussions, and communities of practice allows us to reflect upon, collaborate, safely challenge, and prompt us to explore our experiences in depth, connecting alongside others who are experiencing a similar process.

Benshoff (2001) reminds us that peer consultation is where "critical and supportive feedback is emphasized while evaluation is deemphasized," where the relationship is less hierarchical and provides a variety of benefits including less dependence on experts, greater independence, increased personal responsibility, development of supervision skills, use of peers for modelling, freedom to choose peer consultants, and perhaps most importantly, the absence of evaluation. Faculty-instructors are present to model effective discussion among students. In fact, it's quite normal to see a faculty-instructor actively facilitating near the beginning of the term and then taking a step back and letting students take more leadership roles with the discussions. In the communities of practice you establish outside of seminar, like any forming group, more structure at the beginning allows for less structure and more generativity as you move forward. The Ryerson University School of CYC (n.d.) program lists a variety of ways in-person seminars (and online discussion) benefit us:

- ✓ Learn about other programs and services
- ✓ Brainstorm ideas and solutions
- ✓ Share frustration and joys
- ✓ Discover various ways to deal with a situation or client you're working with
- ✓ Practice learning in a team environment
- ✓ Learn how to give and receive constructive feedback (p. 9)

Not only is peer consultation helpful for the points listed above, but it is also helpful to develop critical thinking capacity. Social service practicum researchers Testa and Egan (2015) looked at students' capacity to critically reflect. In Weeks 3 and 12 of their 12-week practicum placement, students were asked to "name, understand, and challenge hidden assumptions" in an online discussion forum (p. 270). Contrast one student's Week 3 and Week 12 discussion posts:

> If I don't perceive someone as being intelligent, even if they are in a position of authority, I tend to dismiss their views. This is something that I need to be careful with, and figure out ways of working productively around. (p. 270)

I was thinking about things like attachment theory versus the medical model, in terms of diagnosis of children with developmental delays. I thought about how poverty and lack of education affects children, and how cycles of abuse operate. I thought about cultural awareness, and how this comes to play in family work and in assessing situations, as well as drawing on it to explain some family relationships. I thought about how best to help this family in an anti-oppressive way, and how to work with parents with intellectual disabilities. (p. 270)

You can see the layers that are developing as this student challenges herself to consider, connect, and apply. Trust that if you too rise to the challenge, you will also notice this change in your reflective capacity and awareness and your ability to respond to young people's needs. It is through these discussions (not solely the passage of time) that our capacity to critically reflect is strengthened and comes alive.

Performance Evaluation Meetings

You'll likely have at least three meetings with your practicum supervisor and faculty-instructor to review your progress: beginning, middle, and end. As you are the common denominator, you will likely be asked to schedule these meetings. You may even be asked to take a proactive role in facilitating these meetings, as an opportunity to demonstrate your ability to articulate and plan for your learning as well as to seek and receive feedback. See Figure 4.5, which outlines the typical content of these meetings. Read closely so that you can prepare. However, take into consideration other directives you've been given by your supervisor and faculty-instructor.

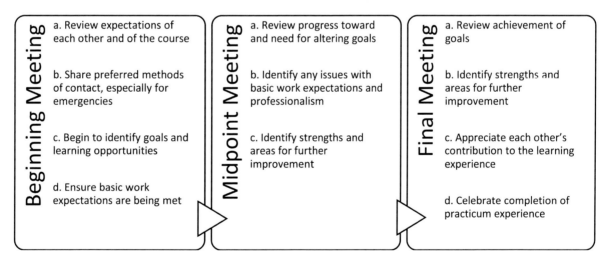

Figure 4.5: Performance Evaluation Meetings—Beginning, Middle, and End

To actively prepare for these meetings, you can reflect on and gather a number of items.

1. Preparing for Your Beginning Performance Evaluation Meeting
   - ☑ Schedule and confirm the time, location, and duration of the meeting
   - ☑ Ask both supervisor and faculty-instructor what to expect during the meeting
   - ☑ Bring all relevant and required documentation (e.g., learning goals notes, practicum manual/syllabi, contact information, etc.)
   - ☑ Reflect on your observations of the site/role thus far and what you want to achieve while you're there
   - ☑ Bring a list of questions and topics that you think would be helpful to explore, regardless of what your supervisor and faculty-instructor will review

2. Preparing for Your Midpoint Performance Evaluation Meeting
   - ☑ Schedule and confirm the time, location, and duration of the meeting
   - ☑ Ask both supervisor and faculty-instructor what to expect during the meeting
   - ☑ Bring all relevant and required documentation (e.g., learning plan, practicum manual/syllabi, examples of strengths and areas of improvement)
   - ☑ Reflect on performance thus far—strengths, challenges, areas for improvement— and where you want to focus your learning for the remaining time

3. Preparing for Your Final Performance Evaluation Meeting
   - ☑ Schedule and confirm the time, location, and duration of the meeting
   - ☑ Ask both supervisor and faculty-instructor what to expect during the meeting
   - ☑ Bring all relevant and required documentation (e.g., learning plan, practicum manual/syllabi, examples of strengths and areas of improvement)
   - ☑ Reflect on performance thus far—strengths, challenges, areas for improvement— and where you want to focus your learning achievements in the future
   - ☑ Bring any appreciative notes for your supervisor and site

Before your midpoint and final performance evaluation meetings, you and your supervisor will likely be required to review your performance according to 1) an assessment form that reviews your skills and 2) a general discussion of your strengths and areas for improvement. Your supervisor will likely be required to submit this form to your faculty-instructor. Most supervisors will want to review this feedback with you before this meeting, so you can be prepared, so there are no surprises, and so the meeting can focus on generating new ideas and sharing insightful reflections, rather than going through a list of checklist items. To be an active participant in this process, review this form beforehand and assess yourself. Take the time to recall examples of your performance according to its evaluation criteria. This preparation will help you in conversations with your supervisor, your faculty-instructor, and assessing your learning plan.

For students who have not been in a practicum performance evaluation meeting before, these meetings can feel intimidating. Further, because the focus is entirely on you, they can be a place of vulnerability and awkwardness, as we don't often have conversations entirely focused on ourselves. Rest assured, these conversations are a chance to celebrate your efforts, learning, and contribution to the site, while also directing your remaining time at the site. Performance evaluations occur because we look forward to hearing your insights and observations; we want the opportunity to support your learning; and we trust your ability to incorporate feedback. We want to see you shine in your own unique way. Ultimately, these are conversations about CYC practice. These meetings are designed to mentor you into the CYC profession. It is time devoted just for you to attend to your development.

> Take out of it as much as you can.
> —Margaret, CYC Student

Performance Evaluation Criteria

All CYC practicum programs will have established criteria in which they expect students to perform. Despite the fact that students will be placed in many different types of settings, these criteria will attempt to cut across all settings, where skills, knowledge, and ways of being will apply (in some way) to them all. Further, each category will likely have examples of how a student could demonstrate this area of ability, such as a Likert scale with examples, where your supervisor could indicate where your skill level falls.

Consider the following common performance evaluation categories: professionalism and professional practice; interpersonal communication and counselling skills; activity programming and intervention planning; relationship development and relational practice; observation and reporting; teamwork and collaboration; advocacy and empowerment; self-awareness and self-care.

How would you evaluate yourself in the performance evaluation categories listed above (or the categories listed in your syllabus), according to the following scales?

- unsatisfactory performance, basic competency, growth and development, quality and consistent growth
- knowledge, comprehension, application, analysis, synthesis
- learning, functional, competent, mastery

Some supervisors will want to complete the form together. Some may want to review their assessment with you before your meeting with your faculty-instructor, while some may have other approaches. Be sure to ask what they prefer. After these performance evaluation meetings and submission of the assessment forms, your faculty-instructor will assign you a grade (at midpoint and/or at final) and it will likely be based upon 1) your participation in these meetings (demonstrating your ability to seek out, receive, and integrate feedback); 2) the verbal discussion of your performance (in general and according to these criteria); and 3) the assessment form itself.

Remember to keep copies of these assessment forms. They will prove useful when evaluating your own progress during practicum, noticing progress for your next practicum, and helping you articulate your skills and abilities when you are applying to work in the field. They will also hopefully have a summary form at the end with a summary of your strengths and areas for improvement, which is useful for when it comes time to seeking a reference and so on. (If not, make sure to ask your supervisor to complete Appendix F).

LEARNING JOURNAL

Keep using your learning journal, developing a consistent, reliable daily or weekly reflective practice. If you have assignments due soon, regarding learning goals, plans, or initial reflective papers or discussion posts, be sure to use your learning journal notes as review material. You'll likely have already touched upon some aspect of what is required of you.

PRACTICE SCENARIOS

Take a look at the Practice Scenarios that conclude this chapter: "Marisol's Goals" and "Students' Supervisors." Use the content that you've read in this chapter to inspire your thinking about each scenario. Notice how a scenario may relate to your own situation at your current practicum placement, even if it is not exactly what you are experiencing. Consider the questions posed at the end of each scenario to help you expand and apply the concepts presented in this chapter.

SEMINAR GROUP AND COMMUNITY OF PRACTICE DISCUSSION QUESTIONS

As you participate in your practicum seminar and/or communities of practice, consider some of the following questions to guide those discussions:

1. What have you learned through actively observing your practicum site?
2. Give an example of when you pushed yourself out of your comfort zone and into the challenge and courage zone.
3. Describe one of your learning goals, its strategies, and measurable outcomes. Listen to others' examples.
4. What are the essential elements to the supervision relationship? What can you do as a student to support that process?

IN CLOSING

In this chapter, we've reviewed how you can approach your learning as an active participant. By understanding the process of learning, how practicum is designed to fully engage you in that learning experience, how you develop as a practitioner, and the methods you can and will participate in to fully engage in learning opportunities during practicum, you will approach and immerse yourself in this practicum experience the best you can. Remember, practicum is not about perfection. It is about learning. It is up to you how you engage with the opportunities in front of you.

PRACTICE SCENARIOS

Marisol's Goals

Marisol has begun her practicum at a residential facility for mandated youth, all who have been referred to the program because of their involvement with the criminal justice system. Marisol is interested in youth mental health issues for youth involved in the criminal justice system, but isn't sure how to translate that into goals. All she knows is that she wants to focus all her goals on youth mental health issues. Her CYC program requires her to develop three goals: one focused on knowledge, one focused on skills, and one focused on self.

Without knowing too many more details about Marisol or her practicum site, what goals would you recommend she set for herself?

_____

_____

_____

Students' Supervisors

Manjit's supervisor expects her to jump in without direction. She'd prefer direction and is worried about making mistakes, despite her supervisor telling her mistakes are welcome. Erin has heard her classmate gets one hour of focused supervision, but at her own site, she just talks to her supervisor in the breaks each day and there's been no discussion of formal meetings. She's a bit envious. Jaslene feels a bit awkward around her supervisor as she feels she's more expressive whereas her supervisor is more reserved. Jen's supervisor has told her he'd like to see her assignments to be able to support her to get a great grade. However, Jen's worried that she won't be able to be as open as she'd like.

Do any of these scenarios with supervisors resonate for you? How would you suggest each student respond to their challenge? How can each student use their seminar group and faculty-instructor to support them?

_____

_____

_____

CHAPTER 5

Reflective CYC Practice

Competencies for Professional Child and Youth Work Practitioners				
Professionalism	Cultural and Human Diversity	Applied Human Development	Relationship and Communication	Developmental Practice Methods
Professional Development and Behaviour Personal Development and Self Care		Practice Methods Sensitive to Development and Context	Relationship Development	

I believe that when we have the chance to experience practice through practicum, to have the privilege of learning through the sharing of others' lived experiences, and then as a group are tasked with developing, critically reflecting, contesting, and collaborating on the ethos/collective ethics we wish for, the worldview that emerges becomes part of who we are.
—Kim Ainsworth, MA CYC Graduate, Practicum Scholar

Child and Youth Care (CYC) professional competencies, foundational attitudes and characteristics, course learning outcomes, fieldwork orientation manuals, and vocational standards explicitly outline reflection and reflective practice as an essential component to our education, training, and practice. Reflective practice facilitates self-awareness and understanding; learning and personal growth; critical thinking; and most importantly, change and improvement to practice, contributing to strengthened relationships that we intentionally develop with the young people and the communities we serve. However, as learners of this practice, we may feel unsure of how to go about this seemingly simple act of reflection.

What do we mean by reflective practice? What does it mean to be a reflective practitioner? What are the benefits and barriers to learning the skill? How can we set up our

Stay curious about everything. I try to point out and ask questions to underline that our assumptions get in the way of our learning as we are too busy proving our hypotheses to accept and really listen.
—Rose, CYC Practicum Supervisor

practicum experiences to best facilitate reflection? Whereas this guidebook continuously encourages reflection through its pages, this chapter will specifically respond to these questions, inviting students to purposefully integrate reflection into their practice, as there is no better place to develop this skill than during practicum.

REFLECTION

At its most concise, to *reflect upon* means to think about something carefully and deeply (Oxford Dictionary, 2018). Clark (2012) describes reflection in the human services as "both an internal state of mediation and rumination and as a process whereby thoughts, actions, and processes are reflected back from other sources, such as supervisors, instructors, and peers," where "reflective practice is viewed as an essential foundational skill that facilitates the linking of theory with practice toward the goals of improving competence and promoting new learning" (pp. 79–80). In Child and Youth Care literature, reflection can be understood as when the CYC practitioner thinks "seriously—about one's actions, the outcomes of those actions, the context in which they occur, and one's immediate experiencing of an event" (Garfat, 2005, para. 4). Snell (2015) comments that "reflection is one of many ways in which we find and make meaning. It is an experience in and of itself which comes when we pause long enough to integrate personal experience with shared relational knowledge" (p. 5). Reflection in this case is purposeful and intentional and its primary goal is to benefit the young person we are working with.

Garfat and Fulcher (2012) turn our attention to practice, highlighting reflection as the action that assists the CYC practitioner in their practice. They ask generative questions to help us consider the encounter we find ourselves in:

- Why am I thinking of doing this?
- What is influencing me to think like this?
- How might my various actions be interpreted by the other person? (p. 15)

Reflection can turn its attention to the self, practice, and the context at large.

SELF-REFLECTION

As we begin to ask ourselves purposeful, reflective questions, the self becomes key. In self-reflection, we reflect *on* and *through* one's self. In previous chapters in this guidebook, we have touched upon the self and its central role in Child and Youth Care practice. We will continue to explore this concept in future chapters, just as you have done in your coursework thus far. Kouri (2015) reminds us that we are not a static, knowable essence, but rather a dynamic, multi-storied way of being, highly contingent on context around us. Thus, we must explore the values, assumptions, and histories that we bring to our work but also understand those in relationship to context and how they are continually in flux in response to context.

Consider the questions posed in Activity 5.1, revealing some of the values, assumptions, and personal experiences we bring to this work.

> Be aware of your biases and everything and how it affects your practice. But don't throw it out the window, just keep it in mind. Use your perspectives to your advantage rather than leaving it at the door.
> —Margaret, CYC Student

Activity 5.1: My Values and Assumptions

1. Identify three values that led you to choose a career in Child and Youth Care.

   _____

   _____

   _____

2. Identify one personal belief or value that has been brought into question since you have learned about your professional role.

   _____

3. List three beliefs that you hold about the role of the Child and Youth Care practitioner.

   _____

   _____

   _____

4. Which aspect of your practicum do you think will most clearly reflect your values?

   _____

   _____

   _____

5. In which aspect of your practicum do you think your values will be most at odds with your working environment?

    _____

6. What personal experiences of adversity may be triggered through this practicum? How will you show compassion for yourself?

    _____

    _____

7. What strengths and resiliency do you bring from the experiences above that help inform your practice?

    _____

    _____

8. What resources do you have to support yourself?

    _____

    _____

9. What hopes and fears do you have for practicum?

    _____

    _____

10. How may those hopes and fears direct your behaviour?

    _____

    _____

Adapted and expanded from Drolet, J., Clark, N., & Allen, H. (Eds.). (2012). *Shifting sites of practice: Field education in Canada* (pp. 80, 92). Toronto, ON: Pearson.

We do not want to end there. In CYC practice, we are not invited to know the self for its own sake (though that is a perfectly acceptable pursuit). Rather, we build self-awareness through self-reflection to know how we show up in our practice, to question the very practices we follow, and to intentionally use our selves through relational ways of being with young people to benefit their lives. This is our responsibility to which we must attend. Garfat and Charles (2007) say a central question that guides our self-reflection should be "Who am I?" (p. 7), and Shebib (2013) adds, "How do others see me?" (p. 26). Because of the transformational learning that occurs in practicum, these questions can be a beacon of light guiding you through.

REFLEXIVITY

With the influence of poststructuralist and feminist thought on our field, we have recently seen the term *reflexivity* enter the CYC vocabulary. Reflexivity can be generally understood as "someone being able to examine his or her own feelings, reactions, and motives and how these influence what he or she does or thinks in a situation" (Cambridge Dictionary, 2018). Reflection and reflexivity have seemingly overlapping definitions. A more complex definition of the term emerges in the caring professions, where reflexivity expands the term *reflection* to accommodate and describe more specifically what we are reflecting upon and with what intention. In their review of reflexivity's varied use in the social services literature, D'Cruz, Gillingham, and Melendez (2007) note its three main components:

1. Critical self-awareness by the practitioner, in how he or she understands and engages with social problems
2. Realisation that our assumptions about social problems and the people who experience these problems have ethical and practical consequences
3. Questioning of personal practice, knowledge and assumptions (para. 20)

In essence, reflexivity becomes reflection's more self-aware and critically minded counterpart. As Newbury (2007) notes, a "reflexive approach is one in which we engage in an ongoing process of identifying, considering, and even questioning the influence of personal and societal values on how we practice" (p. 53). Vradenburg (2007) concurs, concluding that reflexivity is "the act of practicing while having ongoing dialogue about the influences, choices and factors contributing to practice" (p. 29). Interestingly, both Newbury and Vradenburg reflect on their practice from an international CYC practicum placement. Reflexivity often requires us to remove ourselves from the familiar in order to begin noticing the assumptions and taken-for-granted notions we hold within.

> I find a lot of time you're self-reflective when you're insecure and in a state of learning. Critical self-awareness is something you should always fall back on, even when you become comfortable and confident in your practice.
> —John, CYC Student

Table 5.1: Tilsen's Reflective vs. Reflexive Questions

Tilsen's Reflective vs. Reflexive Questions	
Reflective Questions	**Reflexive Questions**
- What did you notice? - What happened? - What was that like? - What do you think about it? - How do you feel about it? - What stood out for you that was interesting or important about it?	- Am I sure about this? What makes me so sure? - What discourses, institutions, or persons would support this certainty? - Which people and communities are included in my understanding, and which are excluded? - How did I come to understand this in this way? - What are other ways to understand this? What other (or whose) perspectives could I consider? - How does my social location influence my reactions and interpretation of this? - What assumptions are behind my reactions and ideas about this? - How do my personal experiences and preferences influence how I see this?

Adapted from Tilsen, J. (2018). *Narrative approaches to youth work: Conversational skills for a critical practice* (pp. 137–138). New York, NY: Routledge.

In her youth work text, Tilsen (2018) demonstrates the shift in perspective when we move from reflective to reflexive questions, contrasted in Table 5.1. Both are important. She states, "reflexive questions invite other perspectives, challenge assumptions, contextually situate your perspective, and interrogate power relations" (Tilsen, 2018, p. 138). As you move through the questions in Table 5.1, Tilsen (2018) recommends that we first not focus on CYC practice. Instead, she recommends that we think about everyday encounters in our life. Ultimately, reflective and reflexive approaches help us become more reflective practitioners.

Can you tell us more about how you connected with that student? What was the response from the young person when you sat and listened? How were you feeling in the moment? I encourage my students to practice asking open-ended questions to their peers.
—Saira, CYC Practicum Faculty-Instructor

REFLECTIVE PRACTICE

Emphasizing the importance of reflection as a core part of a professional's skill set, Schon (1983) formalized the idea of reflective practice. Soon after, health, education, and caring professions adopted and evolved its method to suit their contexts. Reflective practice emerged in response to the dominance of technical, rational, and proceduralized knowledge, and invited professionals to "search, instead, for an epistemology of practice implicit to the artistic, intuitive processes which some practitioners do bring to situations of uncertainty, instability, uniqueness, and value conflict" (Schon, 1983, p. 49). He defined two components of reflective practice: 1) reflecting-in-action, where practitioners reflect during the practice encounter, and 2) reflection-on-action, where the practitioner reflects after the fact.

Schon (1983) offers helpful detail on what reflection can look like, noting that it does not appear one particular way:

> When a practitioner reflects in and on practice, the possible objects of his reflection are as varied as the kinds of phenomena before him and the systems of knowing-in-practice which he brings to them. He may reflect on the tacit norms and appreciations which underlie a judgment, or on the strategies and theories implicit in a pattern of behavior. He may reflect on the feeling for a situation which has led him to adopt a particular course of action, on the way in which he has framed the problem he is trying to solve, or on the role he has constructed for himself within a larger institutional context... In each instance, the practitioner allows himself to experience surprise, puzzlement, or confusion in a situation which he finds uncertain or unique. He reflects on the phenomena before him, and on the prior understandings which have been implicit in his behavior. He carries out an experiment which serves to generate both a new understanding of the phenomena and a change in the situation. (pp. 62–68)

Echoing Schon's ideas, D'Cruz and colleagues (2007) emphasize reflexivity's value in reflective practice, where it becomes "central to working ethically in uncertain contexts and unpredictable situations—as opposed to... following rules and procedures" (para. 21). CYC practice lives and thrives in uncertain and unknown contexts, and thus reflective practice becomes a method and way of being that helps us through its complexity. Stuart (2013) summarizes Schon's ideas, applied to CYC practice, where she describes the process of active reflection: "identify feelings and attitudes; determine how those guide the activities they engage in; learn or identify what needs to be different; and apply that new learning to a new situation" (p. 142). In each encounter, a CYC practitioner notices what is happening, analyzes it according to a set of questions and queries, decides what could be done similarly or differently, and then allows those discoveries to influence future action. The following examples shine light on what the ideas above look like in practice.

> When I started reflective practice it was much more about writing ideas down or journaling. Now it's much more about thinking before I speak. It's almost like forward-thinking but backwards.
> —Cody, CYC Student

REFLECTIVE PRACTICE IN CYC

Reading stories can help expand our awareness, learn reflective skills, and visualize ourselves incorporating reflective practice into our work. Take, for example, the following CYC practitioners, researchers, and writers.

1. In her essay describing an intervention in an emergency shelter, Sauvé-Griffin (2009) experiments with Garfat's reflective practice guidelines when she tries to intervene with a young boy who has locked himself in the bathroom. She joins her knowledge and skills along with high respect for relational practice. She reflects-in-action by thinking about what is happening, her previous experiences, her values and beliefs, the possible outcomes, and her immediate internal experience. As a result of this intentional reflective practice, on her walk toward the bathroom door, she changes her plan. Originally, she planned on requesting that the boy exit the room to talk to her. Instead, she meets the young boy on his terms, slipping a note underneath the door and waiting for his response, resulting in new possibilities and directions for where the interaction could lead. Reflective practice has immediate, different, and desired results: engaging with young people.

2. Winfield (2009) describes a youth worker's encounter with a young boy whose younger sibling is regularly sick. She responds quickly and matter-of-factly to his inquiry about whether his sibling will die. As she lays in bed later that evening, she reflects on her own experience of the death of her sibling. She wonders if she could use the wisdom about her emotional needs and spiritual grieving process to assist with her interactions with the young boy. She becomes curious and looks forward to re-engaging with the older sibling again the next day. Reflecting deeply on this brief but significant encounter offers up endless possibilities and directions for her practice, and she is excited as a result. Interestingly, the author does not share the resulting action, perhaps to encourage the reader to imagine their own response.

3. Newbury (2007) finds her way through an international (graduate) CYC practicum placement. She is asked to conduct a needs-assessment to see if a home hospice program would be helpful for the community. Removing one's self from familiar surroundings can often provide fertile ground for reflection and critical inquiry of our practice. As she listens to various stakeholders' needs, she notices herself impose her values into the assessment. She learns that she "must be as curious and inquisitive about what shapes ideas of 'normal' and 'healthy,'" where for her, reflective practice means that she "must continue to question, to notice [her] judgements and wonder where they come from, and to recognize that anything [she observes] says at least as much about [her], the observer, as it does the observation" in part to avoid "unwittingly ... playing an imperialist role" (p. 52). She stops herself from imposing her personal and professional culture and worldview, and instead pays attention to what the community is saying it needs.

> I need to know why things happen. I like having the whole story. I didn't really know that was my style before. I think it's easier to connect with people with an understanding of seeing the behaviour.
>
> —Heather, CYC Student

As developing practitioners, you may find yourself in similar situations. Often, we are in the midst of a young person's crisis, responding to young people's inquiries on the go, and conducting formal and informal assessments where we are at risk of imposing our own value system, rather than paying closer attention to what the young person really needs. To that effect, Garfat and Fulcher (2012) remind us that even "when a community-based CYC Practitioner meets with a family in their home, it is important to decide how each individual will be greeted on arrival, who will be greeted first and how one will be with them" (p. 11). What may be overlooked as unimportant—a simple greeting—instead becomes a profoundly intentional intervention. We must be intentional about each moment of our interactions and influence. It is through reflection that we can evaluate and change our behaviour to see just how important these seemingly inconsequential encounters are. The challenges a CYC practitioner faces throughout their day offer great opportunities for us to act. By shifting our focus, reflective practice can assist us in being more responsive to the space we find ourselves in and the people we find ourselves alongside. However, we need to be ready to listen.

Benefits and Challenges of Reflective Practice

It is clear the benefits of reflective practice include a wide range of outcomes. Stuart (2013) describes the transformative learning process that occurs, reminding us "we are constantly monitoring and reflecting on experiences in the moment, in order to remain focused on the young person's learning, growth, and development," where reflective practice has the benefit of "refining our skills and adapting our behaviour as a result" (p. 57). Ruth-Sahd (2003) and Davies (2012) list a wide range of specific benefits of reflective practice:

- ✓ Acquisition of new knowledge and skills and improved practice
- ✓ Integration of theory and practice
- ✓ Increased understanding of self, improved confidence, and self-esteem
- ✓ Identification of professional strengths and weaknesses
- ✓ Acceptance of professional responsibility
- ✓ Acts as a source of feedback
- ✓ Enhanced judgement making in complex and uncertain situations

Reflective practice also comes with challenges, ones that will likely shift over time as the practitioner is exposed to the method and its benefits. While evaluating a youth work program, Wiedow (2014) summarizes some of these challenges: not understanding the process, discomfort in evaluating one's own practice, time consumption, and uncertainty regarding what to reflect upon. Knowing this information can help us in the learning process. In the end, reflective practice is not just for reflection's sake. Garfat and Fulcher (2012) remind us "the effective helper is a reflective helper" (p. 15). It is our responsibility as professionals to incorporate reflective practice into our diverse Child and Youth Care approaches for the benefit of the people we work alongside.

Write and reflect on your experiences. A lot. Seek to understand and challenge yourself when you think you 'know.' Resist the comfort of how good it feels to 'know,' and push yourself to consistently explore meaning and alternatives.
    —Mackenzie, CYC Practicum Faculty-Instructor

Go slow to go fast. Get comfortable with being uncomfortable.
    —Natalie, CYC Student

Critical Reflection

Before we move to brainstorming how you can incorporate reflective practice methods into your practicum placement, let's pause and consider some questions and exercises to solidify our understanding of purposeful reflection. Activity 5.2 and Activity 5.3 are designed to engage our ability to think critically about the work we do. Clark (2012) notes that critical reflection and reflexivity "share the key element of critical engagement with how knowledge is created and its relationships to systems and structures of power, in contrast to reflective practice, which focuses on the professional self" (p. 82). In this sense, critical thinking is how we deconstruct, call into question, and do not simply accept the systems, structures, and practices we engage with on a daily basis.

Activity 5.2: What Are We Doing?

In his seminal work, post-structuralist philosopher Michel Foucault (1965) reflects,

> People know what they do; frequently they know why they do what they do; but what they don't know is what what they do does.

Consider this quote for a moment. Replace "people" with "Child and Youth Care practitioners." Now read it again.

> CYC practitioners know what they do; frequently they know why they do what they do; but what CYC practitioners don't know is what what they do does.

Be okay with the level of confusion and existential angst this quote may cause. Then ask yourself: what does this statement mean to you? What does it inspire you to think? What is it that we, as practitioners, do? What does what we do actually do? How can we know? Who and what informs what we know about what we do?

_____

_____

Activity 5.3: Reflexive Questions

Consider D'Cruz and colleagues' (2007) five questions, offered to assist us in the reflection process.

1. How do I know what I think I know about this situation and the problem?
2. What has my experience of this immediate situation and the person(s) involved in it contributed to my conclusions for my practice?
3. Is there at least one other way of understanding this situation and the people involved?
4. Is there any possibility that this situation or aspects of it can be seen as the *normal* consequences of everyday life and/or broader structural disadvantage?
5. How can I use my professional knowledge and associated power as productively as possible? (para. 22)

Now, think of a recent encounter at your practicum site. Move slowly through each question, reflecting on the situation in increasingly more depth. Write your reflections in response to the questions, if you find that helpful. Or discuss them with a fellow classmate. When finished, think of another encounter. Repeat.

_____

_____

_____

_____

Adapted from D'Cruz, H., Gillingham, P., & Melendez, S. (2007). "Reflexivity: A concept and its meanings for practitioners working with children and families." *Critical Social Work, 8*(1), para. 22.

Reflective Practice Methods

So, how can you begin (or continue) to develop your reflective practice skills? The practicum experience provides an excellent opportunity to do this: a carved-out time and space to incorporate new methods to see how they fit, how they need to be altered to fit your individual circumstances, and use all of the learning resources available to you.

First, let us begin by thinking of the context in which you are learning and the sites of opportunity to reflect. As you begin your practicum placement, you may purposefully inquire about

My favourite question to ask is 'what do you think is happening between you and the child/youth/parent in that moment?' The student's explanation gives me a window into their developing theory of practice. I can then follow up with 'how do you know?' and help them to make connections.

—Kristy, CYC Practicum Faculty-Instructor

the systems and structures that are already in place to help facilitate your reflective learning, such as:

- Do you have a class seminar in which open and facilitated dialogue occurs?
- Do you and your classmates, despite being in diverse practicum settings, have a regularly scheduled time to check in with each other to review your learning, challenges, and successes?
- Have you carved out time and space to incorporate reflection into your day? (Daily or weekly journalling, silent reflection time, and so on.)
- Do you have formal or informal meeting times set up with your practicum supervisor or an alternate supervisor depending on their availability?

If you answered "no" to any of these questions, you are encouraged to consider whether you need to be proactive about seeking out these situations. Along the way, you will hopefully come across, be privy to, and learn new practices tailored to your site. Learn them. Experiment. See how they fit for you.

Collectively, through the examples and scenarios described in this and other chapters, we see practitioners and students take different approaches in grappling with reflective practice—silent reflection, peer consultation, supervision, journalling, guided conversations, and so on. These are common methods of reflection that you may (or may not) see at your practicum site too. You may also wish to access the CYC literature—perhaps explore *CYC-Net* or one of our peer-reviewed or professional journals, such as *Relational Child and Youth Care Practice*, where reflection is a common method of written expression, to communicate the complexities of our field. What is important here is that you pay attention to what is (and isn't) available at your site and seminar, and that you attempt to develop this skill. Newbury (2007) reminds us that "reflexivity is not something that can ever be mastered. Reflexivity is a humbling experience and is endless" (p. 55). What matters is that your reflective practice is intentional, continuous, frequent, and open to generative possibilities.

CYC Practicum Students Benefiting from Reflective Practice

Applying reflective practice—in whatever form it takes—can benefit students greatly. It does so not only by developing greater general self-awareness but also by responding to the barriers to learning and triggers that come up in this seminal experience. Ostinelli (2015) believes

> The impact of self-reflection is greatest when students are unpacking their emotional responses to their first placement experience. The first placement often triggers responses, thoughts, and feelings that, if not processed, could halt or inhibit future learning. This information can become the foundation of the enhanced self-awareness students take with them into the classroom, subsequent practicums and their personal development. (p. 38)

Meanwhile, Kostouros (2018) discusses examples of triggers while students are on practicum: students who have experienced bullying in their past who witness bullying at a school placement; students who have experienced negative encounters with the police witnessing the histories or current encounters of young people in the youth justice system; and so on. Recognizing when you are triggered is important, but having a foundation of self-care and wellness is essential. Know your support system at practicum and away from practicum. We need you to be present for the young people experiencing their lives, challenges, and successes. The goal is to have your past experience inform your work, not take away from it or become the focus. Let's look at two CYC practicum students who offer their stories.

1. Take Beneteau's (2002) story. While not presented as a journal, per se, the story draws from his reflective notes and walks his reader through significant learning moments. He reflects on four stories in his CYC practicum experience. First, he describes the nervous, sleepless night before his first shift at a group home. He moves on to share how he spent most of his first day reading policies and procedures and then takes a chance by leaving the office and sitting down with the group for dinner, surprising himself that he felt comfortable chatting with the residents over a meal, as well as afterward over TV. He tells us about the difficulty of differentiating himself between being friendly and being the youths' friend, as well as receiving difficult feedback from a colleague. He ends with a story about taking a resident out swimming, where the youth was surprised that he would actually swim with him and how much they both enjoyed the connection and thoughtful conversation to and from the community centre. Reflecting on each experience as it happened allowed him to notice what was significant, what stuck with him, and what informed his future practice. Meanwhile, it solidified his commitment to his work and improved his ability to integrate feedback.

2. Take Thompson's (2018) story. She lists a number of self-care and discussion-based reflection strategies that worked for her during and after an outdoor education practicum, which involved a traumatic first aid emergency. Her list of reflective, self-care strategies included the following items. (Note the time sensitivity as you read.)
   - Before the practicum, she completed pre-training in first aid and trauma;
   - Immediately after the event, she spent time debriefing with young people, staff, and supervisors;
   - At home she cooked for herself, allowed herself to experience her intense emotions through crying, and got a full night's sleep; and
   - Soon after she checked in with her classmates and instructor.

> Sometimes you just need to take a day. If you don't take that day and you end up burning out, you're no help to anybody.
> —Sam, CYC Student

Both CYC practitioners intersect reflection, self-awareness, and self-care with the experiential, transformative learning experience of practicum. Do any of these strategies sound like they may work for you? What does? What doesn't? What are you doing now at practicum? What would you like to improve upon?

CONTEMPLATIVE PRACTICES

Interestingly enough, many of the reflective and self-care practices faculty-instructors and supervisors encourage students to practise (or what students initiate on their own) are what some people may refer to as contemplative practices. Contemplative practices are approaches and ways of being that promote inquiry and reflection.

Interchanging the terms *contemplation*, *introspection*, and *reflection*, Barbezat and Bush (2014) introduce a variety of contemplative practices for postsecondary students, where students can "inquire deeply into their own meaning and find themselves in the centre of their learning, thus providing them with a clear sense of the meaning of their studies," focus on "introspection and their cultivation of awareness of themselves and their relationship to others," and learn "what they hold most dear," which results in "increased empathy for others and a deeper sense of connection with the world" (pp. xv–5). Some of their examples are listed in overlapping categories in Figure 5.1. What practices do you engage in (or have in the past)? Which practices are you curious about? What would you add to this practice?

> I had one student who listened to specific playlists on his phone on his way home from practicum, as a way to make meaning of his work, and to reflect and give voice to some of the challenges. He would then tell me which songs really spoke to his experience of that day and why.
> —Kristy, CYC Practicum Faculty-Instructor

Interchanging reflective, self-care, and contemplative practices (doing so is common), Kostouros (2018) discusses two concrete strategies that we'd all benefit from practising early on in our careers: compassion satisfaction and leaving work rituals.

1. Kostouros (2018) describes compassion satisfaction as when "knowing that your contribution to others is helpful," gaining "satisfaction knowing we matter to others." It can "contribute to resilience," where "remembering why we do this work and how satisfying it is, can allow us to reframe the negative parts of our work" (p. 43). In other words, don't let these moments pass you by. Do you have a method of noticing and recognizing these moments? Can you create a question in your daily journal that reminds you to notice the good moments, in addition to the challenges? Some practitioners have "warm and fuzzy" correspondence files where they store an appreciative note from a colleague, a card from a young person, a memory of a good moment. What could you do to find satisfaction in the compassion you are practising in these spaces?

2. Kostouros (2018) also describes leaving work rituals, which she says are commonly developed strategies for letting go of the day's troubles, concerns, and reflections when we need to transition from our time at practicum to our life at home with family and friends. She recommends mindful breathing activities, jotting down notes of stressful encounters from that day, then shredding them or "touch[ing] the ground before [students] leave… act[ing] as a symbol that they are leaving their worries at that place" (p. 43). Some practitioners treat their commute to and from work as a focused time to gear up and gear down. Some practitioners

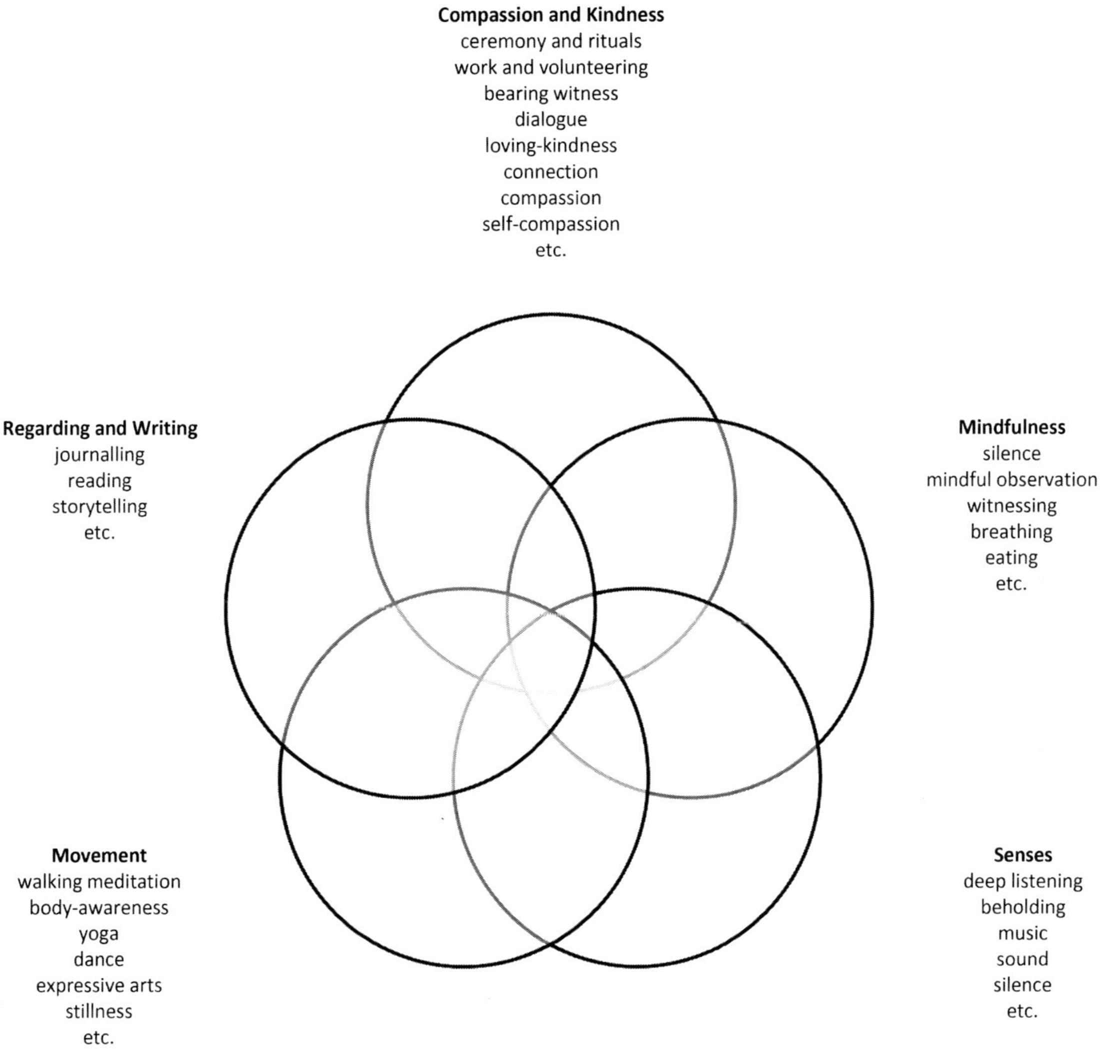

Compassion and Kindness
ceremony and rituals
work and volunteering
bearing witness
dialogue
loving-kindness
connection
compassion
self-compassion
etc.

Regarding and Writing
journalling
reading
storytelling
etc.

Mindfulness
silence
mindful observation
witnessing
breathing
eating
etc.

Movement
walking meditation
body-awareness
yoga
dance
expressive arts
stillness
etc.

Senses
deep listening
beholding
music
sound
silence
etc.

Figure 5.1: Contemplative Practices

Adapted from Barbezat, D. P., & Bush, M. (2013). *Contemplative practices in higher education. Powerful methods to transform teaching and learning* (pp. 10, 95–188). San Francisco, CA: John Wiley & Sons.

listen to music while on the bus leaving the site to physically, emotionally, and cognitively change their body's focus. Some focus their walk home with mindful physical activities, where before they enter their home, they refocus their bodies and minds on what they're heading into, rather on where they're coming from.

> I have a certain way when I'm off work. I would get in my car, open up all the windows and release all that energy I'm taking home to make sure that it wouldn't affect me when I'm at home with my family.
> —Trina, CYC Student

REFLECTIVE PRACTICE—WHAT WILL YOU DO?

We've reviewed a multitude of reflective practices and processes that we may engage in during our practicum experience and beyond. Many of the ideas discussed thus far will be practices you already engage in or are required to do as a part of your course. To shift to the end of this chapter, and as we ground ourselves for the next chapter, review what reflective practices you've done before, what your practicum course and placement have as a part of their practice, and what practices you could intentionally attempt while completing this practicum experience.

LEARNING JOURNAL

In your learning journal, keep moving through the structured prompts and/or unstructured open space. Consider using some of the questions listed above—in the practicum student examples described above or activities—to guide your notes. Observe which questions were more productive to you and which were not.

PRACTICE SCENARIOS

Take a look at the Practice Scenarios that conclude this chapter: "Sean's Idea" and "Anna's Lunchroom." Use the content that you've read in this chapter to inspire your thinking about the scenario. Notice how the scenario may relate to your own situation at your current practicum placement, even if it is not exactly what you are experiencing. Consider the questions posed at the end of each scenario to help you expand and apply the concepts presented in this chapter.

SEMINAR GROUP AND COMMUNITY OF PRACTICE DISCUSSION QUESTIONS

Prepare your responses to the following prompts, for participation in your seminar discussion or community of practice group:

1. As touched upon throughout the chapter, reflective practice can mean many things. What does reflective practice mean to you?
2. What formal and informal processes for reflective practice are in place at your practicum placement? Which processes are you drawn to? Why? Which processes don't fit for you? Why?
3. The practitioners described in the literature and case scenarios throughout this chapter have asked themselves many questions. Some questions may be helpful to you in your own reflective process; some may not. Prepare one question and describe how it helped you create generative reflection for an encounter you experienced at practicum. It may be as simple as asking "why did I do that?" or "what influenced my actions?" Be prepared to share this question with the group and how it was helpful to your process.

It's important for me to be within an environment where my colleagues and my supervisor and I can bounce ideas off each other and maybe you say to one another 'Why are we doing this?' 'Should we be doing something else?' For me, that's reflective.
—Jenn, CYC Student

4. Activity 5.3 asks you to think of an encounter from practicum. Share an encounter at practicum seminar, and ask the group to walk through the same set of questions. Notice how your individual reflections converge and diverge with the group's.

IN CLOSING

Reflective practice intersects with each moment of our practicum experience. It is a complex, challenging, and ultimately rewarding method of meaning-making that benefits us as practitioners and learners, along with the young people and communities we serve. In this chapter, we have touched upon the concept of reflective practice and made space to explore what reflective practice could look like for you. While there are reflective components to all of the questions and activities included in this guidebook, this chapter extends your practicum course's reflective processes, structures, and requirements by inviting you to develop your own reflective practice, surveying a variety of options available to you, and showing you a few examples some CYC practicum students have chosen for themselves.

Engaging in reflective practice is no easy task, as it asks us to focus and make space for the moment-to-moment encounters we experience, as opposed to letting them pass us by. Implicit to this practice is the idea that we will always be improving. Instead of seeing this as a daunting task, one fraught with always feeling like we could be doing better, we should encourage each other to be okay sitting in the uncertainty, the continuous need to change, the endless possibilities for therapeutic practice, and the great effort it asks of us in our movement toward becoming better CYC practitioners that best meet young people's needs.

PRACTICE SCENARIOS

Sean's Idea

Sean was invited to his practicum supervisor's intake and assessment meeting with a youth at the group home. While his supervisor was asking the youth a series of questions, Sean noticed the youth's nonverbal behaviour was somewhat closed, and he wasn't responding very much to the questions. Noticing a book in the youth's half-opened backpack, Sean decides to ask the youth about the book and its recent film adaptation when his supervisor is asking him about his hobbies and interests. After the meeting, Sean's supervisor commends him for taking a risk and breaking up the routine of the interview.

How did Sean use his observations of the immediate environment to help him think on his feet? How may Sean have been using reflection-in-action to inform his decisions?

_____

_____

_____

Anna's Lunchroom

Anna attended practicum seminar with her fellow classmates where the faculty-instructor has just asked them to offer a challenge they've encountered thus far in their practicum. Anna thinks back to the encounter she had at the elementary school staff lunchroom earlier that week. While eating a snack, she overheard a conversation between staff about a young boy whom Anna is just beginning to know. The teacher referred to the boy as "so porcelain" when describing a situation where the boy was being ridiculed by a group of other boys. Anna has felt discomfort since and shares the scenario with her classmates. Her faculty-instructor then asks the group to consider a few questions: what does this word—*porcelain*—mean, and what possible reason would a teacher refer to a student in this way? What is influencing this practitioner's language about this young boy at this time? What historical ideas have shaped and directed how this practitioner thinks of this young boy? If you also have a strong emotional response to this practitioner's description of this young boy, what does that say about your developing theoretical orientation to practice? Do you think it is important for us to think about how we discuss young people, even when they are not present? Why? The group discusses professionalism, ethics, language, gender, intervention, politics, policy, and CYC practice.

Take a moment to consider these questions for yourself. How would you respond and contribute to this seminar discussion?

_____

_____

_____

PART II

In the Midst

CHAPTER 6

Diverse People, Diverse Practices, and Diverse Possibilities

Competencies for Professional Child and Youth Work Practitioners				
Professionalism	Cultural and Human Diversity	Applied Human Development	Relationship and Communication	Developmental Practice Methods
Professional Development and Behaviour	Cultural and Human Diversity Awareness	Practice Methods	Interpersonal Communication	Program Planning and Activity Programming
Personal Development and Self-Care	Relationship and Communication			
Advocacy	Developmental Practice Methods			

As front-line practitioners and practitioners-in-training, we often work in systems that are embedded in colonial histories. In a world increasingly shaped by inequity, a global climate crisis, and growing far-right movements, it is critical that practitioners understand the dynamics of settler colonialism. A decolonial praxis goes far beyond territorial acknowledgements and cultural competency training; it is an ethic that is lived and enacted through daily, concerted commitments to Indigenous self-determination and resurgence. It is a call for practitioners to participate in productive ways in un-settling the settler systems in which we work.

—Sandrina de Finney, Associate Professor,
School of Child and Youth Care, University of Victoria

We work alongside diverse people and communities, we bring diverse experiences, we work on diverse teams with diverse practices, and we desire to keep doing so. As Child and Youth Care (CYC) practitioners, we agree that we are present in the lives of young people to promote their growth, development, and well-being in their unique contexts. Thus, it is of absolute importance to understand how that growth, development, and well-being can, should,

> Diversity is an active and intentional act of learning about the people around you. It is intentionally caring about the people around you. We're both human in this space. What does that look like? What does that mean to us? Being human is being me with you.
> —Cody, CYC Student

and need to be promoted in the spirit of diversity, through all the work we do. Too often we limit, confine, and seek conformity for the lives and possibilities of young people through our perspectives and practices, with massive consequences for their lives. We begin the second section of this guidebook with a discussion on diversity, so as to underscore the critical importance of how we approach our work, what we consider to be a part of our work, how we can change our work, and how we can best support *all* young people in our communities.

DIVERSITY

Put simply, diversity—having variety or difference—is the difference between and among individual people and groups. Different characteristics. Different identities. Different histories. Different experiences. Different goals. Different values. Different motivations. Different knowledges. Different ways of being. Danso (2012) writes that "diversity encompasses the spectrum of observable and non-observable, tangible and intangible differences that shape or define personal and group experiences" (p. 161). It is incumbent upon us—CYC practitioners, scholars, educators, and child and youth–serving organizations (practicum students included)—to intentionally expand our own personal and professional lenses to discover, understand, and appreciate that spectrum of differences and experiences, so as to directly benefit the young people we work alongside. To not do so would be to push our own ideologies, objectives, and ways of being, sometimes brutally so.

Before we circle back to dimensions of diversity—through an analysis of our social location, as well as how we can ensure we are working with diverse practices—let's take a look at the terms culture and worldview to help us get there.

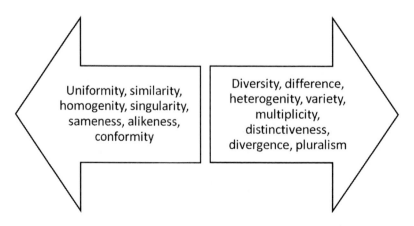

Figure 6.1: Toward Diversity

CULTURE

In simple terms, culture encompasses the socially acquired characteristics, traditions, and ways of thinking, doing, and being shared among groups of people. It is often illustrated as an iceberg, where you will see aspects of "surface culture" above the waterline and aspects of "deep culture" below the waterline, and we understand there are aspects of culture we can easily observe and aspects we cannot easily observe. We could also think of a flower and its root system and the soil that nourishes it, or a community of plants and the rhizomatic structures that connect each plant below the surface of the soil. Culture connects, defines, and differentiates our experience of the world. See Table 6.1 for an example. Take your time considering each point.

Culture is a common way to discuss diversity. That is, we have sought to understand the shared experiences of people within cultures, to attempt to discover the diverse ways people learn to be, despite the fact that we know cultural groups are diverse in and among themselves. Learning about the specific ways in which we define aspects of culture is a helpful pursuit.

In Table 6.1, we can read the numerous ways we learn how to be in the world and things we share with people of a similar culture. Further, over our individual lifetimes, we too become aware of the less visible culture that governs our way of being. The sheer vastness of "deep" or less visible culture should also remind us that we cannot know each and every aspect of each and every culture in the entire world. It is an impossible task. It is the expansive difference in which people have lived over time and across the world that should put us in a position of deep respect and place of "not-knowing." In turn, this place of not-knowing hopefully teaches us to approach our practice from a place of curiosity with each and every person we meet in our work.

> You need to tap into who you are and what your experiences have been. Be aware of why you want to do this work. There's a lot behind that. Be aware of your ethnicity, your socioeconomic background, and understand how that will look to the community you are working with and how that's going to be perceived. Be okay with that and accept that.
> —Jenn, CYC Student

The aspects of culture listed in Table 6.1 not only describe culture in general, they can also inform us as to the ways in which we, as individuals, have

Table 6.1: Aspects of Culture

	Aspects of Culture
Surface Culture (visible)	Language Celebrations Dress/attire Grooming Food and cooking Music Visual, performance, and literary arts Crafts Dance Games

(continued)

Table 6.1: Continued

	Aspects of Culture
Deep Culture (less visible) (unspoken and unconscious rules)	Body language, touching, eye contact, gestures, facial expressions, movement, tone of voice, and nonverbal communication Courtesy Hospitality Contextual conversational pattern Personal space Arrangements of physical space Patterns of group decision-making Approach to problem-solving Family composition Social roles and responsibilities Courtship practice Rules of conduct Fiscal expression Patterns of handling emotions Notions of modesty Concept of beauty Incentives to work, tempo of work, and work ethic Notions of leadership Preference for competition or cooperation Attitudes toward elders Attitudes toward the dependent Ideals of childrearing and parenting Notions of adolescence Theory of disease and definition of insanity Concept of wellness and healing practices Tolerance of physical pain Definition of obscenity Social interaction rate Nature of friendships Relationships to animals Roles in relation to age, sex, class, occupation, kinship, status (assigned and acquired), hierarchy, class, and perceived power Conception of status mobility Concept of "self" Shared history and narratives Values, goals, ideals, priorities, ethics, and ideologies Definition of sin Concept of justice Concept of past and future and ordering of time Notions of logic and validity Beliefs about life and its meaning Reality and consciousness Origin of the universe

Adapted from Hanley, J. H. (1999). Beyond the tip of the iceberg: Five stages toward cultural competence. In S. Martin (Ed.), *Reaching today's youth, 3*; Martin, S. (2014). *Take a look: Observation and portfolio assessment in early childhood* (6th ed.). Don Mills, ON: Pearson; Sensoy, O., & DiAngelo, R. (2017). *Is everyone really equal? An introduction to key concepts in social justice education* (2nd ed., p. 37). New York, NY: Teachers College Press.

Activity 6.1: Aspects of Culture

Myers-Kiser (2016) suggests practicum students in the human services con-sider their own culture and the culture of people they've met and worked with in practicum, by exploring the following prompts in Table 6.2.

First, go through the list and try to think of an example from your life. Per-haps, for "use of space," you write, "as a female I've been taught to take up as little space as possible"; or, under "definitions of success," you may write, "in my family, to be successful means you have a good job." Then, go through the list and try to think of an instance that you've observed at your practicum setting thus far or what you imagine it may be based on what you know about similar settings. When you are finished, notice the similarities and differences. Share your observations with a classmate or member of your community of practice.

Table 6.2: Aspects of Culture in Practicum and My Life

Aspects of Culture	An Example from My Life	An Example Observed at Practicum
Sense of self, including assumptions about autonomy and responsibility		
Communication and language, including verbal and nonverbal		
Understanding of and relationship to authority		
Use of space		
Use of time		
Attitudes toward work (or school)		
Definitions of success		
Beliefs about health and healing		
Beliefs about giving and receiving help		
Beliefs about how relationships should be conducted		
The value placed on appearance and hygiene		
Beliefs about education and the value of education		

Adapted from Myers-Kiser, P. (2016). *The human services internship: Getting the most from your experience* (4th ed., pp. 208–209). Boston, MA: Cengage Learning.

> Recognize and be aware of one's own heritage and cultural values; be able and willing to listen to the stories and experiences of others; expose one's self to other cultures and ways of being; be curious.
> —Deb, CYC Practicum Faculty-Instructor

developed our values, biases, perceptions, and behaviour in the world. They can also inform us as to how the young people (and families) we work with have developed values, biases, perceptions, and behaviour in the world. Further, it should hopefully inspire us to wonder and evaluate how our perspectives and practices have developed as a profession. Professions, fields of practice, academic scholarship, and systems of care have values, biases, perceptions, and behaviour in the world too.

Now that you've read the multiple aspects of culture in Table 6.1, let's turn our perspective toward ourselves, to uncover and bring forth aspects of culture that influence the work we do. Use Activity 6.1 to help.

To not become more aware of our cultural values risks imposing our values on other people. Richmond, Braughton, and Borden (2018) caution that "youth program staff who are unable to examine their own belief system and cultural experiences (i.e., non-dominant versus dominant cultural experiences, and themes of privilege and power) may inadvertently create an environment of exclusion and promote damaging stereotypes" (p. 504). Can you think of an example from your own life where you've witnessed an environment of exclusion, where it may have promoted damaging stereotypes? In this memory, how did the people/program push their own values and beliefs, rather than make space for everyone?

> Students need to be very open to learning from different experiences and different cultures.
> —Harman, CYC Student

CULTURAL APPRECIATION AT YOUR PRACTICUM

CYC practitioner and writer Burns (2006) details a Cultural Inclusiveness and Cultural Affirmation Checklist in his book on therapeutic milieus, suggesting practicum students should take the checklist to their setting and reflect individually and with their supervisor,

Activity 6.2: Culture at Your Practicum Setting

Move through each box in Table 6.3 that highlights different aspects of how your site may or may not support the expression of culture. In no way is it an exhaustive list; rather, it is here to prompt you to observe your setting, to see what is and isn't happening. Note examples of your observations.

including questions and concerns that arise from the activity. Go through the points in Activity 6.2 to reflect on your practicum setting's responsiveness to culture.

Many of our institutions strive to appreciate and celebrate culture and diversity. Some do a better job than others. While reading the following examples, think of your own experiences—at your practicum setting, previous volunteer and work settings, or places where you've received services.

Table 6.3: Culture at CYC Practicum

Do young people talk openly about their cultural experiences? What have you observed?	Do young people appear interested in each other's cultural differences? What have you observed?	Are there opportunities made available to the young people to discuss issues of cultural diversity? What have you observed?	Do members of the group have a unique interest in the diversity among the group members? What have you observed?
Does there appear to be anyone in the setting who is culturally stereotyped? What have you observed?	Does it appear that anyone is neglected or not included by one or more members of the group because of cultural differences? What have you observed?	Do you feel that anyone is discriminated against because of their differences? What have you observed?	If there are multiple cultural groups represented in the setting, do you feel that their differences are welcomed? What have you observed?
Do you feel, hear, or observe in some way any cultural biases coming from anyone at the setting? If so, what have you observed?	Are there visual or auditory representations of cultural diversity in the setting? If so, what have you observed?	Does the setting celebrate holidays across cultures? Which ones are you aware of?	Do the young people and staff within the setting share their differences openly with pride and celebrate them with one another? How so?

Adapted from Burns, M. (2006). *Healing spaces: The therapeutic milieu in child and youth care work* (pp. 128, 131). Kingston, ON: Child Care Press.

- In a recreation centre's drop-in youth centre, we may see activities that focus on the crafts, games, and literature of its participants' cultures
- In a school, we may see celebration of various holidays and rituals across cultures and religions or shared feasts highlighting food from many cultures of its students
- In a health centre, we may see information posters, brochures, and reports distributed and displayed in multiple languages, and possibly staff who are able to speak in multiple languages
- In a child welfare office's reception area, we may see the design and décor reflecting the culture(s) of its families

We can see how these practices stick to the "surface culture" level; they do not attend as much to less visible, unspoken, or unconscious aspects of culture. For example, take an aspect of "deep culture" from Table 6.1, such as "ideals of childrearing." How does your agency view the

> Talk to families about their culture and worldview. Learn from them. Go to Pow Wows and other cultural events. Learn about the history of oppression of Indigenous peoples in Canada, and the world.
> —Farah, CYC Practicum Supervisor

> Learn a little bit. Be curious and ask some questions. Don't make assumptions about their worldview. Just try to build a picture of their worldview and then reflect that back to them and check for accuracy.
> —Sonja, CYC Practicum Supervisor

responsibilities of parents and caregivers? In what ways does it communicate with caregivers? In what ways have you witnessed these unspoken values conflict? What does this tell you about your agency's cultural beliefs, values, and assumptions about caregiving? In the latter half of this chapter, we will continue to deconstruct various values underpinning our CYC practices.

We should caution ourselves, however, when we think of aspects of culture as essentialized, rigid, unchangeable facts. The very opposite is true. Morris (2010) reminds us:

a.   culture is fluid, providing frames of reference for negotiating the world;

b.   culture is systemic, occurring within, between, and across individuals, families, communities, and regions;

c.   each individual carries culture—culture is not simply a construct applied to "others" apart from "us"; and

d.   culture embodies heterogeneity, carries temporal qualities, and cannot be singularized (p. 323).

We would be wise to remember this as we reflect.

FROM MULTICULTURALISM AND CULTURAL COMPETENCE TO CULTURAL SAFETY AND HUMILITY

> We help students see that you can't just judge from what you see. You really have to be having those conversations and getting to know the families you're working with in order to recognize how diverse we all actually really are.
> —Mindi, CYC Practicum Supervisor

For a number of decades, across the helping professions, there has been keen attention to multiculturalism and cultural competence. We have focused our attention on multiculturalism and cultural competence in part because of the continuously changing nature of Canada's demographics, political and economic forces, and our goal to increase our sensitivity to and become more inclusive of marginalized populations. Yoon (2012) brings our attention to Canada's current changing demographics—birth rates, labour shortages, dependence on immigration to sustain institutions, increasing Indigenous population, as well as our projected racial diversity over the next few decades and its significance for CYC practitioners. Canada's cultural profile requires us to respond to the diversity of its people.

In seeking to become culturally responsive to the diverse cultures and worldviews of the young people we work alongside, O'Hara and colleagues (2010) recommend that we learn about the "lived experience of those whose cultural context is different [where] individual and collective narratives are important… to explore the individual history, culture, community, and contemporary realities… [including] history, values, language, family systems, and practices," all while recognizing the heterogeneity within groups of people (pp. 79–82). How do we do this? Danso (2018) reviews key cross-cultural concepts and their attributes, highlighting cultural awareness, appropriateness, competence, sensitivity, safety, and humility. Each concept in Figure 6.2 has evolved from the concept before it,

Cultural Awareness

Here, CYC practitioners can:

examine one's cultural beliefs, values, and ethnocentric views through reflective self-evaluation

understand how culture shapes thinking, behaviour, self-identity, and interactions

respect other cultures and worldviews

appreciate the impact of sociopolitical structures on minorities' experiences of oppression

Cultural Sensitivity

Here, CYC practitioners can:

demonstrate ability to embrace cultural differences, including differences in individual and group behaviour

individualize intervention strategies

examine how one's culture influences professional practice

avoid language, actions, or attitudes that denigrate other cultures

acknowledge that group membership does not determine individual behaviour

Cultural Appropriateness

Here, CYC practitioners can:

ensure that services reflect local traditions and suit cultural context

develop knowledge of the particular issues clients face

acknowledge minorities' historical experiences of oppression

utilize intervention strategies that recognize people's unique characteristics and needs

Cultural Safety

Here, CYC practitioners can:

build working relationships in environments where clients feel comfortable

treat people with dignity and work from a position of respect, humility, and trust

validate and include Indigenous epistemologies in working relationships

empower clients by engaging them as partners in the services offered

embrace the legitimacy of difference and diversity in human behaviour and in society

Cultural Competence

Here, CYC practitioners can:

gain awareness of one's cultural values, beliefs, and biases

acquire sufficient knowledge of cultural groups

demonstrate awareness and knowledge in professional practice

view diversity as a resource, not a problem

acknowledge culture as fluid and dynamic

Cultural Humility

Here, CYC practitioners can:

recognize one's prejudices and cultural misconceptions

engage in continuous self-critique

challenge power differentials

develop an attitude of "not knowing"

Figure 6.2: Key Cross-Cultural Concepts and Attributes

Adapted from Danso, R. (2018). Cultural competence and cultural humility: A critical reflection on key diversity concepts. *Journal of Social Work, 18*: 413–414.

with the aim of the practitioner attempting to be responsive to the diversity of people's experiences.

Cultural Competence

Professions, agencies, and practitioners have largely been focused on the development of cultural competence. Cultural competence is the intersection of awareness, knowledge, and skills. Review Figure 6.3 and jot down what skills, awareness, and knowledge you bring to your practicum experience.

> Students need to embody humility—an awareness that their experience of the world is not universal, and that they need to approach every client with curiosity, humility, and reverence.
> —Kristy, CYC Practicum Faculty-Instructor

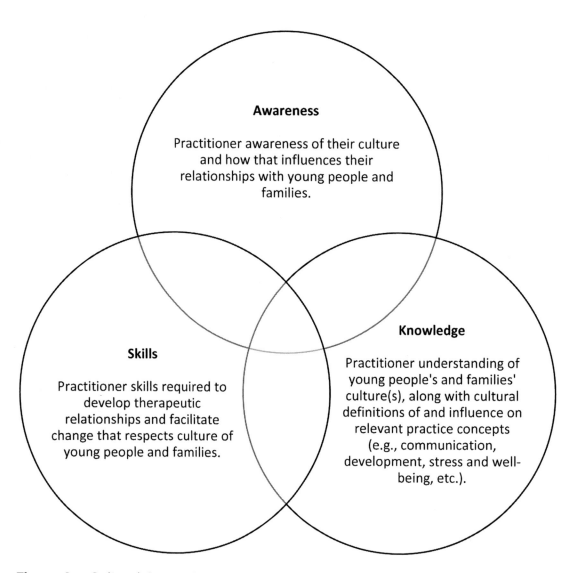

Figure 6.3: Cultural Competence

Adapted from Moleiro, C., Marques, S., & Pacheco, P. (2011). Cultural diversity competencies in child and youth care services in Portugal: Development of two measures and a brief training program. *Child and Youth Services Review, 33*; Richmond, A., Broughton, J., & Borden, L. M. (2018). Training youth program staff on the importance of cultural responsiveness and humility: Current status and future directions in professional development. *Children and Youth Services Review, 93*.

Consider your life experiences, education and training, and volunteer and work experience. Recognize there will be gaps. You're here to learn.

As learners, we are often encouraged to begin in a place of self-reflection to increase our self-awareness as to the experiences we bring to our relationships in the field. Cross (2012) asks us to reflect on "day-to-day behaviours [that] have been shaped by cultural norms and values and reinforced by families, peers, and social institutions," for example, "how one defines 'family,' identifies desirable life goals, views problems, and even says hello are all influenced by the culture in which one functions" (p. 87). In practicum, we have the opportunity to bring forth awareness, conflicts, challenges, struggles, and opportunities.

According to the cultural competence model, we must increase our self-awareness, accumulate cultural knowledge, and incorporate this knowledge into our work with young people. However, that is not enough. There is no point in self-reflection, increasing self-awareness, accumulating any amount of specific cultural knowledge, unless the young people and families we work alongside experience it in a good way.

> What prevents a lot of people from appreciating diversity is the inability to put down your walls and expectations of what you think you know about other people. I think it's just the ability to actually come forward with openness.
> —Margaret, CYC Student

Cultural Safety

There has been a move from cultural competency (where our main focus is on the practitioner's skills) toward an experience of cultural safety, where our focus is on the experience and perspective of the young person or family we're working with. O'Hara and colleagues (2010) state that an "unsafe cultural practice is any action that diminishes, demeans, or disempowers the cultural identity and well-being of an individual," whereas "cultural safety in practice accepts the legitimacy of difference and diversity in human behaviour and social structure," valuing diversity in its own right (p. 83). By focusing on young people's experience of us and the environment we create with them in the services we provide, we have the ability to reduce barriers to access our services, facilitate more meaningful intervention goals and methods, and ultimately create a more trusting, respectful therapeutic relationship. At practicum, you can continually ask yourself: how can I tell if the people my agency serves feel culturally safe? Respected?

> Enter into relationships with curiosity. Ask, 'Who lives at home with you?' as opposed to 'What do your mom and dad do for work?' Build a picture of this person from scratch as opposed to a preconceived notion of what this kid's family is.
> —Sam, CYC Student

Central Skills

Instead of focusing on a predetermined checklist of specific scripts, activities, and culturally specific knowledge, we can consider some *ways of being* will look different, across situations, settings, and time. For example, what do curiosity and openness look like in your practice? Compassion? Respect? Not-knowing? Responsiveness? (For an extended list, see White [2007], Table 3: Some Ways of Thinking about Being in CYC, pp. 239–240). That critical reflection may also encourage us to ask ourselves: what may young people be communicating (verbally,

> Be curious, inclusive, interested and make space for everyone.
> —Rhonda, CYC Practicum Faculty-Instructor

nonverbally) to you that tells you that you are or are not creating a safe space for them to meaningfully participate? How may you address those gaps? How may you repair ruptures?

Eurocentric Values and Worldviews

As we strive for self-awareness, we quickly realize how much we, as a profession, have internalized Eurocentric cultural values and worldviews, whether we have ancestry and familial relations there or not. Briefly, Euro-Western values and worldviews prioritize the needs of the individual over the needs of the group; value competition over collaboration; privilege tasks and results versus relationships and processes; and value individual versus shared ownership. This perspective impacts everything from family structure to education to health and child welfare systems. Euro-Western theories, perspectives, and approaches to practice have dominated what we have come to know and experience as our helping profession. We are not alone in this experience. The fields of education, literature, philosophy, anthropology, and the biological, medical, environmental, and other physical sciences are also dominated by Eurocentric views. We become Eurocentric when we privilege Euro-Western ideals over other worldviews, such as Eastern and Indigenous perspectives.

Yoon (2012) reminds us that CYC's predominantly "Eurocentric worldview impacts everything we do in child and youth care, from the very essence of the pedagogy and curriculum in academic training to the professional standards of practice and competencies in the community. It influences everything" (p. 170). In this light, she asks us to be critically aware of what we agree to be "normal and acceptable," "best practice," and what "exclude[s] the marginalized and minoritized in Canadian society" so that we may better respond to young people in our communities (p. 170). We must critically reflect on how Eurocentric individual and professional values, goals, beliefs, assumptions, and interventions show up in our everyday lives. Then we must critically reflect on how we need to change to better respond to young people. The second half of this chapter will focus on what this means for our practice and how we can go about changing. For now, we will turn to how Canada's helping professions have attempted to educate and train their practitioners to respond to its diversity.

Taking this awareness forward, we circle back to a discussion of diversity through the lens of social justice. A social justice approach to diversity can help us create safe spaces, not only through the individually based interpersonal skills we bring to our interactions with young people but through an analysis of power and oppression of the very systems we work within as well as our efforts to change them, beginning with ourselves. As Sensoy and DiAngelo (2017) warn us,

> Celebrating diversity is important, but because it tends to occur without a study of power, that celebration actually reinforces structural inequality by obscuring unequal power between groups. This allows us to appear as though we are progressive and racially inclusive without actually addressing oppression. (p. 142)

Let's not perpetuate that trend.

CRITICAL SOCIAL JUSTICE

Sensoy and DiAngelo (2017) tell us to both approach our work with critical thinking ("to think with complexity, to go below the surface when considering an issue and explore its multiple dimensions and nuances") and be informed by critical theory (the "approach that analyzes social conditions within their historical, cultural, and ideological contexts"; p. 23). Our work is not neutral. Our interpretations are not neutral. Our institutions are not neutral. Our theories are not neutral. They go on to say that to understand social justice, we must be able to do four things:

1. Recognize that relations of unequal power are constantly being negotiated at both the micro (individual) and macro (structural) levels
2. Understand our own positions within these relations of unequal power
3. Think critically about knowledge
4. Act from this understanding, in service of a more just society (p. 199)

> An analysis of power and privilege is ethically essential here. 'Why do you get to be the practitioner and the person you're working with the client?'
> —Mackenzie, CYC Practicum Faculty-Instructor

Intersectionality

Intersectionality provides a framework for us to understand both the social locations of people (ourselves and others) as well as the power, privilege, and oppression these social locations and their intersections constitute that have very real effects on our lives. Yoon (2012) says that to ground ourselves in an "intersectional framework insists that we cannot separate race, gender, class, rank, ability, age, ethnicity, sexuality, nationality, and religion from political, historical, cultural, social, and economic realities" (p. 178). An intersectional framework sits within a critical social justice perspective, in that it allows and encourages us to analyze and reflect on the stereotypes, prejudices, racism, discrimination, marginalization, violence, and other forms of oppression that the young people we work alongside experience, and then do something productive with that awareness. An intersectional framework allows us to both appreciate the diverse experiences people have as well as analyze the practices and systems we work within to better respond to those diverse experiences.

Social locations reflect the multiple, intersecting identities we all experience, helping us to name them as well as situate them in our current historical, cultural, and political context. To help us explore our and young people's social locations and experience of privilege and oppression, let's look at Simpson's (2009) intersectionality framework in Figure 6.4. Begin in the innermost circle by considering your unique circumstances. Then expand outward to each layer, considering each aspect of identity (e.g., able-bodied), their intersections (e.g., female, person of colour), the types of discrimination each aspect of identity experiences, as well as the larger structural forces that perpetuate these realities. While reading, it may be

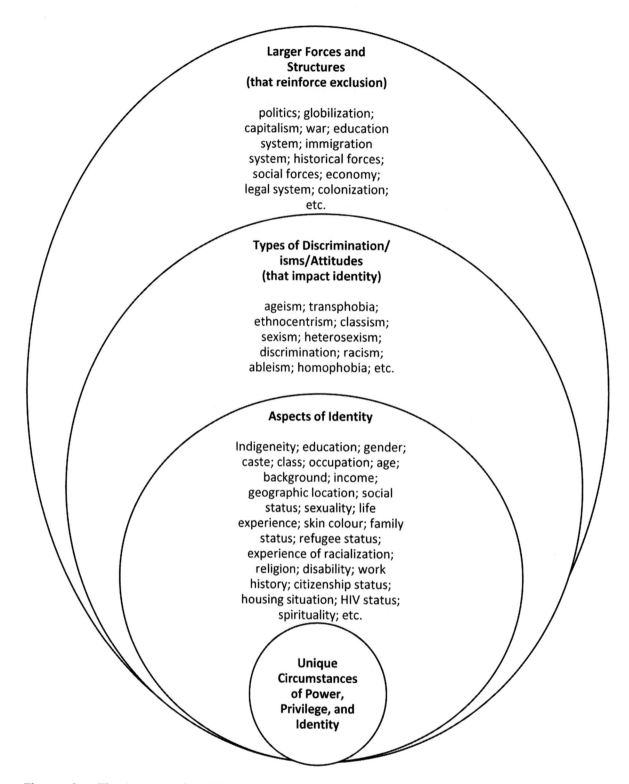

Larger Forces and Structures (that reinforce exclusion)

politics; globilization; capitalism; war; education system; immigration system; historical forces; social forces; economy; legal system; colonization; etc.

Types of Discrimination/ isms/Attitudes (that impact identity)

ageism; transphobia; ethnocentrism; classism; sexism; heterosexism; discrimination; racism; ableism; homophobia; etc.

Aspects of Identity

Indigeneity; education; gender; caste; class; occupation; age; background; income; geographic location; social status; sexuality; life experience; skin colour; family status; refugee status; experience of racialization; religion; disability; work history; citizenship status; housing situation; HIV status; spirituality; etc.

Unique Circumstances of Power, Privilege, and Identity

Figure 6.4: The Intersectionality Wheel

Adapted from Simpson, J. (2009). *Everyone belongs: A toolkit for applying intersectionality* (p. 5). Ottawa, ON: Canadian Research Institute for the Advancement of Women.

helpful to think of your own aspects of identity, or it may be helpful to consider some of the identities of the young people at your practicum site.

If we do not explore our own social location and experience of power, privilege, and oppression, along with the experience of the young people at our practicum settings, we ignore our young people's lived realities. Worse, we risk pushing our own experiences, worldviews, assumptions, biases, and values upon them, where we make young people's experiences invisible and create more barriers in their lives.

Take a practicum student who grew up in an upper middle–class family that valued abstinence as the best way to respond to substance misuse issues. This practicum student was placed at a drop-in youth centre and outreach program in the downtown core. The program's guiding philosophy was a harm-reduction model, which guided their conversations, access to services and spaces, and so on. The practicum student understood that harm-reduction was an evidence-based model, but she found herself not wanting to approach the kids who showed up to the centre high. In what ways is this practicum student struggling? In what ways is this practicum student imposing her worldview, values, and biases? What immediate effects is it having on the space and youth? In what ways is this student missing out on opportunities to connect? What should this student do or consider at this time?

Tilsen (2018) gives us specific questions to help us understand the positions of privilege and oppression we experience. She contrasts positions of power and privilege with positions of oppression, to highlight the very real implications identities have for us.

1. How does your experience as a white person differ from the experience of a person of colour in: passing police on the street? Meeting with a youth worker you have racial affinity with? Being the youth worker for youth of colour?
2. How does your experience as a heterosexual person differ from the experience of a queer person in: expressing affection, love, or comfort in public? Consuming popular culture images and music?
3. How does your experience as a cisgender person differ from the experience of a transgender or gender nonconforming person in: filling out forms for school, the government, jobs, etc.? Using the bathroom? Participating in your school's athletic program? (Tilsen, 2018, p. 82)

We know many people hold privileges that many other people do not enjoy. In fact, many people experience multiple forms of oppression because of their identity-statuses. Keep in mind that we will all likely have aspects of our identity that hold both privilege and oppression. Knowing this helps us become aware of our own experience of privilege and oppression, the experiences of the young people we work alongside, and the systems we have constructed to meet the needs of some but not all people, thus we have the opportunity to change.

Now let's put these reflections together. Consider the young people and families at your practicum setting, their individual and shared experiences. We can focus on one

> We had a practicum student who grew up fairly affluent and from a religious background. This student couldn't understand young people's drug use. It was judgmental and standoffish. They just didn't understand.
>
> —Tom, CYC Practicum Supervisor

young person in our practicum setting, perhaps someone we're getting to know. Using the intersectional framework, let's focus on one young person's social location. What are their aspects of identity and unique life circumstances? What types of discrimination have they experienced? What structural forces are influencing their life? Note your reflections in the space below, as much as you are aware of at the present time. If you need to make some informed guesses, go ahead. If you wish to consult with your supervisor or colleague, explaining the reflection exercise, please do so. Meanwhile, notice any additional reflections you may have about their circumstances. Notice how you may feel compelled to use your position of power and privilege—as an adult, as a student and practitioner with access to knowledge and resources, and so on—to advocate for them and/or change the very systems that we are part of.

Unique Life Circumstances

_____

Aspects of Identity

_____

Discrimination

_____

Structural Forces

_____

We can realize that the people we are working alongside are some of the most marginalized young people in our communities. Take the following examples of social conditions at students' practicum sites:

- A practicum student at an inner-city school where the young people and families are experiencing poverty
- A practicum student at a residential group home where the youth are in government care
- A practicum student at an outreach program where the youth experience (or are at imminent risk of experiencing) homelessness, exploitation, etc.
- A practicum student at an elementary school behaviour support program where the children have been diagnosed with a number of behavioural/physical/mental health conditions

- A practicum student at an involuntary corrections/rehabilitation program, where youth experience criminalization
- A practicum student at a rural or remote setting where young people and families have difficulty accessing food, transportation, health services, etc.

TRANSFORMING PRACTICE

A critical social justice perspective that uses an intersectional framework invites us to deconstruct, transform, and, in effect, diversify our practice. Once we explore the diversity of lived experience, we in turn seek to be more responsive. Because you are new to your practicum setting (and thus in a heightened state of awareness), an active learner (and thus seeking out and focusing upon aspects of practice and systems), and in agreement that attention to diversity calls upon us to ensure we are designing practices and systems to respond to the diverse young people we work alongside, we must consider how CYC practice (and by extension, the helping profession) itself needs to change. You—as a student and emerging practitioner—are in the midst of defining what your practice will look like; deciding where you will devote your time, energy, and influence; and reflecting on why you are doing this work in the first place. Because of this, you have the opportunity to be at the forefront of transforming our practice and systems, defining how the next generation of CYC practitioners will respond to our communities.

> Understand that everyone has a different lived experience and shows up in the world for different reasons and in different ways. Learn how to support those individuals with where they're at.
> —Jasmine, CYC Student

Reconciliation, Decolonization, and Deconstructing CYC Practice

As we look to change the very practice that we're in the midst of learning about, we can look to current movements in practice to get us there. These movements hope to productively dismantle the theories and practices that for too long have privileged some people and oppressed others and redress the historical wrongs that all Canadian institutions have been a part of. Verniest (2006) tells us that we "need help understanding that oppression comes from a worldview that claims superiority" (para. 24), and that in order to engage in acts of social change, solidarity, and empowerment, we must begin with "consciousness-raising regarding oppression" where colonization has caused oppression and "decolonization is the process of the oppressed regaining self-determination and independence in social, economic, cultural, and political structures, and an identity as individuals, families, communities, and nations" (para. 10). Many efforts by marginalized and oppressed communities in Canada—for example, the cultural genocide of Indigenous communities in Canada through state-sanctioned policies and practices such as residential schools, the 60s Scoop, and foster care—have led to a number of movements to redress wrongs. Likewise, critical theory and post-structural fields of thought have influenced our practice perspectives and questioned our ability to respond to all young people, suggesting ways to move forward.

Let's explore some of these concepts, albeit in an introductory manner. You will do the majority of your learning and discovery in future classes, your practicum experiences, and your own self-initiated activities.

Reconciliation and Decolonization

Canada's Truth and Reconciliation Commission (2015) outlined 94 specific and wide-reaching recommendations that we need to become aware of and put into practice in our local contexts. Have you read the TRC's Calls to Action? Its legacy sections—child welfare, education, health, language and culture, justice—and emphasis on the use of the United Nations *Declaration on the Rights of Indigenous Peoples* (UNDRIP) are relevant to and intersect with all of our work in Child and Youth Care practice across child and youth–serving organizations.

> Non-Indigenous students can lack an understanding of the systemic barriers Indigenous youth face, and are unaware of the need to be more culturally competent and to learn about the Truth and Reconciliation Calls to Action and Tri-Council Policies about research with Indigenous communities and how these might apply to their work.
> —Annie, CYC Practicum Supervisor

As a part of the journey in reconciliation, all helping professions are inviting themselves to transform their practice. In their toolkit, the BC Association of Social Workers' Indigenous Working Group (2016) presents reconciliation and decolonization as a new relationship that requires helping practitioners to locate themselves in relation to Indigenous land and knowledge. They ask us to ask ourselves:

- What is your personal and family history that brought you to this land?
- Are you aware of the history of the land you live and work on?
- Were your family or ancestors impacted by colonization, oppression, structural violence, or war?
- What does reconciliation mean to you? What does reconciliation look like to you?
- What guides your own practice framework? What traditional teachings, systems of knowledge, or worldviews inform your own philosophy of practice?
- Have you had the opportunity to learn Indigenous teachings? Are you able to practise these teachings in your profession?
- What are some things you are doing, or can do in the future, to decolonize your personal practice? (p. 4)

Conversations regarding reconciliation—restoring Indigenous self-determination, repairing relationships, redressing wrongs—have led to discussions of decolonizing ourselves and our practices. We can begin by reflecting on our own internalization of colonialist values along with deconstructing the practices we currently take part in. We can ask ourselves, as social service professionals: in what ways have I internalized claims of superiority and control over others?

We certainly do not have to look far to notice how our child and youth–serving organizations, systems, and structures are informed by and replicate colonialist worldviews.

At your practicum setting, notice how some people are privileged and some oppressed via its:

- Infrastructure (e.g., accessibility, inside/outside space, arrangement and availability of furniture, etc.)
- Operation (e.g., school hours and vacations, adult/child ratio, etc.)
- Interventions (e.g., seclusion, age-based separation, government care, etc.)
- Access (e.g., program gatekeeping based on diagnoses, language, etc.)
- Funding (e.g., political variability for program funding, funding that prioritizes restricted measurable outcomes, etc.)
- Policies (e.g., housing availability, welfare policies, etc.)

How have these systems and structures been put into place? How are they maintained? Are they in young people's best interests? Who gets to determine this?

In the spirit of decolonization and reconciliation, we can also ask ourselves: what does decolonization and reconciliation look like at my practicum? Because we are in the middle of defining what these terms look like in practice in local contexts and determining how to move forward from a place of truth and reconciliation, it is okay that these concepts may be new to you, where you may struggle with not only what they mean but also putting them into practice. Nonetheless, let's consider how our practicum settings are participating in these evolving discussions. Students may learn of the efforts their sites are implementing to better respond to Indigenous communities, encouraging practicum students to fully participate so as to bring that knowledge and experience forward with them in their learning.

- At an inner-city elementary school, with a high proportion of its students and families with Indigenous ancestry, staff encourage their practicum students to come to the informal morning welcoming circle, where children's parents and caregivers are encouraged to spend time together, form relationships, and share stories over food.
- At an Indigenous child-family supervised-access site, practicum students are welcome to participate in smudging ceremonies, sharing circles led by Elders, and develop family-centred activities based in song, movement, and arts.
- At a high school outreach program, practicum students are welcome to help coordinate the afterschool Indigenous skilled-arts-based mentorship program, which pairs students with artists in the community.
- At a youth centre, co-located with a number of programs (school, recreation, health, etc.), practicum students learn about Indigenous programming and services at the site and in the area.
- At an alternate secondary school centre, youth-friendly Indigenous literature and media is on prominent display—Indigenous authored and Indigenous central characters in young adult and graphic novels, gaming with Indigenous creators and storylines, and more.

In the examples above, each site has attended to the nature of daily processes, intergenerational relationships, access to services, healing practices, program models, and so on. What do each of these examples mean to you? Do they help you reveal examples from your own setting?

As part of the process of reconciliation and decolonization, as CYC practitioners, we need to take a close look at how colonialist worldviews, values, and structures show up in our everyday lives. As Saraceno (2012) reveals,

> A dominant Western ontology rooted in whiteness and coloniality is embedded in the systems and structures of professional helping, including child and youth care... To engage in transformative social change requires us to challenge professional assumptions and models of helping in CYC and in the legal and socio-political contexts in which CYC operates. (pp. 249, 258)

While we are in the very beginning stages of understanding how our professional (and personal) lives are dominated by these values, one place to begin is understanding how we *position* young people in our work. Skott-Myhre (2008) warns us to not *other* young people through adult privilege and its "acquisition of languages and description such as diagnoses and developmental psychological frameworks that clearly define the youth worker as safely different from the youth served" (p. 170). Have you ever thought of the term *adult privilege*? Meanwhile, Zinga (2012) says we can start by reminding ourselves of the "danger of trying to have genuine encounters with youth if 'you feel that you can interpret their behaviour through a lens of superior expertise'" (Skott-Myhre & Skott-Myhre, 2011, as quoted in Zinga, 2012, p. 273). These CYC scholars collectively ask, "In what ways do we, as adults, as CYC practitioners, as part of the helping profession, practice in ways that assumes superiority to young people?"

Focusing on the CYC profession more specifically, we can look at common practices in CYC. Consider the following worldviews, approaches, and identities that CYC holds.

1. CYC Worldview—How do we define a successful young person?
    *   Compliant with institutions (graduate high school, employment-readiness, "well-behaved," etc.) vs. other visions of success (e.g., youth-activists, change-makers, disrupting and redefining societal norms)
2. CYC Approach—What approaches do we privilege over others?
    *   Privileging verbal communication interventions vs. other modes of communication, connection, and interaction (e.g., expressive arts, nature-based, etc.)
    *   Behavioural modification–based interventions vs. other approaches
    *   Making referrals predominantly to 1-1 counselling vs. other healing practices
3. CYC Practitioner Identities—Do we represent the diverse young people and families we serve?
    *   Who gets to represent CYC teaching, research, and practice? Who is excluded and why?
    *   What effects does this have on young people and their families?

Deconstruction

Deconstructing our foundational perspectives is an important practice, as we question the very perspectives we hold close to our identity and work. Deconstruction means to critically analyze the assumptions, values, systems, and structures. You are already doing this—just look back to Chapter 5, where we focused on deconstructing a situation through critical reflection. Here, we mean that we can also deconstruct our CYC practice as a whole. There is ample opportunity to do so, given that we draw upon a transtheoretical approach, where multiple perspectives inform our practice. Developmental theory, for example, is central to so much of our work—how we understand young people, how we intervene and develop programming and activities, how we track progress, and so on. But how do these theories—any developmental theory or part thereof—serve the young people we work alongside? Are they effective? How can we tell? Are they ethical? How do we know? Whose and what standards are we applying to affirm their use? Applying these types of questions allows us to critically evaluate our work.

Let's get more specific here. Contrasting an Indigenous worldview and a Euro-Western worldview, Zinga (2012) critiques the 20th-century developmental theory that is all too often used in CYC practice. Recall your learning from Maslow's Hierarchy of Needs framework. Zinga (2012) shows that self-actualization (Maslow's highest, ultimate goal and achievement) within an Indigenous mentorship program, through a "culturally relevant framework based on community understandings of traditional teaching," instead "refers to the importance of a young person coming to know and appreciate the gifts the Creator has bestowed on him/her and to start on the path s/he was meant to follow" (pp. 267–268). What shift do you notice has happened here?

Zinga (2012) takes her analysis further. Looking at an Indigenous youth mentorship program in a First Nations community in Canada, she noted that this program's 1) understanding of youth-mentor contact, 2) reasons for initiating services, 3) space where mentorship occurs, 4) duration of their work together, and 5) focus of the mentoring relationship were all more expansive and diversely interpreted than how many Euro-Western worldviews influence CYC service delivery in the field. This example may help us think of our own contexts in practicum—at a school, in a residential home, community centre, shelter, and so on. In what spaces does CYC practice happen? Not happen? Why? Who is involved? Not involved? Why? What timelines are permitted? Not permitted? Why? What is considered part of our practice? What is not? Why? Whose needs does this serve? Not serve? Why?

When we go about the important work of deconstructing our practices and applying a social justice framework, we don't limit ourselves in solely exploring the diversity of people, identities, culture, and experiences. As discussed above, we acknowledge the experience of power, privilege, and oppression. This combination has resulted in a number of social justice practices, including, but certainly not limited to, anti-oppressive practices, reclaiming culture as a way of approaching our work with young people, and the encouragement of all CYC practitioners to become active allies in our work alongside marginalized communities.

Figure 6.5: Toward Socially Just Practice

Anti-oppressive Practices

Many helping professions, programs, and practitioners have been incorporating anti-oppressive practice guidelines. Have you been learning these concepts in your other classes? Lee and Bhuyan (2013) describe anti-oppressive practices as "informed by critical race, feminist, and structural theories, stress[ing] the importance of addressing structural processes that fuel intersecting oppressions" (p. 99). When we look at transforming our CYC practice to become anti-oppressive, we mean that we are committed to ending the oppressive forces that marginalized young people and their families experience. An essential component of both practices is the analysis of power. What do we mean by power? When we look at identity categories (such as the ones listed in the intersectionality framework), we see that power imbalances exist. In anti-oppressive practice, we commit ourselves to changing those inequalities at the individual, organizational, and sociocultural level.

> Courses in Human Rights, Cultural and Human Diversity, and Anti-Oppression practice will help students understand the differences in our field. This will help students understand themselves, their social location, and how to work with others.
> —Saira, CYC Practicum Faculty-Instructor

As you are introduced to your practicum site, observing staff and young people, reading policies, and learning unwritten rules and practice philosophies, you have the opportunity to see how your practicum setting implements an anti-oppressive practice. Use Table 6.4 to help you explore and identify what your practicum site is or could be doing. If these concepts are new to you, don't worry; you can learn by beginning to process their meaning.

Central to anti-oppressive practice descriptions and guidelines is their critical perspective. Critical perspectives question the very "helping" practices we've come to know and suggest concrete, encouraging actions for social change.

Reclaiming Culture

One way we see our practices transform is through reclaiming culture. That is, to recover, reconnect with, recentre, build upon, and enliven one's culture and identity as a holistic approach in attending to developing identity and wellness. We can see many examples of reclaiming culture across programs and services.

Table 6.4: Danso's Guidelines for Critical Anti-oppressive Practice

Danso's Guidelines for Critical Anti-oppressive Practice			
Address the oppressive situation	Challenge oppressive policies and methods	Acknowledge oppression is complex and structural	Situate clients' issues within a wider social context
Avoid attributing client problems as personal deficiencies	Do not assume the expert role	Actively pursue social change	Act when there is a need to do so
Create alliances and coalitions	Use multicultural strategies to create social change	Acknowledge and privilege clients' voices	Advocate for fair distribution and access to power
Understand the change being sought before acting	Develop a clear plan of action	Change can be slow	Adapt strategies to suit the context
Ask, don't assume	Use language that is inclusive and empowering	Promote diversity	Advocate for diversity training

Adapted from Drolet, J., Clark, N., & Allen, H. (Eds.). (2012). *Shifting sites of practice: Field education in Canada* (p. 171). Toronto, ON: Pearson.

Culture as intervention. Culture as strength. Culture as healing. The Canadian Institutes of Health Research (2014) states that cultural interventions—relationships, activities, processes, events, and interventions—are essential to a person's well-being. They list a number of traditional Indigenous cultural interventions. As CYC practitioners, we can learn about a young person's culture and help facilitate their access and connection to their culture through:

- Talking Circles, Storytelling, Dancing, Singing, Feasts...
- Elders, medicine people, and traditional practitioners...
- Land-based activities, hunting and fishing...
- As well as many ceremonies including sweat lodges, fasting... (Canadian Institutes of Health Research, 2014, p. 1)

Using a culture-as-treatment approach, Barker, Goodman, and DeBeck (2017) describe an Indigenous community's response to suicide, which is a "culturally driven community-based approach... emphasiz[ing] the significance of interconnectedness in healing and the revitalization of traditional values (e.g., balance, community, family, culture, meaningful roles, spirituality, etc.) to reclaim community wellness" (p. 6). Reconnecting with culture strengthens identity, belonging, development, and more.

In their discussion of recentring an Afrocentric worldview for Black street-involved youth, Hasford, Amponsah, and Hylton (2018) discuss rites of passage intervention programs that are rooted in traditional practices, that explore and recentre African identity. Through these programs, the identity-based questions explored include:

- Who am I? What values, history, traditions, and cultural precepts do I recognize, respect, and continue?
- How did I come to be who I am? What were/are the forces, events, and people that have come together to frame who I am?
- Am I really who I think I am? To what extent do I understand, internalize, employ, and reflect the cultural authenticity of my origins?
- What is my life purpose? (Hasford et al., 2018, p. 132)

Many minoritized communities and cultures have had dominant culture devalue and systematically restrict the expression of their culture. Programs and practices that reclaim culture strengthen, re-claim, and actively attend to the development of a young person's participation in their culture.

You may already be reflecting on your practicum site and thinking of the young people who have been disconnected from their culture and diverse identities. How are the programs and practitioners attempting to support young people reclaiming culture? In what ways do you see this happening? What are the positive effects this has on young people?

Appreciative and Effective Allyship

We aim to be allies alongside marginalized groups in our communities. Sensoy and DiAngelo (2017) write that "the term *ally* refers to a member of the dominant group who acts to end oppression in all aspects of social life by consistently seeking to advocate alongside of the group who is oppressed in relation to them" (italics original, p. 211). Saraceno (2012), citing Madsen, "invites practitioners to take up the stance of 'appreciative allies... a relational stance characterized by respect, connection, curiosity, and hope [and] a way of being that we actively attempt to bring forward in our actions'" (p. 264). What does this welcoming invitation inspire you to think of? To do?

We can think of many groups in our communities who experience oppression. We may be part of those groups. We may not. Let's consider a group that we all have been in and are no longer a part of, due to its age-based restrictions: children and youth. (Although, considering the socially constructed nature of youth ending and some organizations' push to expand the age limit of youth, you may still be in this category. For now, let's think about the young people we work alongside.)

> My role is to raise everybody up. If we're not all on the same pedestal, then we need to get there.
> —Cody, CYC Student

Young people experience particular oppression, disadvantage, and discrimination that are both unique and overlap with many other groups. Poverty. Violence. Exploitation. Economic dependence. State-based custody. Due to structural, cultural, and developmental factors, young people are not permitted to vote for their interests, fully participate in the decisions made for them, and so on, despite local, national, and international efforts to change these unjust systems of power. Tilsen (2018) asks us to consider: "How do you position yourself to join youth in acts of resistance to unjust systems of power?" (p. 25). In your practicum site, what are the unjust systems of power the young people experience? How do we join with them, rather than replicate unjust systems of power? Take a moment to consider.

Sensoy and DiAngelo (2017) offer a list of actions we can take as allies alongside young people. Reflect on how you may (or may not) currently be acting as an ally in young people's lives in the following text box.

Sensoy and DiAngelo's Being an Ally through Action

✓ Validating and supporting people who are socially or institutionally minoritized in relation to you, regardless of whether you completely agree with or understand where they are coming from
✓ Engaging in continual self-reflection to uncover your socialized privilege and internalized superiority
✓ Working with other members of the dominant group and not positioning yourself as better or more advanced as they are
✓ Advocating when the oppressed group is absent by challenging misconceptions
✓ Letting go of control and sharing power when possible
✓ Taking risks to build relationships with minoritized group members
✓ Taking responsibility for mistakes
✓ Having humility and willingness to admit not knowing
✓ Earning trust through action

Adapted from Sensoy, O., & DiAngelo, R. (2017). *Is everyone really equal? An introduction to key concepts in social justice education* (2nd ed., pp. 211–212). New York, NY: Teachers College Press.

As you read through examples of what being an ally looks like in practice, think about how you show up as an ally alongside young people in their life-spaces at your practicum site. Consider jotting down recent experiences where you did (or could have done) any of these things to bring this awareness to the forefront of your mind. Remind yourself that these examples can be external, observable actions. Likewise, they could be internal reflections that then become external

> Advocacy and social justice— speak with and for youth.
> —Yvonne, CYC Practicum Faculty-Instructor

contributions to the context. This is important work, and we are privileged to be in a position to do so.

How do you show up for the young people at your practicum site? How are you listening to their experience of the world? How do you advocate for their needs? In what ways has the institution you are currently part of—child welfare, educational, health—historically oppressed young people? Are you using your experience of power and privilege—as an adult, as a postsecondary student, and as an emerging practitioner with the knowledge, skills, language, access that comes along with that status—to advance their interests? How do you join young people, rather than control and dominate? Do you listen to young people's feedback when they let you know you've made a mistake? Do you honour that message by integrating that feedback and doing better? We work alongside some of the most marginalized young people in our communities. Every moment you are in the field of practice, you have an opportunity to make a difference for young people. In practicum, you have the opportunity to understand how that can look in one particular context, with the young people you are meeting and the programs in which you participate, in the complex system they are part of. What will you do with that opportunity?

DIVERSE POSSIBILITIES

In many ways, our historical and many current practices limit the possibilities of encounters with young people. This is not to discourage you; rather, it is to encourage you to critically evaluate the limits and possibilities of practice. Who we engage with, how we engage with them, what spaces we do and do not occupy, what we do and do not do in our time together, where we take our conversations, and what we consider worthy of focus. We do not need to rid ourselves of everything we have ever known. Our theories and practices contribute good things to the wellness of our communities. But we do need to consider a more responsive, productive way of engaging with young people, if only for the fact that the world is changing and we need to change alongside it.

Radical Youth Work

Let's take this focus on *action* further. Let's not limit our action to being an ally alongside marginalized young people. Let's also reconsider every aspect of our work, aligning ourselves with a more expansive approach to Child and Youth Care theory and practice.

Skott-Myhre (2005) contrasts radical youth work and colonial youth work. *Colonial* youth work "has its central premise in the disciplining of youth bodies and youth minds to comply with the interests of the nation, the corporation, the family, or the agency" (para. 3). We only have to look to the developmental stages we expect all young people to progress through, the movement we expect from them through our institutions, how we construct a well-behaved young person, and the goals we hope they achieve. A *radical* "youth work would show how youth as pure creative force produces itself as a revolutionary effect," where youth work becomes a "relational force," "purely creative, as sheer affirmation," "always engaging in the multitude," "an encounter of potential" based in community and love (Skott-Myhre, 2008, pp. 178–184). We only need to look to today's young people for their voice, perspective, innovation, and leadership to see this creative force at work.

When we open up our practice to consider other ways to engage young people, the diversity of our experience together becomes exponential, with possibilities unknown at the outset of the encounter. To this end, Yoon (2012) encourages us to work "together for our collective liberation from the shackles of the dominant mainstream discourse of power and privilege" where "we need to make transformative personal change that will impact social change from the ground up" (p. 165). This collective liberation, this radical CYC practice can begin to take shape as you situate yourselves in your practicum setting, participate in lively, engaged discussion with your peers, and deconstruct, experiment with, and make sense of the ideas that existing CYC practitioners, scholars, and educators present to you, as tentative, precarious, and fluid as those offerings are.

Let's begin with this practicum experience, in this moment in time, in these spaces we find ourselves, with these people we learn and work alongside, with these experiences we bring to the present moment. Let's open our worlds, minds, practices, and profession, step into this space, and embody diversity—people, practices, and possibilities—to better respond to the needs of young people, families, and their communities.

LEARNING JOURNAL

You have completed numerous reflection activities, considered a number of social justice frameworks, and applied some of these ideas to the young people at your practicum setting. Take the opportunity to record in your learning journal what you've learned from doing all this purposeful reflection—where it brought you from and where it may be taking you.

PRACTICE SCENARIOS

At the end of this chapter are two practice scenarios to give you more examples of practicum students grappling with the topic of diversity and diverse practices: "Lincoln's Invitation" and "Anika's Observations." Read the examples and consider the reflective questions at the end. By the very nature of imagining the scenario the practicum student finds themselves in, you will hopefully be encouraged to think of your own situation and the relevant themes, issues, problems, and possibilities the scenario brings forward in your own context.

SEMINAR GROUP AND COMMUNITY OF PRACTICE DISCUSSION QUESTIONS

You have completed a number of reflection activities, question prompts, scenarios, frameworks, and more in this chapter. Most of them have been internal reflections. That is, you've been asked to do this work on your own. Now take the time to share in your seminar discussion or community of practice what you've learned, what you found difficult, where you'd like to apply these ideas in your practicum setting, and so forth. Listen deeply to your classmates and group members. They too have done purposeful, reflective work, opening themselves up to bringing various issues, identities, and experiences to the forefront of their mind. This takes courage, vulnerability, and trust. Treat that with respect and encouragement.

1. How does your practicum setting demonstrate an appreciation for diversity?
2. How has reflecting on your social location (including aspects of your identity and the privileges and oppressions you experience) helped you better serve young people and their families?
3. Think of a perspective, approach, policy, or practice as a part of your CYC work that you believe to be oppressive in some way or that privileges a Euro-Western worldview over others. Analyze it accordingly: how does it have very real effects on the lives of young people and their families? What will you now do with this awareness?
4. How do you show up as an ally for the young people at your practicum setting?

IN CLOSING

We end this chapter recognizing the vast territory we've explored. We've engaged in this journey to approach our work differently. We've repositioned ourselves not just as active learners, applying the theories and perspectives we've been keenly studying in our classes thus far, but to approach our practice with a critically informed lens. We desire to respond to the diverse needs of people in our diverse communities. We need to become more aware of how we show up to that work. We must participate in our work with a socially just approach, deconstructing the very practices we hold dear. You are encouraged to approach the rest of this guidebook with this chapter in mind. How can we welcome diversity in our settings? How can we ensure we're meeting the diverse needs of young people? How can we diversify our practices? How can we create spaces for diverse possibilities to occur? Ask these questions, and while doing so, know that you are at the forefront of this change. That what you do here, in this practicum, at this time, makes a difference to young people and redefines what we mean by CYC practice. We are all in this together.

PRACTICE SCENARIOS

Lincoln's Invitation

Lincoln is a white, male CYC student in his early 20s placed at an Aboriginal Friendship Society, in its youth recreational programs. While most of his time spent there is in the youth-designated space—drop-in room with couches, games, books, and open space—he has been encouraged to get to know the entire organization by visiting different programs and events. When he was told he could bring his partner to the weekly Family Night, where the community gathered over food, games, storytelling, music, and dance, he noticed he was surprised that he was invited to do so. He was self-aware enough to reflect and discuss with his supervisor and instructor, telling them that he'd always been taught that his personal life (family, interests, etc.) was separate from his work life (practicum, school) and that the boundary should be set. Upon discussion, he was encouraged to notice the Indigenous worldview of the Friendship Society, where holistic understanding of relationships and vocation do not have such rigid lines and to welcome the interconnectedness across relationships and spaces.

In your practicum setting have you noticed any cultural or worldview differences, between what you were raised or taught to hold as good or important, that have been challenged, expanded, or changed?

_____

_____

_____

Anika's Observations

Anika is a South Asian, female CYC student in her mid-30s, with a background in early childhood education. Placed in a child-development centre for her practicum, she's involved with many of its programs—family outreach, assessment and referral—spending a lot of time in the various program rooms and alongside many of the specialists there, learning about their resources. In the childcare room, she notices that many of the books show family composition with two parents (male/female), two children (boy/girl), and one pet (cat/dog). In the interviews she's attended, she's noticed that some of the assessment tools (questionnaires, interviews, etc.) assume particular things about what "good behaviour" means (compliant, quiet, not disruptive). She also notices that almost all of the staff at the centre, especially the ones with advanced professional de-grees, are white, yet many of the families who attend the centre have multiracial and multicultural backgrounds. She feels that these practices do not create a welcoming environment for families.

What values do these examples—literature, assessment tools, staff profile—directly and indirectly communicate to families? What do the materials, re-sources, and staff diversity at your practicum setting directly and indirectly communicate to the youth and/or families at your site?

_____

_____

_____

CHAPTER 7

Facilitating Therapeutic Change in CYC

Competencies for Professional Child and Youth Work Practitioners				
Professionalism	Cultural and Human Diversity	Applied Human Development	Relationship and Communication	Developmental Practice Methods
	Relationship and Communication Developmental Practice Methods	Contextual-Developmental Assessment Contextual Development Practice Methods Access Resources	Relationship Development	Genuine Relationships Intervention Planning Program Planning and Activity Programming Activities of Daily Living

It doesn't matter whether you are an experienced worker, or a student undertaking a practicum placement at PLEA, you have the opportunity to make a positive and long-lasting impact on the young people... Accepting youth unconditionally and developing caring relationships based on mutual trust, you are fostering the opportunity for positive change. By continuing to offer support and encouragement, and adopting a non-judgmental approach, the seeds are being planted for positive outcomes down the road.

—Mike Jeffreys, Senior Program Director,
PLEA Community Services Society

In our work as Child and Youth Care (CYC) practitioners, we have the opportunity to affect meaningful change in young people's lives. Do not think you are *just a practicum student*, shadowing practitioners. Even though you're placed in this particular setting for a relatively short time, not only do you have the chance to learn how your previous course work is applied in practice, while observing and learning from your supervisor and other CYC and aligned professionals, you also have the ability to make a difference in young people's lives. And, like a researcher immersed in field observation, your very presence—pursuing goals, completing requirements of the course, and bringing yourself to the space—will have an impact on the site, its staff, and its young people.

This chapter will focus on the ways we facilitate therapeutic change in micro-level systems and environments, where many practicum students are placed. The following chapter will focus on the ways we facilitate therapeutic change in macro-level systems and environments, where some of you will be placed, but many of you will have the opportunity to participate in this work through specific tasks and responsibilities. Figure 7.1 outlines the topics we will explore in the micro- and macro-systems; note, however, that there are hundreds more topics we could explore. This chapter will end with some theories and models of change that will guide these approaches.

In your courses thus far, as well as remaining courses in your certificates, diplomas, and degrees, you have been exposed to numerous theories, approaches, and areas of practice to affect therapeutic change—depending on a number of factors including your faculty's expertise, provincial requirements, specific local context's needs based on geography, demographic, social conditions, politics, and more. Notice what approaches, methods, and models are useful and relevant to your current practicum setting, and make note for future practicum placements.

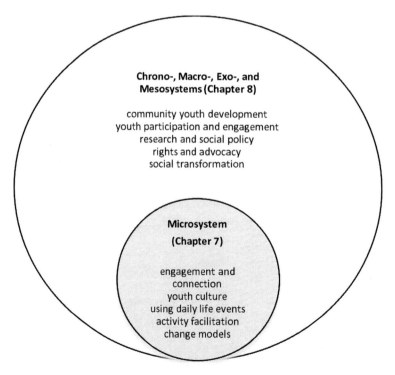

Figure 7.1: Therapeutic Change across Systems—Microsystem

ECOLOGICAL THEORY AND MULTI-LEVEL INTERVENTIONS

As an organizational frame with which to approach a discussion of change, we will draw upon the familiar Ecological Theory (Bronfenbrenner, 1979). Typically, we use this theory to understand a young person's context and factors influencing their life, from the immediate environments they're situated within (micro), to the relationships between those environments (meso), to the environments in which they're not present but nevertheless influence them (exo), to the wider societal conditions (macro) that impact them over time (chrono). Here, we will instead use this theory to discuss the systems and environments we have the opportunity to affect change within, using our CYC perspectives and approaches in practicum.

Derksen (2010) encourages us to view the potential scope of our CYC practice through a lens of multi-level interventions, using ecological theory to inform our perspective; we are encouraged to see CYC practice across the environmental systems that influence young people's lives. White (2007) reminds us that "CYC work involves intervening with individual children, youth and families *and* their social environments. This requires skills in professionalism, direct client care, program planning, social justice advocacy, plus an ability to strengthen social environments and analyze social policies" (p. 236). While Anglin (2000) divided CYC work into two categories—direct service to young people and organizational activities—we often have the opportunity to work across the spectrum, whether we're in a "direct service" or "organizational" setting and/or role. Wherever you are placed in practicum, do not let that limit your perspective of CYC practice. Notice the potential for all places, spaces, and systems where CYC practice can be valuable.

Micro-Level Systems and Environments

For the most part, for your first and second practicum experience, you will be working directly with young people in their life-space. As detailed in Chapter 2, CYC students are typically placed in school, community, or residentially based programs, working with children, youth, and their families. Across these spaces we have the opportunity to build relationships and facilitate therapeutic change directly with young people. How do we purposefully enter into these spaces and engage in CYC practice? Whether we're at a group home, a youth drop-in centre, an elementary school, or street outreach program, we all *begin* through engagement and connection.

It is this engagement and connection that we often spend our first few weeks at practicum focusing upon, struggling through, and noticing moments of success and opportunities for more connection.

> I encourage students to see themselves as caring, connected adults who are in the space to be in relationship with young people. Their job is to make connections, and to communicate care for the young people they come into contact with.
> —Kristy, CYC Practicum Faculty-Instructor

RELATIONAL ENGAGEMENT AND CONNECTION

Students should look for opportunities to move from the shadows and onto the sidelines, then from the sidelines to areas of assistance, then from assistance to co-facilitation.
—Andrew, CYC Practicum Faculty-Instructor

We must begin somewhere. We enter into the practicum space. We are new to the people around us. We are concurrently learning about the organization and environment as we immerse ourselves in it. We want to connect with the young people. Find out who they are. Spend time with them. Perhaps influence their growth, development, and wellness. And at the very least, offer them a positive experience, however that may end up looking.

When first connecting with young people, we can sometimes feel stuck, worried, incompetent, or general unease. McGrath (2018) lists the questions that ran through her mind when first meeting with young people: "Will I connect with them? Will we have anything in common? Will I know what to do? Will they learn to trust me? What will they think of me?" (p. 124). Do these reflections resonate for you in some way? Are you feeling these uncertainties too? McGrath reminds students that "feeling nervous and anxious can also be healthy because it shows that you care about what you are doing" (p. 124). We do care. That is why we're here. As you spend the first few weeks in practicum, how are you feeling about your connections with young people?

Often, and depending on the context, there is a slow pace; it takes multiple points of contact, sharing meaningful moments over multiple interactions. If it didn't—if connection was "quick," for example—we may actually have different concerns. What we are doing in our engagement with young people is in fact an opportunity for learning and intervention in and of itself. We are modelling to young people how relationships form. Pacing, approach, and more are all factors in these moments. They are observing us too.

A Note on Structured and Unstructured Settings

Further, depending on your site, connections can happen at different paces. There are formal and informal structures in place that facilitate these connections. There are settings that are more structured with more formal opportunities to connect. There are settings that are less structured with more informal opportunities to connect. Mainstream schools are sometimes more structured, whereas alternative schools may be less structured. Group homes are typically less structured, whereas a residential treatment facility may be more structured. Youth drop-in centres can be across the spectrum, depending on programming. What is your practicum program, and do you find it more structured or unstructured?

Consider the following list of practicum student scenarios and their first few weeks of opportunity for engagement and connection with the young people at the site:

- A practicum student at a supervised-access site shadows her supervisor when meeting families and playing with the kids, is introduced, and given clear direction on what activities to do with the families.
- A practicum student is instructed to facilitate a sports game at the recreation centre and immediately meets and has the opportunity to get to know many young people at once.
- A practicum student at an elementary school is introduced to a number of children in the drop-in support room and immediately begins to play games with them, then has the opportunity to wave and say hello when she sees them in the hallway the next day.
- A practicum student at a group home notices that one of the residents never comes out of her room. Another girl leaves the home for a few days at a time.
- A practicum student at an emergency youth shelter notices the same youth do not show up each evening at curfew/check-in.

If the latter two students in the list above come to practicum seminar and compare their situation to the first few students, how may each one of them feel? Is anyone really "connecting better" than the other? No. Are all students learning about connection and engagement in the context of their sites? Yes. Should all students have faith that their "hello" or "nice to see you today" or "so glad you're here" or "I brought a game with me today, I wondered if you may want to play later?" (even if they are received with silence or swearing) is making a difference? Yes! It is wise to not judge or evaluate the connection too early on. Remember, you are planting seeds for connection. You may not witness the results of these efforts for some time. You may not even witness the results of these efforts while you're there. But you must trust that your efforts to engage, altered based on the immediate feedback you're getting at the site, will lead somewhere meaningful.

> Just engage the young people. Figure out the atmosphere and environment you're in. Figure out what your place is going to be. Find the best techniques and strategies that you're going to utilize to engage young people. Find out their interests. See what you can bring. Ask questions.
> —Tom, CYC Practicum Supervisor

Engagement and Connection Skills

We can look to the guidance of practitioners and scholars who compile recommendations for us as we practise our engagement skills. Sapin (2009) offers suggestions on maintaining dialogue with young people, a way we often connect and engage across CYC settings:

- ☑ Focus on the young person
- ☑ Approach young people positively rather than prejudging or labelling
- ☑ Allow young people to find their own examples and demonstrate their knowledge rather than showing off and scoring points
- ☑ Expect to learn from the young people rather than telling them "how it is"…
- ☑ Check understanding of the situation rather than interpret possible meanings
- ☑ Acknowledge what the young person says rather than disagree

☑ Ask about opinions rather than providing them; ask for suggestions rather than giving them

☑ Check young people's own feelings or responses rather than demonstrating your own

☑ Design activities with high levels of participation and creativity; don't just control or divert attention and energy

☑ Invite feedback; don't resist criticism

☑ Encourage young people to express themselves; don't talk too much

☑ Allow young people time to explore their ideas; don't move into decisions or actions too soon

☑ Encourage young people to share their experiences and feelings; don't problem-solve (p. 63)

> Simplify your language. Get down to their level: Do you really want to have people stare up at you? Do you enjoy staring up at someone?
> —Donna, CYC Practicum Supervisor

In the recommendations above, we can see the active application of interpersonal skills: listening, checking in for accuracy and understanding, genuinely summarizing and paraphrasing information, all from a place of curiosity and positive regard (Shebib, 2013). So, what does engagement look like at your practicum site? Think about those first few moments and encounters you have with young people. Consider the following examples from practicum students.

✓ A practicum student at a group home asks one of the young girls if she wants to go outside and play some basketball in the cul-de-sac

✓ A practicum student at a youth centre positions herself at the table at the centre of the room, begins to play solitaire, and asks if a young person wants to join and play a card game together

✓ A practicum student at an alternative school program sits next to a youth at the computer stations, explores some music-streaming websites, and eventually asks what they're working on

✓ A practicum student at an elementary school joins the class in playing a game of soccer

✓ A practicum student at a group home asks a young resident to help her fix a bike together

✓ A practicum student at a shelter says hello and introduces herself to each of the young people as they arrive in the evening

✓ A practicum student at an elementary school takes the time to memorize three young people's names and one strength or interest about each student each day

Now consider your own practicum placement. What are you actively doing to connect? What are your classmates actively doing to connect?

_____

_____

EXPLORING YOUNG PEOPLE'S INTERESTS AND PARTICIPATING IN YOUTH CULTURE

In CYC, we speak and write a lot about "meeting young people where they're at" and we do this in many ways. Not only do we begin our engagement and connection in their life-space, basing our work on their development and strengths, and work toward more socially just conditions, we also enter through their interests. Oftentimes, these interests intersect with pop culture—music, dress, literature, social media, and so forth. Our knowledge of and ability to connect on this level serves us well in our efforts to engage. Tilsen (2018) says, "youth workers know that pop culture is youth culture, and showing interest in youth's interests is central to relationship-making" (p. 121). Children too. We are curious about, recall our own experience of, engage in, and utilize pop culture as a site of meaningful, engaged connection with young people.

> I remember closer to the end of practicum one of the young people said they appreciated that 'You actually knew my name and came up to me compared to other staff who sat there and didn't really want to talk to me. They didn't seem interested in me.'
> —Cody, CYC Student

Think of a recent encounter with a young person at your practicum site and the potential it may have had for engagement. Did you use the opportunity to connect through a sports team logo on a hat or sweatshirt? A toy or game? A comic book or well-worn novel clutched close? A television show? A new hairstyle or colour? A website or social media post? Song lyrics or a dance move? Slang/lingo? Add examples to the list you see in Figure 7.2: pop culture artifacts, experiences, and behaviours you see every day in your practicum.

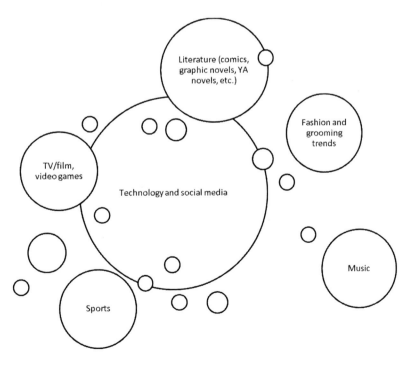

Figure 7.2: Youth Culture

> It was down to the point where I was on the ice rink and I can barely skate. I was getting on their level so on the following Monday I could then sit down and help them build a resume.
> —Jasmine, CYC Student

Drawing upon the interdisciplinary nature of cultural studies, Tilsen (2018) doesn't stop with just learning about what young people are engaged in. She goes on to use young people's culture as a place of inquiry and intervention. What meaning do young people make of the cultural products they are interested in, interacting with, and influenced by? She offers a model to use pop culture to encourage young people to be active agents in deconstructing the meaning of pop culture in their lives. She divides her approach into three types of inquiry: 1) the meaning young people take away from their experience of the cultural product, 2) an analysis of the system that is producing the cultural product and experience, and 3) deconstruction of the messages and stories young people are experiencing. Imagine how engaged a young person may be, and how much you may learn about their perspective of the world, through a conversation based on any pop culture artifact in the immediate environment (a novel, a hit song, a video game, or a television series). Think about asking the following questions:

- What are some things you've learned from the characters in this story?
- If you were in charge of the music on a popular label, what kinds of songs would you produce?
- According to this film, what are the rules for being a man or woman? (Tilsen, 2018, pp. 128–129)

Young people are often at the forefront of sociocultural change. They quite literally introduce new vocabulary, dance, and fashion to our wider culture. They drive industry change, such as with their behaviour on social media. We can look to young people internationally and in our communities who are young leaders and change-makers, giving voice to unjust conditions and demands for social change regarding educational, civil, justice, and environmental rights, to name a few. Think of the youth-coordinated walk-outs across North American secondary schools, or the Indigenous youth who led the Idle No More movement. How can we join young people in their efforts to make a better world? How can we use our access to power (age, communication, bureaucracy, systems, etc.) to benefit their vision of their future world? Immersing yourself alongside young people at practicum gives you a window into their world. Let's pay close attention.

A Note on Social Media

Social media in particular offers us opportunities and challenges to connect and engage with young people. Stuart (2013) invites us to become "present through social media—the use of which is a daily life event—provid[ing] opportunities for therapeutic use of daily life events, often without physical presence" (p. 296). For better and for worse, young people are online, using the internet, social media platforms, and related technology in many ways. Perhaps because of the lack of clear direction on how to manage engagement in online environments, CYC students, graduates, and practitioners are across the spectrum with regard to how they approach social media and online matters. Perhaps because of the current societal discussion of the benefits and harms of social media (focusing all too often on the latter), there is a general lack of support to engage young people online, or too rigid boundaries are recommended or drawn. Consider the responses from CYC students regarding how they engaged young people on social media during or soon after practicum, in Figure 7.3. (While reading the examples, consider what influenced their opinions.)

What would you do? What are your own positions? What creative approaches do you take? How does your agency support you in this goal? How is it informed by theory? How can we use social media platforms to engage young people, while also modelling boundaries and acting ethically?

There are many possible moments for meaningful encounters using technology. Cech (2015) reminds us that connection "can happen when the worker shows an interest in the child's phone or game rather than trivializing it or shutting it down"; we may be surprised where the conversation leads, such as when "the child may begin to feel more comfortable talking about real and virtual friends, multiple online identities, aggressors and problems, time wasters and threats, and a host of other challenges in the digital world" and where "digital technology can be a stimulating way to engage children in activities that prompt them to learn more, engage actively with others, and advocate for structural change" (pp. 228–229). It's what we do with these encounters that becomes CYC practice, where we can let our perspectives and approaches transition from in-person to online.

USING DAILY LIFE EVENTS

Whether online or in-person, as CYC practitioners, we use the opportunities that daily life events afford us. The purposeful use of daily life events is and has been central to CYC practice. Because we find ourselves in the life-space of young people, we have ample opportunity to use the daily rituals, processes, events, activities, conflicts, challenges, connections, movements, and goings-on as a site of connection and intervention. Unlike the helping practitioners who limit their connection to the four walls of the office and the hour (or less) a week (or less) of appointment time, we have, in some cases, 24 hours of opportunity to connect. Further, we do not limit our time to recall and reflection—such as a counsellor might do, recalling and reflecting with a young person on a conflict experienced the day/week before. We are in the life-space, in the moment of events happening, in real time, with real opportunity to continue, alter, change, evolve, and strengthen new behaviour, experiences, opportunities, and possibilities in young people's lives. Just think of the possibilities!

Charles, Freeman, and Garfat (2016) state, "a child and youth care practitioner's engagement in the daily life events of another person allows her to

> One youth I got to know, I noticed got left out of a lot of interactions with the kids. So I would just jump in and start playing a game with the other kids already playing. I'd go out of my way to draw this other kid into the game. It's just trying to get other kids to think about not leaving people out of their game.
> —Adrian, CYC Student

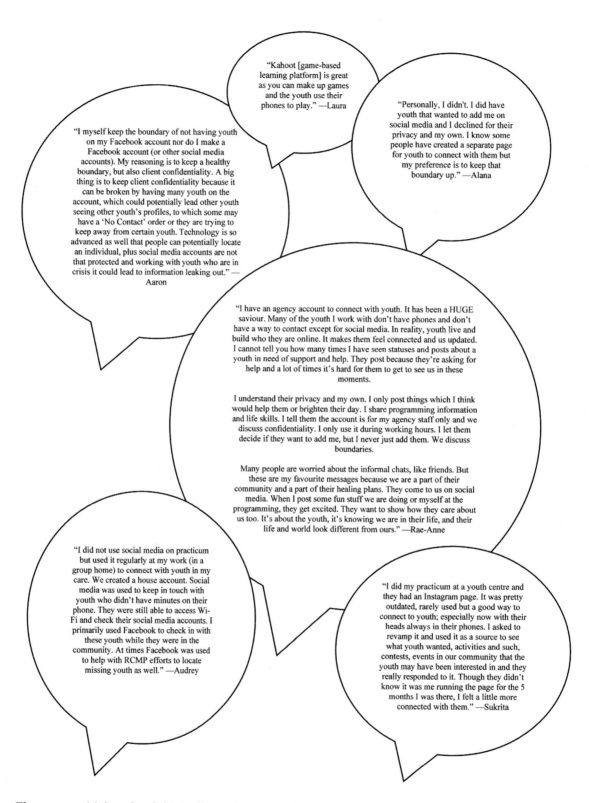

"Kahoot [game-based learning platform] is great as you can make up games and the youth use their phones to play." —Laura

"Personally, I didn't. I did have youth that wanted to add me on social media and I declined for their privacy and my own. I know some people have created a separate page for youth to connect with them but my preference is to keep that boundary up." —Alana

"I myself keep the boundary of not having youth on my Facebook account nor do I make a Facebook account (or other social media accounts). My reasoning is to keep a healthy boundary, but also client confidentiality. A big thing is to keep client confidentiality because it can be broken by having many youth on the account, which could potentially lead other youth seeing other youth's profiles, to which some may have a 'No Contact' order or they are trying to keep away from certain youth. Technology is so advanced as well that people can potentially locate an individual, plus social media accounts are not that protected and working with youth who are in crisis it could lead to information leaking out." — Aaron

"I have an agency account to connect with youth. It has been a HUGE saviour. Many of the youth I work with don't have phones and don't have a way to contact except for social media. In reality, youth live and build who they are online. It makes them feel connected and us updated. I cannot tell you how many times I have seen statuses and posts about a youth in need of support and help. They post because they're asking for help and a lot of times it's hard for them to get to see us in these moments.

I understand their privacy and my own. I only post things which I think would help them or brighten their day. I share programming information and life skills. I tell them the account is for my agency staff only and we discuss confidentiality. I only use it during working hours. I let them decide if they want to add me, but I never just add them. We discuss boundaries.

Many people are worried about the informal chats, like friends. But these are my favourite messages because we are a part of their community and a part of their healing plans. They come to us on social media. When I post some fun stuff we are doing or myself at the programming, they get excited. They want to show how they care about us too. It's about the youth, it's knowing we are in their life, and their life and world look different from ours." —Rae-Anne

"I did not use social media on practicum but used it regularly at my work (in a group home) to connect with youth in my care. We created a house account. Social media was used to keep in touch with youth who didn't have minutes on their phone. They were still able to access Wi-Fi and check their social media accounts. I primarily used Facebook to check in with these youth while they were in the community. At times Facebook was used to help with RCMP efforts to locate missing youth as well." —Audrey

"I did my practicum at a youth centre and they had an Instagram page. It was pretty outdated, rarely used but a good way to connect to youth; especially now with their heads always in their phones. I asked to revamp it and used it as a source to see what youth wanted, activities and such, contests, events in our community that the youth may have been interested in and they really responded to it. Though they didn't know it was me running the page for the 5 months I was there, I felt a little more connected with them." —Sukrita

Figure 7.3: Using Social Media with Young People

intervene responsively and immediately to help the other person learn new ways of being and acting in their world" (p. 30). Stuart (2013) describes daily life events as "any eventful moment [that] is opened to a therapeutic moment. A daily life event is open for therapeutic use when the practitioner and young person engage in exploring its meaning together," where the CYC practitioner empowers "the child within his/her life space, seizing opportunities through seemingly unimportant events out of which a young person's days are constructed" (pp. 295–296). They include wakeups, meals, transportation, homework, conflicts, interactions, struggles, and successes. There are literally endless opportunities. What are the daily life events of the young people you're working alongside?

Let's go through some examples of daily life events to see how they provide opportunities for connection, learning, growth, development, and intervention. Activity 7.1 provides examples of daily life events and the possible opportunities for intervention. Remember, intervention does not have to be complex. It can be a learning opportunity, a moment to connect and strengthen relationship, and so on.

> Rather than taking time away from the parents and children at the visitation centre, we decided to do activities with the families that connect parents with their children.
> —Harman, CYC Student

Activity 7.1: Daily Life Events at My Practicum Setting

Look at the following examples of daily life events across multiple settings—both expected and unexpected—and brainstorm the opportunity that avails itself to you and the young people there. After completing the examples below, add specific examples from your own setting.

Table 7.1: Opportunities in Daily Life Events

Expected and Unexpected Daily Life Event	Learning/Intervention Opportunity
Children in the schoolyard have a conflict in a game.	An opportunity for de-escalation, emotional awareness, problem-solving, connection, and modelling relationship repair.
The youth at a group home need to wake up from their sleep overnight to attend school, appointments, and activities.	Autonomy and dependence, responsibility, self-care, wellness, sleep habits, motivation, attention to physical needs.
The staff and group of kids become disoriented while downtown after attending an event together. Some people are worried they're lost.	

(continued)

Table 7.1: Continued

A young person invites their support worker to attend their medical appointment.	
A child "acts out" in the classroom.	
Some of the children at an after-school club are excluding another child.	
A parent is late for pick up.	
A youth doesn't want to join the group activity at the drop-in centre.	
A young person is new to the community and wants to take the bus to get to the community centre but hasn't used public transportation on their own before.	
Dinner needs to be made, served, and eaten at a group home or shelter.	
A young person is lounging alone in the living room, watching television.	
A youth has been missing from their group home and calls the overnight worker to let them know of their location and requests a drive home.	
Example:	
Example:	
Example:	

ACTIVITY FACILITATION

Another way we as CYC practitioners support and facilitate therapeutic change is through the purposeful use of activities. When we refer to activities, we include a wide interpretation of what this means: facilitating a group activity in the school yard, an ice-breaker activity for children at a recreation centre camp, a life-skill activity with one or a few youth at a group home, taking a trip to a rally or protest with a young person, or decorating the room with a new resident of the group home.

VanderVen (2012) contrasts activities as a way of passing time and keeping kids busy for busyness's sake versus activities that "can promote positive developmental outcomes… and might actually be one of the primary cornerstones of learning, overall development, positive mental health, and successful adulthood" (p. 209). She tells us that CYC activities (such as play, sports, games, arts, crafts, service, music, hobbies, rituals, etc.) promote identity, industry, mastery, self-regulation, frustration tolerance, physical skill, body image, empathy, perspective-taking, teamwork, sharing, co-operation, and more (pp. 209–210). Meanwhile, Damsgaard (2011) discusses activities as a therapeutic medium in building relationships, facilitating self-awareness, and promoting developmental change with young people, where she offers numerous reasons CYC practitioners use activities as a site of intervention. She states that they aid in assessment, promote engagement, facilitate relationship building, promote child empowerment, facilitate a sense of belonging, fit with children's developmental stages, aid in learning, aid in the expression of feelings and emotions, reduce stress and anxiety, offer positive experiences, and are effective (pp. 49–59). Remember these outcomes when it comes time to plan, facilitate, and evaluate your own activities. Young people's activities are quite literally contexts for development. We connect through activity. Development occurs through the activity. The activity becomes the opportunity for therapeutic change.

> One of our students took on a youth as her mentee and empowered the youth to grow into a strong and independent woman. She did this by one-on-one engagement, joined her on outings, lunches, shared stories, and grew from their experiences together.
> —Farah, CYC Practicum Supervisor

What activities are you part of with the individuals, groups, and/or families at your practicum setting? What activities have you been invited to join, alongside your supervisor or other staff? What activities are you planning to do with the young people at your site? Work through Activity 7.2 to analyze an activity at your site.

Activity 7.2: Facilitating and Evaluating Activities

Take an activity from your site. Any activity that you or another practitioner facilitated. Analyze its components according to information in this guidebook and/or theory and approaches from your activity facilitation class work.

What was the activity?

_____

Whose idea was it to initiate the activity? And why?

_____

What was involved in the preparation for the activity?

_____

Who did the activity involve?

_____

What did the activity involve?

_____

_____

What did you notice about the motivation and interest of the participants throughout the activity?

_____

What developmental needs did the activity attempt to meet?

_____

What daily life events did the activity build upon?

_____

What outcomes did the activity create for young people?

_____

What changes did the young people want made to the activity?

_____

What changes would you make to the activity? Why?

_____

When we deconstruct activities in this way, we become more aware of the multiple factors involved in facilitating meaningful activities that promote growth and development.

You are likely required to facilitate an activity—with an individual or a group—as part of your practicum experience. What are you planning to do? What's been suggested to you? What would the young people at your setting like to participate in? Remember to apply your developing knowledge of CYC practice in all aspects of activity planning, facilitation, and evaluation.

As we transition to a discussion of models for change, keep in mind the immediacy of our practice and the infinite opportunities for connection and therapeutic work. You are at your practicum setting, observing, noticing, experimenting, and trying new things. You are also observing how people change, their environment's influence on them and their influence on their environment, the effectiveness of interventions, and the precariousness and tentativeness of it all. This is complex work. Our learning is immense. We ourselves are going through much learning and change. Let's blend these two worlds—young people's change, our change—and move to a discussion on change models, one that will certainly not begin nor end in this course.

> We give students the opportunity to plan a workshop. Some practicum students think 'this is going to be the best workshop' but they haven't talked to the young people about it or if it's even something they're interested in. They haven't promoted it. Some kids say they'll be there but they don't show up. We connect with the student afterward: 'How will you do it differently next time?'
> —Tom, CYC Practicum Supervisor

MODELS FOR CHANGE

Across your CYC certificates, diplomas, and degrees, you will be introduced to many models of change that will guide your work with young people. What have you been introduced to? There are hundreds to draw upon, whether they are central to CYC or borrowed and adapted from aligned professions and schools of thought. Sometimes they are called theories, perspectives, models, or approaches. What matters is how they can be helpful to you with the young people at your site. If they are not, consider them for your toolkit of strategies and approaches for another time, another space. Know that most theories can help us understand a situation so as to act in a meaningful way. We offer a few models here, but know that there are numerous models that you've studied, and more will be introduced over the coming months and years. Meanwhile, so too will your practicum site supervisors and staff have models that they draw upon and guide their work. Ask them! They will like the chance to explain their work.

> Come in and engage with the youth, develop relationships, hang out, and figure out what interests them. Without the relationship—without developing that connection—you're not going to be able to move on to the next steps.
> —Tom, CYC Practicum Supervisor

Stages of Change

When working directly with young people and their families, we draw upon models and theories of how people change and develop, so as to support them on that journey. In CYC, we are drawn to theories that allow for the greatest reflection of the human condition, as we work with diverse people with diverse experiences. One model is the Transtheoretical Stages of Change model, used across settings, demographics, needs, programs, and roles, as seen in Figure 7.4. Cech (2010) looks at this theory of change, focusing on young people. She highlights that a CYC practitioner who understands the underpinnings of this model is more apt to recognize the child's location in the events unfolding around her or him and the child's capacity for change. The worker is more apt to identify which processes of change might be more useful for that child at that location and capacity, interpreting a child's reaction to a suggested program as a stage of change rather than simply as a behaviour that is intransigently defiant or aggressive. (pp. 131–132)

We often enter into young people's lives at the pre-contemplation, contemplation, and sometimes action stages. But too many social services programs assume that people are ready for action. Let's look at how this model may help us understand how to observe,

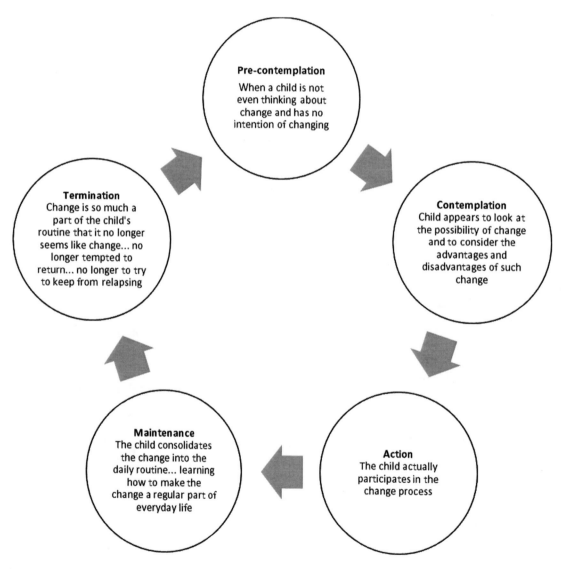

Figure 7.4: Stages of Change

Adapted from Cech, M. (2010). *Interventions with children and youth in Canada* (p. 132). Don Mills, ON: Oxford University Press.

notice, engage, and intervene with young people. Consider what behaviours we may observe in a young person and how that may reflect the stage of change they're in. Read the following list of scenarios, which you may find yourself observing in practicum:

- An adolescent boy has been hanging out near the entrance of a youth drop-in centre but doesn't come inside.
- Kids are in a social-emotional skills group at school, each learning mindfulness strategies to use at home and school.
- An adolescent girl is working with her support worker after substance misuse relapse. She's learned many things that help and hinder her recovery process.
- A group of parents are in a parent support group, offering each other guidance to help them negotiate conflict with their kids.

Now, go back through this brief list and note: 1) the developmental or behavioural change they (may) want to address, 2) their possible stage, and 3) what idea you have to support them in their continued growth. Stuck? Have a conversation with a classmate. When you've completed this reflection, move to Activity 7.3.

While this model is often applied to individuals, individuals in groups, or families, we can also think of team, organizations, professions, communities, and societies in terms of their engagement with change. Think about our community's awareness of the opioid epidemic, our agencies' adoption of trauma-informed practice, institutional efforts to engage in reconciliation with Indigenous communities, and so on. What stage of change would you put your city as a whole? What about our country? We can see how these social movements, efforts, and issues come into the public awareness, are sometimes slow to adopt, and require multi-level interventions and systemic support to maintain change and its results. This model of change allows us to adapt our understanding of, engagement with, and interventions alongside young people *and* communities.

> Looking from the outside in, you won't be able to see any change. But when you're in a relationship, doing programming and activities, you can see where the person started and where they ended. If you don't have that relationship, you wouldn't have known.
> —Margaret, CYC Student

Positive Youth Development

Akin to CYC's central practice approach—a strengths-based perspective—are strengths-based theories and frameworks to approach our work with young people and communities. Many schools of thought, fields of practice, organizations, and practitioners have shifted their approach from abnormality, deviance, pathology, problems, and risk toward strength, capacity, assets, wellness, opportunities, and resilience. One such framework is positive youth development. By the very fact that you're drawn to CYC practice, you're likely already using this framework, whether you're aware of it or not. Programs and practitioners coming from a positive youth development framework seek to foster and promote a number of strengths-based outcomes, listed in Figure 7.5.

Activity 7.3: Observing Change

Now that you've gone through some examples in the text above, let's turn our attention to the young people at your site. Choose one young person you're getting to know. Recall your observations of them, interactions with them, what you've learned about them from other staff and supervisors, and so on. What are they struggling with? What are they aware of/unaware of with regard to a helpful or more prosocial way of being? What are they working on or through? What are they tasked with figuring out? What would be a positive addition into their world? What are some barriers standing in their way? Try not to get too complex. By the very nature that young people are developing, growing, and attending to their well-being, there are limitless ways we can support them in that process.

In Table 7.2, read the questions, along with the example given. Next, read through the questions again and apply them to a young person at your practicum site.

Table 7.2: Applying the Stages of Change

Relevant Stage Observation	Example	Your Practicum
1. What's your observation?	Sam hangs out at the entrance of the youth drop-in centre every Friday night but doesn't enter.	
2. What is a possible developmental need or behavioural change that could benefit their life? Or what change are they working on?	Sam could possibly be struggling to connect with friends, find belonging in his community.	
3. What stage do we think is relevant to the young person's situation?	Pre-contemplation or contemplation	
4. What support could you provide, keeping in mind this stage?	Recognize and welcome his presence, encouragement to see him next week, bringing an appropriate game outside the centre, hanging out outside the centre, invitation into the centre, etc.	

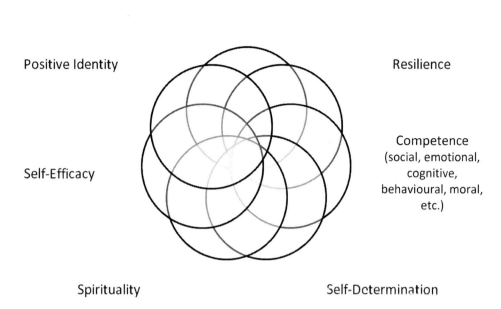

Figure 7.5: Positive Youth Development

Adapted from Catalano, R. F., Berglund, M. L., Ryan, J. A. M., Lonczak, H. S., & Hawkins, J. D. (1998). Positive youth development in the United States: Research findings on evaluations of positive youth development programs. *The Annals of the American Academy of Political and Social Science, 591,* 98–124.

Hartje, Evans, Killian, and Brown (2008) write that "positive youth development emphasizes youth strengths, building youth competencies, and strengthening youth protective factors… [where] organizations are able to create environments that reduce at-risk behaviours and teach youth to become responsible adults" (p. 28). Through conversations, focus, activities, groups, referrals, and more, we can implement this framework. How is your practicum setting implementing a positive youth development framework to support the growth, development, and wellness of the young people at your site?

Resilience

Resilience is one aspect of positive youth development, which we refer to often. Ungar (2008) tells us that resilience "is a concept that changes our focus from the breakdown and disorder attributed to exposure to stressful environments, to the individual characteristics and social processes associated with either normal or unexpectedly positive psychosocial development" (p. 21). He goes on to state five principles of resilience relevant to practice:

1. Resilience is nurtured by an ecological, multileveled approach to intervention
2. Resilience shifts our focus to the strengths of individuals and communities

3. Resilience shows that multifinality, or many routes to many good ends, is characteristic of populations of children who succeed

4. Resilience has shown that a focus on social justice is foundational to successful development

5. Resilience focuses on cultural and contextual heterogeneity related to children's thriving (pp. 25–30)

The young people we work alongside often experience (or have experienced) trauma, crisis, adversity, and stress. While we support them through those experiences, we often focus on their strengths—their resiliencies—that get them through. As described above, resilience is both internal and environmental, and we can identify and support the development of resiliency through all of the work we do. How does your practicum site focus on resiliency?

_____

_____

In the following chapter, we look at a community-level approach to applying positive youth development. For now, let's complete our discussion of models of change in the micro-level system and environment, focusing on the Circle of Courage.

> So many people focused on his negative behaviours. Then he would react by not doing his work. So I said 'we're going to play guitar at the end of the day, so we're just going to get through this activity right now.' I shocked myself that I was able to get him to get his work done. Especially because he was deemed one of the 'difficult' students.
> —Trina, CYC Student

> Everyone is looking for some place to belong and if you can help them to feel as though they belong, that they're interesting, and that they're cared about, you can't ask for more than that.
> —Chris, CYC Practicum Supervisor

Circle of Courage

Aligned with and predating positive youth development is an Indigenous-informed worldview and framework to young people's development and well-being. Presented holistically and with attention to the balance and interrelatedness between areas of young people's lives and their community, the Circle of Courage focuses CYC practitioners' attention to four areas that blend both the needs and resilience of young people. Building on work by Brendtro, Brokenleg, and Van Bockern (2002) and Brendtro and Larson (2006), Figure 7.6 shows how generosity, independence, mastery, and belonging form together to meet those needs and develop that resiliency. Notice how we can take its guidance and apply these concepts for different contexts, ages, and spaces of young people. Notice how resilience and strength is embedded throughout, with an assumption that young people have the capacity to attend to this need, and we as CYC practitioners have the opportunity to support this need, interconnected within young people's communities.

Using the Circle of Courage framework, we may be inspired to approach assessment and intervention in the following ways:

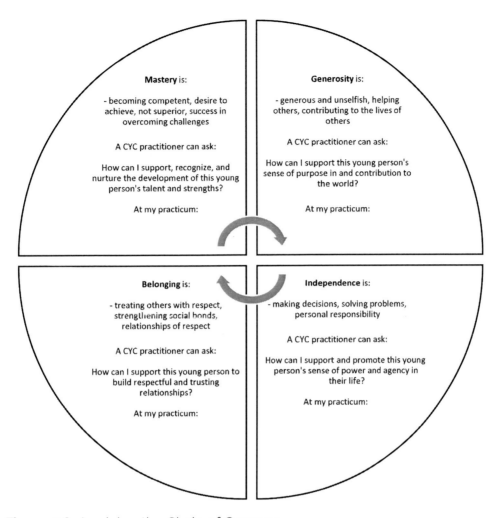

Figure 7.6: Applying the Circle of Courage

Adapted from Brendtro, L. K., Brokenleg, M., & Van Bockern, S. (2002). *Reclaiming youth at risk: Our hope for the future.* Bloomington, IN: National Education Service; Brendtro, L. K., & Larson, S. J. (2006). *The resilience revolution: Discovering strengths in challenging kids.* Bloomington, IN: Solution Tree.

- Belonging—we may support a young person to connect with their cultural roots; develop relational skills to develop connections with family; etc.
- Generosity—we may help a young person explore volunteer experiences in the community; we may involve young people in group activities that contribute to the school, neighbourhood; etc.
- Independence—we may support young people to develop problem-solving skills; access resources and support; etc.
- Mastery—we may notice a young person's interest and skill and invite them to join a class or program or connect with an Elder in the community; make a referral to an apprenticeship program; etc.

What do each of these concepts look like for young people at your practicum setting? Focus your attention on one young person at your practicum site. Maybe it's a young person your supervisor has been working with for some time, a young person you've been matched with, or a young person you've been getting to know and you'd like some direction. Think of this young person and notice strengths and needs. Jot those ideas down under the "at my practicum" sections in Figure 7.6.

Having reviewed a few models of change, notice your experience of that process. Which models are you drawn to? Why do you think that is? What was it like to frame your understanding of young people through *this* model vs. *that* model? Did it allow you to explore new ideas for connection and intervention? Why do you think that is? Noticing these reflections will help you articulate your theoretical orientation. As you develop as a practitioner, notice which theories, perspectives, frameworks, approaches, and models help you and the young people you work alongside. These are the ideas that guide you as a practitioner. They will be similar and different to each classmate who is developing their own unique, evolving, eclectic orientation to their work. And it is ongoing.

PLANNED AND DEVELOPMENTALLY APPROPRIATE INTERVENTIONS

We have reviewed a number of perspectives, approaches, frameworks, and models. We're not solely reviewing them for the sake of building your toolkit of strategies to approach and develop your practice. We're also surveying these perspectives—showing you how they inform our work from what we observe and notice to how we engage and connect, to how we assess and plan, to how we intervene—to help you articulate a planned rationale for your work. In our practice, across all types of agencies and roles, we need to be able to articulate a planned, intentional, and informed approach to our work. We need to be able to explain this to our supervisor, so they can support that work. We need to be able to explain this to young people and their families, so they are informed as to our involvement in their lives. We need to be able to explain this for ourselves, to help guide our time with young people. This is part of our professional responsibility.

Articulating your approach and rationale on a continual basis helps us advocate for both our continued work together and communicate to other professionals—your supervisor, colleagues, and others—to help them understand our contribution to young people's lives. Further, regularly checking in on how we understand a young person's situation and how we are participating in facilitating therapeutic change helps us track the progress of that intervention and whether it is effective. When we observe the outcomes of our work, we can then continue our work, alter it, and make decisions to best meet the needs of young people.

Listening to Young People

What experience do young people have of us attempting to engage and connect with them and support and facilitate therapeutic change with and alongside them? Iwasaki (2014) listened to young people as they reported on their experience of positive change. They highlighted the significance of "learning from experiences as life lessons," that "from suffering can come beautiful things," how "lived experience help[s] youth grow and develop," how "essential [it is] to find out strengths/talents of youth in order to 'love yourself and stand up on your own,'" "to discover and identify abilities, skills, and talents," "having an inspiring person and having a person who 'cares about you and trusts you'" who can "help generate strong hope and determination for a better life and positive growth," and to have opportunities "to help other youth" (p. 32). As we can see, our presence combined with the intentional use of skills, knowledge, and ways of being have significant impact on young people's lives—sometimes more than we will ever know.

Many Theories, Many Approaches to Change

We've explored many central and common perspectives of CYC practice in Chapter 1 and now many theories, models, and approaches to facilitating therapeutic change in this chapter. As we explored in Chapters 1, 6, and others, the eclectic approach of CYC practice includes many perspectives. What is central to yours? What have you learned in your CYC courses that you're now connecting with practice in your practicum setting?

Do not be surprised if you find these models of change and CYC approaches repeated throughout your credential and practicum placements. Despite the passage of time and your development of competency, learning is not linear in the sense where we move from Point A to Point B, to Point C. Rather, informed by experiential and transformative learning theory, learning can be viewed as a spiral—where we learn, shift, move around, circle, and return to the same concepts over and over, to greater degrees of depth and complexity—or a meander, with journeys, U-turns, and tangents wherever our learning needs to take us.

Be an adult role model. Finding housing or temporary shelter. Find a place for a young person to hang out after school. Finding out about other programs. Give out condoms. Have a conversation. Connect with the youth clinic. Finding a place where they can find something to eat. Getting kids in school. Helping older kids get jobs or plan for postsecondary. Helping with transit. Sharing a life skill. Challenging young people to think about what interests them and where they may go in the future. Getting kids home. Helping them get home with each other. Getting them rain jackets to stay dry. Dealing with teenage drama. Working through relationships. Developing confidence about body image. There is so much we do on a daily basis.
—Tom, CYC Practicum Supervisor

LEARNING JOURNAL

Keep writing in your learning journal to see how it can take you from observation and recall into a space of reflection, learning, and transformation. Try to focus this entry, and those for the next few weeks, on how you are participating in facilitating therapeutic change.

PRACTICE SCENARIOS

Take a look at the practice scenarios that conclude this chapter: "Lara's Names" and "Students' Strengths." Use the content in this chapter to inspire your thinking about the scenario.

Notice how the scenario may relate to your own situation at your current practicum placement, even if it is not exactly what you are experiencing. Consider the questions posed at the end of each scenario to help you expand and apply the concepts presented in this chapter.

SEMINAR GROUP AND COMMUNITY OF PRACTICE DISCUSSION QUESTIONS

We've covered a lot of territory in this chapter. Use this expansive territory as an opportunity to connect with your classmates and communities of practice. Consider addressing the following questions, then take the conversation from there and move it to where it needs to go.

1. What successes and challenges are you experiencing as you engage and connect with young people? What works? What doesn't? Under what circumstances?
2. What youth or pop culture are you seeing children and youth engage with? How are you using those observations to assist you in connecting and intervening?
3. Share an example of a daily life event you're using at your practicum site as an opportunity to connect, observe, and facilitate therapeutic change.
4. Share an example of an activity you plan to facilitate or have already facilitated at practicum. What went into the planning, facilitating, and evaluation stages? How did it go? What would you change and why? What would you do again and why?

> Change takes place in relationship. Unless you have built rapport or established trust that's positive, you're going to get nowhere.
> —John, CYC Student

IN CLOSING

This chapter has reviewed the multiple ways in which we have the opportunity to facilitate therapeutic change alongside young people, their families, in their communities. As you continue to learn what our foundational perspectives and approaches look like in greater depth in future coursework, you will also continue to be exposed to more advanced models and theories of change. Know and trust, however, that in your first year of coursework, which sets the foundation of your practicum courses and the rest of your credential, you are being exposed to the foundational concepts and skills you will need to be an effective practitioner. You are out in a practicum setting, experimenting, learning, and evolving your practice, and we trust that you have the ability to connect with youth. At its simplest—and yet significantly meaningful and complex—you are connecting with youth, offering them experiences that they might not have had the opportunity to explore if not in your presence. What you do with that privilege and responsibility is up to you.

PRACTICE SCENARIOS

Lara's Names

Lara is in the first few weeks of her practicum placement at the recreation centre. Her main goals are to develop strong relationships with a few kids, facilitate a few activities, and learn about helpful community resources. Her supervisor recommends that she try to learn at least three names of the kids she meets each day and at least one interesting thing about each of them.

Why would a supervisor advise a new practicum student of such a seemingly simple goal?

_____

_____

_____

Students' Strengths

Daniel considers himself a decent hockey player, so he was happy to learn his supervisor supported him taking the kids to the local ice arena for a field trip. Jay was excited to learn that her supervisor would connect her to the school's Gay-Straight Alliance club, as she attributes her high school's club as one of the main reasons she felt safe to come out at a young age. As an international student whose first language is not English, Huang felt language may be a barrier to connecting with the youth; however, her supervisor immediately connected her with a group of international students and her supervisor has already noticed how Huang is able to empathize with many of the challenges they experience. Suze is into graphic novels and notices many of the youth are too, so she connects with the librarian at her practicum to find out more.

Is there anything about your identity, personal interests, skills, hobbies, passions, or life experiences that may offer something unique to your practicum site and people?

_____

_____

_____

CHAPTER 8

Community and Organizational CYC Practice

Competencies for Professional Child and Youth Work Practitioners				
Professionalism	Cultural and Human Diversity	Applied Human Development	Relationship and Communication	Developmental Practice Methods
Law and Regulations Advocacy	Foundational Knowledge Cultural and Human Diversity Awareness and Inquiry Developmental Practice Methods	Contextual-Developmental Assessment		Program Planning and Activity Programming Community Engagement

Effecting change is about exploring all angles to a situation, and any input and commentary students can lend would surely be welcomed with open arms as it expands the scope of perspective for the organization. While it can be intimidating for students to speak up, particularly those who have minimal work experience, they should always be encouraged to voice their thoughts, opinions and insights during their time with an organization. This supports not only the organization, but also the student's own learning experience, which is the intent of the practicum itself.

—Malcolm McAuley, National Senior Director, Big Brothers Big Sisters

While much of our practice occurs in the immediate environments in which we find young people, working directly with children, youth, and families, we also bring our CYC practice and worldview to settings, roles, tasks, and activities in which we do not find young people but nonetheless influence their growth, development, and wellness. Particularly if you come to your Child and Youth Care (CYC) certificate, diploma, or degree with considerable experience, you may be in a practicum focused on organizational experiences. Or you may be in a direct care practicum working with young people but you nevertheless

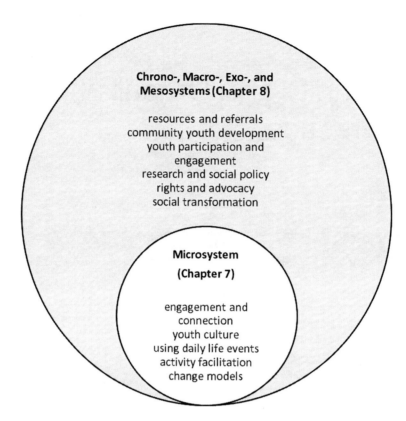

Figure 8.1: Therapeutic Change across Systems—Macro-System

have the opportunity to explore organizational activities at your site. In this chapter, we will explore the macro-level systems and environments in which we have the opportunity to support young people's therapeutic change. We will move through practice concepts including community development, youth participation, research and policy, rights and advocacy, and social transformation in order to expand the possibilities in which we see CYC practice applied. Meanwhile, we know you may have not yet taken courses on policy and legislation or rights and advocacy. Here, we will focus on what you may experience in your first or second practicum so that those courses may resonate even more when you take them.

> I encourage all students to meet with every member of the staff team to learn about their roles and see the bigger picture of how the organization operates.
> —Annie, CYC Practicum Supervisor

ORGANIZATIONAL SETTINGS, TASKS, AND ACTIVITIES

Leaders in the CYC field remind us that our practice exists on multiple levels. Particularly if you come to your certificate, diploma, or degree's first practicum with considerable work experience, you may be placed at a setting and/or in a role where you may not be working directly with young people but rather the environments and systems that influence their lives. Or you may be at a practicum setting where your primary role is to work directly with young people, but you may also be encouraged or ask to participate in tasks and activities that influence young people's lives but do not involve them directly. Or you may not be involved in these roles or settings, but you may be curious for the future. Any which way, it's important to see how CYC can provide a meaningful perspective to creating change across systems and settings.

Consider the following practicum placements that were more organizational in nature:

- A practicum student was placed at a foster care support site and developed a feedback survey for the families and children to complete regarding their experience of the services
- A practicum student was placed at a recreation centre working with youth in various programs but also spent time shadowing her supervisor in his supervisory role, learning about staff scheduling, interagency collaboration and planning meetings, and so on
- A practicum student was placed at a youth-research centre, where she looked at large datasets of health and developmental information of young people, exploring her own subject matter interest (e.g., help-seeking behaviours amongst youth, etc.)
- A practicum student was placed at a government representative's office, shadowing and learning from the policy analyst and constituent outreach program, focusing on child, youth, and family matters
- A practicum student wrote curriculum for a social-emotional support group from an Indigenous framework within an alternate school program for Indigenous children
- A practicum student at a street-outreach program actively involved himself at the interagency collaboration and planning meetings, contributing to the planning of a youth event
- A practicum student developed, wrote, and submitted a grant proposal for a summer youth employment program, while also working within a recreational centre

What does this list inspire you to do at your practicum site? What could you ask to be involved in before your practicum placement ends? Let's take a look at Figure 8.2 to see some organizational settings, tasks, and activities for inspiration.

COMMUNITY RESOURCES

When we widen our scope to all of the environments young people are influenced by, we can begin by looking at the community the practicum is located within. In the guidebook, you've been asked to reflect on a number of factors related to community: its diversity, its resources, and so on. Before we move forward, let's consider your practicum setting's community in more detail.

Once you develop relationships with the different agencies, they're more able to hear what the issues are.
—Donna, CYC Practicum Supervisor

Figure 8.2: Organizational Settings, Tasks, and Activities

One way we get to know our community is to learn more about its characteristics. While this information may seem distant from the moment-to-moment encounters we have at practicum, learning about our communities can provide context, especially when it comes to many of the successes and challenges young people and families face. Consider the questions listed below to understand your practicum's community in more detail. Ask your supervisor or colleagues for information and direction when needed.

What is the history of this community?

_____

How would you describe the community geographically? And what is it like to physically move through your community (e.g., public transit, roads, sidewalks, and other infrastructure)?

_____

What can you learn about this community's profile (e.g., Statistics Canada, etc.)?

_____

What Indigenous ancestral land is this community occupying? What is your practicum setting's relationship with the community's Indigenous representation (e.g., band, governance, etc.)?

_____

Who is the community represented by (e.g., municipal, provincial, federal, Indigenous representatives)?

_____

How does this community communicate to/among its members (e.g., local newspapers, forums, etc.)?

_____

What educational institutions, health authorities, and social services serve this community?

_____

Where are they located in relation to your practicum setting? How do they intersect with your practicum setting?

_____

Does this community have shared public spaces? Are they child-friendly?

_____

What are this community's unmet needs, social issues, or problems?

_____

What are this community's public assets and strengths?

_____

How are your practicum organization's clients' needs represented in the community?

_____

> Every school has their own way of working. You really have to ask questions about the system in place and how it works and how you can be a part of the system.
> —John, CYC Student

Community Assets

Understanding your community's assets is a valuable tool to help you support young people. Community assets are people, qualities, policies, resources, facilities, services, expertise, physical spaces, and more. Meanwhile, an asset is something that can be used to support people and develop solutions to social issues. Not all communities are the same. Through the eyes of young people at your setting, what are the community strengths and assets? A number of organizations across Canada have explored their community's strengths and assets geared to a particular topic (e.g., food, recreation, mental health) and/or to a particular population (e.g., street-entrenched youth, immigrant and refugee families). For example, Toronto's Danforth-East York community created a Healthy Kids Community Challenge (2016) and the Winnipeg Outreach Network (2018) created a Winnipeg Street Guide for street-involved youth. There are many, many more examples. Does your practicum's community have a strengths and assets map that could be of use to you in getting to know your community in more depth? Where could you find one? You could begin with neighbourhood, municipal, and First Nations band organizations. You could move on to specific educational institutions, health authorities, and prominent non-profit organizations in your area.

Meanwhile, you could create your own map. Complete Activity 8.1 to explore your practicum's community in more depth.

Activity 8.1: Asset Mapping in My Practicum Community

To explore your practicum's community in more depth, let's focus on a population and issue you're interested in.

1. Determine Your Scope

To narrow the scope of what you will explore, let's focus on a population and issue you're interested in. A population could be adolescent girls at a group home, parents of children at the school, support workers at the youth health clinic attached to the drop-in centre, and so on. A social issue could be food, leisure, shelters, and more. Then combine the two. Some examples are:

- free recreation and leisure activities for kids and their families in your area
- youth-friendly outdoor spaces in your area
- immigrant and refugee programs and services in your area
- youth recreation and leisure programs in your area
- subsidized/funded summer camps for kids in government care

- supports specifically helpful to street-entrenched youth (housing, food, medical, advocacy, legal, etc.)
- mental health programs and services for children and families

What population are you interested in supporting?

_____

What topic or social issue are you interested in exploring?

_____

2. Research Your Community

Brainstorm what you already know about the assets in your community that exist to support this population. Ask supervisors, staff, and young people about what resources exist in the community. Cross check with classmates for inspiration and ideas. Explore online by using relevant search terms and any mapping applications that could help your search. If possible, walk, drive, or transit around your community for the purpose of exploring resources. See the physical space, be surprised by what you find. Take notes.

_____

_____

_____

_____

3. Map It Out

Create a visual representation of what you find. A map suitable for a brochure? A small laminated card to fit in a wallet? A drawing? An infographic? Be creative. Try to make it youth-friendly, where the young people and families who you would want to show it to could easily read it, or perhaps take a copy with them for their own use.

Community Resources and Referrals

One reason to get to know our practicum placement's community is so that we can connect young people with appropriate supports and resources. One way we do that is through referrals. We work with young people and families who may need a variety of specialized supports and resources. In fact, we are often a referral from another resource. However, as we get to know them, through our work with them in one setting, we may decide that a particular resource, program, or service may be of additional support, particularly if it's outside our scope of practice or competency. Examples include:

> Students will meet other professionals in the area at agency meetings. Then all of a sudden they're able to say to me that they 'met a counsellor from this place and this young person was talking to me about some stuff going on with their medical condition and maybe I could connect them.'
> —Tom, CYC Practicum Supervisor

- A group home resident may be exploring her cultural roots
- You think a child may benefit from subsidized spring break or summer camps
- An elementary school child may be struggling with literacy
- You think a youth at risk of becoming involved in the criminal justice system may need some support for their mental health
- You notice a family may benefit from interpretation services
- You may wonder if a young person is being exploited
- A family may need some support dealing with conflict
- A young person needs help finding emergency shelter

Whatever the need we observe that may benefit from external supports—if we do not have the capacity to address it within our own program—we can look for other child and youth-friendly resources in the community. Work through Activity 8.2 to begin to develop your knowledge of various resources in your practicum's community. In this activity, we'll focus on one young person at your practicum site.

Activity 8.2: Making Recommendations and Referrals

In CYC practice, we will make recommendations and referrals with or on behalf of young people and their families. For this activity, think of one young person at your site you're working with and have come to know. Think of their situation, what unmet need you think would benefit from a referral to a resource. Perhaps it's a new group home resident and they've been asking you about fun and free activities in the neighbourhood. Maybe you've had a conversation with your supervisor about possible mental health services for a family. Notice that the referral or recommendation could be formal (i.e., requiring a formal referral from the caregiver or practitioner) or more informal (i.e., not requiring a formal referral, but you wish to recommend it to the young person you're working with). Whatever it is, begin by exploring your community's resources related to this need. Then move through the following steps.

1. Identify a young person you're working with.
2. Think of an unmet need in their life.

3. Identify three resources that you'd like to explore in more depth.

4. Explore their online presence first. Try to navigate each agency's website from the perspective of a young person or family's point of view.

5. Learn how to get to each resource via walking or transit and visit each resource.

6. Where appropriate,* visit the site. Introduce yourself to the person at the front desk, and ask for any information you can take away (e.g., a pamphlet, brochure, etc.).

7. Observe the interior and exterior space. What are people doing? Where are people hanging out? Is it child- or youth-friendly?

8. Return from the space and challenge yourself to describe it to a young person by practising with a classmate or your supervisor. How would you describe the program and space so as to help break that barrier for the young person?

(*Note that some resources on your list may not be possible to access physically, if, for example, their location is private. In that case, try to do the best you can to find out the information you need to know. Try to make contact in some way. In most cases, this will be a hypothetical exercise for research purposes. It may not be appropriate to make these recommendations at this point in time. Keep this knowledge in your toolbox, ready to retrieve when needed.)

COMMUNITY YOUTH DEVELOPMENT

When agencies are tasked with creating child- and youth-friendly program delivery and design, we can look at community-wide or interagency approaches. When looking at developing the community centres in Metro Vancouver, Martin and Tennant (2008) prioritized the importance of city-wide service planning that took into consideration:

1. Creation of a safe youth friendly environment;
2. One-to-one work to promote individual growth;
3. Integration of high-risk/special needs youth into community programs;
4. Collaborative planning both within the community centre and especially with other services involved in the life of the child/youth and family;
5. Small group development;
6. Advocacy for children, youth and their families;
7. Opportunities for children/youth to take on leadership and volunteer roles;
8. Support to resolve interpersonal conflict between children, youth, families and other community members; and
9. Assessment of crisis situations [with] appropriate interventions and referrals. (p. 22)

In other words, they looked at the community as a whole from the perspective of young people's needs. Does your practicum program fit into a wider initiative to meet the needs of young people? How so? Your supervisor will be a great resource to learn the connections between and among other child and youth-serving organizations that may be part of a community-wide strategy to meet the needs of young people. For example, the playground in the neighbourhood may be the result of a number of groups coming together to identify a need for children. Your in-patient hospital unit may be linked with the wider health authority's desire to meet the needs of children's specific developmental and mental health needs. Your street-outreach program may be the result of multiple levels of government coordinating with a group of non-profit organizations in the city. The skate-park your youth regularly access may be part of a city-wide initiative to create more public spaces for youth. The addition of an Elder to your community programming may be a part of a wider effort to meet the needs of Indigenous young people. The public health campaign

> We have to know how systems work and how the current system is working for the person we're working with and how it is not working to benefit them and the history of why this is.
> —Cody, CYC Student

you see on the walls of your practicum's entryway may be a result of prioritized funding to address the health of families across settings. The interagency collaboration group may be a result of multiple agencies coming together to address gaps in the system. Learning how your program, practitioners, and interagency connections fit within the community is essential for you to understand how we support (and do not support) its young people.

Positive Youth Development

One model we use to meet the needs of young people in our communities is through positive youth development. In Chapter 7, we touched on positive youth development from a micro-level system and environment. That is, using a positive youth development framework, we attempt to promote resilience, competence, self-determination, and more in our interactions with young people to foster growth, development, and wellness. We can also look to community-level planning that helps our young people thrive. Huebner (2003) outlines five Ps of positive youth development with the central questions we should be exploring (see Figure 8.3). As you read Figure 8.3, consider your practicum's community and what you've learned about it thus far. While this model uses youth-centric language, replace youth with "young people" or "child" or whatever is relevant to you.

Now, you probably will not be in charge of program planning at the city-wide level. However, your supervisor and practicum colleagues may be. Wouldn't it be a great opportunity to find out how they're involved, learn what conversations they're part of, and observe the necessary factors that go into making our communities more open, available, and inclusive to our young people? Whether you are involved in community-level planning or not, considering the questions above may help you widen the scope of your own practice with young people, making you more knowledgeable of, curious about, and facilitative of relationships among young people and their community.

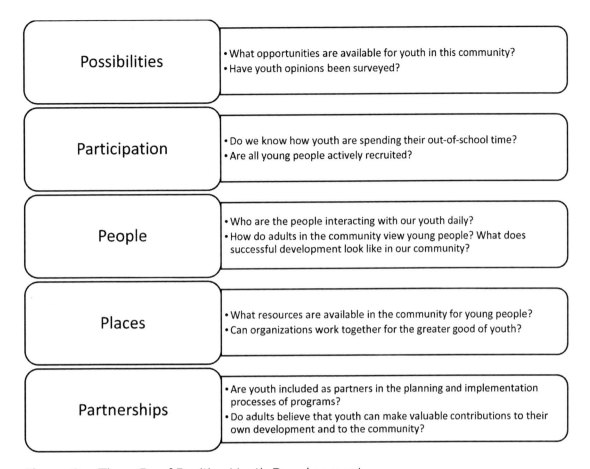

Figure 8.3: The 5 Ps of Positive Youth Development

Adapted from Huebner, A. J. (2003). Positive youth development: The role of competence. In F. A. Villarruel, D. F. Perkins, L. M. Borden, & J. G. Keith (Eds.), *Community youth development: Programs, policies, and practices* (pp. 352–353). Thousand Oaks, CA: SAGE.

YOUTH ENGAGEMENT AND PARTICIPATION

More and more, organizations are inviting a historically ignored yet crucial stakeholder into their organizational governance processes—the young people themselves. Engaging and involving young people in the design, implementation, and evaluation of programs, services, and practices that impact them seems like common sense. But until a few decades ago, it wasn't a thought that crossed people's minds. Gharabaghi and Anderson-Nathe (2015) give examples of involving young people in organizational activities including, but not limited to:

- Youth on advisory boards
- Youth advocacy groups
- Networks of young people in government care
- Youth presence in policy development and decision-making bodies

Why look at young people's participation in your practicum's organizational structure, service delivery, and policies? Not only do they affect young people directly, participation also quite literally builds the very capacities and skills we hope to promote in our direct work with young people. When young people participated in organizational decisions and governance, Ramey, Lawford, and Vachon (2017) noticed that young people were engaged; built relationships; improved interpersonal, self-regulation, leadership, and problem-solving skills; adopted new roles and responsibilities; and had greater knowledge of their community with opportunities to give back. Further, Iwasaki (2014) says that not only does meaningful youth engagement support youth development, it also helps change systems. (Later in this chapter, we will highlight the specific children's rights that advocate for young people to participate in the decisions that impact them.)

Before we look at your practicum site and how it involves young people, let's remind ourselves of what meaningful participation can look like. Figure 8.4 illustrates categories of participation and non-participation.

Looking at Figure 8.4, we move from non-participation to participation. For example, some programs have advisory boards with youth representatives. Some of those boards meaningfully engage those representatives in decisions. Some do not. When they do not involve young people in decisions, despite their physical presence on the board, this type of participation is referred to as *tokenism*. It all depends on the *meaningfulness* of the participation itself.

Your practicum setting—or the agency it is part of—will involve young people in some way in its decision-making. However, the depth, quality, meaning, authenticity, and impact of that involvement will vary across organization and groups. How has it come to be this way? Where would you put your practicum's agency on this ladder? Does it tokenize youth representation on the advisory committee, or does it actively involve young people in decisions? Have the young people themselves initiated involvement and influence, advocating for structural change? How is the agency thinking of changing? We can look to

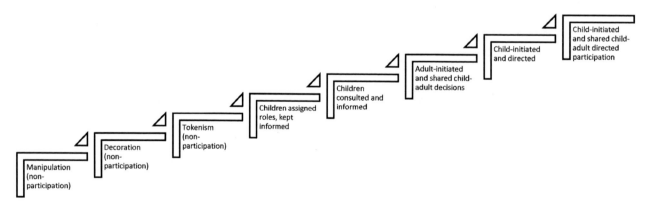

Figure 8.4: Hart's Participation Ladder

Adapted from Ramey, H. L., Lawford, H. L., & Vachon, W. (2017). Youth-adult partnerships in work with youth: An overview. *Journal of Youth Development, 12.*

many children- and youth-in-care networks for leadership on that front. While you're at practicum, take the opportunity to learn. Then check in with your practicum classmates to see how youth participation varies. You'll get a snapshot of what participation looks like, which will hopefully progress over time.

RESEARCH AND PROGRAM EVALUATION

When it comes to the macro-level factors that influence our work, we can look to research that guides our practice. By the very fact you're in practicum, you've been exposed to enough coursework, textbooks, course packs, and instructor expertise to see what research informs our practice. In this guidebook alone, we survey (albeit briefly) many CYC practice topics and the relevant literature.

Let's recall a course that CYC students take early on in their programs: lifespan development or child and youth development. You take this foundational course so you are exposed to developmental knowledge that you can then integrate into your practice. We apply this knowledge each day we work alongside young people and their families: the words we choose, the activities we design, the observations and assessments we make of young people, and the goals we set with them. All of this should be based on research: studying the needs, trajectories, issues, and interventions with young people, hopefully across settings, contexts, and cultures. Over the completion of your certificates, diplomas, and degrees, including your future practicum placements, you will also be exposed to a wide variety of best practice, evidence-based practice, and practice-based evidence. You may also get to take courses understanding and facilitating research in CYC. But how does research inform your practicum setting? Ask. Just as your practicum program and its practitioners will have a theoretical orientation that guides their practice, they too will have practices—program designs, interventions, and more—informed by research. In fact, you may consider yourself an active participant in the research and knowledge dissemination chain: you are being exposed to research, you consume research, you seek out research to inform your practice, and you actively apply knowledge from that research in the settings and roles you find yourself in. Did you know that is what you are doing?

Take, for example, Deanna, a CYC practicum student placed in a residential group home for adolescent girls in government care. As she immersed herself into the site, she quickly learned that the staff was evolving to integrate trauma-informed practice into every aspect of their work with the residents. Many organizations are adopting trauma-informed principles and practices at their direct-service, staff-team, leadership, and policy-making levels. At its core, trauma-informed principles of practice include 1) trauma-awareness without a need for trauma-disclosure; 2) an emphasis on safety (physical, social, emotional, spiritual, cultural) and a focus on building trust; 3) creating environments that provide "opportunity for choice, collaboration, and connection" by fostering "a sense of efficacy, self-determination, dignity, and personal control"; and 4) strengths-based practice focusing on skill building and empowerment (Centre of Excellence for Women's Health, 2013, pp. 13–14). While Deanna was at her practicum placement, she decided to invite herself to a trauma-informed workshop for the agency staff, find current peer-reviewed research on trauma-informed practice for adolescent girls in residential group homes, and take an active role in the weekly team meetings where they discussed the needs of the residents. You can hopefully see how aligned trauma-informed practice can be alongside foundational CYC practices.

Nathan, a CYC practicum student placed at an elementary school supporting kids deemed to have behavioural issues, noticed mindfulness practices were being adopted by individual practitioners (teachers, support workers, etc.), as well as by the school itself. He noticed that during morning announcements, they practise mindfulness breathing. There were group activities that practised mindfulness techniques. The classrooms were stocked with colouring books, stress balls, as well as mindfulness apps on the classroom tablets. During one-on-one conversations with support staff, kids were encouraged to practise mindfulness to de-escalate crisis, encourage emotional awareness and literacy, and so on. He even saw that some of these mindfulness practices were being communicated with parents through the school's monthly newsletter. Not entirely aware of mindfulness techniques and philosophy, or the research behind it, he decided to ask the principal, his supervisor, some support staff, and some teachers he'd gotten to know. He was given some articles to read and some videos to watch about the outcomes of these activities for children, was encouraged to visit the classrooms to observe more, and began to practise mindfulness techniques himself.

What research—principles, standards, best practices, evidence-based practice, practice-based evidence, and so on—guides and informs your practicum site? Is it positive youth development? Trauma-informed practice? Mindfulness? Attachment? Harm reduction? Restorative justice? List them on the lines below. How can you observe this research being implemented? How do the young people at your site experience these practices? Write your observations below. Ask not only your supervisor but various support staff at the site, from different disciplines, if you can. Have conversations and get enough information to see threads that form. There may be one overarching practice, or there may be many. If the research is unfamiliar to you, ask to learn more. Hopefully your supervisor will link you to resources. Meanwhile, don't stop there. Bring these ideas back to the classroom as you take more classes.

_____

_____

_____

_____

_____

Connected to research is program evaluation. Programs are required to evaluate their services now more often than not, due to accreditation and other standardized quality assurance practices. How does your program check in with itself to see if it's effective? Does it survey its young people or families? Does it follow particular standards? Does it measure outcomes or track progress in some way? Find out! The next time you meet with your supervisor, be sure to ask them. One way to search on your own is to look at your program's agency's Annual General Reports. They'll have basic information shared within that document—sometimes a combination of program descriptions, descriptive statistics (e.g., number of people served, program attendance), participant voices and feedback (e.g., quotes from young people and their families), and other administrative reports and information (e.g., funding revenues and service expenditures). Pause reading this guidebook right now, and go look for a recent report. What did you learn that you did not already know about the program and its agency? Write the name of the report and a few new things you learned in the space provided.

> Students are offered the opportunity to attend outside events and meetings to better understand the work of the agency in the context of the systems and agencies operating in the province.
> —Annie, CYC Practicum Supervisor

_____

_____

_____

SOCIAL POLICY AND LEGISLATION

Just as research and program evaluation informs and guides the practicum settings we're currently participating in, so too does social policy and legislation. Social policies are the guidelines, principles, and actions of governments and groups concerned with improving the social conditions of people in communities. Legislation is one form of social policy: collective laws put forth by governments that direct practitioners, programs, and services. Social policy includes areas of education, welfare, justice, social services, health, and more, intersecting with some of the most complex issues of our communities.

> Learn about the foster care system as well as advocates at provincial and local levels.
> —Farah, CYC Practicum Supervisor

Hann (2017) transitioned from a direct care environment to a policy development agency during her CYC graduate-level practicum, saying she'd dreamt of "generating change at a systemic level, participating in the development of policies that attempt to guide and govern CYC practices on the ground" (p. 30). In this practicum, she wasn't sure what to wear, had to read more background material and files than she wanted to, felt intimidated by the overuse of acronyms and impossible timelines, felt isolated, and missed developing relationships with young people. Thankfully, this soon shifted. In fact, she found where her "CYC approach could be beneficial; respectfully engaging stakeholders by meeting them where they were at, considering the developmental stages and utilizing cultural competency, to name a few," as well as understanding the intricacies of written and oral communication, developing relationships across departments and purposes, and perhaps, most importantly, beginning to "recognize opportunities to amplify the voice of the young people." She found herself re-energized for her work when she returned to direct work with young people (p. 33). You may not be in a practicum that focuses on research and policy, or have the chance until your own graduate work or after a few years in the field. However, you may want to think about what it might look like, as more CYC practitioners are entering into various levels of service delivery, including the top of many organizations and institutions, as political representatives, advocates, and ministry executives and so on.

While we're not always aware of them, social policies and legislation directly impact the young people and families we work alongside and the work we do with them. As you move through your CYC programs, you will become more informed about these policies and legislation, perhaps even with a goal to become more involved in their development in your future career. (We certainly hope you do!) For now, however, let's survey the social issues, social policies, and legislation that intersect with your practicum site. When you take a future course on policy and practice, you'll be glad you did.

What social issues impact the young people and families at your practicum setting and/or its surrounding community? Pay attention to conversations, newspaper articles, and complaints you've learned about since beginning at your practicum setting. What are they?

✓ Public transportation?   ✓ Access to health care?   ✓ Climate change?
✓ Social isolation?   ✓ Sex education in   ✓ Violence?
✓ Affordable housing?   schools?   ✓ Poverty?
✓ Affordable child care?   ✓ School closures?   ✓ Racism?
✓ Program cuts?   ✓ Shared public space?   ✓ _____
✓ Youth employment?   ✓ Safe drinking water?   ✓ _____

Take, for example, Jordie, a CYC practicum student placed at a mentoring program for Indigenous youth. During his time there, he participated in a number of discussions, read many newspaper articles, and saw several consequences of the unjust conditions many of the youth experience on a daily basis, including racism and micro-aggressions in public spaces and discrimination while attempting to obtain employment. He noticed how the Indigenous youth were also disproportionately in government care, experienced less success in the school system, and did not have full access to their culture because of the long-standing effects of cultural genocide of Indigenous peoples and intergenerational effects of trauma. What social policy and legislation supports and hinders their experience?

Consider the situation of Selena, a CYC practicum student placed at a neighbourhood support program, working primarily with immigrant families with young children. On a daily basis, she sees the effects of the lack of quality affordable housing, access to affordable child care, low wages and unstable employment, difficulty accessing family health care, high levels of stress, and so on. What social policy and legislation supports and hinders the experiences of these families?

In our work, social policy and legislation will directly and indirectly impact the lives of the young people we work with, including municipal, provincial, federal, and international laws; principles; conventions; and agreements. These can include:

- Municipal: by-laws, etc.
- Provincial: child welfare acts, social assistance acts, etc.
- Federal: *Canada Health Act*, *Youth Criminal Justice Act*, Jordan's Principle, etc.
- International: United Nations *Convention on the Rights of the Child*, *Declaration on the Rights of Indigenous Peoples*, *Convention on the Rights of Persons with Disabilities*

Since we work alongside some of the most vulnerable, marginalized people in our communities, we notice how young people and families are struggling and how some social policy and legislation supports them; some does not go far enough, and some entirely neglects their needs and well-being. Continue to explore the social policies that relate to your practicum agency's young people.

> They would take me to the courts, meetings, and to the social worker's office. I saw the whole picture and how the agency is working with other agencies providing the service they do.
> —Harman, CYC Student

CHILDREN'S RIGHTS AND ADVOCACY

Throughout our CYC education, we discuss the rights of children and youth. We often find ourselves in the situation where, because of our work in their life-space, we have the opportunity to advocate on their behalf. When we take an advocacy role, we can look to international conventions and agreements, such as the United Nations *Convention on the Rights of the Child* (UNCRC), the United Nations *Declaration on the Rights of Indigenous Peoples* (UNDRIP), and the United Nations *Convention on the Rights of Persons with Disabilities* (UNCRPD). While you may not have explored all these conventions and agreements in depth, you likely have been exposed to or learned briefly about some of their contents. Do you remember the articles included within them?

Ramey, Lawford, and Vachon (2017) and Cech (2015) remind us that within the UNCRC there are specific articles to help us form positions and arguments as we advocate for young people's needs:

- ✓ Article 12 (give opinion and be listened to)
- ✓ Article 13 (find out things and share what you think)
- ✓ Article 15 (join or set up a group)
- ✓ Articles 12 and 23 (full participation)
- ✓ Articles 16 and 17 (rights to information)
- ✓ Article 18 (accessible and affordable care)
- ✓ Articles 19, 28, 34, 37, and 38 (protection from harm, abuse, and exploitation)
- ✓ Article 24 (protection from environmental toxins)

When we see the daily consequences of structural barriers and systemic oppression that influence young people's well-being and access to opportunity and success, we become advocates for change. Walker (2003) reported youth workers believe advocacy is their central responsibility, where

> They feel passionate about connecting young people to resources, advocating for their rights, battling negative community perceptions about youth, generating support for youth development programs, speaking out against injustices, and promoting partnerships and inclusion of young people in the spectrum of community affairs. (p. 386)

Meanwhile, our standards of practice—including both our code of ethics and competencies—state that advocacy is part of our role and responsibilities. We can be advocates for people, causes, issues, and change, on the individual, group, or societal level.

Hamlet (2017) reminds practicum students—in this case, in school settings—there are many opportunities for micro- and macro-level advocacy efforts.

Hamlet's Micro and Macro Advocacy

1. Advocate with or for a student
2. Remove barriers restricting access to resources and opportunities
3. Use consultation, collaboration, or referrals
4. Collaborate with a local group or organization
5. Create an advocacy plan
6. Identify a problem within a system
7. Collaborate and consult to effect change in a specific system
8. Inform the public of issues
9. Communicate through reports and committees
10. Collaborate with councils and community groups
11. Address policies, laws, and legislation
12. Present at boards and in front of legislators
13. Involve oneself in a professional association

Adapted from Hamlet, H. S. (2017). *School counseling practicum and internship: 30 essential lessons* (p. 79). Los Angeles, CA: SAGE.

How do you advocate for the young people you work alongside? How does it empower the young people you work alongside, helping them develop their voices, rather than disempower by speaking for them? How does advocacy fit within your current practicum placement? What does advocacy look like? If advocacy is not part of your practicum setting, why not?

SOCIAL TRANSFORMATION

When we think about our practice—the moments we share with young people, the services we design for them, the advocacy we do to promote their well-being, and so on—ultimately, we are calling for a more caring, responsive society to meet the needs for all its people, especially its most vulnerable and marginalized. To do so, we call for transformation of the very systems and society of which we are a part. Tilsen (2018) asks, "What does it look like when youth and youth workers work for social transformation?" (p. 147). In her youth work text, she describes two scenarios of child and youth practitioners who consider social transformation central to their roles, and who creatively applied advocacy into their work directly with young people. As you read, notice how they integrate community youth development, participation, social policy, and advocacy into their work.

> I got to take part in the annual staff meeting and I saw their CEO talk about the goals for the agency and funding. We had the opportunity to speak our own voice about it. It shows that your voice does matter.
> —Trina, CYC Student

Tilsen's Transformational Youth Work

Marjaan was part of a community group organizing a forum for mayoral candidates. He created a youth panel that participated in the creation of the forum. As a staff member of a transitional living program and drop-in centre for youth, he also collaborated with the youth to bring their concerns to the forum. Marjaan held conversations with the young people to discuss the election and solicit their ideas about what issues they thought the candidates should speak to. He made a poster titled, "If You Could Ask the Mayor a Question, What Would It Be?" on which youth wrote questions on sticky notes. Marjaan curated their questions for the forum so that the moderator was sure to ask them. He provided transit tokens for young people who wanted to attend the forum. Marjaan and the organizers prioritized the youth in attendance who wanted to ask a question directly of the candidates.

Emily works in a youth-led organization that challenges and seeks to transform conventional institutional structures that maintain a hard line between staff and youth. Her program features a youth advisory board. The agency pays the youth members and provides training and support for them, just as it does for the adult staff members of the management team. The youth make program and policy decisions, including those related to contracts and funding, and have direct access to the executive leadership of the organization. For example, the rapid rehousing program for queer and trans youth run by the agency is the brainchild of queer youth who identified culturally specific housing as a need and brought this to management. Youth served as consultants advising the creation of the program.

Adapted from Tilsen, J. (2018). *Narrative approaches to youth work: Conversational skills for a critical practice* (pp. 147–148). New York, NY: Routledge.

After reading about Marjaan and Emily's efforts, what do they inspire you to do? You do not have to think of a new program or initiative, nor would you typically have the opportunity to do so as a practicum student in a first- or second-year practicum placement. Instead, think of your context, your practicum site. Think of the young people's (or just one young person's) needs. What social transformation do you feel compelled to participate in? Have your practicum experiences thus far heightened your awareness?

_____

_____

_____

You do not have to know the answer. What you must do is consider and become aware of the systemic barriers and oppressions that do not serve the young people we work alongside. Then try to do something about it.

Truth and Reconciliation

As briefly discussed in Chapter 6, individuals, groups, and communities in Canada are engaging in a process of truth and reconciliation with Indigenous communities. As all social service, health, and educational institutions engage in this discussion too, it's incumbent upon us, as CYC learners, to learn about this discussion and what we are responsible for participating in, to redress many of the historical wrongs and present conditions that have been perpetrated by Canada as a nation, along with its institutions, social policy, and legislation. This includes us, as a profession. We can begin with the Truth and Reconciliation Commission of Canada's (2015) Calls to Action as a place to enter this discussion. Or we can begin by listening and learning. Wherever we start, we have the opportunity to understand, in a very real way, what our practicum agencies are doing to engage in this ongoing dialogue.

What does truth and reconciliation mean to the people at your practicum site? What does it mean to its Indigenous people, its settler-visitors? What does truth and reconciliation look like? How are wrongs addressed? Who is involved? What is being done? What will be done? What does this process look like?

_____

_____

_____

The TRC (2015) outlined 94 Calls to Action, many of which are relevant to the educational, social service, justice, and health settings in which CYC practicum placements exist. Consider the following excerpts and how they may relate to your practicum setting, keeping in mind that our roles and programs often intersect through multiple domains and institutions.

Table 8.1: The TRC's Calls to Action

The Truth and Reconciliation Commission of Canada Calls to Action		
Call to Action #5 Child Welfare "develop culturally appropriate parenting programs for Aboriginal families" (p. 1)	Call to Action #10 Education "developing culturally appropriate curricula" (p. 2)	Call to Action #22 Health "recognize the value of Aboriginal healing practices and use them" (p. 3)
Call to Action #23 Health "provide cultural competency training for all health-care professionals" (p. 3)	Call to Action #38 Justice "commit to eliminating the overrepresentation of Aboriginal youth in custody" (p. 4)	Call to Action #66 Youth Programs "establish multi-year funding for community-based youth organizations to deliver programs on reconciliation" (p. 8)

Adapted from TRC. (2015). *Truth and Reconciliation Commission of Canada: Calls to action.* Winnipeg, MB: Author.

We see evidence of successful and unsuccessful attempts at this process as we move forward in this discussion. In elementary and secondary schools, you may see the presence of more historically accurate narratives of Canada's history, or you may see an increase of Indigenous support workers. In child welfare, health, and youth justice settings, you may see more culturally responsive programming and intervention and cultural safety training for staff. In community recreation settings, you may see more celebration of Indigenous communities. Or you may not. We see evidence of successful and unsuccessful attempts in this ongoing dialogue. Pay attention to the settings in which you take part as a CYC learner, whether it be your postsecondary classrooms, your practicum setting, or your friends and family at home. As CYC practitioners with a vested interest in caring for vulnerable and marginalized young people and their families, we have the opportunity to be at the forefront of this conversation and this change.

Ultimately, we attempt to enact socially just change at micro- and macro-levels, which of course there is endless opportunity to do so. This change is only limited by our ability to perceive and be responsive to the unjust conditions in which people live along with our ability to move through complex systems designed to work better for some people than others. In essence, we work within the constraints of the systems we are part of, hoping to change those very constraints to allow for greater liberation for young people. Modlin and Newbury (2016) list socially just practices in CYC that can include:

- Re-considering what constitutes foundational knowledge in our field of practice

- Working relationally with leaders and policy-makers to ensure support for important opportunities for informal connection in communities
- Forging partnerships with young people so they can represent themselves when it comes to decisions or programs that have direct implications on their lives
- Ensuring access to important cultural practices and teachings that might not (presently) be part of mainstream education or interventions
- Lobbying to eliminate barriers to access or succeed in activities or events to which certain young people are often excluded for reasons beyond their control
- Ensuring young people have opportunities not only to receive services but to contribute to social life on the basis of their own gifts and passions (p. 18)

The community and organizational efforts we engage in can be wide-scale or narrow, big or small. It can be the march you organize or the march you attend with a young person. It can be the policy you write or the policy you use to advocate for your young person's rights. It can be the program you design or the program you refer a young person to. Whatever it is, it is our job to become increasingly aware of the systems of which we are a part, in order to change them.

LEARNING JOURNAL

Keep using your learning journal to reflect on your experiences at practicum. As you approach assignment due dates, remember to use your learning journal as "field notes." Case studies, agency profiles, and learning plans will be more detailed and informed with the learning you've done in this journal.

PRACTICE SCENARIOS

Take a look at the Practice Scenarios that conclude this chapter: "Jenna's Advocacy" and "Truth and Reconciliation." Use the content in this chapter to inspire your thinking about each scenario. Notice how the scenarios may relate to your own situation at your current practicum placement, even if they are not exactly what you are experiencing. Consider the questions posed at the end of each scenario to help you expand and apply the concepts presented in this chapter.

SEMINAR GROUP AND COMMUNITY OF PRACTICE DISCUSSION QUESTIONS

Conversations and discussions are endless when we expand our perspective to include macro-level systems and environments in our CYC practice. Consider the following questions for your discussion groups:

1. What social issues are influencing the lives of young people at your practicum?
2. How are young people involved in the design and delivery of programs at your practicum site?

3. What research and best practices guide your program's delivery, and how has that changed over time?

4. What legislation, acts, policies, and rights are relevant to the young people at your site? How are they implemented?

5. How are your practicum setting's leadership, programs, and practitioners participating in Canada's Truth and Reconciliation Commission's Calls to Action?

6. What acts are you taking part in to create more socially just conditions for the young people at your practicum?

IN CLOSING

This chapter has focused on the macro-level systems and environments in which we work and influence young people. Through a discussion of community development, youth participation, research, social policy, advocacy, and social transformation, we have journeyed through more environments that have the opportunity to effect change. You will be exposed to these concepts throughout your future classes, as you advance in your studies and practice. Continue this learning. Continue this effort. Our work is not limited to the immediate environments with young people, though it is always informed by this practice-based knowledge. We too can have an impact on the macro-system around us, thereby promoting the growth, development, and well-being of young people and families.

PRACTICE SCENARIOS

Jenna's Advocacy

Jenna's practicum placement is at a secondary school from September to June. Since beginning just a month or so ago, she's noticed it is more of a conservative community, which is different than what she has experienced at school herself. For example, she's overheard that during the recent municipal election, there was a lot of debate at the school district level and by city councillors who were not supporting the move to gender-neutral bathrooms. She read some recent newspaper articles and social media posts to see what people were saying. Jenna feels committed to trans-advocacy because she's learned that youth who identify as transgender experience disproportionate levels of violence at school, mental health struggles, disengagement from school, and increased risk for suicide. Jenna's partner identifies as nonbinary, and she's becoming more aware of just how unsafe schools can be for gender nonconforming students. She's noticed her supervisor, a few teachers at the school, and the youth at the alternate program where she spends most of her time are mad about these political discussions and feel they do not represent their opinions or experience.

They are brainstorming how they can advocate in ethical and effective ways to increase school safety.

What types of advocacy activities would you suggest Jenna bring to the group that are youth-friendly, participatory, and focus on trans-youth safety in schools that Jenna could contribute to within the scope of her practicum?

_____

_____

_____

Truth and Reconciliation

At the students' most recent practicum seminar, their faculty-instructor asked everyone to reflect on what truth and reconciliation means to them; during the following seminar, they will discuss their reflections. Tara believes it means to become a good ally alongside Indigenous people. Davina believes it means to tell the stories of her grandparents and great-grandparents so that no one will ever forget the cultural genocide that happened through centuries of racist assimilation policy. Seth believes it means working through his struggles with his relationship with organized religion and reaffirming his commitment to spirituality. Junie and Ari believe it means connecting with stories from communities across the globe and across time, from people who have experienced similar historical atrocities and current sociopolitical conditions. Simon doesn't know where to begin.

How would you participate in a conversation on truth and reconciliation? What does it mean to you? How do you see truth and reconciliation discussed in your practicum seminar and/or community of practice? How can everyone's voice be included?

_____

_____

_____

CHAPTER 9

Challenging and Challenges in CYC Practice

Competencies for Professional Child and Youth Work Practitioners				
Professionalism	Cultural and Human Diversity	Applied Human Development	Relationship and Communication	Developmental Practice Methods
Awareness of the Profession Professional Development and Behaviour Personal Development and Self-Care Professional Ethics Law and Regulations			Relationship Development Teamwork and Professional Communication	Behavioural Guidance

The most important lessons to be learned is that certainty and "easy shifts" are overrated; good practice always unfolds in the context of not knowing and feeling slightly overwhelmed!
> —Kiaras Gharabaghi, Associate Professor and Director, School of Child and Youth Care, Ryerson University

There is no question about it. We work amid challenge. We respond to challenging situations, navigate challenging relationships, are governed by challenging policy and practice, and practice within challenging systems, with the opportunity to challenge taken-for-granted worldviews about our very practice itself. By *challenge*, we do not necessarily mean a negative experience (but it can mean that). Rather, we mean that our practice involves complexity, contradiction, conflict, complication, messiness, uncertainty,

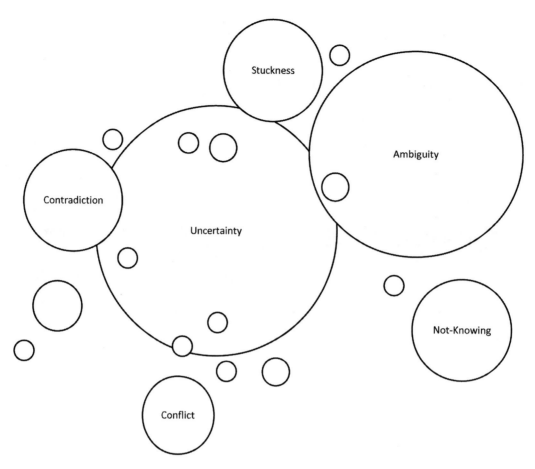

Figure 9.1: Challenges and Uncertainty

discomfort, ambiguity, and the feeling of being stuck. It also involves matters of ethical considerations, violations, dilemmas, and choices. By challenge, we mean that we must recognize this complexity as a central part of our practice, rather than work against it as something that comes up once in a while. Some may say that challenge *is* our practice and being able to respond well within challenging encounters and environments is an important way of being that we are developing as Child and Youth Care (CYC) practitioners. Many scholars, practitioners, and leaders in the CYC field have written on the inherent complexity and challenges in and among our practice, with guidance for new practitioners. This chapter calls attention to some of the challenges we may experience in practicum and the opportunities available to us to navigate those challenges.

CHALLENGES

Before we review challenges that we can expect to encounter in practicum, let's begin with reflecting on the challenges you have already experienced or are currently experiencing. Don't let them pass you by. To help you reflect, consider looking through your learning journal or recalling conversations from your seminar discussion, community of practice, or with your supervisor, colleagues, and instructor. Ask yourself the following questions:

- When have I felt stuck, not knowing what to do?
- When have I felt discomfort or unease?
- When have I felt at odds with or questioned an action, decision, or policy?
- When have I noticed a conflict or contradiction between points of view?
- What situations have I encountered where there was no clear way to respond?
- What has seemed messy and unpredictable?
- When have I witnessed clear violations of ethical standards or unclear or competing paths forward?
- What has challenged you: your practice, your values, your knowledge, ways of being?

_____

_____

_____

If you give yourself enough time, your list could become quite extensive. (And that's okay. It does not signify incompetence, inability, or that you're not in the right place.) If you analyze your list, you may see the challenges that can be felt at both the micro- and macro-levels. We respond to challenging situations, navigate challenging relationships, are governed by challenging policy and practice, and practice within challenging systems, with the opportunity to challenge taken-for-granted worldviews about our very practice itself. Let's look at Figure 9.2 to see some common types of challenges. If you wish, mark up the figure and categorize the challenges you've brainstormed above into the various sections. Note any themes that emerge. Meanwhile, let's explore some of these challenges in more detail and depth along with the opportunities they present.

> Recall past experiences where they have overcome challenges that seemed insurmountable at first, and what resources they called upon to be able to do so.
> —Kristy, CYC Faculty-Instructor

CHALLENGING SITUATIONS AND BEHAVIOUR

In day-to-day CYC practice, we will encounter many challenging situations. When it comes to early practicum placements, the following examples of interpersonal, engagement, and behavioural challenges are common:

- ✓ We may have a difficult time relating or connecting to the young person.
- ✓ We may be yelled or swore at or ignored and may personalize these interactions.
- ✓ We may not like the young person or they may not like us.
- ✓ We may try to "do for" rather than "do together."

Figure 9.2: Challenges across Systems

✓   The young people we work with may display behaviour that we consider problematic, disruptive, or inappropriate.

✓   The young people we work with may be struggling with a behaviour in a way that makes us uneasy in some kind of way, and so on.

In these kinds of challenging situations, Stenbeck (2018) encourages self-reflection, where we may encourage ourselves to explore where the anxiety is coming from, learn more about the young person's background and the environment. Moore (2019) speaks directly to new practitioners' internal struggle to separate themselves from young people. New practitioners, regardless of context, are at risk to "interpret the actions of youth as a measure of their own success or failure," such as a CYC practitioner who describes a "good shift' [as] one in which there were no escalated behaviours from the youth" (Moore, 2019, pp. 34–35). The goal is to get to a place of focusing on the relationship and its learning opportunities, as opposed to personalizing the encounter. Kostouros (2018) shares a story from her time as an emerging practitioner, working with young offenders. After regularly being told off by a teenage boy, she snapped, yelling back at him. Later on, when she drove home, she felt awful about her behaviour and realized that his behaviour could have been coming from a place of seeking connection. She put aside her ego and connected with him the next day to apologize for her behaviour and also inquire about his behaviour. It led to an opportunity for repair, insight, vulnerability, and further connection. She learned that he was acting out toward her because he wanted to work with her, because he'd seen how she connected well with the other youth. This was the only way he knew how to command her attention. This CYC practitioner provided an added opportunity for relationship development: repair (one we often overlook).

> We encourage our students to not take things personally. Make sure you debrief it with staff. Never leave feeling that you're the worst person, that you're not a good person, that you messed up. Talk to staff right away. I want students to leave thinking that they did so many incredible things today with so many incredible youth.
>
> —Tom, CYC Practicum Supervisor

Think of the young people you work with in your practicum setting. Do you have an example of when you interpreted an action of a young person as your own failure? Is there a time you can recall when a young person was perhaps trying to connect, but not doing so in a way you noticed at the time? How can we look through these challenging encounters and behaviours to see the opportunity that resides within them? Reflection is key, and it doesn't have to happen in the moment.

Problems

Since practicum is an opportunity to apply what you're learning in the classroom to practise, observe, experiment, and develop as a practitioner, then take that learning back to the classroom, it is important to hover around this idea of problems. Often, the very fact that our position as a CYC practitioner has been created, or the program in which we operate exists, is because someone identified a problem and decided to allocate funds to address that problem. It is important to be aware that this is the context in which we are working. Thus, it is difficult to disrupt and bring in new perspectives. "But I'm a strengths-based practitioner," you may say. Yes, we hope you are. However, we continue to work within services and among practitioners who maintain a focus on problems. Further, we work within contexts that situate problems inside young people, which then becomes the focus of intervention. This has consequences for how we practise. Where are we locating the problem?

From Deficit-Finding to Strength-Building

Looking at CYC as a whole, Gharabaghi and Phelan (2011) challenge the worldview and practice approach where "problems are seen as behaviours to be shaped, controlled, and stimulated at a very surface level" (p. 89). Looking at residential care programs specifically, Brockett and Anderson-Nathe (2013) observe a preference for "behaviour modification and rule-compliance over opportunities for authentic relational engagement and facilitation of new insight with young people whose problematic behaviours may also demonstrate resilience and agency" (p. 7). They say that, as CYC practitioners, we have opportunity to see the many meanings of behaviour including "understanding how young people adapt to and make sense of themselves in context… [where] workers can reframe all behaviours, even problematic ones, through a lens of strength and adaptation" (p. 10). Across practicum settings—educational, residential, and community—do you observe practices that value control and compliance rather than connection and relationship? How so?

Focusing on resiliency as opposed to problematic behaviour, Ungar (2004) tells the story of "the foul-mouthed, conduct-disordered young girls they encounter, though arguably more at risk by conventional standards, are less stereotypically passive and view themselves… as healthier than their peers who express themselves in gender-appropriate ways that result in their remaining silent" (p. 360). Can you recall a situation where a young person was "acting out" or being "disruptive" in some way at your practicum? Could their behaviour instead be interpreted as strength and resilience?

> We walk students through a challenge the same way we walk the kids through their challenges. By believing in their inherent worth. Helping recognize their strengths, and empowering them to make a decision that works for them.
> —Farah, CYC Practicum Supervisor

Anglin (2002, 2014) looks at young people's problematic behaviour through a lens of pain. That is, we interpret young people's "acting out" through a place of understanding: a young person could be moved to anger because they are experiencing pain in the present or from the past. If we see behaviour through pain, it encourages us to be compassionate toward a young person and understand why they may be behaving in a disruptive way. He says, "responding with understanding and respect does not necessarily prevent such outbursts, but can turn problems into learning opportunities" (Anglin, 2014, p. 54). We can be responsive rather than reactive; use influence rather than control; challenge young people with choices; and do with, not do to, all while reading young people's actions through a lens of pain-based behaviour (Anglin, 2002).

As a result, we can change our practice from a place of deficit-finding to a place of strength-building. Because one of CYC's core perspectives is strengths-based practice, we offer a lot to many settings, which continue to be dominated by deficit-finding practices. Strengths-based practice tells us we cannot only identify and build on young people's capacities, interests, abilities, and so on, but we also come from a place of respect and dignity, with an inherent hope and optimism for their growth and wellness. This is not to say that by focusing on strengths, we ignore problems. Rather, it means problems can help to inform our perspective and response, where we trust that focusing on and building strengths will impact and address those very problems. How can a focus on resilience, strength, and a re-interpretation of problematic behaviour help us to connect and intervene with young people? How does your practicum context focus on building strengths, rather than finding deficits?

CHALLENGING RELATIONSHIPS

Since we develop relationships as well as work relationally, we will encounter challenges relational in nature. It is all part of our work.

Above, we read the story of how Kostouros (2018) engaged in relationship repair with a young person. This was a challenging situation, but it also yielded opportunity for modelling relationship repair, where this CYC practitioner gave this young person the opportunity to see what a relationship can look like through conflict with a positive outcome. The young people in our lives may not always get to see these kinds of outcomes. Have you had the chance to do repair work with a young person with whom you experienced any kind of conflict? What was that like? How was that just as important as the engagement and connection you first developed with them?

Another example of a challenge in relationships with young people is the development of boundaries. In Chapter 3, we explored developing healthy boundaries in CYC practice. How have boundaries shown up in your practicum site? Consider some of the following examples of boundaries showing up in early practicum experiences. We may notice:

- We feel pulled to describe our relationships with young people as friends, rather than our way of being as friendly
- We are compelled to disclose personal experiences, information that may not be in young people's best interest
- We are compelled to over-extend our role, and, for example, give out our personal phone number or social media information
- We are compelled to say, after the end of our practicum, we will stay in touch with a young person

In what ways have boundary issues shown up in your practicum experience thus far?

_____

_____

Not only do we develop relationships and work relationally with young people and their families, we also develop relationships and work relationally with colleagues, supervisors, and the wider community network to support young people's growth, development, and wellness. This comes with some challenges, too, that you may or may not be experiencing at your practicum.

Effective multi- and interdisciplinary teamwork is essential to supporting young people. However, challenges can emerge. For example, Gharabaghi (2008) discusses conflicts and challenges between CYC practitioners, which can take the form of complaints that the other practitioner isn't doing something the other person believes is appropriate or

> It was great being able to be aware of my own worldviews and how they came into play. Sometimes you kind of just want to fix everybody. Being able to realize that you're not going to be able to handle every single situation. You're not going to be able to fix every single problem. Learn to be okay with that.
> —Adrian, CYC Student

essential for the young person's care. He writes, "a school-based child and youth care worker complain[s] that the residential child and youth worker is not sufficiently consistent with expectations… the hospital-based child and youth worker complain[s] about the outreach child and youth worker not being sufficiently vigilant about the child's nutrition," and so on (p. 238). Have you found yourself (or observed others) doing this? In such cases, he suggests that practitioners:

- Engage in reflective practice
- Understand that young people experience and behave differently across environments
- Must expect different outcomes and behaviours at any given time
- Have a strong understanding of each other's roles
- Commit to avoid getting caught up in perceived hierarchies (p. 238)

> There was an incident with another practitioner. A lot of things were said to the client that were not okay and ethical. I bounced ideas off my supervisor. The practitioner had a lot going on. One of the things I saw was if you said something it can hurt the client more than anything. I felt super helpless.
> —Heather, CYC Student

Discussing professional issues in CYC, Gharabaghi (2010) also reviews conflicts and dynamics amongst practitioners in general, stating,

> Adult dynamics are not typically any more or less functional and positive than dynamics amongst children and youth or between children and youth and specific adults. Inter-personal conflict, issues of intimacy and boundaries, professional disagreements, perceptions of incompetence, personal likes and dislikes, judgment, racism, sexism, homophobia, competition and a host of other issues and problems emerge when adults try to work together toward a common goal. (p. 59)

We would be wise to remember this while working on teams, where we each have an idea as to how to meet young people's needs, what their best interests are, what approach will work best, who and when and how and why we do what we do. To respond to these complexities on teams, Gharabaghi suggests:

- A great deal of effort on the part of every team member
- Open and honest communication
- A strong sense of and a shared vision of professional conduct
- A common vision for ethical conduct (2011, p. 59)

> All professions need to be on the same page when working with the family.
> —Trina, CYC Student

While we focus a lot on young people, focusing on the team indirectly benefits young people. Developing and maintaining relationships among teams and across our networks is part of our work. How do you see this need in action at your practicum site? Do you see your supervisor connecting with colleagues in and outside of the organization? How is conflict managed when it arises? Observing these challenges is a significant learning opportunity for you during your time at practicum.

Another challenge that can present itself differently across practicum settings is how well-established the CYC role is within an organization. Due to a number of factors, organizations and their various professionals' understanding of what a CYC practitioner is will vary from site to site. These reasons include, but are not limited to, CYC developing as a professional body; the performance of many roles, with different titles for our roles; expertise being valued differently across social services; and our roles emerging because of different needs across different communities.

Let's take schools as an example. Many of you or your classmates will be placed in schools on practicum, or you'll be working with schools in some way (e.g., finding a good fit for an alternate school program for a youth, attending a school planning meeting, supporting pro-social behaviour in young people to strengthen relationships and attendance at school). Some schools will have an established CYC presence, where teachers, principals, guidance counsellors, nurses, and social workers will know what the CYC practitioner contributes to the young person and team. They'll also utilize our set of skills, knowledge, and ways of being in the culture of the school and include us when planning interventions for its young people. On the other hand, some schools may have a CYC practitioner in a supporting role at the school but will not utilize them to their fullest capacity and scope of practice. Here, CYC practitioners' contributions can be minimized or overlooked; we may be treated as though we're an extension of another role (e.g., educational assistant, etc.); we are excluded from important plans or interventions; or other staff are unaware of our role and how we can contribute to positive change.

Do you or does your supervisor experience any of these? Even if you're not at a school, you're still likely on a multidisciplinary team of some kind supporting a young person. For example, you could be a youth worker at a group home, and one of the youth at the home has a large team of professionals supporting them. Do other professionals know your role, utilize it to its fullest capacity, and invite you to contribute? Gharabaghi (2008) refers to this phenomenon as CYC credibility, where the contribution of a CYC practitioner will increase when other practitioners learn how much we can benefit the team's goals for the young person. You may wish to ask your supervisor at your next meeting how the CYC role and contribution are known, included, and valued (or not) at the organization or across the multidisciplinary teams that exist. If it is well-established, ask your supervisor what it took to get to that place. Without a doubt, past CYC practitioners will have put in a lot of effort to make themselves known, develop and strengthen relationships, and so on. We should acknowledge this work. As a CYC practicum student, you're an ambassador of CYC and have an opportunity to continue this work at this setting in our communities.

CHALLENGING POLICY AND PRACTICES

When it comes to the challenges we can experience at the policy and practice level, White (2011) reminds us that many scholars have "called attention to the ways in which organization and system-level requirements, like narrow mandates or the practices of labelling and categorization, create numerous ethical challenges and constraints for child- and youth-serving professionals" (p. 44). Hare (2010) extends these challenges to include the problem with externally imposed mandated transitions embedded in policy and practice: "chronologically determined imperative of transition (whether at age 16 or 18 or 21) is artificial and unreasonably early in comparison to normative data on transition from the family home" (para. 3). For example, youth aging out of foster care face many challenges. Arguably, if we extended that age-based transition, it would create more time to develop life skills, learn to live independently, begin advanced training or education, and so on. Advocates will argue that the current transition is unjust and unethical. These types of policies—criteria for beginning or ending services—have significant consequences for the young people we work alongside. All too often, because CYC practitioners exist within the various life-spaces of young people, we catch young people in these systemic gaps.

Meanwhile, there are other policies, procedures, and practices directing our work that may exist for very good reasons, but nonetheless have undesired or unintended consequences for young people. Consider some of the following examples to help you think of the gaps and barriers you notice at or connect to your practicum site.

- Your practicum may be in a group home, where a young person is open to a referral to mental health services; however, the mental health services program says they think the more appropriate referral would be to a substance misuse program, due to the young person's concurrent struggles with post-traumatic stress and marijuana use. Then, you find the substance misuse program refers the young person back to the mental health services program. You feel like you're going in a circle.

- You may be at a recreation centre, and you've been told your role is not to provide counselling support to young people but to make referrals where needed. However, one young person only connects with you because of your relationship and is not interested in being referred.

- You may be at a supervised visitation centre, supporting young people and their families. You notice conflict between the agency's stated or implied expectation of parent engagement or child discipline and the family's expectations.

- Your practicum site's hours of operation make it difficult for some parents to visit, due to their working hours.

- Your practicum may be in an elementary school, based primarily in a behavioural support program. In order for a child to be accepted into the program, they must have a diagnosed disorder or disability, but the waitlist for a psychiatrist or pediatrician is at least six months. A family with a child who may benefit from this program just moved to the area and does not have a family physician who could make the referral.

- You may be at a centre where language interpretation services are provided, but, in some cases, they rely on the children of parents to interpret information.

- You may be in a street outreach program and notice many youth (who have recently exited government care) are experiencing homelessness because of the age cut-off, ending funded services.
- At an elementary school practicum placement, you notice that one way some practitioners respond to children who are "acting up" and being "disruptive" is to isolate and seclude them from their peers for various lengths of time.
- Your practicum site occupies an older building not originally meant for the program, and there are not many open shared spaces for young people to play or hang out.
- At a residential care facility practicum placement, you notice physical restraint policy that seems to escalate, rather than de-escalate, young people's violent behaviour.
- You may be at a short-term youth shelter that requires young people to check in at certain times of the day in order to ensure a bed continues to be available. Some young people have a hard time making it back.

Obviously, we could go on. Wherever you find yourself completing your practicum, there will be mandates, requirements, and other policies that pose barriers for young people and their families. What have you noticed thus far? If you're stuck, ask your classmates for their observations at their site to help you delve deeper, or ask your supervisor for what they've observed in your program or wider agency. Make a list here.

_____

_____

Once you've brainstormed a few examples, reflect on values, perspectives, and other factors that could be influencing these policies. For example, in many cases, funding will determine how many practitioners can be hired. Criteria needs to exist to determine who receives support and who doesn't. A program may be designed to serve young people who are ready for making a change and not young people who are contemplating or struggling with making changes. Bureaucratic and institutional needs are prioritized over young people's needs and realities. And so on. Look at your list. What could be happening for your scenarios? Once you've brainstormed a few possible reasons for these policies' existence, consider how this sits with you. Does it make sense to you? Are you okay with this? Do you think it should change? Why or why not?

Becoming aware of factors that influence young people and your practice with them can help us to understand not just the context in more depth but also how and where we may influence change to better respond to young people's needs. While you may not have the opportunity to do so in the relatively short time you're at your practicum placement, you will nonetheless develop the ability to understand these influential factors to prepare yourself for future work that you do.

Policies, procedures, and practices impact not only young people but also our work. Challenging work environments can impact our practice (including ourselves). Gharabaghi (2008) describes specific factors that can be experienced in residential group home environments, including roles not being taken seriously, crisis-driven environments, a risk of losing boundaries between staff members, as well as the informality of working in the lifespace of young people leading to a disregard of professional conduct. Further, Barford and Whelton (2010) describe challenges within our field, stating, "CYC work is exceptionally stressful," where "the combination of low salaries, poor working conditions, inadequate training and supervision, lack of support from policy makers and the general public, and a difficult and challenging work environment has led to tremendous turnover in the CYC field" (p. 274). This is not to discourage you. Rather, it is here for you to realize the factors within the environment that are influencing our work. In practicum, we have the opportunity to observe these factors. Barford and Whelton follow up with a number of practical recommendations to some of the challenges in our work. While as practicum students we may not have control over many of these factors, we can notice which environments better support our work, while advocating for better working environments over time. Their examples include:

- Increasing number of staff-per-child ratio, allowing the staff more breaks, debriefing with staff members after difficult situations, [and] reducing the expectations and responsibilities of CYC workers
- Ensuring CYC workers are well-trained and knowledgeable regarding their roles and responsibilities
- Establishing a sense of pride and loyalty toward the organization
- [Fighting] to establish a sense of [professional CYC] pride and identity
- [Encouraging] employers to reward and encourage staff for their hard work and dedication
- Generating a sense of interest and involvement in the field through the establishment of committees, extracurricular activities, awards banquets, and various other social events
- [Mentoring opportunities] by older, more experienced employees... to discuss feelings of disenchantment, frustration, and emotional detachment (Barford & Whelton, 2010, pp. 284–285)

CHALLENGING SYSTEMS AND FORCES

We've reviewed a number of behavioural, relational, policies, practices, and work environments that we can experience as challenging and that no doubt impact the young people we work alongside. We can also experience challenges at the systemic and sociocultural level, where we are challenged by the inequities and barriers the young people we work alongside face on a daily basis. Flip back to Chapter 6, where we discussed some of the types of discrimination that impact young people's identity and larger forces and structures that reinforce exclusion (Simpson, 2009). What are the children, youth, and families at your practicum setting experiencing?

- Children and families living in poverty
- LGBTQ+ youth experiencing homophobia and transphobia at school and barriers to access health services
- Black and Indigenous youth overrepresented in the Canadian foster care system
- Refugee families experiencing the trauma of war and dislocation and an inaccessible immigration system
- Gentrification of urban communities
- Rural and remote communities' access to basic needs (housing, health care, water, food)
- Young people impacted by the effects of toxic masculinity
- Race-based criminal profiling of Black and Indigenous boys and young men
- Exploitation of young girls
- Colonialist institutions and institutional histories, structures, and attitudes
- Difficult to navigate, exclusionary, and discriminatory health, educational, welfare, and justice systems
- Young people excluded from decisions and processes that directly impact their well-being

Do any of these barriers impact the young people and families you are supporting at your practicum? What is life like for them, to face these barriers on a daily basis? What is it like for you, as a support person in their lives, to witness these systemic inequities and barriers? What is it like to navigate these systemic influences, with the goal of creating a more just and responsive environment for young people? Are you, or the organizations you are part of, perpetuating any of these inequities, or are you contributing to the dismantling of systems and barriers as part of your work?

In her CYC practicum journal, Fraser (2013) describes her experience of an international CYC practicum placement, ultimately asking herself, "what does ethical CYC practice look like when practicing in different contexts deeply implicated by poverty, racial discrimination, social class, and political forces?" (p. 101). She writes in her learning journal:

We go in, learn, reflect, practice, give back in some way, and then we leave without promise that we will ever return to that organization…Were my promises built with good intentions? Had I created expectations to stay connected to the school because of my own moral dilemmas? Perhaps the purpose of fieldwork in any context is to reach out to students like me—to get me thinking about how ethical issues are constantly circling around me in my practice and cross-cultural encounters. It is a messy journey, which boldly ignites larger intersectional issues of class, gender, race, and power that I (the CYC student) am deeply entangled in. It is a messy process. (p. 102, italics in original)

> We learn most from our struggles. I don't want to hear everything that's going well and what's going right. I want to know where students are struggling and where their self-doubt is and what keeps them up at night.
> —Sonja, CYC Practicum Supervisor

There are no easy answers to any of these questions. This is the complexity of our work, where we concurrently attempt to support young people in their contexts while attempting to change the conditions that negatively impact their lives. We live in these contexts too. We are not immune to these inequities and barriers. Let's join alongside young people and their families to create better lives for everyone, amid and despite the great challenges we face.

ON STUCKNESS AND NOT-KNOWING

We can see just how uncertain, messy, complicated, conflicted, and stuck we can become in our work, responding the best we can to its complexity. This is not to discourage you; rather, it is to support you in your attempts to articulate those challenges so that we are better able to respond. There is no doubt, however, we can feel challenged by many situations, contexts, and influences. These challenging feelings can cause all kinds of discomfort. Feeling paralyzed, uncertain, isolated, conflicted, unsure, helpless, and powerless can be part of our experience of our work.

Meanwhile, our need to *figure it out* will be strong. We will likely want to leave this place of discomfort as quickly as possible, which often has unintended consequences (e.g., not responding well, responding from a place of fear, etc.). This is not to say that as you develop as a practitioner, you will not develop more helpful ways of understanding and responding to situations and contexts. You will. However, we also need to keep in mind the value of staying in the place of being stuck, encouraging ourselves to take a not-knowing stance so that we may approach situations and contexts less from a place of problem-solving and work toward a place of generating possibility.

> If I'm uncomfortable with something it's forced me to become direct and to really address the things in the moment.
> —Jenn, CYC Student

Anderson-Nathe (2010) confirms that we "operate in environments that are in constant states of change, often chaotic, and utterly unpredictable," where we "often associate [our] own experiences of not-knowing what to do as indications of incompetence" (pp. 135–136). Meanwhile, de Finney, Little, Skott-Myhre, and Gharabaghi (2012) underscore the importance of "uncertainty, because people who are certain ask fewer questions and [they] think creativity thrives in the rich atmospheric of the unknown that is generated by and generates the question" (p. 134). So too does Hillman (2018) remind new CYC practitioners that "the best theory and practice frameworks in the world will not fully prepare students for CYC practice in these incredibly complex times… one of the most important feelings to become familiar with is being in the tension of not knowing" (p. 69). Finally, Anderson-Nathe (2010) warns us that "*knowing* has the potential to blind professionals to unexplored possibilities in their practice, and that a deliberate stance of not-knowing may open these possibilities" (p. 132). Not-knowing is *not* a state where we lack knowledge, skills, or ways of being, nor does it discard knowledge. Rather, it is the

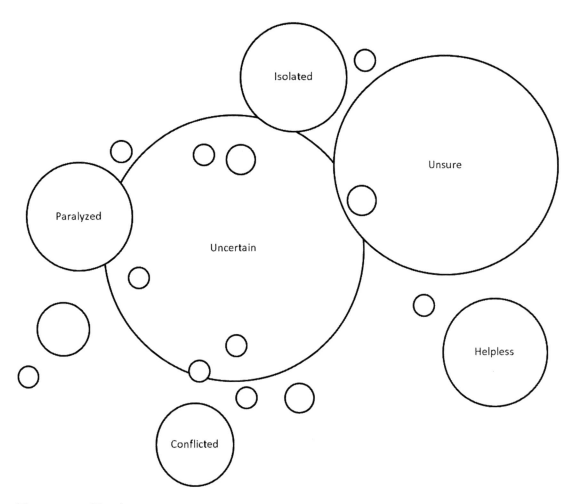

Figure 9.3: Stuckness

rejection of needing to be an expert, along with the appreciation of, the ability to endure, and the openness to possibilities that present themselves in complexity.

Ultimately, as CYC practitioners, we are encouraged to move from knowing, certainty, and prescribed solutions toward a place of not-knowing, uncertainty, and the creative responses that become available to us, when we no longer are restricted by needing to know.

ETHICAL CONSIDERATIONS

With this invitation in mind—to stay in a place of not-knowing—we re-enter into a space of ethical considerations. As professionals, we aim to do good work, make good decisions, all in a good way, in and among unpredictable, complex environments. In Chapter 3, we discussed the concept of ethically sensitive practice, where White (2011) invites us to:

- Recognize the value-laden quality of CYC
- Discern morally relevant issues
- Critically reflect on [our] own social and cultural situatedness and professional assumptions

- Practice articulating moral positions
- Anticipate and respond to ambiguity and uncertainty
- Engage in critical debate
- Generate creative responses, and
- Recognize that taking ethically responsible action is much more demanding than conforming to standards or consulting a code of ethics (p. 47)

In essence, White (2007) describes CYC practice as "characterized by choices and dilemmas, ambiguities, ethical tensions, and competing sets of interests about what constitutes good and right action" (p. 242). Further, Ricks and Griffin (1995) remind us that ethical practice includes decision about practice issues—that is, how best to do our jobs—and ethical issues—that is, the right action to take when someone's welfare is at stake—where what we consider as *best* and *right* are very much influenced and constructed by our own experiences. We make these choices in challenging contexts every moment of the day. Many of the challenges described in this chapter have been ethical in nature. Some may argue that all our practice has ethical considerations: how we show up to the work, the decisions we make, the actions we take, the frameworks and values that guide our practice, what we attend and don't attend to, and so on.

> When in the midst of a challenge, I encourage students to be open and honest with themselves and their site supervisors and to seek out a well-rounded understanding of the situation. To check out any assumptions the student might have. All challenges can be opportunities for learning and growth.
>
> —Rhonda, CYC Practicum Faculty-Instructor

When we are in our early practicum placements, we have the opportunity to observe ethical practice: practice that lives up to the expectations we set forth for ourselves through our actions, choices, and decisions, the dilemmas we find ourselves in, as well as practice that violates those ethical standards. You will likely witness a spectrum of what we consider good and not good practice and a spectrum of straightforward and complex situations.

Let's explore two central principles of ethical practice—respect and do no harm—and relate these concepts to our practicum settings. We are likely quick to agree with both statements—that practitioners should respect the young people they work alongside, and they should not inflict harm upon them. But both of these principles are not as simple as they sound.

What acts of respect have you seen in your practicum setting? There may be many—interactions with young people, program design, spaces, policies, and more. But you may also observe acts of disrespect in your practicum setting—interactions with young people, program design, spaces, policies, and so forth. List some of both.

_____

_____

Isn't this interesting? How has it come to be this way? What is your understanding of respect informed by? How has it developed? What do you consider respectful? Disrespectful? Do you interpret interactions with young people, program design, spaces, and policies the same way as a colleague, a youth, a classmate? These are all important questions to consider as you develop how you as a CYC practitioner will act respectfully toward young people.

We can also look at another central principle of all ethical codes and standards of competency: do no harm. Again, many of us may be quick to agree with this statement, that practitioners should not inflict harm upon young people. It is more complex than that, however. What harms have you witnessed or become aware of within the helping field, at your practicum or otherwise? For example:

- Not keeping a commitment to a young person
- Not preparing oneself to be present for the work
- Lack of planning for youth's expected transition
- Poor outcomes of young people exiting government care
- Overlooking acts of racism and discrimination
- Perpetuating certain value-systems or worldviews over others

We can see how harm occurs on a regular basis, despite the best intentions of programs, policies, and practitioners. What, in your opinion, is creating conditions for harm to occur? What are the consequences of these harms?

When it comes to ethical choices and ethical dilemmas, what have you been learning in your courses thus far? Flip back to your Introductory to Professional CYC Practice coursework (or elsewhere), where you perhaps were introduced to ethical decision-making models. Many frameworks for ethical decision-making follow a similar process as seen in Figure 9.4.

While you'll explore ethics in more depth and specificity in other classes, focusing on ethical practice and choices at practicum gives you an opportunity to learn the complexity

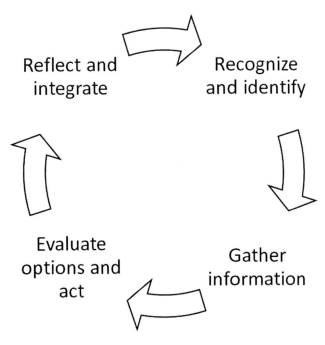

Figure 9.4: Ethical Decision-Making

first hand. You may stay in an observation role; you are nonetheless learning the multiple factors involved when practitioners are tasked with making decisions and hard choices in their work. We move from:

1. recognizing and identifying the ethical issue involved in the situation, to
2. gathering information, through reflecting on the situation, who and what is involved, and what is required and/or expected of us, to
3. evaluating our multiple options, considering the consequences of each, and then acting, to
4. reflecting on the outcomes of that action, while integrating that learning for the next decision that we encounter.

It is an ongoing journey.

First and foremost, as practicum students and emerging practitioners, know you are not alone (and never should be put into a situation where you are alone) in responding to violations of ethical standards or ethical dilemmas and choices. When you began your practicum, your supervisor told you who to connect with and the procedure to connect with them if you encounter an ethical violation or dilemma. They may have even run through scenarios where you may need to call upon them (or someone in their place). They might have also shared their agency's procedure for responding to a violation of ethical standards or an ethical dilemma. If they haven't already done so, take it upon yourself to learn. Review Activity 9.1 to apply their process, and incorporate what you've already learned in your introductory CYC classes.

> Talk about it! Make sure to tell your faculty-instructor. We are here to support you, advocate for you. It's not okay for students to be unsafe or creating unsafe environments. Be sure to utilize faculty to support you with the tools and language when handling challenges.
> —Saira, CYC Practicum Faculty-Instructor

Activity 9.1: Ethical Violations and Choices at My Practicum

Flip to Appendix H to remind yourself of the ethical code that CYC practitioners in North America follow. Go back to notes from classes where you were given a step-by-step process for responding to ethical dilemmas or making ethical choices. Review these notes, documents, and guidelines.

Meet with your supervisor, and ask them what types of violations and/or dilemmas they typically encounter at the organization. Ask them about both simple and complex scenarios, how they and their team responded, and how each scenario turned out. Ask them for any policy or procedural expectations regarding how you should respond to these situations. Write your notes here, ensuring you do not record confidential/sensitive information.

_____

_____

_____

_____

Now, think of what you've observed at practicum thus far. Ethical violations you may observe in practicum may relate to issues of confidentiality, consent, competence, boundaries, and respect. Ethical dilemmas you may be involved in at practicum could relate to issues of safety versus autonomy, needs of the individual versus needs of the group, competing values as to what is in the young person's best interests, and so on. Reflect on any of these situations, and think about how it was handled. Record your observations here, ensuring you do not record confidential/sensitive information.

_____

_____

_____

_____

Practicum is an opportunity to observe, contribute, connect, and learn. Outside the classroom and textbooks, and within the specific contexts of your practicum placement— alongside your cohort of classmates in other specific contexts—you have the opportunity to see what your ethical standards of practice and processes for making decisions can look like. We can notice similarities and differences. We can notice how for one context, an act or decision may be right, but in another, it would be different. And we have the privilege to learn from multiple professionals doing their best to meet the needs of young people in challenging contexts. It is often these challenging situations that define who we are as practitioners and how we wish to work with young people and their families, reconfirming our developing theoretical orientation to CYC practice.

When it comes to professional issues, students can struggle to recognize the complexity of some of the situations students find themselves in and the need to get support from site mentors and faculty.

—Deb, CYC Practicum Faculty-Instructor

POTENTIAL AND OPPORTUNITY

Snell (2015) reflects that our work can "feel unpredictable, volatile and even ambiguous," which can tempt us to "create structures, make predictions and set goals," but we could instead think "about where we are in the moment, and less about where we think we are going next" (p. 7). In de Finney and colleagues' (2012) conversation, de Finney contributes that among social change's "messiness and contradiction, I see great potential… I think finding our way out of this requires radical imagining and hope, and a commitment to work in uncharted waters through the 'damned hard' parts of it" (p. 143). Meanwhile, across Canada, CYC students are being invited to be agents of change where a student can take up an "attitude of reflective noncompliance" (Shaw & Trites, 2013, p. 13) and "[adjust] their practice to be an agent of change in the ecological system" (Child and Youth Care Education Consortium of British Columbia, 2018, p. 19).

What will you do with these invitations?

_____

_____

_____

Reframing challenges, Weston (2006) invites us to "take the ethical problem before us not as a difficulty to be overcome or gotten rid of but as an actual *opportunity* to be welcomed," asking us to ask ourselves "can I think of any way in which this 'problem' might actually be *welcomed*? Are there *opportunities* in it? For what?" (p. 39, emphasis in original). He warns that the opportunity may not be evident at first, then shares a story, encouraging practitioners to expand their perspective.

In an elderly care home where a lot of idle time exists, professionals are tasked with filling the time with activities, often, he argues, just for the sake of filling time. In this way, the problem is *lots of time* and the solution is *to fill the time with activities*. When he reframes the problem as an opportunity, he allows himself to see *time* instead as a community resource and the elderly community as a valued part of the community. When he reframes it this way, it allows him to think of a different approach to the situation. Time becomes an opportunity, rather than a problem, and he brainstorms and imagines elderly people connected to libraries, historical museums, and child care centres, where their wisdom and abilities are considered contributions to the community. Relationships are strengthened, people are valued, and new opportunities are created.

What does Weston's (2006) story inspire you to reflect on? Are there challenges at your practicum site that could instead be seen as opportunities? How so?

LEARNING JOURNAL

Focus on some of the challenges you've identified throughout this chapter, to take advantage of the learning opportunity in your learning journal. What helps you move through each challenge well? What hinders the process? Focus your reflections on challenges.

PRACTICE SCENARIOS

Take a look at the Practice Scenarios that conclude this chapter: "Different Schools" and "Sadie's Seclusion." Use the content you've read in this chapter to inspire your thinking about the scenario. Notice how the scenario may relate to your own situation at your current practicum placement, even if it is not exactly what you are experiencing. Consider the questions posed at the end of each scenario to help you expand and apply the concepts presented in this chapter.

SEMINAR GROUP AND COMMUNITY OF PRACTICE DISCUSSION QUESTIONS

In your seminar or community of practice group, consider the following questions for discussion:

1. Take a look at the challenges you listed in the beginning of the chapter, where you found yourself stuck, uncertain, or conflicted in some way. Bring one example to your seminar discussion or community of practice. Share your experience, listen to others and notice how your peers sit in the stuckness and learn from it. Appreciate each other's experiences.

2. What systemic forces influence the lives of the young people at your practicum setting?

3. What is an example of an ethical dilemma that you or your supervisor have experienced at your practicum setting? What procedure is required at your practicum setting for responding to an ethical dilemma?

4. Weston (2006) invites us to "take the ethical problem before us not as a difficulty to be overcome or gotten rid of but as an actual *opportunity* to be welcomed" (p. 38). What does this mean to you? What opportunities have you noticed within ethically challenging situations?

IN CLOSING

We end this chapter encouraging you to view challenge and uncertainty as an opportunity for possibility. There are challenges everywhere—challenging situations, behaviours, relationships, policies and practice, systems and forces. Challenge *is* the work. Ethical practice and ethical issues *are* the work. And if we approach challenge—uncertainty, complication, conflict, ambiguity, and contradiction—in a state of reaction, personalization, fear, or perceived lack of competence, we miss an opportunity. Listening to CYC practitioners, scholars, and leaders in the field, we are invited to work within the complexity, rather than avoid it.

> I learned to be comfortable with the unknown, not being in control, and being able to just roll with it.
>
> —Jenn, CYC Student

PRACTICE SCENARIOS

Different Schools

Wendy's secondary school seems to not know what to do with a CYC practitioner. Most of the teachers treat her like she's in the class to support students finishing their homework. Wendy notices that her practicum supervisor divides her time between three different schools. Melanie, on the other hand, notices that her supervisor has been integrated into all parts of her secondary school. She's on a number of teams, flows in and out of classrooms all day, seems to know all the youth, and has a resource room with a lot of activities, couches, and room to facilitate groups. Melanie has been introduced to the staff, and they almost immediately asked her to visit their class, help them with an event, and say hi in the halls. Wendy is struggling to be noticed, feels she's not being utilized at all, and worries she may not be able to meet her goals as well as her classmates.

Setting aside the specific practicum expectations of each of these students for a moment, consider their school contexts. What micro-to-macro factors would lead to both of these contexts? How well is the CYC practitioner known, utilized, and valued in your agency? Or on the teams in which your supervisor is involved? What is the historical context for this current reality?

_____

_____

_____

Sadie's Seclusion

Sadie is completing a practicum at an elementary school where there are a few young children who struggle with emotional regulation and sometimes act out aggressively. On a few occasions, Sadie has noticed that one young child in particular will be brought to a private, dark room, even if he isn't behaving violently. On one occasion, he was left there alone for over 20 minutes. On another occasion that room was being used, and he was left in a boys' washroom unattended, though not for long. Upon Sadie's inquiry, her supervisor has explained that they don't have enough educational support workers to help intervene early and de-escalate aggressive behaviour. She's unsure of the school district's policy on seclusion, but these practices don't sit right with her.

What ethical issues are of concern in this scenario? Are there any policies and procedures that cause you discomfort? How may this point of discomfort be a good learning opportunity to explore an issue further?

_____

_____

_____

CHAPTER 10

Observing, Documenting, Writing, and Reporting in CYC

Competencies for Professional Child and Youth Work Practitioners				
Professionalism	Cultural and Human Diversity	Applied Human Development	Relationship and Communication	Developmental Practice Methods
Awareness of Law and Regulations

Advocacy | | Contextual-Developmental Assessment

Access Resources | Teamwork and Professional Communication | Intervention Planning

Community Engagement |

> Review documentation, ask about what they are reviewing, and seek understanding of the documentation practices that are often times unique and tailored to each organization's needs. Request to write "ghost logs" where you write what you think matches the documentation practices of the organization as well as what you've been taught in class and request feedback from practicum supervisors. Learners often enjoy the opportunity for practice as they are often fearful of missing details within their first attempts… It is important that the whole story of the young person is represented—ensure that the young person is able to have a clear picture of their life story while they were within the care of the organization.
>
> —Michelle Chalupa, CYC Faculty, Practitioner, and Writer

Practicum is often the first time where we have the opportunity to formally participate in observation, documentation, writing, and reporting. These tasks and activities require the intersection of a number of skills, attitudes, and awareness, including attention to professional ethics. Across Child and Youth Care (CYC) roles and settings there are numerous opportunities to do so, including:

- Observing a young person to understand how they interact with their environment

- Observing a young person for the purpose of communicating development or achievement of a goal to a particular audience
- Writing an incident report or communication log
- Communicating an event or activity to its intended audience
- Consulting with a professional team regarding a young person

In practicum, you have the chance to practise your observational skills every day. Depending on the site, you may or may not be invited to participate in writing and reporting activities. We encourage you to ask to be involved as much as you can.

From observation, writing, and documentation, to the multiple ways that oral and written communication and reporting can take across practicum settings, this chapter will focus on potential opportunities for you to participate, as well as guidelines that may help you along the way.

OBSERVATION

We are continuously observing the environment and integrating these observations into our work to benefit the young people, families, programs, and the wider contexts we work within. How we determine what is helpful or unhelpful, how we conceptualize a young person's situation, how we communicate with our colleagues about how to move forward, and so on, all comes from observation. Whether we recognize it or not, we are always observing. We can do this informally, as we move through our days. Or we can do this formally, where we focus on someone or something specific, using those observations for a particular purpose.

First, we observe our environment, including people, interactions, behaviour, and other contextual factors over time. Then, we reflect on those factors in the moment or afterward. Next, we conceptualize what those observations mean, integrating existing knowledge with our observations. Then, we decide to engage, act, or intervene in a specific way. Finally, we return to observing the environment again and repeat the process (see Figure 10.1). This process can happen within a few moments, such as during an interaction. Or this process can happen over time, such as during a formal process of assessment and intervention planning.

When it comes to planned observations, we can turn to guidelines to tell us why we observe and how we should approach this task. Why do we observe? Gronlund and James (2005) say that ultimately, we observe to "consider each young person's accomplishments and needs and to plan effectively for the next steps to support continued growth and development" (p. 25). More specifically, Martin (2014) tells us we can observe young people in order to:

- Learn about them and their development
- Identify issues of concern and respond appropriately
- Learn about their family and culture
- Monitor progress
- Help determine how we become involved in their lives for planned interventions and improvement of our programs

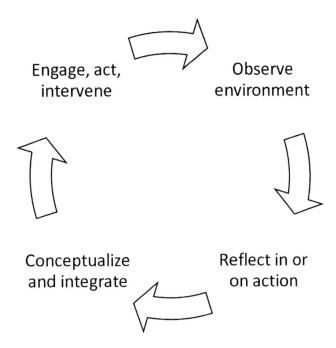

Figure 10.1: Observe, Reflect, Conceptualize, and Act

Gronlund and James (2005) refer to observation in terms of where our *attention* and *focus* are directed. There are hundreds of factors we can pay attention to. Just think of the microsystem/mesosystem/exosystem/macrosystem/chronosystem factors we've considered in previous chapters. It's our professional responsibility to make decisions about what we attend to, as well as to become aware of what we are and are not focusing upon. We cannot pay attention to everything. We are always making decisions. We need to cultivate the ability to do this intentionally and responsibly.

What is it that we actually pay attention to and focus upon? Gronlund and James (2005) list some examples, including ones that you may encounter in your practicum:

✓ A moment with a young person or group of young people
✓ The various routines, activities, and areas of your setting
✓ A specific life skill or domain of development
✓ Young people's skills, abilities, behaviour, choices, preferences, and expressions of identity
✓ How a young person navigates the setting
✓ The success of planned activities
✓ The flow of daily routines
✓ A challenge that a young person experiences
✓ Circumstances surrounding problems that may arise

Meanwhile, while we are observing these moments, we have the opportunity to approach observation from a CYC framework (as discussed throughout this guidebook and your previous and concurrent classwork). Using a CYC framework of practice, we can look to the young person's:

- Growth across physical, emotional, social, cognitive, cultural, spiritual development, and functioning
- Expression of identity (cultural, gender, etc.)
- Strengths, capacities, interests, abilities, and wishes
- Responses to challenge, conflict, etc.
- Progress and setbacks over time
- Experiences of discrimination, oppression, disadvantage, and struggle
- Engagement, interactions, and interpersonal dynamics within relationships (social/peer, staff, family) and activities
- Wider ecological context that surrounds and influences them

> Put yourself in the place of a child, youth, or family that you're working with. Try to understand and experience a behaviour or circumstance from the inside out vs solely through an observer lens.
> —Mackenzie, CYC Practicum Faculty-Instructor

Meanwhile, we can also observe agency-related activities for multiple purposes. For example, we count the number of people who attend activities and who we provide services to; we observe events to notice their success and areas for future improvement; and we record pertinent information in agency meetings (team, case planning, interagency). We do this for the purposes of gathering, recording, and reporting information. Why? To demonstrate and evaluate the effectiveness of services, provide continuity of care over time and across service providers, meet the requirements of a funding or accreditation body, and so on. This is important work.

At your practicum experience thus far, what have you had the opportunity to formally observe and document? Read the following list to help you brainstorm. You may not have even noticed you're already doing this!

1. A practicum student at a child development centre is invited to observe a group of young children play and document their skills—emotional functioning, and behaviours in or across a particular developmental domain—to keep on file.
2. A practicum student at a middle school is asked by their supervisor to focus their attention on one youth throughout the week and present their observations to the intervention team at the school to help with the next steps in planning to support her.
3. A practicum student at a group home is invited to observe events of the day and record salient information in the group home's communication log for the evening shift staff.
4. A practicum student at a recreation centre observes and records the names, interests, and strengths of a number of children, so as to recall that information for the next time they see them.

5. A practicum student at a youth shelter is invited to an intake meeting with an adolescent boy and document vital information—name, government care status, age, suicide risk, and so on—according to a set intake form.
6. A practicum student at a youth drop-in centre may observe an event or activity and report some details—attendance, participation, success, areas of improvement—to their supervisor to plan for a future event.
7. A practicum student at a family development centre is invited to observe interactions between a child and their parent and document those interactions in a progress log sent to the family's social worker.

Across all these examples, the practicum students (1) were invited to complete an observation, (2) which has a particular purpose (3) for a specific audience (4) that must be communicated in a specific way. What observation, documentation, and reporting activities have you completed or participated in thus far? Perhaps your practicum course requires you to do a planned observation. Be sure to count the informal and formal examples. If you're stuck, consult with your classmates or community of practice. If you have not had these opportunities thus far, check in with your supervisor to ask what you could become involved in at your practicum site.

WRITING AND DOCUMENTATION

What do we do with our observations? We incorporate that knowledge into all of our work with young people at the setting. We also have the opportunity to document and report that information for different purposes. Before we get too ahead of ourselves, let's take a step back and focus on writing and documentation. Complete Activity 10.1 to focus on everyday writing and documentation activities.

> For my supervised access practicum, we had to write how the visit went. I got to see how other workers wrote and then I was able to write up my own and then I got feedback from the workers.
> —Trina, CYC Student

Activity 10.1: Everyday Writing and Documentation Activities

Recall the past few days where you wrote something (anything). Now, make a list.

_____

_____

Your list may include notes for a research paper, a grocery list, an email to an instructor, a text to a friend, notes in class, a post to social media, and an upcoming event in your day planner. We could go on. Let's focus on the process of creating one item for a moment: a grocery list. What is involved in this seemingly simple written task? A lot. Consider the following steps that we may take as a part of this process.

After reading Steps 1 through 7 in Figure 10.2, consider the following questions:

1. What is this list's intended outcome? Is it to obtain the correct groceries? Or is it that people are well-nourished, enjoying meals together?
2. What has occurred to create this grocery list? Meal planning, calculations of portions and product types, an observation and assessment of items in the relevant environment, and so on.
3. Who is it communicated to? Yourself or others, for when you or they are at the store?

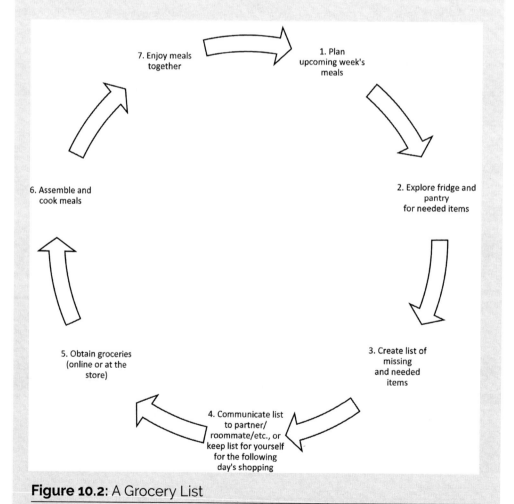

Figure 10.2: A Grocery List

At least, this is how we hope this process goes. What if a step is skipped?

1. What happens if you show up to a grocery store without a list of needed items, selecting items purely from memory? What if you've neglected to record the amount of or specific type of item? You may purchase too little or too much or not obtain the correct item.

2. What happens if you give that list to your partner, parent, roommate, or child to obtain the groceries themselves, but they show up to the store and are confused as to which product to purchase? What if they cannot read your messy writing? Do they return with the incorrect items, missing items, or items you were not expecting? Does the misunderstanding lead to a potential conflict?

3. What happens if you attempt to assemble and cook meals, but an item is missing? Your meal must go without the item or you must return to the store to obtain it.

Reading through these questions and process, did you recall a time where you missed a step and encountered difficulty, misunderstanding, inconvenience, disappointment, conflict, or worse?

What we decide to observe and record is important. What environmental factors we take into account is important. How we decide to record and communicate that information is important. What potential challenges the process has is important. What benefits and outcomes the process has are important. Attending to each part of the process is important.

When it comes time to document an observation, we need to consider a number of factors. Consider the following basic recommendations for writing and documenting in the human services field (Cech, 2010, 2015; Hoffmann, 2013; Myers-Kiser, 2016):

☑ Avoid jargon, slang, abbreviations, and acronyms without original word, expletives, broad and vague phrasing, unclear references, and trendy words (unless it's a direct quote)

☑ Be honest, accurate, factual, based on observations (what is seen and heard by you)

☑ Use clear, professional language

☑ Attend to grammar, spelling, syntax, sentence structure, and organization of ideas

☑ Complete documentation as promptly as possible, to preserve memory and meet needs of young person and/or agency

☑ Include enough detail but be concise and to the point; use concrete descriptors

☑ Decide on the difference between salient and non-salient information, based on the purpose and goals of the observation and report

☑ Stay away from problem-based language (labels, deficits, blaming, problems); focus on strengths-based language (solutions, responses, outcomes, progress, needs, interventions)

☑ Use person-first language (e.g., write "a person experiencing psychosis," not "a schizophrenic")—don't label, describe

☑ Note the difference between objective, observation-based statements vs. subjective judgements (opinions, conclusions, etc.)

☑ Preface feelings, assumptions, and perceptions with "it seems" or "it appears" or "it was suggested"

☑ Where conclusions are made, support with evidence (direct quotes, specific and detailed examples and reasoning, etc.)

☑ Be clear on sources—are these your observations, a report from a young person, or third-party observations?

☑ Maintain confidentiality, guided by setting requirements

☑ Be aware of and consult with the team regarding personal bias

☑ Be mindful of who may read the report, now and in the future

> I see a lot of those mistakes: emotions being put on families when we actually don't know. Instead, use the word 'seem' or 'appeared' or 'presented as.' Or, if mom does say she is happy, then you would write 'Mom says she was happy.' Focus on the observable behaviour.
> —Mindi, CYC Practicum Supervisor

While you may immediately agree with these recommendations, understanding what they look like in practice, completing what is required of you, and developing your own approach takes time. Be patient with yourself. Learn from your supervisor(s) and colleagues. Participate in mock documentation. Ask for and integrate feedback. Keep learning. These skills are not learned overnight.

WRITING AND REPORTING

Moving back to examples from the field, we can encounter numerous opportunities where writing, documentation, and (oral and written) reporting is required. While we may not be involved in the majority of these opportunities in practicum, we will nonetheless benefit from becoming aware of their existence. While you're at your practicum site, you can pay attention to both what is expected of your (or your supervisor's) role, as well as by the program, agency, and the field at large.

> Look at the style and content of what others report and seek out opportunities to practice writing in that style. Learning to write in neutral and respectful ways which respect confidentiality and avoid judgmental language is a skill which needs to be learned.
> —Annie, CYC Practicum Supervisor

Before we get to specific examples, we can look to the rationale for various types of reports (and the observations behind them). McAleer (2009) states that practitioners write reports for a variety of reasons, including:

- Workers need to document changes in clients' behaviour, emotional states, and attitudes to monitor, anticipate, and head off problems. These problems could be risk-taking behaviours such as criminal activity or substance abuse, or they could be dangerous behaviours such as self-harming or harming others.

- To develop treatment plans that need to be followed and adjusted when necessary. Treatment plans are effective only when goals and progress are well-documented.
- Workers must also protect themselves by documenting their actions and decisions. There will be occasions when you are asked to justify your actions or decisions, and your reports will be invaluable references for you.
- You must write reports to meet the accreditation, licensing, and legislation standards of your profession (p. 3)

We document and report to measure change; note progress and setbacks; provide continuity of care across time, practitioners, and service providers; and demonstrate and evaluate effectiveness of services. Further, we write and report not only individual and group activities and interventions, we also write and report for organizational purposes.

Review Figure 10.3 for examples of writing and reporting across systems. Here, you'll note there are immediate practice environment requirements and agency requirements. There are also writing and reporting activities done at the community and organizational level, as well as in our CYC profession. By no means is this list exhaustive; rather, it gives you examples of reporting in and across different contexts. Your agency and supervisor will not be involved in all these tasks; however, while you're reading through the figure, you may wish to list the equivalent examples at your practicum site. If you're struggling for examples, discuss this with your supervisor and/or colleagues.

Practising Writing Reports

Practising various forms of reporting will be useful, especially if you haven't had the opportunity to participate in oral or written reporting. The following activities encourage you to become more involved at your practicum site in terms of observation, documentation, and reporting. While not all examples will be relevant to each practicum setting or role, there will nonetheless be similar opportunities for you to participate in. From the following activities (or suggested activities), pick and choose what is relevant to you, based on the individual factors at your practicum site. These categories include: 1) day-to-day observations and documentation; 2) education and marketing; 3) presentations; 4) proposals for funding and support; and 5) professional writing and communication. Each category's activity will provide a number of relevant examples so you can explore different reports, meant for different audiences and purposes.

Day-to-Day Observations, Documentation, and Records
As discussed earlier in the chapter, across settings and roles we have the opportunity to observe young people in their life-space, as well as document and report on these observations so as to inform our continued work with them.

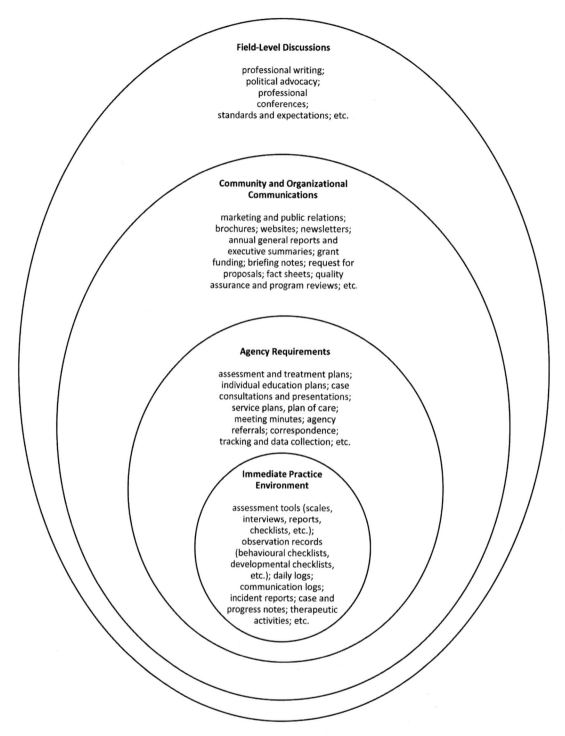

Figure 10.3: Examples of Writing and Reporting across Systems

Consider the following examples that practicum students may encounter in a first or second practicum experience regarding observing, documenting, and recording.

- A practicum student at a supervised visitation centre is required to observe parent-child and practitioner interactions and activities and report that information in a progress note that focuses on strengths and development over time.
- A practicum student at a group home is asked to contribute to the daily communication log—summarizing the afternoon interactions, events, activities, significant interactions, and the coming and going of its residents—to communicate to the evening shift workers.
- A practicum student at a middle school was witness to a physical fight between two students and is asked to write up an incident report of the situation.
- A practicum student at an elementary school helps facilitate a social-emotional skills group with her supervisor and is asked to summarize the session's content, process, and significant interactions, contributions, behaviours, and growth of its participants for her supervisor's files.
- A practicum student at a group home is asked to help complete a referral form for a new youth resident seeking mental health services, and needs to review her file and reflect on recent interactions for required information.

In these day-to-day observations and reports, the practicum student needs to identify the steps that must occur to complete the observation and accompanying documentation or report. They must consider the situation they need to observe or recall, as well as any other information they needed to gather. They consider where they need to focus their attention and for what purpose. They hopefully have the opportunity to look at previous examples of the type of report in question where they could notice the language, phrasing, and types of information that is included and excluded. They hopefully will receive feedback from supervisors and colleagues and have the opportunity to integrate that feedback and try again.

Experiment with Activity 10.2 to learn how to write an incident report. Each setting will have its own incident report form. If you prefer, ask to see this form at your site and complete one as practice in lieu of this activity.

Activity 10.2: Observing and Recording for an Incident Report

Across many first- and second-level CYC practicum settings, we will be tasked with writing an incident report. Incident reports document a significant incident that took place at the organization, during provision of its services, involving young people in its care. Its primary audience is likely other professionals and sometimes caregivers.

Depending on the policies at your setting, incident reports are required for different situations, typically when safety is a concern. A young person was injured during an activity. Two or more young people had a physical altercation at school. A young person ran away from the setting. A young person had an allergic reaction while on a field trip. Illegal substances were found in a young person's possession. And so on.

Incident reports require us, as CYC practitioners, to have observed the initial situation—and any relevant precursors and consequences. We also have to include pertinent information and exclude irrelevant information. Some of this information will be administrative (e.g., dates, names, etc.), and some will attend to the process of the incident (e.g., interactions, behaviour, conversations, etc.).

In response to the following incident description, complete the subsequent incident report. When writing the report, recall the basic recommendations for documentation (see pp. 249–250).

You are a practicum student in a middle school, working alongside your supervisor, the youth and family support worker. On February 20th, at 2:55 p.m., you were walking down the hallway saying goodbye to students as they gathered items from their lockers at the end of their school day. You notice a group of students gather down the hall, beginning to yell loudly. By the time you approach, you see two students you know—David and Amin—being pulled off each other by other students. David held his cheek and looked like he was in pain. Amin was holding his fist. Both continued to yell at each other. You are aware that these boys have had altercations before. As the vice-principal and guidance counsellor arrive and take each boy to the side, you overhear some kids say that David was whispering racist and homophobic slurs while pushing Amin. They have lockers next to one another. The vice-principal asks you to complete an incident report for his file, as you were the only staff member present.

HILLSIDE MIDDLE SCHOOL—INCIDENT REPORT

Date, time, and location of the incident:

_____

Type of incident:

_____

Report completed by (name and role):

_____

Names of person(s) involved in the incident:

_____

Description of the incident (including sequence of events):

_____

_____

_____

_____

Action taken:

_____

_____

Recommended follow-up:

_____

Signature of report author:

_____

Date and time report completed:

_____

When you've completed the incident report, compare your entry with a class-mate's and notice the similarities and differences.

Now let's move to other forms of communication in CYC practice.

> No one can argue with your observation but they can argue with your interpretation.
> —Jasmine, CYC Student

Education and Marketing

This type of communication includes posters, flyers, hand-outs, calendars, newsletters, and so on. Notice what's on the walls, bulletin boards, and shared in the communal spaces at your site. In practicum, we have the opportunity to see what kinds of educational materials are presented in this space. We also see our organization's marketing, done to promote its programs and activities for young people. Marketing materials are created to get the word out that activities, events, and services exist. Those activities, events, and services have been created based on practitioners' observations of what young people need.

Consider the following examples that practicum students may encounter in a first or second practicum experience.

- A practicum student at a youth centre creates a calendar of events to distribute on social media, bulletin boards, and via email to other practitioners to get the word out about the upcoming month of activities at the centre geared to youth.
- A practicum student at an elementary school creates a kid-friendly poster for the upcoming Lego Lunch Club to distribute across the school.
- A practicum student at a recreational centre creates a poster for social media safety, reinforced by a group activity she facilitated with the kids, inspired by some of the conversations she had with the kids.
- A practicum student at an emergency youth shelter creates a poster on substance use safety guidelines for youth, focusing on some of the recent opioid overdose risks facing the residents.

Learn how to create educational and marketing materials. If you are required at practicum to do so or required for your practicum course, share among your classmates for suggestions and ideas.

Presentations

Presenting information to groups of people can often cause us to experience performance anxiety. However, it's important to know that audiences are interested in what we have to say. They're curious to know about our expertise, observations, and insights. They have the ability to help us solve problems and implement any recommendations or suggestions we may have.

Consider the following examples that practicum students may encounter in a first or second practicum experience.

- A practicum student at a youth outreach program for youth at risk or involved in the justice system researches outdoor education, adventure, and summer camps for the agency's multidisciplinary team, including the locations, referral process, and costs. He presents this information at a team meeting.
- A practicum student at a group home who has made a good connection with one of the new residents is invited to present a summary of activities, engagement, and youth functioning at an upcoming team meeting, to discuss the next steps in planning this young person's care.
- A practicum student at a child development centre who has connected well with a young boy, who struggles with a developmental disability, researches best practices, watches training videos, and summarizes this information for a multidisciplinary team meeting.
- A practicum student at a group home attends a municipal government council meeting with her supervisor to advocate for youth-friendly spaces in the community. The student helps her supervisor prepare persuasive, evidence-based information, including observations of the community.

From case consultation to municipal advocacy, the following steps will help you prepare for a presentation:

1. Identify and Understand Your Topic: determine the scope of the topic, what you can convey in the time allowed, and your personal and professional intersection with the topic
2. Interpret Your Audience: who are they, how many people will be present, what may they want to know, and why are they there
3. Gather Material and Research: gather relevant stories, research, and practical information, keeping in mind what your audience will be most compelled by
4. Organize Your Talk: include an engaging beginning, substantive middle, and powerful end; in what format you will be able to present the information; and what you want to ask of your audience

Consider these steps for any presentation that may be required of you through your coursework or practicum site and complete Activity 10.3 for practice.

Activity 10.3: Five-Minute Presentations

Developing presentation skills is essential in many CYC roles and settings. To brainstorm a possible topic, consider the following list or look to what may be required of you in your practicum setting or course. For example, you may already be expected to present a scenario for discussion at a team meeting. Or you may be expected to formally present to your practicum seminar group about your practicum agency.

- Think of an issue relevant to the young people at your practicum setting that you think your classmates may be interested in learning about (e.g., the impact of overdoses on first responders, young people aging out of care, or a specific developmental disability and evidence-based intervention).
- Think of a young person you've been working closely with, where you've experienced some successes and setbacks; what would you like some help with for deciding future direction with the young person? Think of your classmates as your professional team and how they could help you.
- Think of a gap in community services or infrastructure that you believe could be addressed at a political level. Imagine your classmates are the municipal government city council, hearing from its community members. Advocate for change.

Based on the topic and audience (following the presentation preparation guidance above), develop a five-minute presentation. Practise with your seminar classmates or community of practice. Imagine they are the intended audience—a staff team, a multidisciplinary case planning group, or city council. Instruct your classmates to take specific roles in order to make the experience more authentic.

Once you've presented and observed your classmates' presentations, practise providing and receiving constructive feedback. In this case, constructive feedback could include responses to the following questions:

- What resonated for you?
- What did you learn?
- What seemed like essential information?
- What seemed like unessential information?
- Were there any disruptions to the presentation's flow that could be changed for next time?
- Were there any gaps of information that would have been helpful to include?
- How will you take the information forward in a useful way?

Proposals for Funding and Support

Across practicum settings, CYC practitioners have the opportunity to participate in funding proposals to support the work they do. While you may not be involved in a large funding proposal, you may have the opportunity to review past proposals for your own learning and/or identify a much smaller-scale project that you would like to seek funds to support.

Consider the following examples that practicum students may encounter in a first or second practicum experience.

- To learn how special projects are funded at the elementary school, a practicum student attends a Parent Advisory Committee meeting, reviews funding proposals the principal has written in the past, and meets with a few supervisors within the school district.
- A practicum student at a kids' drop-in recreational centre wants to facilitate an event for the kids but needs funds to purchase materials, food, and an honorarium for a performance group. He writes a short letter—including an event description, rationale as to how the event fits within the mandate of the centre, an outline of benefits to the kids, and a budget—to his supervisor to seek funds for the event.
- A practicum student at an alternate school notices their small library doesn't have many books other than the standard curriculum. After noticing some barriers within the school system's budgets, she canvasses her friends to see if they want to donate their young adult literature—graphic novels, comic books, and so on— that has more diverse characters and storylines. She presents them proudly in the school room.

- A practicum student at a group home notices that the house has a large backyard as well as a basketball hoop in the cul-de-sac; however, all the sporting materials (soccer balls, basketballs, field hockey sticks, etc.) are deflated or broken. With permission, he decides to write a letter to the local sporting goods store, formally asking for donations in kind to support the residents' wellness through physical activity and connection.

> When I hear a student say they want to do something I ask them for a proposal. I give them some examples and templates. I don't want them to copy and paste. I want them to use their own words and own thoughts. Use the thoughts of the kids. Do it as thoroughly as you can. Ask big! All we can do is scale it down.
> —Tom, CYC Practicum Supervisor

Whether it's a one-time activity, large event, or new service, developing proposals to fund activities and programs is complex and requires you to use CYC in new ways. Start small. Use Activity 10.4 to brainstorm what you could propose at your site.

Activity 10.4: Proposal Brainstorming

What programs, activities, supplies, or initiatives would you like to propose to your practicum supervisor? What gap have you noticed? What challenges and needs have you identified? What outcome would you like to see? Brainstorm here.

_____

_____

If you were to propose this idea to your supervisor, what form would your proposal take? Email correspondence? A letter? A formal proposal? Ask what is required at your site.

_____

To help you brainstorm how you will ask for support, consider the following questions:

- What is your idea?
- Who will it benefit and how will it benefit them?
- What research or evidence is available to support this idea?
- How will you make your idea happen? What resources do you need?
- Who do you need to communicate this idea to for support?
- Why is this idea important?

_____

_____

_____

Use these ideas to help inform your email, letter, or proposal. Draft your message to your supervisor here, and get feedback from your peers.

_____

_____

_____

_____

_____

_____

_____

Less words than more. Have an introduction and a conclusion. Know what you're talking about, do a bit of research. Have a tagline, something that grabs people. Make sure you've got your budget aligned and know where the money is coming from. Make sure you address the positive impacts. Use testimonials to personalize it.
—Chris, CYC Practicum Supervisor

Professional Writing and Communication

Finally, as CYC practitioners, we engage in oral and written communication that supports dialogue across settings, communities, and countries. As we participate in these conversations, we describe our experiences and observations of practice, integrate theory with practice, highlight trends and challenges, and advocate for change. We take those experiences and communicate to a wider audience for a more general purpose: to improve our practice. When we attend workshops and conferences, we engage in dialogue about observations of practice. When we conduct research, we share our findings with a wider audience. When we communicate with the public, we disseminate knowledge and advocate for the needs of young people based on our observations. Do not think that these activities are out of reach for you as an emerging practitioner.

Consider the following examples that practicum students may encounter in a first or second practicum experience.

1. A practicum student at a social service agency reads the agency's website, program descriptions, and annual general reports for the last few years, including summaries of programs and budgetary expenditures.
2. A practicum student at a policy centre creates an info sheet for her classmates on a new child-, youth-, and family-related policy and its implications for social service, health, and educational organizations' practice.
3. A group of practicum students attend a CYC (or aligned professional) conference/workshop to learn more about a specific topic or issue related to their practicum setting's population's needs.
4. A practicum student at a research centre creates a fact sheet about supporting young moms in the community, based on the research she completed with the large datasets on youth health across the province.

5. A practicum student at a group home writes a "letter to the editor" for their local newspaper advocating for compassion, increased funding, and more youth-friendly services for youth struggling with opioid substance use (with permission of the agency).

6. A small group of practicum students placed at educational settings decide to co-write an article for a CYC publication, with their faculty-instructor's guidance and advice, about their learning experience in practicum, tying theory to practice.

While some of these examples may be out of the scope of your practicum course and learning objectives, they may still be important to consider as you move forward in your education and in the field. If you're drawn to these ideas in any way, perhaps a practicum at a policy development centre, advocacy group, or research setting is in your future.

Staudt, Dulmus, and Bennett (2003) encourage all social service practitioners to participate in knowledge sharing, including publishing ideas from their practice. They noticed the factors that contributed to front-line practitioners' interest in publishing included a desire to contribute to practice, encouragement or mentoring from a faculty-instructor, support from colleagues and family, the enjoyment of writing, and more (p. 77). When it comes down to it, publishing is about dialogue. When you read something, you are participating in that dialogue. When you write, you are contributing to it. Luckily, we have multiple accessible venues to participate in local, national, and international discussions. Practicum is a big focus of CYC right now in Canada. Accreditation boards are discussing it. Faculty teams are designing it. Scholars are researching it. And students are experiencing it. Why not share your experiences to influence that discussion?

Past *Relational Child and Youth Care Practice* journal editor Thom Garfat (2008) directly invites all readers to contribute: "perhaps you might wonder if you too, might not like to give back to the field in this way. For there is always room for more and you will always be welcome here" (p. 4). The field is calling for diverse voices, representative of the current directions, needs, and desires of the field.

Sharing your experiences does not have to be extensive or complicated. Start where you are: what you learned in practicum, what successes you had, challenges you overcame, the critical lens you bring to your experiences, and where you think CYC should be heading. Tell us a story of how you connected with a young person (keep their identity anonymous—focus on your learning). Tell us a story of how you became more aware of the values, assumptions, and biases you bring to your role. Tell us a story of how you used critical theory to become more aware of the privileges you carry and/or oppression you've experienced and how you're using those life experiences to directly benefit young people. Tell us a story of a program in your community that you think the wider CYC profession should know about. Tell us a story of how you discarded some historical theories and welcomed new ones (and make sure to tell us how we can see theory being helpful in our practice). The opportunities are endless.

Why not start with your practicum experience? If you were to write an article for one of our journals—*CYC-Online*, for example—what would you write about? What stories would you want to share? Who could help you formulate and communicate your ideas?

Remember, you're the expert on your learning and development process. We learn from sharing stories. We want to read and listen to yours.

We have now had the opportunity to review numerous examples of opportunities for your current (or future) practicum placement, where you will take practice observations and communicate those for different audiences, in different formats, for different purposes. Again, these opportunities may present themselves at your practicum setting, you may have to advocate on your behalf to participate in them, or you may not have the opportunity to do them just yet. However, one form of observation, documentation, and reporting that we all need to learn about—no matter what the practicum setting or role—is the disclosure and reporting of abuse and neglect.

DISCLOSURE AND REPORTING OF ABUSE AND NEGLECT

We turn to what can be an intense experience for many practitioners: encountering young people who disclose abuse or neglect while in our care. We work with vulnerable young people and are more likely to encounter young people who have experienced or are experiencing abuse and/or neglect. It is up to us to learn how to respond the best we can to their needs in the moment and afterward. In your experience in the field thus far, you may have already encountered a situation where you have had to report suspicions of child abuse and/or neglect. While you may not come across this experience in your practicum, you are nevertheless responsible to know what you may encounter, what you may observe, and how you should respond, both to the young person's disclosure as well as how and to whom you should report that information. You should never be alone in this process. Your supervisor and colleagues should be there to support you throughout.

Across all provinces and territories of Canada, as community members, but especially as practitioners who perform professional duties with heightened awareness of the signs of abuse and neglect, we have a duty to report this information to maintain the safety and protection of young people. It is important to understand your professional, agency, and provincial requirements to report reasonable concerns of abuse and/or neglect.

Let's first explore what we may observe with young people—through our interactions, conversations, and observations—who may be experiencing abuse and/or neglect. Abuse can take many forms and involve different people: from parents and caregivers (including responsible adults involved in the care of young people's lives) to siblings and peers, and so on. Abuse can be physical, where a child is injured or harmed by a caregiver or if a caregiver is unable or unwilling to protect the child from injury or harm. It can be emotional, where a caregiver injures a young person's self-worth. It can be sexual, where a young person is exploited sexually, from inappropriate sexual boundaries to assault. Abuse can also take the form of neglect, where a young person's basic needs are not provided for by the person responsible for their care, such as housing, food, safety, clothing, access to health treatment, and more. Further, children can also be witness to multiple forms of abuse in their home environment.

While we may not directly witness this abuse, in our roles we can be witness to the indicators of potential abuse. In Table 10.1, Martin (2014) provides an extensive list of indicators of potential child abuse or neglect but also cautions practitioners to see all behaviour within the context in which it appears. She reminds us that we should not arbitrarily take one of these signs or symptoms and assume anything; rather, we should see clusters of behaviours to inform our conclusions. We work with vulnerable populations often in the context of poverty, and it is our responsibility to not view poverty through a lens of neglect and maltreatment. Rather, we need to see the effects of poverty as a social justice issue that we can respond to, to improve the conditions in which families live. As you look through the list in Table 10.1, consider what you have witnessed in your practicum, and the meaning you've attributed to it.

Provincial Policy and Legislation

Across provinces and territories, child, family, and community services legislation will drive the rules you—as an adult community member and practitioner providing professional care to young people—are expected to follow. Whether you're a practitioner in Ontario consulting the guidelines of the Ministry of Children, Community, and Social Services and Children's Aid Societies; Saskatchewan consulting the guidelines of the Ministry of Social Services; British Columbia consulting the guidelines of the Ministry of Children and Family Development; or another province, all governing bodies will have legislation and accompanying guidelines to help you understand your duties and responsibilities. You must then integrate that knowledge into your own relational approach, in the context of your specific agency, with specific factors involved, in the specific scenario you encounter with a young person. If you have not already consulted these documents through your Introduction to CYC Practice or a related course, stop what you are doing right now and go read them.

What provincial or territorial act contains legislation regarding your responsibility to report abuse and neglect?

What ministry website contains the general guidelines that you are responsible for knowing and following?

Agency Policy and Procedure

All health authorities, educational institutions, and social service agencies and organizations will have integrated their governmental legislation and guidelines for their specific context. They will have created policy and procedure regarding the observation or disclosure of abuse and neglect for their specific setting. Depending on the contextual factors

Table 10.1: Indicators of Child Abuse and Neglect

Indicators of Child Abuse and Neglect	
• Noticeable changes in behaviour • Frantic behaviour, particularly associated with bathing or changing clothes • Regression • Confusion • Expressions of anger • Increased activity or restlessness • Fear of being left alone • Physical symptoms (stomach ache, nausea, etc.) • Isolation from peers • Clinginess, whining, crying • Performance deterioration • Being unwashed and lacking personal care • Bite marks • Expressions of guilt and shame • Rope burns/lashings • Toileting problems • Feces smearing • Seeming intimidated • Phobias • Urinary tract infections • Runaway attempts • Fear of going home • Bruises • Welts • Cuts • Burns • Fractures • Poor memory and concentration • Disorganized home life • Cannot recall how injuries happened • Fatigue/sleep problems • Sudden weight change • Difficulty walking or sitting • Torn, stained, or bloody underwear • Injuries to the mouth, genital, or anal areas • Pain in any area of the body • Acting out sexualized scenarios • Atypical changes in personality • Stress	• Bizarre, sophisticated, or unusual sexual knowledge • Reverts to bedwetting/soiling • Fearful when startled • Need for constant companionship • Lack of trust • Inability to have fun • Lag in emotional development • Fear of failure • Excessive neatness/compulsive behaviour • Unattended medical/physical needs • Consistent hunger • Nutritional deficiencies • Erratic program/school attendance • Steals food or other items • Takes over adult caring role • Inappropriate dress for the weather • Bald patches on head • Vacant stares/frozen watchfulness • Indiscriminate affection-seeking • Overly compliant or willing to please • Acts out alarming scenes imitating parents/others • Lack of boundaries in physical contact • Unsafe and risky behaviour • Emotional dependence • Unusual inability to communicate • Unexpected/unexplained fears • Atypical attachments • Marks on arm (possible handprints) • Self-abusive behaviours • Sleep and eating difficulties • Excessive masturbation • Inappropriate sexual behaviour • Dramatic mood swings • Outbursts of anger or hostility • Sexually abusive toward others • Drawings with sexualized content • Disclosure of abuse

Adapted from Martin, S. (2014). *Take a look: Observation and portfolio assessment in early childhood* (pp. 307–308). Don Mills, ON: Pearson.

of the organization—residential care settings, correctional or rehabilitative institutions, recreational centres, schools, and so on—its practitioners will need guidance and support in order to support the young people in its care through this process. For example, some agency procedures could (or could not) look like the following:

> In my first practicum, I had to call the Ministry because one of our youth came in and was under 18 and that was the policy, just in case they were missing.
> —Heather, CYC Student

- Stay with the young person
- Do not ask investigative questions; just listen and observe
- Immediately consult with a supervisor (or another responsible person in their absence)
- Recall as many facts, observations, and so on that you've been privy to, and record them for reporting purposes
- With your supervisor's support to ensure the safety of the young person, call your local ministry office to walk through a reporting conversation that will include an assessment of the young person's immediate risk
- Record the incident as per the requirements of the agency (i.e., an incident report)

These steps may not include attention to the relationship between you and the young person. This is where our CYC approach—our relational practice—assists us in maintaining our connection with young people through this process.

CYC Professional Practice

As to our professional responsibilities to respond well to young people who have experienced abuse and/or neglect, we can look to the relationship and relational approach that is foundational to our CYC practice. We can also look to our ethical standards for guidance and expectations on, for example, respect and the limits of confidentiality. Ultimately, young people expect us to care for them, show compassion and understanding, and ensure their safety. We can do this through our connection with them, walking them through difficult situations. While the reporting of abuse and neglect can seem procedural, what should be at the centre is our relationship with the young person and our relational approach to each encounter. What is important to any process of disclosure and reporting of abuse and neglect is what is important through any other therapeutic encounter with young people. We need to ensure that young people trust that we will walk alongside them through their life journey, conveying to them that we care for them and believe they deserve to live their life not with abuse and neglect but with wellness and care.

Your Practicum Context

Of course, integrating these factors will look different across practicum sites. Learning from others will help us along the way. Because practicum is focused on learning from others, we can look to supervisors, colleagues, faculty, and classmates to help us through.

Activity 10.6: Disclosures of Abuse or Neglect at My Practicum Site

At the beginning of your practicum, you likely reviewed policy and procedure at your organization related to disclosures of abuse and/or neglect. It will be helpful to review those documents to refresh your memory. Next, if you have not already done so, take the time to have a focused conversation with your supervisor to understand how disclosures of abuse/neglect have or may happen at your practicum site. Processes will vary slightly, depending on contextual factors. For example, a disclosure of abuse from a youth at a group home will be different than a disclosure of abuse from a child at a recreational centre. Why? Consider the multiple factors in these two situations. Age, development, custody status, government involvement, proximity to risk, and organizational policy are just some of those factors.

Ask your supervisor for some examples of their experiences so you can move beyond the abstract processes and guidelines. During this conversation, you may consider asking the following questions to more fully comprehend the situation. Take some notes to help you recall important guidance, but do not record identifying personal information.

- What was your existing relationship and connection like with the young person?
- In what context was the abuse/neglect observed or disclosed?
- What happened during this interaction with the young person?
- How did you explain to the young person that you had to tell someone to ensure their safety?
- What policy and procedure did you need to follow?
- What steps did you have to take? Who was involved throughout each step?
- What was the outcome of reporting the abuse/neglect?
- How did that situation impact your relationship with the young person?
- What was it like for you, as a practitioner, to go through this process?

_____

_____

_____

_____

_____

After your conversation with your supervisor, you may wish to confidentially debrief with your classmates. What was it like to listen to this situation? What did you learn from the process? You may also wish to focus your learning journal reflections on what you learned.

Work through Activity 10.6 to explore how disclosures of abuse and/or neglect may show up at your practicum site and how you can responsibly respond.

While we cannot anticipate the exact conditions in which we will observe signs of abuse and neglect, nor can we anticipate if and when a young person discloses abuse or neglect to us, we certainly can be prepared to understand how we may encounter this situation at our practicum site. We can then learn from our colleagues and classmates about the varied conditions in which we may encounter disclosures of abuse or neglect and the requirements to report this information. Ask your colleagues and ask your classmates across different practicum settings: how have you encountered observations of or disclosures of abuse and neglect? What was required of you in these situations? How did you maintain your relationship with the young person through this difficult situation?

> Think about what 'duty to report' actually means and how do we do it without causing harm to the families in the long run.
> —Farah, CYC Practicum Supervisor

CRITICAL THINKING IN OBSERVATION, DOCUMENTATION, AND RECORDING

As we near the end of this chapter, let's again consider observation, writing, and reporting as a chance to contribute to the growth, development, and wellness of young people. To achieve this goal, we can approach each of these processes with a critical lens, reflecting upon what we observe and why, how we describe and communicate young people's lives, and the purpose and intentions when reporting information about and to young people.

In her review of decades of documentation practices in a residential care setting, Chalupa (2015) witnessed the evolution of practice standards and expectations. She noticed that, in the past, documentation practices were considerably unprofessional, whereas current practices were changing for the better (see Figure 10.4).

In her reflections, she concluded, "good record-keeping and documentation of child and youth care practices ensure accountability around practice standards but they also preserve life stories and personal achievements" (Chalupa, 2015, p. 77). You are at a practicum setting at a particular time in the helping profession's development. We practise observation, documentation, and reporting in particular ways, influenced by factors including time. What will our practices look like in 20 years? How will they (hopefully) be more respectful, accountable, and helpful to young people and their families? What about today's "best practice" may shock us when looking back?

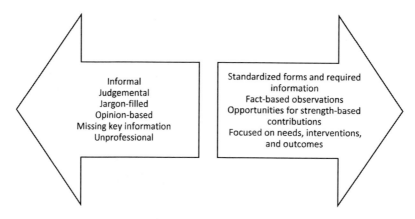

Figure 10.4: Past and Present Documentation Trends

Look at the language. Why is this written? How is it written? What purpose is it meant to serve? How is it being used? How would I like to read it? What would I do the same or differently?
— Yvonne, CYC Practicum Faculty-Instructor

We can also look to theoretical assumptions embedded in our observation, documentation, and reporting practices. For example, Pacini-Ketchabaw (2011) warns that when "developmental theories are treated as facts… [and] these 'facts' lead us to construct certain views about children, and we use these views to interpret observations of the children and youth we encounter in practice," we are shaping, limiting, and including certain understandings of young people, while excluding others (p. 19). Snell (2015) goes on to reflect that she believes "reflective assessment and thorough documentation is vital to our work," but that she is "dismayed by the implicit assumption that a young person 'should' be somewhere else and that our role is to 'get them there'" (pp. 7–8). She is highlighting our contribution to a particular understanding of what observation, documentation, and reporting processes are for. Do they exist to support young people in their wellness, or do they exist to prescribe certain assumptions of where young people should be?

Highlighting the opportunity for strengths-based practice, Leon and Pepe (2010) state observation and subsequent documentation and recording give us the chance to "practice identifying client strengths, conceptualizing those strengths for the written context, and documenting the strengths objectively" (p. 366). To that end, we could ask ourselves: if and when this young person reads the report, would they feel they've been respected and their dignity as a person upheld? The practice of communicating about and for young people— written, oral, and so on—is a matter of ethics. We should develop these skills to expand our competency, but we should also embody this responsibility with an ethical stance. As we have been reminded throughout this guidebook, everything is a matter of ethics.

Young People's Files

One way of critically assessing observation, documentation, and reporting practices is to look at files. Files include paper or digital collections of correspondence, observations, reports, and other information about an individual young person, held confidentially at an organization. Files can contain a spectrum of information—as simple as contact information and consent for participation in a specific program or as complex as multiple reports, incidents, interagency documents, and other information over time. Complete Activity 10.7 to engage thoughtfully and respectfully when reading and contributing to files of young people at your site.

Activity 10.7: Respectfully Reading and Contributing to Young People's Files

When in practicum, we have access to privileged and confidential information in young people's files, depending on our roles in the setting. Reviewing and contributing to young people's files needs to be approached with the utmost respect. For this activity, you will need to ask your supervisor for access to a file. It is preferred that your supervisor select a file of a historical client; that is, a case that's been closed, such as a past student no longer attending the school or a resident no longer at the group home. If this is not possible, then ask to review a file of a young person you know of, and ask your supervisor to omit any information they believe you should not see. (If your site does not keep individual files—for example, at a recreational centre—ask your supervisor for access to equivalent information.) Show your supervisor the questions below, so they are aware of the activity's purpose.

In a private space at your site, review this file, considering the list of questions. If you take notes or write about this experience, take extra precautions to exclude confidential information. Focus on your learning experience, not their information.

- What information is included in this file? What is excluded?
- What are your impressions of this person, based on reading their file documents?
- What story does this file tell about the young person? What story does it not tell?
- How do you think reviewing this person's file helps and hinders your connection with them?
- Do you find that the documents in this file have followed the basic recommendations listed earlier in this chapter? What examples would you give to support this assessment?
- Do you experience the documents in this file as respectful, non-judgemental, and strengths-based? What examples would you give to support this assessment?
- How will you respect confidentiality as part of the process of reviewing this file?
- What was this experience like for you?

_____

_____

_____

_____

_____

_____

_____

> Written documentation is permanent. It matters what we write and how we write it. I invite students to think about the young person while they are documenting, and how they think the young person would respond if they were reading the words the student is writing about them. This helps keep them strengths-based and cognizant of the impact of their words.
> —Kristy, CYC Practicum Faculty-Instructor

As we become more involved in observing, documenting, and reporting—for a variety of audiences and purposes—we must keep young people at the centre of these actions. Chalupa (2015) speaks to the significance of this work, when she reflects,

> Every youth has a right to their own history, to be represented, and to have the respect of professionals who ensure that reporting is accurate, complete, and retrievable... [where] each file represents the life of a human being, and provides a chronicle of relationships with carers, teachers and peers during periods of out-of-home care. (pp. 79–80)

As emerging CYC practitioners, this is the responsibility we carry forward into our work.

LEARNING JOURNAL

You've been observing your practicum environment for a while now, including the people and activities happening within it. What have your informal and formal observations taught you? What opportunities have you had to document, write, and report? What was that process like for you? What did you learn? Focus this week's learning journal entry on this chapter's topics. Use the opportunity to work through any challenges you're experiencing.

PRACTICE SCENARIOS

Take a look at the Practice Scenarios that conclude this chapter: "Differing Views" and "Strategic Writing." Use the content in this chapter to inspire your thinking about the scenario.

Notice how the scenario may relate to your own situation at your current practicum placement, even if it is not exactly what you are experiencing. Consider the questions posed at the end of each scenario to help you expand and apply the concepts presented in this chapter.

SEMINAR GROUP AND COMMUNITY OF PRACTICE DISCUSSION QUESTIONS

In your seminar and community of practice groups, consider the following questions for discussion:

1. What types of written communication are required in your role at your practicum site? Explain each type, then compare and contrast with your classmates' examples.
2. Many of the reports, assessments, and documentation we complete are for the purpose of sharing with other professionals (for assessment and planning, staff communication, case management, service referrals, etc.), as opposed to being for young people and their families. When we write these reports, what if we keep in mind that young people are going to read them? Does this change how you write? How so?
3. What is the process at your site for disclosure of abuse and neglect?
4. What are the pros and cons of looking at a file before getting to know a young person? What does your practicum site advise? What is your opinion? What are the factors that go into your decision?

IN CLOSING

In this chapter, we've had the opportunity to review a number of tasks and activities that encourage you to immerse yourself into the world of observation, documentation, verbal and written communication, and reporting. In a first or second CYC practicum, how immersed you become in these tasks will depend on your role and setting. Whether you've had the chance to write a mock incident report, present on a particular issue at a team meeting, or write a proposal for funding, we invite you to consider the great responsibility you have—to give care and consideration to the ethics involved—and the significant impact all these tasks have on young people's lives. Not only are we tasked with finding the words that reflect the lived reality of young people, while communicating to diverse audiences with diverse interests, we must also consider the bigger picture. What is communicated, how it is communicated, and to whom and with what intention have very real implications for young people and their well-being. How can we use that influence to benefit their lives? That is what we are figuring out as we avail ourselves to these opportunities at practicum.

PRACTICE SCENARIOS

Differing Views

In seminar, Nasser shares that he believes he shouldn't read a young person's case file before meeting them. He says it may influence how he views that young person before he forms an opinion himself. Kaley thinks it's valuable to view a young person's case file before meeting the young person, so that it can help her to get to know the person, what they're like, what they may need, and if there are any important things she should know before meeting them.

Think through the pros and cons of each opinion. How do you think each person has arrived at their opinion? What do you think is right? Does your opinion change if the contextual factors change? How could each person's concerns be addressed? What have you decided to do or what were you told to do at your agency?

_____

_____

_____

Strategic Writing

Ahmad obtained permission from his group home supervisor to ask a local retail store for donations of sporting goods. He plans to write a letter and visit the store. Penny offers to begin a social media account for the recreation centre's youth drop-in centre, posting youth-friendly information, including free events in the community, jobs and volunteer opportunities, other community resources, public health info, and inspirational quotes. Char's supervisor asked her to accompany her to an open community forum, co-hosted by the municipal government and transportation authority. Char was asked to prepare some current research on youth-friendly transportation initiatives and gather some quotes from youth at their agency about their needs for her supervisor to present.

Is there something at your practicum site you could be advocating for through the strategic use of writing?

_____

_____

_____

PART III

Ending and Moving Forward

CHAPTER 11

Wellness and Self-Care in CYC

Competencies for Professional Child and Youth Work Practitioners				
Professionalism	Cultural and Human Diversity	Applied Human Development	Relationship and Communication	Developmental Practice Methods
Personal Development and Self-Care				

Focus on and explore personal feelings that are enhanced throughout the practicum experience. This is emotional work. Triggers that we never knew we had, feelings of disappointment, sadness, happiness, feeling overwhelmed, worries for our clients. The better we reflect and understand ourselves in the work from the beginning of our work, from practicum to retirement, the better we will fare in this field and the better we will support and honour our clients' journeys.

—Jennifer Hanrahan, Director of Operations and Residential Services, St. Leonard's Youth and Family Services

What does it mean to care for oneself? What does it mean to be well? How does one go about pursuing, maintaining, and strengthening wellness? Why do self-care and wellness matter to our practice as emerging Child and Youth Care (CYC) practitioners? This chapter discusses reflecting on our own experience of wellness, reviewing recommended strategies in the pursuit of wellness, and identifying stressors and risks to our wellness if we do not attend to ourselves. Meanwhile, this chapter also hopes to shift us from a focus on individual self-care strategies to a discussion of collective and sustainable wellness as a community.

You may ask, shouldn't this chapter on wellness and self-care be first? Yes! While we touched on this topic in a few earlier chapters, it is often not until we reach the end of our first practicum experience that we have the embodied experience of the effects of *attending* and *not attending* to our wellness. If this topic were placed at the beginning of

> I don't think I was even aware what my internal resources were at the time.
>
> —Jenn, CYC Student

this guidebook, it may risk being looked over as an abstract concept, easy to gloss over. As you're coming to the end of your practicum experience, you have now gained valuable experiential learning to reflect upon. You also have the opportunity to set further goals for any upcoming placements and positions in the field.

WELLNESS AND SELF-CARE

What exactly does wellness mean? What is self-care? They are the deliberate attitudes, activities, and actions we perform that attend to one's holistic health and well-being. These are life-long journeys we take as we learn more about ourselves and our needs, immerse ourselves in different contexts with different demands and responsibilities, and experience successes, challenges, losses, and changes over time. Wellness and self-care is essential to our CYC practice so that we show up for young people and families with presence, are able to focus our attention on and respond to their needs and not our own, model the pursuit of holistic health and well-being, and increase our self-awareness as to when we may need additional support.

1. What does wellness and self-care mean to you?

   _____

   _____

2. How have you attended to wellness and self-care throughout your practicum thus far?

   _____

   _____

3. How have you neglected wellness and self-care throughout your practicum thus far?

   _____

   _____

4. What have you learned about your wellness and self-care needs through the particular challenges, responsibilities, and expectations you have experienced in practicum thus far?

   _____

   _____

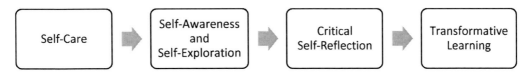

Figure 11.1: Burns's Self-Reflection Learning Progression

Adapted from Burns, M. (2012). *The self in child and youth care: A celebration* (p. 13). Kingston, ON: Child Care Press.

Burns (2012) connects self-care to our learning process (Figure 11.1). He highlights that self-care is the essential first step to achieve transformative learning. When we attend to self-care, it provides the foundation for awareness and exploration of one's self, which leads to the capacity and opportunity for critical self-reflection. This opportunity then opens up space for transformative learning to occur.

Have you noticed this connection in your learning experiences at practicum thus far? Have you noticed that when you have not attended to your wellness, you have been less able to reflect, less able to meaningfully and authentically learn? Less able to respond well to the young people around you?

STRESS AND WELLNESS

Working in any helping profession can be stressful, and that stress can interfere with our ability to be well. Further, with academic, family, and financial responsibilities, it may seem obvious to say that students experience a unique kind of stress. Meanwhile, the hours you must complete for practicum are often *in addition to* your regular responsibilities, rather than *in lieu of.*

Stress—tension, strain, pressure, weight, and so on—includes the pressure put upon us, the effects of that pressure, and how we embody that pressure. In what ways do you experience stress? How does stress show up in your life?

> We had a student who wanted to quit the program, because they were feeling overwhelmed. After having a good cry, and being able to talk things through with their supervisor, they were able to process, and fight to get back on track. This student ended up working for the agency, because they embraced how we show empathy for all people.
> —Farah, CYC Practicum Supervisor

Many people thrive under stress and spend a lifetime learning how to pursue challenges while staying well and sustaining themselves in this complex field of work over time. Each of us has indicators that tell us when we need to slow down, check in, and attend to ourselves. These indicators could include frequent physical illnesses, variability in emotions, adoption of unhealthy habits, sleep disruption, difficulty focusing attention, missing or being late for deadlines and meetings, decrease in efficiency and performance, negative interactions with those close to you, withdrawing or avoidance, feelings of helplessness, constant complaining, the denial of stress in one's life, or a desire to flee the stressful situation (Birkenmaier & Berg-Weger, 2011, pp. 39–40). Which of these indicators do you recognize in your life? What are your internal and external experiences of stress?

Recall a stressful time in your life—current, recent, or past. What was happening? What was involved? How did you experience stress?

_____

_____

Now think of that same stressful time in your life. What helped you through it?

_____

_____

How stress shows up in practicum students' lives can look very different. Consider the following practicum students' situations.

1. Sonia is trying to do everything. She arrives at the residential group home early. She stays late. She's asked to be involved in multiple programs and projects while at practicum. In the first 2 weeks, she's completed 60 hours of an 8-week practicum that requires a total of 150 hours (while also taking 2 elective courses and working part-time on the weekend). She hasn't yet informed her supervisor or faculty-instructor of her schedule. She's sure she'll need an extension for an assignment for one of her elective classes. She hasn't seen her friends in a few weeks, she is skipping meals, and she has noticed she's quite irritable while driving.

2. Ina knows she experiences the world through emotion, empathy, and compassion. She is in a practicum placement at an elementary school that works closely with the kids at the neighbourhood house and recreation centre, and sometimes conducts home visits to support its families. Ina notices that when she returns to her home and family, she often reflects on the children's lives, the daily barriers they face, and the crises she has been and anticipates being involved in. Ina's children and partner notice that she has been frequently distracted, distant, forgetful, and quick to become upset.

3. Francis likes getting to know the youth at the street outreach centre, in the youth drop-in room offering food, games, and a warm place to hang out. He also goes on outreach visits to offer street-involved youth food, clothes, access to services, and so on. Francis told his supervisors that he eventually wants to work in child protection, working to support kids in government care, so he feels lucky that they began inviting him to interagency and case-planning meetings for some of the youth they support. He notices, however, that at many of these meetings, some of the professionals only increase their involvement when there's a crisis, don't speak very respectfully of the youth, and seem to be more preoccupied with following bureaucratic procedure than connecting with the youth. As a former youth in care, he feels discouraged and disappointed, to say the least. Now he's not so sure his voice will be welcomed, and he's beginning to question his future career directions.

Do you recognize any aspect of these practicum students in yourself? What strengths do these students bring to the challenges they find themselves facing? How is stress showing up in their lives? What difficulties are they currently experiencing? What difficulties may they encounter in a few weeks? A few months? A few years? What words of encouragement would you give to Sonia, Ina, and Francis right now? What guidance would you give to them before practicum began? What would you invite them to reflect upon regarding wellness and self-care?

Self-Care Strategies

One way we respond to stress in our lives is to implement self-care strategies to reduce or manage stress. In Chapter 2, we reviewed Birkenmaier and Berg-Weger's (2011) list of general self-care recommendations for practicum students. Go back and re-read this list, and consider how you attended or did not attend to these recommendations.

How we engage in these particular self-care pursuits is put into practice individually and looks different from person to person. Consider the following list for more specific recommendations. Myers-Kiser (2016) asks practicum students, "what stress-relieving activities are you engaging in during the course of your internship?" while also offering the following list as a place to start experimenting (p. 272). As you read through this list, consider which activities you enjoy doing and/or are beneficial to your health and well-being.

> Self-care is needed the most when you don't think you need self-care.
> —Margaret, CYC Student

> Make sure you're using time outside of practicum and work to engage in activities that you like, want, and enjoy.
> —Jasmine, CYC Student

> Check in and check out.
> —Yvonne, CYC Practicum Faculty-Instructor

> Get a good night's sleep. Eat something yummy. Indulge in something.
> —Donna, CYC Practicum Supervisor

- ☑ Talking with friends
- ☑ Walking
- ☑ Bike riding
- ☑ Playing with pets
- ☑ Swimming
- ☑ Sitting outdoors
- ☑ Internet surfing
- ☑ Playing individual or group sports
- ☑ Running
- ☑ Online social networking
- ☑ Working out
- ☑ Playing electronic or video games
- ☑ Pleasure reading
- ☑ Spending time with friends or family
- ☑ Eating dinner out
- ☑ Praying
- ☑ Meditating
- ☑ Taking a nap
- ☑ Watching a movie
- ☑ Lying in the sun
- ☑ Working on puzzles
- ☑ Knitting
- ☑ Listening to music
- ☑ Playing an instrument
- ☑ Gardening
- ☑ Doing yoga (pp. 271–272)

What else would you add to this list of self-care wisdom from students, supervisors, and faculty-instructors? What happens when we do not attend to our wellness and experience the cumulative effects of stress over time?

Mindfulness breathing. Yoga stretches. Smudge. Come to the office, close the door, and vent. Drink water. Eat healthy. Know your own trauma triggers and how you carry pain. Be aware of your own history.
—Sonja, CYC Practicum Supervisor

COMPASSION FATIGUE, VICARIOUS TRAUMA, AND BURNOUT

We work in challenging environments, supporting young people and their families in their life-space who face significant adversity. Supporting people through these challenges requires us to practise wellness and self-care to show up well to this supportive role *and* to navigate difficult terrain alongside young people and families encountering difficulty. Compassion fatigue. Vicarious trauma. Burnout. Where have you learned these terms before? What do they mean to you?

A lot of my self-care is done with my kids, going on a walk in the park or to museums or to the arcade or just going for a SkyTrain ride. I have all these areas where I travelled as a kid and just being able to bring my kids and watch them walk in the same footsteps, I just love it.
—Adrian, CYC Student

In his discussion of self-care in CYC, Burns (2012) reminds us that

> Compassion fatigue or vicarious trauma is an accumulation of the stressors inherent in becoming emotionally involved with one or more psychologically troubled individuals. After certain amounts of exposure to individuals who are in psychological pain or distress, you begin to not only empathize with their situation, you often begin to internalize some of their psychological stress… This internalizing of the psychological pain or distress is termed compassion fatigue or vicarious trauma. It is characterized by physical and emotional fatigue to the point of exhaustion, sharp decrease in the ability to empathize, increasing lack of interest in otherwise enjoyable experiences, and frequent episodes of physical, psychological and/or emotional pain. Burnout is the culmination of compassion fatigue to the point where you are unable to function adequately either in your personal life or your professional life. (p. 59)

Looking at burnout within CYC practitioners, Barford and Whelton (2010) notice that "it was the employees who were experiencing a high degree of work pressure, a poor understanding of their roles and expectations, and who felt the least commitment to their jobs that experienced the highest amount of emotional exhaustion" (pp. 282–283). First-time practicum students face a unique combination of stressors too: students can be unsure of their role, unsure of learning expectations, and unsure of how to contribute what they know to the practice environment. Meanwhile, Kostouros and Briegel (2018) notice the unfortunate trend that "some [practicum] settings are extremely under-resourced and that can mean that they rely heavily on staff for extra duties. In some cases, as a student, you too may be asked to take on more than anticipated" (p. 119). All the hard work you've already done in your practicum experience thus far—to know your role and what is expected of you, reduce pressure by having a support group and advisors, and develop a strong commitment to your practicum site—is all work that helps us reduce the chance that we enter into a place of exhaustion. Oates (2016) reviewed the practicum experience itself and suggested that a combination of supervision and other formal and informal supports reduced levels of burnout: seminar group, connection with students and instructor, purposeful reflection, self-care activities, connection with friends and family. Not only is your practicum course designed to facilitate your learning experience, its main components—seminar group, supervisor and instructor availability, reflection activities and assignments, and so on—are also there to support wellness.

> Self-care used to be football for me or other sports. It turned into podcasts. Or sometimes I do spoken word. It's finding different pieces that turn your brain off.
> —Cody, CYC Student

> There's going to be experiences where information may affect you on a personal level. Acknowledge that and how it affects you is important. Then know what supports you have if it does have an impact on your life.
> —Trina, CYC Student

WELLNESS ACROSS SYSTEMS

Zak (2015) recommends we look to our ecological system to see what does and does not support wellness, noting that there are individual, agency, and systemic factors. Some of these factors are included in Figure 11.2. As you read each factor, consider how it can either contribute to an environment of stress or an environment of wellness. Meanwhile, as you read, add more.

For example, when time is disrespected within a workplace—people consistently showing up late for work, being asked to stay beyond the end of a shift without pay, expecting staff to accomplish too much within the time available, and so on—it can contribute to the stress individuals feel in a setting. When adaptations are made for staff experiencing burnout—such as counselling support, temporarily altered caseloads, and increased social support—it can contribute to the support and wellness individuals feel in a setting. When the organizational culture of an agency is based on crisis and fear, the experience of individuals contributing to that agency will be very different than those contributing to an agency with an organizational culture based on continuous learning and development. Notice how, in all these scenarios, it is the practitioner who carries the effects of those stressors. It's the practitioner who feels the effects of poor sleep habits, and it's the practitioner who stays up at night because of the fear-based organizational culture. Like the young people we work alongside, we must address change at multiple levels of systems.

SUPPORTING WELLNESS AND SELF-CARE

Some CYC educational programs have a dedicated wellness course as part of your credential. Others will have wellness content threaded through the courses. What have you been learning thus far? What have your faculty-instructors been encouraging you to attend to, as you introduce yourself and immerse yourself in this field?

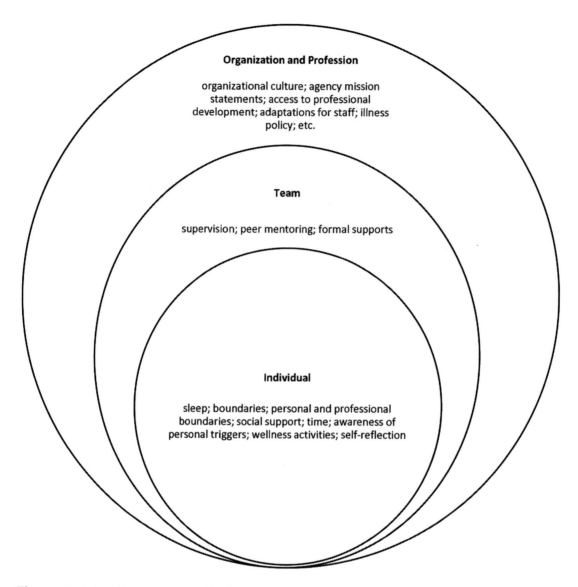

Figure 11.2: Wellness across Systems

Heaney Dalton (2018) encourages new CYC practitioners and practicum students to develop our resilient selves, to "know without a doubt that the resilience you develop now will help sustain you day-in and day-out and keep you around long enough to reap the rewards of all the time and effort you are investing in your future" (p. 123). All the care you devote to your wellness now—including reflecting on mistakes, setbacks, and lack of care—will be important in attending to your practice over time. What you learn about yourself now will inform your future self. What you care for now will help shape what you need in the future.

> It's one thing to think about it and another to do it.
> —Rhonda, CYC Practicum Faculty-Instructor

Wellness Wheel

In CYC, we often look to holistic frameworks and models of young people's development and wellness. It makes sense for us to look at our own wellness through this lens as well. Loiselle and McKenzie (2006) describe a wellness wheel for human service practitioners, which is an Indigenous approach to wellness that is

> Achieved through individual effort toward the attainment of balance and harmony in life and the fulfilment of personal potential… [a] holistic approach that aims to promote well-being at all levels of society as well as in all realms of human functioning, i.e. the body, the heart, the mind and the soul. (p. 3)

As described in Figure 11.3, the wellness wheel includes the physical, emotional, mental, and spiritual realms.

The wellness wheel walks us through meaningful, guided self-reflection and purposeful planning and action. It assists us in our ability to be present for young people, sustain ourselves and our practice, and model wellness in complex environments. While the following activities will focus on your wellness as a student in practicum, you could also reflect on how this framework could be useful when working with young people and families, facilitating and supporting their wellness. Central to the wellness wheel framework (and the traditional Indigenous medicine wheel teachings it

> It's life balance, not work-life balance.
> —Andrew, CYC Practicum Faculty-Instructor

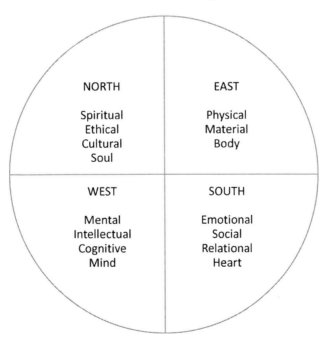

Figure 11.3: The Wellness Wheel

Adapted from Loiselle, M., & McKenzie, L. (2006). The wellness wheel: An Aboriginal contribution to social work. *First North-American Conference on Spirituality and Social Work*, Waterloo, Ontario, Canada, pp. 13–18.

derives from) is the "principle that all things are interconnected" (Verniest, 2006, para. 6). That is, wellness exists and is in relationship across the four realms as well as across individual-collective-structural contexts.

   Activities 11.1, 11.2, and 11.3 will walk you through a current assessment of your wellness in each realm: from reflection and assessment to brainstorming and planning, and then to action. Keep in mind that there will and should be overlap between areas. Further, while you may identify many areas in need of development, do not feel the need to pressure yourself by addressing all those areas at one time. We are, after all, talking about wellness and self-care. Address what you feel is important, possible, and promotes wellness, rather than adding pressure and stress in your life.

Activity 11.1: Step One: My Wellness Today

Without jumping ahead to Steps Two and Three, consider each area in your life—physical, emotional, mental, and spiritual. List the ways in which you attend to or care for each area of your life. In your reflections, include how you, the people in your life, and the contexts in which you take part support your wellness. For each area, ask yourself:

1. What are you presently doing to care for your physical/emotional/mental/spiritual well-being?
2. What environmental factors contribute to your physical/emotional/mental/spiritual well-being?
3. What activities, practices, thoughts, and other factors support your physical/emotional/mental/spiritual well-being?

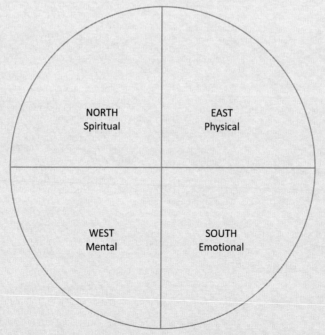

Figure 11.4: Step 1: Wellness Wheel

Keep in mind Figure 11.3's descriptors as you brainstorm, and be sure to think widely. For example, in the physical realm, you may put "getting enough sleep" and "nature walks," but you also may put "my college scholarship" and "body positivity" to ensure you're listing all the things contributing to this area of your wellness. Again, don't worry about overlap or in which category to list an item. Where the item goes is not as important as the meaning you attribute to it. If you're unsure, put the item in multiple categories. Do not rush through this activity. Consider taking notes for this activity throughout your week. Whenever you notice something you're doing to care for yourself, list it. See what you come up with.

When you are done, notice the balance between and across all four areas. Ask yourself: have you considered each of these areas before? Are some areas full of items and others sparse? Do some areas feel "easier" to care for than others? Remember, this is not a competition nor is it about quantity. It is about quality, meaning, and balance. Move to Step Two when you are ready.

Adapted from Loiselle, M., & McKenzie, L. (2006). The wellness wheel: An Aboriginal contribution to social work. *First North-American Conference on Spirituality and Social Work*, Waterloo, Ontario, Canada, pp. 13–18.

Activity 11.2: Step Two: Reflecting on My Wellness Today

Loiselle and McKenzie (2006) list a number of thoughtful, complex, and guiding questions you can ask yourself about each realm of wellness. Move through each realm and its listed questions. Notice the questions move from an assessment of your current life to your needs, desires, and wishes for your life, then toward what you could be doing (or avoiding) to enhance each area. Jot down your reflections. These questions are not simple; take the time you need. When you've completed this step, move to Step Three.

Table 11.1: Step 2: Wellness Questions

North: Spiritual
Do I have meaning and purpose in my life?

Do I live up to my principles, beliefs, and values?

_____

_____

What are my spiritual/religious beliefs and practices?

_____

_____

Do I take time out for prayer, fasting, silence, meditation, or enjoyment of nature?

_____

_____

Do I have a grateful attitude about life?

_____

_____

Am I honest, loving, caring, sharing, respectful, trustworthy, humble, and helpful?

_____

_____

In what ways am I respectful of nature?

_____

_____

Do I feel a sense of connectedness to and pride for the values of my culture?

_____

_____

What positive activities can I do to nurture my spiritual life?

_____

_____

East: Physical

In what condition is my physical health?

_____

_____

What are my physical needs right now?

_____

_____

What does my body language tell me? Do I like myself?

_____

_____

What are my priorities to improve my physical well-being?

_____

_____

What positive activities can I do to enhance my physical well-being? (e.g., nutrition, sleep, personal hygiene, exercise, appearance, posture, rest and relaxation, clothing, home tidiness, financial situation)

_____

_____

What harmful things must I avoid to achieve health? (e.g., various dependencies)

_____

_____

What do I see about my future on the physical and on the material planes?

_____

_____

What are my goals? How do I see myself in two years from now?

_____

_____

South: Emotional

In what condition is my emotional health?

_____

_____

What are my emotional needs at this time?

_____

_____

Do I have a positive self-esteem and a strong sense of self-worth?

_____

_____

Am I able to express my feelings and do I have someone I can confide in?

_____

_____

Do I trust people?

_____

_____

Do I feel the need to control others/situations?

_____

_____

Am I maintaining healthy relationships? (e.g., with my life partner, family, relatives, friends, co-workers, neighbours, etc.)

_____

_____

What positive things can I do to enhance my emotional and social well-being?

_____

_____

_____

Am I taking time to nurture the relationships in my life?

_____

_____

Do I have unresolved issues from the past?

_____

_____

What do I feel about the future?

_____

_____

West: Mental

What is my self-talk (or inner dialogue) usually like? (e.g., is it affirmative, positive, and optimistic, or is it self-deprecating or generally negative about others?)

_____

_____

What are my general intellectual activities?

_____

_____

What are the mental stimulations in my life? (e.g., creative activities, reading, writing, studying, puzzles, crosswords, etc.)

_____

_____

What are my creative abilities and how do I foster them?

_____

_____

Am I satisfied with my level of education as well as intellectual and cognitive development?

_____

_____

Am I satisfied with the kind of work I am doing?

_____

_____

Do I take time to reflect and analyze what is happening in my life?

_____

_____

What are my problem-solving skills, and how can I improve them?

_____

_____

Is time management a problem in my life?

_____

_____

What positive activities can I do to enhance my life in the mental, intellectual, and cognitive spheres?

_____

_____

Adapted from Loiselle, M., & McKenzie, L. (2006). The wellness wheel: An Aboriginal contribution to social work. *First North-American Conference on Spirituality and Social Work*, Waterloo, Ontario, pp. 13–18.

Activity 11.3: Step Three: A Wellness Plan

In Step One, you assessed your current wellness and all the things contributing to your wellness in each realm of your life. In Step Two, you expanded that assessment with guided questions that hopefully widened what you considered part of your wellness. You brainstormed things that you may need and/or could be doing to enhance each area of your wellness. In Step Three, we put this together by setting achievable goals to maintain an area of wellness, consulting with your peers to help, and setting a timeline to check in with yourself.

☑ Consider the activities you included in Step One and the activities brainstormed in Step Two.

☑ Meanwhile, consider the example activities listed in Figure 11.5.

☑ Identify one or two goals you have for yourself for each area. Record them around the circle.

☑ Next, check in with your practicum seminar group or community of practice. Share what you feel comfortable sharing. What are they doing? Could you offer ideas for support? Could you seek their guidance regarding what is realistic to accomplish, introduce, or maintain? Do they have ideas you did not think of, that you believe would be a good fit for your life?

☑ Finally, recognize challenges will arise. Adjustments will need to be made. Environmental factors will change. As such, it's important to make a plan to check in with yourself (and each other) to see how your wellness plan is going. What timeline would work best for you to check in with yourself regarding how your wellness plan is going? Daily, weekly, monthly, each term? Decide on a timeline and follow through.

Recognize that a wellness plan may look different for each person. For example, while many practicum students focus on getting enough sleep as part of their physical wellness plan, for each student what is "enough sleep" will be different. One student may set a goal of eight hours of sleep each night. Another student may set a goal of having no screen time before she goes to bed. Another student may set a goal of visiting his physician to address his sleeping difficulties. Another student may set a goal of saving money to purchase a new pillow to address their back pain. Further, remember you are likely already doing many things to support your wellness. Having a goal to continue to do something is perfectly acceptable. Do not reinvent the wheel.

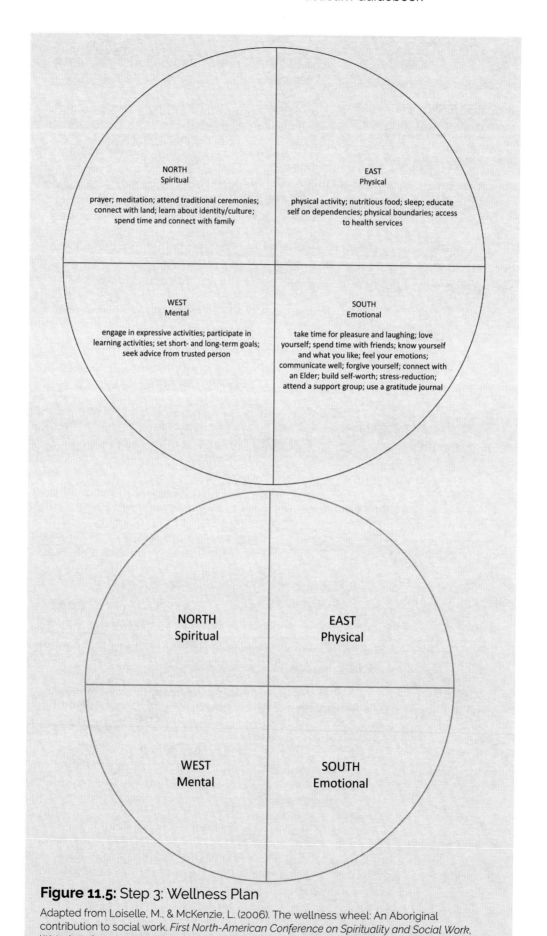

Figure 11.5: Step 3: Wellness Plan

Adapted from Loiselle, M., & McKenzie, L. (2006). The wellness wheel: An Aboriginal contribution to social work. *First North-American Conference on Spirituality and Social Work*, Waterloo, Ontario, Canada, pp. 13–18.

SUSTAINABLE PRACTICE

Focusing on our individual wellness can help our practice, but it is also important to look at wellness from a collective and systemic level too. Further, the ability to critically think about self-care and wellness in our field of practice can help to address both individual struggles and problematic systems that we experience.

Keynote speaker at the 2018 National CYC Conference and social justice activist Vikki Reynolds critiques the traditional concept of burnout, saying it is problematic because it privatizes pain "as if workers somehow aren't tough enough or aren't doing enough emotional sit-ups or something like that to get us ready for the work, when, in fact, what's happening is we are working in contexts that lack social justice" (Reynolds, n.d., para. 3). She invites us to refrain from diagnosing practitioners with compassion fatigue, vicarious trauma, and burnout, stating these conditions are *responses to unjust structures*. She asks us to change our focus and reframe our questions (see Figure 11.6).

When we move away from self-care as a way to survive this work and avoid burnout toward a place of sustainability and wellness, Richardson and Reynolds (2012) suggest we will find a place "amazingly alive in our work" (para. 3). Here, there is spirited presence, genuine connectedness, rich engagement with social justice, and openness to transformation amid difficult work (Richardson & Reynolds, 2012, p. 3). In this conceptualization of wellness, as CYC practitioners, we

> I have a 10 for 10 list that I suggest: list 10 things you enjoy doing, that bring you a sense of joy, relaxation, and connection that you can do easily for 10 minutes. Do at least 3 of them each day. It's easier to find 10 minutes than it is to find 30, but if you do the 10 minutes 3 times a day, you've given yourself 30 minutes of time for you.
> —Kristy, CYC Practicum Faculty-Instructor

> It really clicked for me when Vikki Reynolds said a professional saying they're 'burnt out' from the families they're working with is actually placing blame on the families. And you are revictimizing them. It's putting that on the families and it's not actually the families.
> —Mindi, CYC Practicum Supervisor

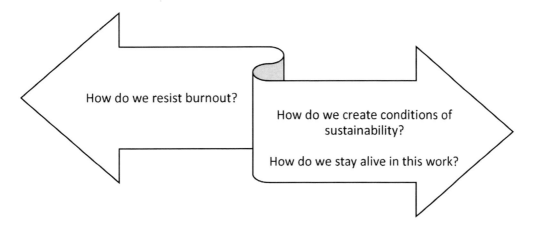

Figure 11.6: Reynolds's Sustainable Practice

Adapted from Reynolds, V. (n.d.). "Zone of fabulousness": Q & A with Vikki Reynolds. University of Calgary, para. 32.

join alongside young people and families in our communities in our collective efforts to change the very circumstances in which we all find ourselves.

To that end, Gharabaghi (2018) encourages us to resist the conversation about self-care becoming operational, rather than meaningful activities and processes that sustain and improve practice. He goes on to say that self-care should be

> First and foremost a commitment to "exercising" the imagination… a way of re-imagining everything one encounters in practice… about story-telling to oneself, re-creating oneself as a character in one's story who finds pathways to meaningful engagement, meaningful relational practice, meaningful care, nurture and love, and meaningful outcomes. It is even about imagining oneself as a warrior of social justice, an ally or participant in anti-racism, a revolutionary in the "un-doing" of institutional control and oppression. In our imagination, we can create pathways for being with young people that render them partners rather than clients. We can overcome barriers to social justice that have been embedded for decades and even centuries. (Gharabaghi, 2018, pp. 62–63)

Too often, self-care and wellness recommendations encourage us to break away from practice—leave practicum at the door, go take a bath, exercise three times per week, see a counsellor when stressed, and so on. Here, Gharabaghi (2018) reminds us that through an imaginative stance, "self-care does not mean to escape our practice. It means to build our practice in a way that is just… When we do this, we gain hope, we gain strength, and we gain strategies for being in the world that doesn't reproduce the oppression of what we may currently experience" (p. 64). Don't escape. Build. Don't survive and avoid. Become amazingly alive.

When we think of our practice in this way, what does this open up space for? What does this allow you to consider? About your wellness? About the wellness of the environments we work within? About the wellness of our communities? About the wellness of our practice? What if we were to create a wellness wheel for CYC practice? What would that entail? Consider the following questions to help us apply a critical lens to our practice.

What legislation, policies, professional competencies, and procedures support young people's physical, emotional, mental, and spiritual wellness? What doesn't? What needs to change?

_____

_____

What interagency connections, interdisciplinary practices, and practitioner relationships support young people's wellness? What doesn't? What needs to change?

_____

_____

What CYC ways of knowing, doing, and being support young people's wellness? What doesn't? What needs to change?

_____

_____

What can you do as a practicum student right now to contribute to that change?

_____

_____

Practicum is a good opportunity to notice and learn. Some practicum settings will have considered and integrated wellness into every aspect of their systems. Some will not. We will align with some practitioners' ways of tending to wellness; others, not so much. What practicum gives us the chance to do is observe and notice how we function within these spaces. It gives us the chance to experiment with strategies and ways of being to see what fits for ourselves. And it gives us the chance to offer new ideas. In practicum, we have a window of opportunity to envision just what kind of practitioner we wish to be, and how we will sustain ourselves and the work we do.

LEARNING JOURNAL

Take any of the activities, questions, or concepts in this chapter and reflect on them in your learning journal. What part of the learning journal itself contributed to your wellness as you completed practicum?

PRACTICE SCENARIOS

Take a look at the practice scenarios that conclude this chapter: "Shaheena's Wellness" and "Michelle's Learning." Use the content in this chapter to inspire your thinking about the scenario. Notice how the scenario may relate to your own situation at your current practicum placement, even if it is not exactly what you are experiencing. Consider the questions posed at the end of each scenario to help you expand and apply the concepts presented in this chapter.

SEMINAR GROUP AND COMMUNITY OF PRACTICE DISCUSSION QUESTIONS

In your seminar or community of practice groups, consider the following questions for discussion:

1. How has your wellness been challenged in your practicum experience thus far? What have you learned about yourself as a result?
2. What self-care strategies work well for you? What have you learned from your classmates, supervisor, faculty-instructor, and the young people you work with about taking care of yourself?

3.   At your agency, what supports wellness? What neglects wellness?

4.   How can we build our practices in ways that are just and sustainable? At your practicum, what have you observed that embodies just and sustainable practice? What doesn't?

IN CLOSING

What does wellness mean to you? What helps you sustain wellness amid challenging work? How can we encourage collective wellness? How can we support each other in changing the very environment and work that we do to encourage wellness? Of course, this is a long journey, the beginning for some students, in the midst for others. What we learn about ourselves and our practice in our practicum helps inform our next steps. Developing holistic wellness practices will assist us in showing up well to our work and doing challenging work. But so too will considering the very environments and systems we work within. Remember, that we—ourselves, our classmates, our supervisors, our instructors, and the young people and families we work alongside—are all in this together.

PRACTICE SCENARIOS

Shaheena's Wellness

Shaheena focused on wellness as part of her goals during her practicum placement at a group home for adolescent girls. At first, her goal was somewhat separate from the site itself: she wanted to ensure she was sleeping well, was well nourished, and made time outside of practicum and work for rest and relaxation. As she moved through practicum, she began to notice ways to integrate wellness into the girls' daily lives. She would ask the girls if they wanted to go for walks, make meals together, do morning and evening stretches, spend time reading, watch comedy shows together, and so on. Eventually, the girls began to engage in wellness activities without her prompting.

How do you model, integrate, and focus on wellness in your practicum site that builds upon young people's needs and is appropriate to the context?

_____

_____

_____

Michelle's Learning

Michelle feels like she didn't attend at all to wellness and self-care during her practicum. Nearing the end of her practicum at a hospital, she feels she neglected this aspect of her learning and is feeling the consequences. She's been at the hospital five days a week. She's done a variety of shifts to experience the 24/7 nature of the unit. She's sat in on numerous interdisciplinary case meetings, she's gone on every activity and outing possible, and she's gotten to know each of the kids at the unit. Over the past two months, she's hardly seen her roommate, her mother keeps texting to see how she's doing, and she cannot count how many times she's visited the fast food restaurant down the street from the hospital. She cannot recall the last time she had a good night's sleep. Something's always on her mind. Now, she just wants practicum to end. She needs to get back to her part-time job so she can pay next term's tuition. She's desperate to see the light at the end of the tunnel and has almost forgotten that upon ending her practicum, she also has to submit assignments. She's unsure how she'll have the energy to do so.

How can Michelle take this learning and use it for future planning? What do you think she's learned about herself and her needs? What have you learned about yourself and your needs during this practicum placement? How may that help you for your next practicum?

_____

_____

_____

CHAPTER 12

Closing Relationships and Closing Practices in CYC

Competencies for Professional Child and Youth Work Practitioners				
Professionalism	Cultural and Human Diversity	Applied Human Development	Relationship and Communication	Developmental Practice Methods
Professional Development and Behaviour Personal Development and Self-Care		Sensitivity to Contextual Development in Relationships Practice Methods	Relationship Development	Intervention Planning Program Planning and Activity Programming Group Process

Whenever possible, we encourage talking openly about endings and transitions that are on the horizon, and exploring thoughts and feelings related to these events. An openness to discussing these concepts helps young people to develop their social and emotional skills for the future, and to maintain healthy attachments despite the reality that endings and transitions will occur. In some cases, providing a healthy ending or transition experience can help with healing past experiences of negative or unanticipated endings.
—Avril Paice, Organizational Development, Boys and Girls Clubs

Before you know it, practicum will come to a close. Just as you are getting to know the organization, the staff, your role, and the young people, your hours will be completed; your time will be up. Whether your practicum lasted one or eight months, whether it was part- or full-time, you will enter into the process of leaving practicum. Just as you attended to the beginning of practicum—getting to know the agency, meeting and connecting with new people, learning what is expected of you—you will also need to attend to the end.

Ending your time in your Child and Youth Care (CYC) practicum offers the opportunity to reflect on endings in general—what they mean to us, how we can be intentional with this opportunity, and how we may learn new ways of leaving well. We encounter many endings in our lives—intentional, unintentional, planned, and unexpected. In practicum, we need to attend to many factors as we prepare to leave. Hopefully, you know when your last day at the practicum site will be, so you can plan ahead. The seemingly administrative task of setting a schedule is actually quite important to attend to in terms of relational practice. There are many relationships we need to attend to as we plan to end our time at practicum. There are many formal and informal closing practices that we can create and participate in as a part of our departure. And there are many ways we can leave something behind.

> Prepare yourself and the youth that you're leaving.
> —Margaret, CYC Student

This chapter is divided into two parts. The first part focuses on the process of ending your time at your practicum site, attending to the relational aspects of your departure. Here, we will focus on closing relationships and closing practices. The second part will examine how you can make a lasting contribution to your practicum site through a legacy—whether this is an academic requirement or not—giving back to the agency that contributed so much to your learning experience. The final chapter of this guidebook will also attend to ending, but more so the pieces that come after you've ended your time at practicum. This chapter will focus on the time that you're there.

ENDING

Everything ends. We experience death, loss, and change. We shift, we discontinue, we leave. When we think about ending, you wouldn't be faulted if your mind immediately went to sadness, grief, or loss. Across the helping field in general, the literature on ending takes a very clinical, pathology-based approach. In this way, ending is frequently viewed through the lens of loss with a restricted focus on the grief-laden feelings we and young people experience. The focus has been on sadness, anger, confusion, conflict, and abandonment. Further, the administrative terms we attach to the process—discharge meeting, termination report—are harsh, reflecting scenarios analogous to the theories which inform them: severing or cutting off relationships. When we notice the number of theories, articles, and practices that attend to the beginning of relationships or working through change as compared to the theories, articles, and practices that attend to the ending of relationships and processes, the latter is almost entirely eclipsed. The lack of literature and the focus on pathology excludes many perspectives. However, CYC has much to offer the helping field in terms of our approaches to practice in young people's life-space, including endings.

> The CYC profession is one of 'hellos' and 'goodbyes'—practice saying both in healthy ways as this needs to be role modelled.
> —Andrew, CYC Practicum Faculty-Instructor

In contrast to the descriptions above, CYC opens up space for the closing process to be full of opportunity to:

- Model good endings for young people who may not have had the opportunity
- Attend to the spectrum of emotions we and young people experience

- Incorporate a developmental understanding of people's needs
- Celebrate connection, accomplishment, and change
- Appreciate the space and people who provided us a context for our learning
- Move forward with new learning, acknowledging the place we came from

OUR EXPERIENCE OF ENDING

To enter into a discussion on the closing process, we can begin with ourselves and what we bring to this encounter. What personal and professional experiences of ending come to mind when you think about ending? Complete Activity 12.1 to explore some of these experiences.

> I believe we need to have honest discussions about how our personal experiences with endings influence the way we do this professionally.
> —Kristy, CYC Practicum Faculty-Instructor

Activity 12.1: My Experience with Ending

Move through the following three steps to reflect on some of your experiences of ending and separation.

Step One

Our lives are full of endings. Identify three significant endings that you have experienced in the past. It could be the time you quit a job, graduated school, ended therapy, finished a project, said goodbye to a group of campers at an outdoor camp, broke up with a romantic partner, or experienced death for the first time.

Ending #1

_____

_____

Ending #2

_____

_____

Ending #3

_____

_____

Step Two

For each of the situations above, ask yourself the following questions. As you reflect, take some notes next to the list you've made in Step One.

- What was involved in this ending?
- How did you respond emotionally and behaviourally to this ending?
- How did others respond emotionally and behaviourally to this ending?
- Did you have time to prepare for this ending? What was involved?
- What did you think, feel, or do to deal with the losses involved in this ending?
- What went well? What didn't go well?
- How do you make meaning of this ending in your life now?

Step Three

Looking at your notes from Steps One and Two, what do you notice? What conclusions could you make about what is helpful and unhelpful to the process of ending? How might your experience inform your ending at practicum?

Write a few words of wisdom—recommendations, insights, dos and don'ts—on what you have learned about endings based on these experiences.

_____

_____

If you feel comfortable, share with a seminar classmate or your community of practice group. Share for the purpose of learning from others' experiences. Listen to how they have experienced ending. Notice points of similarity and difference compared to your own experience. Notice particularly similar situations that are experienced differently.

Adapted from Myers-Kiser, P. (2016). *The human services internship: Getting the most from your experience* (4th ed., p. 297). Boston, MA: Cengage Learning.

How we carry these experiences forward impacts how we engage in closing practices. What we focus on at the end of practicum is influenced by these experiences. How will you bring this wisdom forward?

Lawrence-Lightfoot (2012) highlights that "our societal neglect of the rituals and purposes of exits is not only [a] puzzling contemporary phenomenon; it is also strange when we consider the history… a history that has been primarily defined by leave-takings, departures, and journeys away from home" (p. 7). How have we come to be this way? What is lost when we do not focus on endings as a part of "normal development" and "normal processes" young people will experience in their life-space? Are we missing an

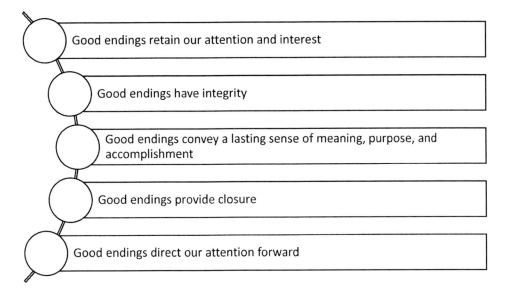

Figure 12.1: Characteristics of Good Endings

Adapted from Dunn, D. S., Beins, B. C., McCarthy, M. A., & Hill, G. W. (Eds.). (2010). *Best practices for teaching beginnings and endings in the psychology major* (pp. 338–339). New York, NY: Oxford University Press.

opportunity if we skim over or overlook the experience? Lutsky (2010) underscores the significance of endings, saying, "endings have the power to transform how we remember and evaluate parts of our lives and how we tell the stories of our lives" (p. 337). He states that even conversational endings tend to involve "statements that review an interaction, justify its termination, plan for continuity, and express positive affect and well-wishing" (p. 337). Whether it's a conversation, postsecondary course, relationship, or life, he suggests good endings have five common characteristics, as seen in Figure 12.1.

Compare the characteristics in Figure 12.1 with the examples you reflected upon in Activity 12.1. Was anything missing in your experience?

PERSPECTIVE AND TIME

Beginning, middle, end. These terms involve time. But whose beginning, middle, and end are we referring to? Yours? The young person's? Considering who the ending belongs to is an important factor in how we plan. Practicum often has an arbitrary ending. That is, you leave your practicum site when your academic requirements are completed. While that may correspond with a pre-existing ending at the practicum site, it more often does not. Pre-existing endings for a young person could include the end of a school year, the end of a therapeutic group, the end of a project or competition, the end of a young person's time with a program or service, and more. Which pre-existing endings exist at your site?

> Think about the young people first, remind them that you are a practicum student, and you will not be here forever. Have a count down and a strong separation activity.
> —Saira, CYC Practicum Faculty-Instructor

For the most part, practicum students typically end their time at a practicum setting when they've completed their required hours, however many hours that may be. These hours often correspond with the beginning or ending of your institution's academic term. Is that in young people's best interests when it comes to leaving (or for that matter, beginning)? While it is not always possible to predict a pre-existing ending, we nevertheless must consider the impact. What is the impact of us leaving for young people? How can we intentionally end our time at the practicum site to correspond with another naturally occurring ending? How can we ensure we're attending to any additional disruptions our departure has on the setting or its young people? These are all factors to consider when ending your time at your practicum site.

When we think about time, we make space for ourselves to consider how each person (including ourselves) will experience our departure. We should consider each person's point of view.

Let's begin with the young people at our practicum sites. Who have you connected with? Try to think of everyone you've connected with during your time at your practicum site. This may be easier for some sites than others. For example, at a group home or small alternate school program, you may only encounter a handful of young people. At a youth drop-in centre, school, or street outreach program, you may have encountered hundreds of young people. In that case, try to think through all of the meaningful connections you've made with the young people and families. Consider reviewing this list with your supervisor, as they may have observations or information you may not yet have.

Looking at this list of young people, what do you think they need in response to your leaving? Keep this list of young people in mind as you move through the questions and activities in this chapter.

Now, let's think about your supervisor and staff. Who have you connected with? Try to think of all the staff you've made meaningful connections with across the programs in which you've been involved. You may have one direct supervisor, but you may also have had the opportunity to be supervised by other staff throughout your practicum experience or for a particular project. Also consider the leadership who indirectly supported your practicum by making it possible in the first place—the principal at the school who encourages supervisors to take on practicum students, the HR person who gave you an orientation, and so on. Try to write a comprehensive list.

Looking at this list of supervisors and staff, what do you think they need in response to your leaving? Keep this list of supervisors and staff in mind as you move through the questions and activities coming up in this chapter.

Then we have yourself. What are your needs? How do you process endings? What do your previous experiences of endings teach you as to what you need now? While your practicum course will be designed to include closing practices that help you process its end, what do you need above and beyond this to close your experience? For example, your seminar class may have a potluck for the last class, your final performance evaluation meeting will give you an opportunity to thank your supervisor and faculty-instructor, and you will submit your final assignments, hopefully relieving some pressure so you can move on to your next step. Maybe you need something beyond this experience. Do you need to celebrate a job well done with friends? Does your community of practice need to have an informal ceremony acknowledging each other's support? Consider these pieces as you close.

ENDINGS IN PRACTICE

When we refer to closing relationships and closing practices in practicum, we are referring to many layers: ending an activity or intervention with a young person or group of young people, ending a relationship with a young person, and ending a relationship with supervisors and staff at the site. Let's explore some of these experiences in more depth.

Therapeutic Endings

While you may not have taken a course on group dynamics or helping skills yet, practicum offers the opportunity to learn how we end therapeutic processes with young people and their families. When we refer to the end of a therapeutic process, we can mean the end of an activity or event, the end of a group, the end of an intervention with a young person, or the end of the involvement in a service. In your practicum setting, you may have encountered numerous endings:

- A "Games Night" ends at a drop-in youth centre
- A spring-break camp for kids finishes
- A 12-week social-emotional skills group for elementary school children ends
- A group home resident leaves the facility and returns to their family or moves to independent living
- A child is discharged from a hospital psychiatric unit
- A family ends involvement with a family development outreach program
- A child finishes services at a child development centre
- A youth ages out of government care

All these encounters need to be attended to. All these situations have the potential to end on good or bad terms. They all provide an opportunity for therapeutic intervention. Many of the programs CYC practitioners participate in have established closing practices for these and other endings. Think through what your practicum site offers in terms of intentional, planned endings. If you're stuck for examples, ask your supervisor. List them here.

Ending Relationships with Young People

Whether it's because a young person has completed a program or is ending a service or it's because we're leaving a practicum setting, we also need to attend to the closing of that relationship. Flip back to the list of young people you wrote a few pages ago. What do they need as you plan to depart? From a youth mentoring context, Keller (2005) recommends practitioners follow five general guidelines with young people, outlined in Figure 12.2. Consider how these apply to your practicum site.

As you read Keller's (2005) guidelines in Figure 12.2, you could ask yourself the following questions:

1. How are you openly acknowledging that the relationship will be ending?
2. How have you attended to the young person's and your own feelings about the relationship ending?
3. Have you highlighted the time you spent together including their accomplishments?
4. Have you planned a way to mark the occasion?
5. Have you created a way to preserve memories of your time together?

Similarly, Peterson (2011) focused on the conversational exchanges that occur during the closing process, where successful ends were marked with 1) successes that were praised, 2) a reflection on the relationship, 3) an acknowledgement of the spectrum of emotions experienced by young people and practitioners, 4) clear boundaries about future contact, 5) an evaluation of what was learned through the relationship and time together, and 6) hopefully closed with a formal celebration appropriate to the relationship and setting. Spencer and

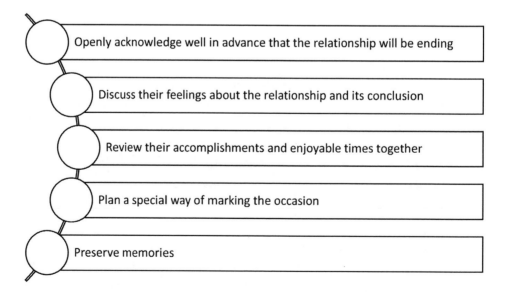

Figure 12.2: Guidelines for Ending Relationships with Young People

Adapted from DuBois, D. L., & Karcher, M. J. (Eds.). (2005). *Handbook of youth mentoring* (p. 95). Thousand Oaks, CA: SAGE.

Basualdo-Delmonico (2014) emphasize that using the closing time as an opportunity to evaluate time together is helpful. They say that questions as simple as "what did you like best about the time we spent together?" or "what one thing do you think we should have done differently?" provide time to reflect, as well as benefit future practice (p. 477).

As you read through these characteristics and recommendations, consider how the existing closing practices at your practicum site (using your list above) meet or do not meet these guidelines. Pay attention to how a guideline can look different across contexts. How we "convey a lasting sense of meaning, purpose, and accomplishment" depends on the work we focused on with young people. How we "preserve memories" looks different for a 7-year-old child versus a 16-year-old youth. How we "mark the occasion" looks different at a group home, a hospital, or a recreation centre. Consider your context.

Bad Endings

We shouldn't minimize the consequences of bad endings, as "failing to provide some sort of resolution or closure ritual at the end of a relationship can be damaging for youth, particularly for those who've been let down in their relationships with adults in the past" (The National Mentoring Partnerships, 2015, p. 10). Review Table 12.1 to understand young people's feelings that can result from poorly timed, dysfunctional endings. Then contrast that with the well-timed, functional

> Never promise you're going to be back, even if it's for volunteer work. I would much rather they come back as a surprise than to promise and never follow through. The young people see that all the time in their lives. Don't be another person doing that.
> —Tom, CYC Practicum Supervisor

Table 12.1: Functional and Well-Timed Endings

	Early Relationship Ending	Well-timed Relationship Ending	Overdue Relationship Ending
Functional Ending	Expected and structured (unplanned but completed ending)	Expected and structured (planned and completed ending)	Delayed and structured (unplanned but completed agency ending)
(associated feelings)	sadness, pensiveness	satisfaction, admiration	frustration, acceptance
Dysfunctional Ending	Unexpected and unstructured (unplanned and not completed ending)	Expected and unstructured (planned and not completed ending)	Delayed and unstructured (unplanned and not completed agency ending)
(associated feelings)	abandonment, fear, anger	anticipation, confusion	resentment, dissatisfaction

Adapted from The National Mentoring Partnership (MENTOR). (2015). "They always come and they never say goodbye": Understanding healthy closure in youth mentoring (p. 10).

endings. First, consider how these apply to your practicum site. Also, look back to the beginning of this chapter where you reflected on your experience of endings. Do you recognize any feelings listed in this chart?

As you can see, there is a lot of opportunity to not do things well. This is not meant to scare you; rather, it is to underscore importance. While we may have good intentions, how young people experience endings is important to consider. While Table 12.1 comes from a youth mentoring context, take any ending that is relevant to the young people at your practicum site and consider it through this framework.

While these examples focus on young people and the ending of services, programs, or relationships with practitioners—rather than practicum students leaving a practicum site—they will hopefully inform you as to how you can attend to the closing process as you plan to depart.

These are the factors we need to keep in mind. Where do we go from here?

End at the Beginning

In practicum, we should be ending as we begin. That is, since we know our departure date, the young people and staff at our practicum site have a right to know this too. Don't assume that because you and your supervisor know when you are leaving that everyone will know.

When you introduced yourself at the practicum site, you likely introduced yourself as a practicum student. Perhaps you said something such as "Hi. My name is Sanj. I'm a practicum student; I'm with the program until February" or "I'm a student at XYZ College; I'll be at the school for a few months; I'm looking forward to getting to know everyone." Maybe your supervisor or colleagues introduced you in this way as you were oriented to the site. When we say these types of things, we help young people and their families understand our role at the organization. It also helps them understand our capacity and involvement in its programs. Not only is it important for them to know your role in terms of consent and so on, it is also important in terms of relational work. Young people have the right to know that the person who is keenly wanting to engage with them is going to be leaving. Failing to do so can cause relational harm.

> Ending their time at a practicum placement is an opportunity to work on endings and to model this for children and youth.
> —Rhonda, CYC Practicum Faculty-Instructor

Too many of the young people we work alongside have experienced difficult relationship endings. Think of a young person in government care—the relational disruptions and losses, the worker turnover, the service changes, and so on. We can either contribute to vague, unclear, and disruptive relationship losses, or we can facilitate an alternate experience. Obviously, we want to avoid harm. Yet, everywhere we look, this happens. We hear it from young people. We witness it. We may have even experienced a harmful relationship loss with a practitioner in our own life.

From the beginning, we prepare to leave. If you feel you have not done a good enough job at preparing them, ask your supervisor for support. Check in with your seminar classmates. Ask your faculty-instructor for help. That's what they're there for.

Consider the following reflective questions as you prepare to end your time at your practicum:

1. What have you done thus far at your practicum to prepare the young people at your practicum site for your departure?

    _____

2. What will you do to mark the occasion of your departure?

    _____

3. What individual, site, environmental, and systemic factors have you considered that inform these closing decisions and actions?

    _____

4. Are there young people at your practicum site who you feel may experience your departure with difficulty? If so, how are you attending to their needs?

    _____

As you approach the end of your time at practicum, you can refer to when you will be leaving. You could say, "I hope you'll come to my goodbye lunch next week, as I've really enjoyed connecting with you" or "I'll be leaving at the end of the month, so I hope to see you again at the drop-in centre before then to say goodbye" or "Friday is my last day at practicum"; this information can be integrated seamlessly into your conversations. These simple advance notices of your departure help prepare young people.

Good Endings

Your efforts to conclude your work with specific individuals, create gifts or objects to give to the young people, plan a ceremony of some kind, and appreciate the people who have contributed to your learning is part of the work of closing.

You must pay attention to context. For example, how you prepare youth at a drop-in recreation centre, many whom you see once a week, will be different than how you prepare children at an elementary school whom you work closely with every day. Further, how you prepare one child at that elementary school whom you've worked closely with will be different than the group of children in a classroom you once visited during your orientation. Meanwhile, how you prepare one child with different developmental needs compared to another will also be different. Don't forget about the staff. Only you and your supervisor will know the specific contextual needs of the young people and staff at your site. It's important to give time to prepare.

When it comes time for you to end your time at the practicum setting, plan accordingly. Make a plan with your supervisor. Think of the connections you've built. Think of the impressions the young people have made in your journey. Think of the impressions you've made in theirs. Think of the learning the setting has given you.

Have a party. Make a video for them. Write something nice to each of the kids. If you want to give them something, it doesn't need to be fancy. Tell them how you feel about them. Tell them all the nice things.
—Donna, CYC Practicum Supervisor

I've seen practicum students give painted rocks with messages. Inspiring or positive words. We've had students do paintings and put it up in the centre. They've left binders of resources of fun activities. We never expect a gift or for a student to spend money. Leave something meaningful.
—Tom, CYC Practicum Supervisor

Closing Practices

Closing practices offer the opportunity for young people and practitioners to formally and informally end their time together through a purposeful, planned process. Examples of closing practices from practicum students include, but are certainly not limited to, the following list:

- A goodbye lunch with young people or staff
- A school announcement in the newsletter or over the public address system
- A going-away party
- One-on-one conversations with young people and staff
- Cards or letters of appreciation that include well wishes for the young person, what you've learned in your experience with them, and appreciation of your time together
- Goodbye notes highlighting the young person's strengths and your time together
- Giving objects to remember you by (a painting or illustration for the group home's living room or office wall, a painted rock with a significant word written from a conversation with a young person, etc.)
- A gift for the program that reflects your time there

What would you add? Ask your supervisor for examples of what past practicum students have done. Ask your seminar classmates and community of practice for examples of what they're preparing to do. While the examples here are somewhat general, remember to incorporate yourself. Do you like to illustrate? Are you a writer? Are you more introverted or extroverted? Do what feels authentic to you. Make note of these ideas here.

Any connection made with a student can be long-lasting for them. At the end of my practicum I drew a picture of something I knew the student liked. Something simple that I knew I could draw but that was personal for them.
—Sam, CYC Student

Notably, many therapeutic endings incorporate an appreciative element, are marked by an informal or formal ceremony, and include something for the young person to take away. Why? When young people have an object (a card, a letter, a rock, a picture, an item of some significance), they're better able to remember the experience, attach meaning to the object as it represents your relationship and time together, and integrate that meaning into their life as it unfolds. Whether you are working with a young person or a group of young people, there's ample opportunity for closing practices that utilize the closing process to benefit young people. Conveniently, it helps us CYC practitioners process the encounter too.

Your Process

Many practicum students will feel a combination of sadness and accomplishment at the end of their practicum experience. You will hopefully have connected closely with several young people and staff. You will likely also feel sad to not be at the site to continue to get to know people, contribute, and learn from them. You will also likely feel satisfied by a job well done. Practicum is a lot of work, a commitment beyond a regular course at school. Finishing practicum will hopefully bring a sense of pride to your life. You may also be anticipating future expectations in your life: a new course load, a different schedule, changes in employment, and so on. This can be exciting, daunting, and more. Often, our feelings at the end of practicum relate to our experience of practicum itself. If we had a strong connection with our supervisor, we may be sad to say goodbye. If we didn't engage well with some of the people at practicum—for whatever reason—we may leave feeling ambivalent and unsatisfied. If we had some difficult relationships with staff or a supervisor, we may feel a sense of relief. This is all expected and important for you to process in the way that feels authentic to you. Always remember to link any experience to your learning.

> Remember that young people don't have the best recall and retention. Students can give something tangible that commemorates and symbolizes their time together but also be a reflection about all the wins they've made and the strategies they've learned. While they're with us, we expect them to do a lot of hard work. Give something that represents all that hard work.
> —Sonja, CYC Practicum Supervisor

Through this difficult or enjoyable experience, what did you learn about yourself, relationships, and your practice? What are you feeling as you come to practicum's close?

_____

_____

_____

Acknowledge these feelings. Feel the sadness, loss, accomplishment, relief, ambivalence, and excitement. Celebrate your accomplishments. Share the impact that practicum has had in your life. These are all important pieces to attend to as *you* process the end. It'll arrive quicker than you think.

Now let's switch gears: from closing practices to leaving a contribution to your practicum site.

LEAVING SOMETHING BEHIND

We participate in our practicum settings for a relatively short period of time. Our presence at practicum settings offers additional support to young people, opportunities for staff to supervise and support the field's growth, and passionate student voices with fresh enthusiasm about theory and practice. Meanwhile, the program, its staff, and its young people and families contribute so much to our learning as we develop as practitioners. Those experiences stick with us and continue to inform our practice years after we've left the practicum site. As a way to give back to the site that has and will continue to have such an impact on our professional journeys, we often encourage practicum students to leave something behind.

Many CYC programs require practicum students to contribute legacy projects, something that students leave behind as a contribution to the site. Some CYC programs do not require this, but they nonetheless recommend that practicum students offer a "final project" of some kind. As well, some practicum sites ask students to contribute a legacy project as a way to focus their learning and present a final product to the site. Legacy projects (sometimes referred to as capstone projects) are as diverse as the sites they're meant for and the students who create them. In all cases, legacy projects are one way to end your time at the practicum site that:

1. Express appreciation
2. Last beyond your presence
3. Synthesize what you learned from the experience
4. Incorporate your own interests
5. Offer something to the site that it needs

Is a legacy project a required component of your practicum assessment package? If not, is a legacy project something you may be interested in doing? If so, thoroughly check your assessment package's instructions. The following guidelines and recommendations are here to help you brainstorm and widen the scope of what you think you can contribute. They should not override any instructions you receive from either your faculty-instructor or supervisor.

Legacy Projects

Most legacy projects combine site and student needs in order to benefit the young people at the practicum site (see Figure 12.3). It is worth spending some time developing a number of ideas and checking in with your supervisor as to what works for you both and to ensure it'll benefit young people, families, and/or the staff at the site. Most supervisors are thrilled to know that you'll be able to devote some time and energy to create a legacy project of some kind, but do not want it to become a make-work project. (No more resource binders! We have Google for that now.) Supervisors also like being consulted as to what they think the site needs. Start with your own reflections. You may also be happy to learn that at least a portion of the work you do to create a legacy project will likely count toward your practicum hours (check with your

> Especially when doing a project, there's a lot of ownership around that. The goal with legacy projects is to create something and then let it go so that it can be for the community.
> —Chris, CYC Practicum Supervisor

Figure 12.3: The Legacy Project Equation

faculty-instructor). Where appropriate, it may be helpful to consult with the young people at your site to ask what they think the program needs.

With that said, what have you noticed your practicum site may need? Has a staff person complained that "if only I had the time to…"? Have you noticed that your classmate's alternate school has certain helpful materials that your alternate school does not? Begin by noticing a gap, a complaint, or a need of some kind. Then focus on your own interests, skills, and goals. What do you want to contribute? What do you like doing? How could your personal interests, hobbies, and skills contribute? What do you think would benefit the site?

Dunn, Beins, McCarthy, and Hill (2010) discuss capstone projects in applied psychology programs, similar to legacy projects, which included developing curriculum for social-emotional themed groups for various ages, designing websites, compiling resources, and researching topics for supervisors. Take a look at the extensive list of actual legacy project examples in Table 12.2 from CYC practicum settings. Ask your faculty-instructor for ideas and guidance as to what is expected of you. If your legacy project is a required component of your assessment package, you'll want to keep in mind its instructions, as well as how you'll report on the process.

Whether you are required to contribute a legacy project to your practicum site or not, they can provide a lasting contribution and are often quite fun. Don't forget to mention this legacy project on your resume and include it in your portfolio. (More on that topic in the next and final chapter.)

LEARNING JOURNAL

As you come to the end of your time at your practicum site, focus your learning journal on the experience of ending. However you arrive to the place of ending, experience it. Experience it through purposeful reflection so that you may be able to more closely understand the endings young people experience.

Table 12.2: Examples of Legacy Projects

At a youth outreach program, a practicum student researched summer camps for youth in care (no cost, subsidized, or low cost, and researched internal and external government resources for financial support) and provided that brief **REPORT** to the child welfare workers and other staff at the program.	At an Aboriginal Family Services site, two practicum students researched and created an **ACTIVITY BOOKLET** that focused on high-participation nutritional, spiritual, musical, cultural, social, and emotional connection activities that could be done with young children and their parents and grandparents (that were no cost and had no barriers). They created multiple copies and had it spiral-bound.	At a group home, a practicum student brought her own slightly damaged **SCOOTER**, and she and the young male group home resident worked on its repairs: went to the home repair centre together for items, worked on it in the backyard, etc. When it was repaired (at the end of the placement), she gifted it to him.	At an emergency shelter for youth, a practicum student created a **POSTER** on a new substance that was emerging as particularly unsafe, with practical tips, youth-appropriate language, and safety info, as well as some cards with emergency info for the youth to take away.
A practicum student at a recreational centre completed a **FUNDING PROPOSAL** for a youth-employment grant.	At an elementary school undergoing significant renovations, a practicum student created a **QUESTIONNAIRE** and report regarding safety concerns from the children.	At a victim services centre with an unused office space, a practicum student proposed a **DESIGN PLAN** that researched child- and family-friendly furniture and design items within the agency's budget and with developmentally appropriate rationale.	A practicum student at a high school did a workshop on cultural heritage (with a group of English and Social Studies classes), and the large **POSTER** paper they worked on stays hanging on the wall in the classroom.
As a part of a group she was co-facilitating for youth, a student created a **COLLABORATIVE PIECE OF ART**, and it hangs on the wall of the room of the teacher who was supervising her.	At a group home, a practicum student noticed their activity equipment was damaged, so he went to a local store with a formal request letter and they donated a **BASKETBALL**.	At a mental health residential facility, a practicum student created a **WELCOME and ORIENTATION BOOKLET** for new youth arriving to the centre.	At a mental health residential facility, a practicum student created a Practicum Student **ORIENTATION BOOKLET** for new practicum students (including checklists, who's who, maps, do's and don'ts, etc.)

In an elementary school that was incorporating iPads into its curriculum, a student researched and experimented with age-appropriate social and emotional **APPLICATIONS** and presented a list of recommendations to the teachers and support workers.	With the permission and budget at a school, a practicum student who enjoys gardening helped create a small **GARDEN PLOT**, while also creating a life-skill activity with the youth, focusing on indigenous plants in the region.	At an alternative high school, a student noticed the lunch food budget was being spent on fast food. She researched and prepared a **RECIPE BOOKLET** with easy-to-make recipes (within the food budget) and then practised with the youth a few times.	At a group home, a student researched and created an age appropriate **WELLNESS BOX** for the residents that contained easily replaceable activities (colouring sheets), and stress-reducing objects (playlists, stress balls, etc.) from a dollar store.
At a youth centre, a practicum student noticed the male youth connected over exercise routines, so he made a **POSTER** with exercise visuals, benefits, and notes on safety.	At a transportation outreach program, a practicum student created an easily printed and laminated **MAP** of resources that surrounded each train station that could fit in a wallet or pocket.	At a policy and research placement, a student created a **FACT SHEET** for their website, focusing on their youth-health research.	A student at an outreach drop-in centre painted a **MURAL** on the wall with open space for youth to write inspirational quotes.
A practicum student created a **SOCIAL MEDIA PAGE** for the youth outreach program and began posting event calendars and related items on its page, sharing the log-in information and guidelines for posting with the staff at the site.	A student at a youth wilderness outreach camp made a short **REPORT** to be distributed to the probation officers and social workers who may be interested in referring their clients to the program.	A practicum student at a non-profit community centre made a **MANUAL** for an independent-living life-skills group, with an outline of a few sessions focused on cooking and nutrition skills for older youth.	At a specialized education site (school, family development, and counselling), they lost a **SENSORY BOARD** and a practicum student created a new one because no one had the time to replace it. (It included velcro, snaps, zippers, buttons, and other materials.)

PRACTICE SCENARIOS

Take a look at the practice scenarios that conclude this chapter: "Raya's and Selena's Goodbyes" and "Legacy Contributions." Use the content in this chapter to inspire your thinking about the scenario. Notice how the scenario may relate to your own situation at your current practicum placement, even if it is not exactly what you are experiencing. Consider the questions posed at the end of each scenario to help you expand and apply the concepts presented in this chapter.

SEMINAR GROUP AND COMMUNITY OF PRACTICE DISCUSSION QUESTIONS

In your seminar and community of practice group, consider the following questions for discussion:

1.   What are the risks of ending your time at your practicum site and telling young people "let's stay in touch" or "I'll visit soon"?
2.   What closing activities would be appropriate for your site and the relationships you've built, as well as the needs of the young people at your site?
3.   How is modelling good relationship endings in and of itself a benefit to the young people we work alongside?
4.   What would be a meaningful legacy contribution to your site? Something that you could leave behind that captures some piece of your learning and yourself to benefit the people and programs at the organization?

IN CLOSING

Attending to closing is an important part of our practice with young people. Not only do we need to develop this skill and attend to this process as part of the therapeutic work we do with young people, we also need to pay attention to the process of leaving the practicum setting as a student. When ending, consideration of contextual needs is of the utmost importance—time, age, emotions, history, setting, and so on—just as with any other phase of a relationship or encounter. Through engagement and connection we pay attention to beginnings. Through intentional change, challenge, development, and conflict we pay attention to the middle. So too should we pay attention to the end. Endings introduce opportunities for us as practitioners and as practicum students. How one practicum student ends at one site will look different than another. They all will have one thing in common: a recognition of the time you have spent and the learning you've experienced through an appreciation of your supervisor, the program and its staff, but most of all its young people.

PRACTICE SCENARIOS

Raya's and Selena's Goodbyes

Raya has had a wonderful time in her practicum at the recreational centre. She has enjoyed her time so much, she's asked if she can stay on in a volunteer capacity. Her supervisor supports this idea and has passed her along to the volunteer coordinator. As she wraps up her time at the centre, she's been telling the kids "I'll be back to volunteer, so we don't have to say goodbye," but she's uncertain of which programs she'll be part of and when she'll begin this role. Meanwhile, as Selena approached the end of her practicum at the elementary school, she made sure she did a closing activity with the social-emotional skills group she helped facilitate, wrote thank-you cards for her supervisor and colleagues, gifted small rocks with aspirational words for the kids she felt she connected with, said goodbye at the team meeting, and reflected on the spectrum of emotions she felt, from sadness to satisfaction. On her last day, however, a young boy she saw and said hello to at the school every day but who had never really responded to her, came up to her and asked "How come you're going?" and "Will you be back?" Selena was surprised that he also knew her name and that he seemed upset that she was leaving. She told him how much she appreciated seeing him every day, but she left practicum feeling that she inadequately anticipated his needs.

What should Raya attend to when she communicates her changing role to the kids at the centre? What may Selena have learned about the impact we make on kids? How should both students attend to the uncertainty as we depart a practicum site?

Legacy Contributions

At the specialized education centre for children with developmental disabilities, Sonia noticed many of the teachers referred to a tactile "busy board" that had gone missing months ago. In her free time, Sonia enjoys arts and crafts—in particular felting and sewing—so she asked if she could make a replacement. Cain noticed that the youth at his group home didn't go outside to the home's large open yard, and wondered if it was in part because the basketball, soccer ball, and volleyball were deflated and torn. He also knew that budgets were limited. He asked his supervisor if he could approach the local sporting goods store to formally ask their manager if they would consider donating some replacements. His supervisor told him she would review any letter he drafted. Taryn noticed that the alternative high school program often took the youth out to fast food for lunch, something she was quite frustrated by because she'd recently read how much food impacts energy and mood. Sticking within the daily food budget, she decided to make a recipe booklet, with easy-to-make recipes for the youth, including grocery lists, current costs, and instructions. She consulted with the youth, took note of the school's kitchen appliances and other details, and created a visually engaging booklet for the youth. She then facilitated a few meal activities, taking a few youth to the store, cooking, and eating together, revising the booklet based on their feedback. She felt proud writing "by Taryn, Practicum Student."

What did these students do (observe, consult, reflect, act) in their process to create a lasting contribution to the site? Do they inspire you to create something that lasts past your presence? Is there something that frustrates you about your site that you can turn into an opportunity?

_____

_____

_____

CHAPTER 13

Consolidating Your Learning and Working in the CYC Field

Competencies for Professional Child and Youth Work Practitioners				
Professionalism	Cultural and Human Diversity	Applied Human Development	Relationship and Communication	Developmental Practice Methods
Awareness of the Profession Professional Development and Behaviour Personal Development and Self-Care			Teamwork and Professional Communication Skills	Community Engagement

As a student, it is essential to look for and create intersections for learning. Remember both that practicum and your classes are vital in your learning to be a practitioner so you cannot experience them as parallel processes. When in practicum, practise what you are learning in your classes and share new information with your team. When in your classes, think about what you see happening in your practicum and critique incongruence. Be curious and reflective in both spaces and be honest about how these experiences influence your thoughts, your feelings and your actions. Recognizing and exploring these intersections as a student will help you navigate the complexities of child and youth practice throughout your career.

—Jenny McGrath, Assistant Professor and Practicum Scholar, Child and Youth Care, MacEwan University

Congratulations! You made it! Your first Child and Youth Care (CYC) practicum experience is complete. It is often our first few experiences with practicum that stay with us throughout our professional career. Here, we zoom into all of the learning opportunities, are hyper-aware of the expectations of us to develop as practitioners, and make meaningful connections with young people and families who have generously allowed us to enter into their lives for a short period of time. This experience was a chance to not only observe and practise how your previous course work is embodied in practice but also to critically reflect on what CYC practice is and could be. It is also an opportunity to understand yourself as an emerging practitioner. In practicum placements, we spend a lot of time in the active observer role, moving from shadowing to trying things out. In this space, we

> In my first two practicums, I was figuring out where I was and where I wanted to be.
> —Jasmine, CYC Student

have the opportunity to see how we as people show up authentically in the relational work that we cultivate with young people and families. We formulate our emerging theoretical orientation to practice. We observe how CYC perspectives take shape. We reflect and question and reflect again. Before we know it, it's over.

Before you rush to finish your practicum assignments, take a break between terms, or re-focus your energy on what is ahead, there are a few more items to manage to make the most of your practicum learning experience. In that spirit, this chapter splits into three parts: consolidating your learning and completing the requirements of your practicum course; exploring options for working in the field; and finally, bringing your learning back to the classroom as you move forward in your CYC certificate, diploma, or degree.

CONSOLIDATING YOUR LEARNING

Not long after our practicum experience has ended, we immerse ourselves in our next plans: work, courses, professional and personal responsibilities. While impactful experiences we had during practicum will stay with us, we may forget some of the day-to-day activities, celebrations, people, tasks, responsibilities, and learning we may have had. Keeping evidence of your learning—in this guidebook, your learning journal, your assignment package, and so on—will help you recall these moments. So too will going through a process of post-reflection help you consolidate this learning. It is particularly helpful to do this reflection after you've completed your time at practicum, but perhaps before your final assignments are complete, so you can make the most of this learning. Let's begin that process by moving through a number of post-placement reflective questions, in Activity 13.1.

Activity 13.1: Post-Placement Self-Assessment and Reflection

Re-familiarize yourself with your practicum experience as a whole. Scan your learning journal, your performance evaluation meeting notes, and your learning plan. Recall significant moments you experienced. Reflect on the connections you made with young people, families, and staff. Recall how you felt approaching the beginning of practicum, as you began, getting your stride, and then its end. Reflect on the following questions to help solidify the learning you experienced throughout practicum.

What did you learn about yourself? As a learner, as a practitioner, as a person?

_____

_____

What were you most surprised to learn about yourself?

_____

_____

Where did you struggle?

_____

_____

Where did you shine? What are you most proud of?

_____

_____

Who helped you in your learning process?

_____

_____

What learning do you want to take forward to your next practicum?

_____

_____

Where do you think would be a good next practicum placement and why?

_____

_____

What do you imagine you'll never forget about this experience?

_____

_____

> What I thought I wanted to do when I graduated was not what I actually wanted to do when I graduated.
> —Jenn, CYC Student

In Heaney Dalton's (2018) reflection on her career in CYC, she notices how she remembers her firsts: how she felt about herself; how her choice of vocation would be tested deeply; how helpless, anxious, or afraid she felt at times; how heartbroken she felt when a young person died; how she attached to mentors; how she developed her determination; how she became more assertive; and how she created moments of humour and joy. Approaching retirement, she looks back and reflects, "I hope that one day, you too might sit in the warm sun, next to a meandering river, and reflect on the varied textures and beautiful colours of your long and success-filled life in CYC" (p. 123). She tells practicum students and emerging practitioners that your experiences here are the ones that will stick with you the longest, the ones you will remember when you retire. So, don't think this is only a course you're completing, checking it off your list of requirements to move through to graduation. Know that it is something you'll remember forever—the challenges, the successes, the learning.

GOALS AND LEARNING PLANS

One assignment that all CYC practicum students will complete in some form or another is stating, progressing toward, re-evaluating, and achieving your learning plan and its many goals. In Chapter 4, we reviewed a number of goals that practicum students develop, so they can focus their learning at practicum through these goals. Of course, you will have many, many moments of learning; however, by focusing on a handful of goals that attend to different outcomes that you want to achieve for your learning, we then have the ability to transfer that goal-centred learning to all of our practice. Using the SMART model—specific, measurable, attainable, relevant, and time-bound—we looked at how we can set goals for ourselves and work toward achieving them, remembering that the desired outcome is not perfection but learning.

> Be kind to yourself and forgive yourself when it doesn't turn out to be exactly what you think it'll be.
> —Cody, CYC Student

1. Did you achieve the goals you set for yourself?

    _____

    _____

2. If so, how can you tell you achieved those goals? If not, what factors influenced you not achieving those goals?

    _____

    _____

3. What supported you in pursuing your goals?

    _____

    _____

4. What hindered you in pursuing your goals?

    _____

    _____

5. Did you need to alter your goals at any point in time? If yes, how so?

    _____

    _____

6. What did you learn about the goal setting process itself?

    _____

    _____

PERFORMANCE EVALUATION

By the end of your practicum placement, you've likely experienced at least three performance evaluation meetings with your faculty-instructor and primary supervisor. You've set goals and oriented yourselves to the expectations of practicum at your meeting at the beginning of practicum. You've reviewed your goals, strengths, and areas for improvement at a mid-point performance evaluation meeting. You've done the same in your final evaluation meeting. Not only are these performance evaluation meetings required to assess your learning, they are also useful in terms of reflecting how you'll take that learning forward. In the short term, they can help you submit your assignments and prepare for job searches. In the longer term, they can help you identify preferred future practicum placements and reflect on the direction you want to take in the field. While performance evaluation meetings can be intimidating at first, it is important to know that not all jobs in your future will devote focused time dedicated to assisting you in your achievement of your individualized goals. Take this opportunity to use these meetings to aid you in multiple ways. The following list gives a brief overview of how some practicum students have used the performance evaluation meetings to help them in ways beyond the meeting itself. Meanwhile, if your practicum does not already require it, consider asking your supervisor to complete Appendix F to help you. Include it in your portfolio or use it for a job application.

- Jean took copious notes during his performance evaluation meetings so he could list all the skills his supervisor mentioned as his strengths and contributions, which helped him write a better resume.

- Sarah used the form that her supervisor completed, which summarized her strengths and areas of improvement, to help her apply for a job when the job posting required her to submit a reference letter along with her application.
- Ella took the performance evaluation form, which she and her supervisor reviewed together and in the meeting with her faculty-instructor, to help understand what may be required of her in her next practicum.
- Nav reflected on his performance evaluation meetings to help him brainstorm where he'd like to do his next practicum and which elective courses he'd like to take to develop his skills.
- Francis is applying to a specialized certificate in mental health, which she intends to complete alongside her CYC diploma. She's going to use her performance evaluation summary forms as part of her application.

> Reflect and identify how successful they've been. Try not to look at 'I could have' or 'I should have.' It's time to be celebrated. You just put in a hundred or more hours. You came from here to there. Look at the growth. Reward and celebrate yourself.
> —Chris, CYC Practicum Supervisor

Some CYC programs require that the practicum student facilitate these meetings or that they increase their participation so that by the end performance evaluation meeting, they're facilitating the meeting. Take initiative! Make these meetings meaningful to you. While the added pressure to facilitate this meeting may cause alarm or performance anxiety of some kind, reframing it by considering it as an opportunity for you to get what you need is recommended.

PORTFOLIOS

Another component to completing your practicum course requirements may be a portfolio. Portfolios demonstrate your collective learning in an organized, thematic way. Zubizarreta (2009) suggests that to demonstrate learning in a portfolio we must have the following three components: 1) reflection, 2) documentation and evidence, and 3) evidence of collaboration and mentoring. That is, we must show not just what we did but how we learned. Portfolios are not created for the sole purpose of demonstrating your learning; they are a learning activity in and of themselves. While not all programs require a portfolio, reviewing typical portfolio components can be helpful, so you can develop ways of recording, tracking, and recalling your experiences for when you need to complete reflective papers later on in class or when it comes time to apply for jobs (see "Career Files" later in this chapter). Some typical components and organization of a portfolio are listed in Table 13.1.

Zubizarreta (2009) suggests we consider the following questions to help us enter into the portfolio assignment with purpose:

- What, how, when, and why did I learn?
- What have I accomplished with my learning?
- What products and outcomes do I have to demonstrate my learning?

Table 13.1: Typical Practicum Portfolio Contents

Typical Practicum Portfolio Contents	
Component	**Example**
Organizational items	Cover pages, table of contents, dividers, etc.
Administrative items	Contact info, timesheets, orientation checklists, basic work habits checklists, etc.
Evaluation items	Self, supervisor, faculty-instructor from midpoint and final performance evaluations
Learning and professional development plans	Draft and final plans
Agency profile	Program pamphlets, maps, organizational charts, etc.
Demonstration of learning themed by: Learning activities Learning goals Course outcomes Performance evaluation categories CYC Competencies Another framework	Supporting materials/evidence: • Narratives: theoretical orientation, significant learning experiences, journal excerpts • Summaries of learning experiences and evidence—descriptive and reflective • Work products—reports, activity plans, projects, photos, etc. • Appreciative items—cards, etc. • Relationship and engagement—cards, notes, approved photos, etc. Along with descriptive narratives of the significance of the item.
Graded assignments	Assignments and evaluation
Career and profession-related items	Practicum and supervisor job description, resume, references, membership certificates, and professional development activities (e.g., first aid, food safe, nonviolent crisis intervention certificates, agency-based training, etc.)

- What measures and accounting do I have of my learning?
- What difference has learning made in my life?
- What plans do I have to continue learning?
- How is the evidence of my learning integrated with my reflections and self-assessment in the portfolio? (pp. 22–23)

Review your syllabus, seek consultation from your faculty-instructor, check in with classmates, and invite your supervisor to support you to gather materials to demonstrate your learning. Students can get stuck when trying to think of supporting materials and

Be creative, diverse, introspective, momentous, and professional.
—Andrew, CYC Practicum Faculty-Instructor

evidence for their portfolios. The following list may help you collect relevant items that demonstrate your learning. (Keep in mind that staff and young people's confidentiality must be maintained by redacting/omitting information or obtaining permissions.)

- ✓ Online discussion threads
- ✓ Maps
- ✓ Photos
- ✓ Relevant physical objects (flower, poem, shoe-lace, balloon, etc.)
- ✓ Activity plans
- ✓ Notes and cards from young people
- ✓ Gifts of appreciation
- ✓ Research/journal articles and news articles
- ✓ Resume (before and after)
- ✓ Program brochures
- ✓ Business cards
- ✓ Skills inventories and checklists
- ✓ Job descriptions from agency
- ✓ Video/audio transcripts
- ✓ "Case studies" and reflective commentary
- ✓ Ethical decision-making models and commentary
- ✓ Copies of agency policy and procedures
- ✓ Copies of work products (e.g., artwork, documentation, reports, and research)
- ✓ Case presentations
- ✓ Feedback from supervisors
- ✓ Excerpts of learning journals or voice-recorded journals
- ✓ Workshop/training certificates
- ✓ Legacy and capstone projects
- ✓ Assignments (drafts and final) and feedback
- ✓ Performance evaluation summaries

This can all seem very administrative. However, portfolios should be the culmination of your learning experience, holding meaningful documents that represent your learning. This is an opportunity for you to show your faculty-instructor what you've learned. Read the following stories of practicum students' learning and how they decided to demonstrate that learning in their portfolios.

1. Later in Jocelyn's practicum placement at a recreation centre, she had to follow workplace and provincial procedure regarding a young person's disclosure of historical abuse. Her practicum portfolio required her to demonstrate her learning through the knowing, being, doing CYC framework as related to the CYC competencies, including professionalism. To demonstrate her learning in terms of what knowledge she gained, what skills she learned, and how she embodied respect, presence, responsiveness, and care with the young person, she prepared the following items for her practicum, along with narratives of each item's significance:
   - A copy of the agency policy and provincial guidelines regarding reporting abuse

- A copy of an email from her supervisor appreciating Jocelyn for her contribution to the process, identifying a number of skills she practised
- A narrative description of the events
- An excerpt from her learning journal regarding her reflections from that incident

2. Aaron developed a number of meaningful connections with the kids at the elementary school. His practicum course required him to report on the course outcomes as they related to his learning goals, one of which was to facilitate a planned activity. He decided to include the following items to demonstrate this learning, along with narratives of each item's significance:
   - A photo of the classroom, identifying the materials and space he used for the activity
   - A copy of the activity plan with post-activity commentary on how the activity went
   - A photo of the artwork produced from the activity with the group of kids
   - A summary of quotes from the young people, when Aaron sought feedback from them as to how he could improve the activity for the future

3. Placed at a youth outreach program and shelter, Mandeep developed a strong connection with two Indigenous youth. Wanting to work collaboratively with them, she asked if she could come along to a Missing and Murdered Indigenous Women and Girls vigil they were planning to attend in the downtown core. Afterward, she took them to tea to connect with them and reflect on the community event. Mandeep's practicum course required her to demonstrate CYC competencies as related to her learning goals, one of which was advocacy and social justice work. As such, she included the following items in her portfolio, along with narratives of each item's significance:
   - A copy of the United Nations *Declaration on the Rights of Indigenous Peoples*
   - A copy of the website's event page, describing the community vigil information
   - A copy of the group photo that the girls posted to their social media page (with permission)
   - A copy of the song lyrics and online video link that was playing at the vigil, along with a reflection on its significance
   - An excerpt from her learning journal

In the scenarios above, each student was tasked with finding material that represented their learning, communicating that learning, and organizing this information according to the framework required for their portfolio. It is a big job. Make time and space to do it well.

PROFESSIONAL DEVELOPMENT

Completing our first practicum can help us direct our professional development in the short and long term. Professional development includes any activity, experience, education, training, and involvement in our CYC profession that contributes to our continuous development as a practitioner. It can be informal, formal, and whatever is meaningful for you. The most obvious professional development you're doing is completing your credential in CYC. Do not discount the massive amount this effort and its multiple components—courses, practicum, postsecondary institution involvement, mentoring from faculty and staff, special projects, and so on—can take. Be sure to understand how your credential is contributing to your development. For example, you may be required to take elective courses. Be purposeful in that planning.

Beyond the credential you're working toward, CYC has many opportunities for you to engage in continuous learning and contribute to the profession. Your practicum experience may have identified specific or general areas of development you'd like to pursue. Let your own preferences guide you. Gharabaghi (2010), Moscrip and Brown (1989), Szewello Allen and Robertson (2012), and others list a number of professional development activities that CYC practitioners may want to consider, particularly as you reflect on your learning plan and set future goals for yourself:

- ☑ Attend a local, national, or international CYC (or aligned) conference
- ☑ Become a member of your provincial CYC association
- ☑ Attend or participate in an association workshop or gathering
- ☑ Begin a professional network at your postsecondary institution
- ☑ Read
- ☑ Continue a community of practice group for ongoing peer consultation
- ☑ Find a mentor
- ☑ Become a certified CYC-Professional through the North American Association of CYC Practitioners
- ☑ Develop cultural competency and experience working with anti-oppressive frameworks
- ☑ Acquire advanced certifications in trauma-informed care, wilderness education, mental health, and more
- ☑ Acquire short-term training, including driver's licence, food safety, first aid, non-violent crisis intervention
- ☑ Get on mailing lists for seminars, events, and conferences
- ☑ Build information technology, business development, organizational change, program evaluation, political, or aligned knowledge and skills
- ☑ Make a plan for new skills and how to obtain them
- ☑ Invite support and feedback
- ☑ Develop interests outside of work that generate energy
- ☑ Surround yourself with people who you can talk to and who understand your work

Which of the ideas above will you pursue?

_____

_____

Instead of creating an arbitrary checklist of professional activities you think you *should* do, consider a different approach. As you immersed yourself in practicum, you likely noticed what you were drawn to and what you weren't. What did you gravitate toward? What did you think you'd like to learn more about but perhaps just didn't have the time? If you were to explore one facet of practicum further, what would that be? What is a particular issue that children, youth, and families face (e.g., mental health, developmental disability, etc.)? Was it an age group or specific population (e.g., younger kids, young parents, kids in government care, newcomers, etc.)? What conversations did you gravitate toward? What topics did you want to learn more about? What training do you wish was offered?

_____

_____

As you take the time to reflect on your significant learning, consider how to create a SMART professional development plan to move forward. Take Jenna's and Simon's stories below to help you brainstorm specific, measurable, attainable, relevant, and time-bound goals.

Jenna completed her practicum at a residential group home for older adolescent girls. At first, she wasn't sure if she'd like the placement, as she thought she really wanted to work in schools. After the placement was over, she realized just how much she likes the flexibility and unpredictability of the life-space of adolescent girls. As she developed relationships with the girls, worked on daily life skills, assisted with report-writing, attended case-planning meetings, and so on, she became very interested in the worlds of young people in government care and the systems that intersect with their lives. As such, she has enthusiastically and tenaciously decided to devote all possible learning opportunities in this direction. Her plan includes:

- ✓ Read about provincial policy and legislation that impacts kids in government care and youth aging out of government care
- ✓ Become more knowledgeable about overrepresented populations in government care, including Black and Indigenous children and youth
- ✓ Where possible, focus course assignments related to issues the older adolescent girls face
- ✓ Join *CYC-Net* social media groups and participate in online forums discussing issues, practices, and advocacy efforts related to the issues the older adolescent girls face
- ✓ Join a local group that advocates for kids in government care or leaving government care
- ✓ Read and collect news articles, blog posts, and other literature to stay current on what's happening in the community that impacts these kids
- ✓ Watch documentaries, arts-based performances, and other media about kids in care

✓ Attend a rally, protest, or awareness-building event advocating for youth in care

✓ Sign a petition advocating for the age of government care services to extend beyond 18–19 years

✓ Apply for a relief worker position with the residential group home's agency

> There was one instance with a girl who signed and inspired me to learn. Sign language is hopefully an elective I can take so I can better serve a more diverse group of people.
> —Trina, CYC Student

Simon completed his practicum at a youth drop-in centre at a recreation centre, located in an inner-city hub of services and resources, including other recreation services, a library, and a high school. While Simon was at the youth centre, one of the staff members took him to a neighbouring community resource centre that supported Indigenous youth. Simon noticed how strongly connected the Indigenous youth were to the centre and how essential it was to have the youth workers at both centres linked to each other in order to support the youth. As a post-placement goal, Simon decided he wanted to learn more about becoming an ally alongside Indigenous youth. In order to do this, he decided to:

✓ Enroll in elective courses that focused on Indigenous youth, perspectives, and history

✓ Use course assignments to focus on topics impacting Indigenous youth

✓ Participate in gatherings and events in his community including environmental rallies, cultural gatherings, scholar guest lectures, and so on

✓ Understand the Indigenous lands his community sits upon

✓ Read newspapers, blogs, and non-mainstream literature about issues pertaining to Indigenous youth

✓ Read young adult novels and graphic novels, which tell stories about the lives of fictional and actual Indigenous youth

✓ Research resources in the community that support Indigenous youth—educational, land-based, spiritual, artistic, health, family, and so on—and identify potential volunteer opportunities

✓ Explore potential sites for his next practicum experience

> When I started talking to the refugee students who came from Syria and the stories they were sharing and what they went through: it really hit me. You can see the impact that it was having, they were trying to adjust into the school environment and it was difficult for them. I realized I want to work with refugees and immigrants. They need so much support. I was an immigrant myself.
> —Harman, CYC Student

What do you think of Jenna's and Simon's plans? What have they inspired you to think of in terms of your professional development? How can you too use the existing structures you're part of—school, social media, and more—to your advantage? List a few ideas here.

_____

_____

_____

CERTIFICATION

Finally, as we shift toward a discussion of working in the field, as our field professionalizes, it may be worth looking into preparing for certification as a CYC-Professional with the CYC Certification Board or your provincial association's certification process. Why? You may be strongly encouraged to prepare for certification upon your departure from your credential. It may be a helpful designation to have when applying for jobs. When it comes to supporting young people and families across contexts, it is a membership interested in ensuring that the public can understand the breadth and depth of competency and unique contributions of CYC practitioners. Having a glimpse of what will be required of you will be helpful.

> Through my practicum placements I realized that I was really interested in mental health. I dedicated most of the rest of my degree looking at mental health.
> —Heather, CYC Student

The Child and Youth Care Certification Board (2019) describes the certification process as a multimethod, comprehensive approach to demonstrating CYC competence, which includes, among other administrative application material, the submission of:

- A scenario-based exam
- An outline of your training and experience in a number of areas
- Completion of eight portfolio assignment activities
- References and supervisor assessment
- Proof of association membership

It is comprehensive. You'll be glad to know that Curry, Eckles, Stuart, and Qaqish (2010) learned that graduates from CYC programs in Canada did exceptionally well on the exam. The various portfolio assignment activities may even align with a practicum or other CYC course assignments you're already doing.

As our field engages in discussions of professionalization, advocates for increased awareness of how CYC practitioners contribute to the wellness of young people across contexts, and continues to define and expand our role, it is worth spending time in your CYC credential also thinking about how you are and will be involved in the profession at large.

WORKING IN THE FIELD

While completing certificates, diplomas, and degrees, quite often CYC students will be working in the field. Students may decide to work not only to afford the increasingly expensive tuition and skyrocketing costs of living but also to gain experience. Hopefully CYC students learn early on that their skill set is invaluable to many contexts. These jobs will likely be entry-level and temporary/casual positions, but they are valuable stepping stones to one's desired career path. Working in the field has the additional benefits of staying current with practice issues, getting to know your local and provincial systems and structures, and contributing to your community. Don't exclude volunteer experience. It's a great way to expose yourself to different contexts, develop skills you may not have the opportunity to do in school, and contribute. Meanwhile, students can bring examples from the field into their classes to inform, critically evaluate, and shape what they're learning in class.

The following section reviews some activities that may help you as you explore how to enter into the field and continue to shape your experiences as you develop as a practitioner.

KNOW WHAT YOU OFFER THE WORLD

When approaching working in the field, it is important to review what job possibilities are out there as well as what you bring to these potential positions. As CYC practitioners, gaining practice experience as you complete your education benefits you in a number of ways. Not only is it a chance to continue to develop your skills and contribute to your community, it is also a great way of bringing your practice into the classroom. Your ideas, challenges, issues, and critical thinking developed in the field will help your education become even more meaningful. As a student in an applied credential, with at least one practicum completed, you may be surprised to know how many jobs you are now eligible to apply to.

As you have learned by now, CYC practitioners do not hold the same job title. Child and Youth Care Worker, Family Support Worker, Neighbourhood House Assistant, Youth Support Worker, Youth and Family Counsellor, Child Care Counsellor, Crisis Support Worker, Outreach Worker—the list goes on. Cech (2015) lists Educational Assistant, Family Support Worker, Youth Outreach Worker, Respite Worker, Child Care Provider, Residential Care Worker, Foster Care Worker, Child Protection Worker, Welfare Worker, Service Worker, and Child Life Specialist (some require certificates, some diplomas, and some degrees). For each practicum student placed with each supervisor in each context, there may be a different job title associated with it. It can be confusing.

> The beauty of the child and youth care profession is that there's so many different ways you can branch off and avenues that you can take.
>
> —Jasmine, CYC Student

The Government of Canada (2011) lists common CYC practitioner jobs under its "Social and Community Service Workers" category in its National Occupational Classification list (#4212). See Table 13.2 for examples of these positions as well as typical tasks and responsibilities. (Keep in mind that this list is not exhaustive.)

Reviewing general and specific job descriptions such as this one can help us brainstorm the skills, knowledge, and ways of being 1) that we have been practising in school and practicum thus far and 2) that may match up with the skills listed on job postings that we hope to apply for. As you read the list in Table 13.2, you hopefully saw a few items that overlapped with what you did in practicum.

Regardless of position or setting, there are essential skills you are developing in your coursework and practicum thus far that align with national skills and competencies that organizations hope job applicants possess. The Government of Canada (2015) lists essential skills, which are considered the building blocks for other skills and competencies: reading, document use, writing, numeracy, oral communication, thinking, digital

Table 13.2: Government of Canada Social and Community
Service Workers (NOC: 4212)

Social and Community Service Worker Job Titles

Government of Canada (2011) states that "social and community service workers administer and implement a variety of social assistance programs and community services, and assist clients to deal with personal and social problems. They are employed by social service and government agencies, mental health agencies, group homes, shelters, substance abuse centres, school boards, correctional facilities and other establishments" (para. 1).

Job Titles

- Aboriginal outreach worker
- addictions worker
- child and youth worker
- community and social services worker
- community counsellor—social services
- community mental health worker
- crisis intervention worker
- drop-in centre worker
- drug addiction worker
- family service worker
- group home worker
- mental health support worker
- neighbourhood worker—social services
- residential counsellor—group home
- settlement worker—community services
- street outreach worker
- transition house worker—social services
- youth development co-ordinator
- youth worker—social services (para. 2)

Tasks, Duties, and Responsibilities

- Review client background information, interview clients to obtain case history and prepare intake reports
- Assess clients' relevant skill strengths and needs
- Assist clients to sort out options and develop plans of action while providing necessary support and assistance
- Assess and investigate eligibility for social benefits
- Refer clients to other social services or assist clients in locating and utilizing community resources including legal, medical and financial assistance, housing, employment, transportation, day care and other services
- Counsel clients living in group homes and half-way houses, supervise their activities and assist in pre-release and release planning
- Participate in the selection and admission of clients to appropriate programs
- Implement life skills workshops, substance abuse treatment programs, behaviour management programs, youth services programs and other community and social service programs under the supervision of social services or health care professionals
- Meet with clients to assess their progress, give support and discuss any difficulties or problems
- Assist in evaluating the effectiveness of treatment programs by tracking clients' behavioural changes and responses to interventions
- Advise and aid recipients of social assistance and pensions
- Provide crisis intervention and emergency shelter services
- Implement and organize the delivery of specific services within the community
- Maintain contact with other social service agencies and health care providers involved with clients to provide information and obtain feedback on clients' overall progress
- Co-ordinate the volunteer activities of human service agencies, health care facilities and arts and sports organizations
- May maintain program statistics for purposes of evaluation and research (para. 4)

Adapted from Government of Canada. (2011). *National occupational classification: 4212 Community and social services workers.* Ottawa, ON: Author.

technology, working with others, and continuous learning. You may have already noticed how many job postings list these essential skills in some way that is relevant to the position. It is your job as an applicant to clearly communicate how you have developed these capacities. You may wish to reflect on how you've developed these skills in your practicum and how you are practising these skills throughout your credential.

Why review lists of job titles, essential skills, and duties? Emerging practitioners of all types aren't always aware of the scope and specificity of their skills, knowledge, and ways of being. Part of what you're learning in your coursework and practicum is how to communicate these skills, knowledge, and ways of being. Reviewing this information will help you prepare to search for jobs, develop a resume and cover letter, and discuss your abilities in an interview.

What are some other ways to help articulate the concrete, tangible tasks and responsibilities CYC practitioners have? Here are some sources you could review:

- ✓ Your course syllabi learning outcomes, objectives, or curriculum guidelines
- ✓ Your practicum manual or field guide
- ✓ Yours or another CYC program's program or course descriptions
- ✓ Your postsecondary institution's career services website's handouts or guidelines
- ✓ The North American Competencies for Child and Youth Work Practitioners (Appendix G)
- ✓ Job descriptions from your practicum agency
- ✓ Job descriptions available online that are comparable to your practicum position
- ✓ Your performance evaluation assessment forms from practicum

Take a look at job descriptions. Look at how you engaged kids. Reflect on the things you learned: did I learn about budgeting, reports, other agencies? Did I facilitate a group? There's so many things practicum students may not think of.
—Tom, CYC Practicum Supervisor

Something that I previously knew—but it wasn't at the tip of my awareness of how valuable it—is my ability to remain calm and cool.
—Adrian, CYC Student

Underline. Highlight. Circle the phrases, active verbs, tasks, responsibilities, competencies, and ways of being you are developing. As you develop this inventory of skills, knowledge, and ways of being, you may be surprised about just how much you can do! Keep this brainstorming work, as the "data" will inform your job search and application materials.

CAREER FILES

Related to portfolios, but not entirely the same, are career files. Career files collect relevant CYC education and practice experience so as to best represent that information when it comes time to seek future practice education and experience. A portfolio for practicum is meant for your faculty-instructor to evaluate your learning in practicum. We can also create portfolios for our education and practice as a whole, building upon each course, practicum, and work experience we gain. Career files (or general portfolios) can take many shapes: an online LinkedIn profile, a web-based portfolio, or a private digital or paper-based file with materials that demonstrate your education and practice experience that you keep at home and consult when applying for jobs. While some information should be kept private (young people's identity, staff names, etc.), as we engage in a technology-based world, many employers are interested in seeing these representations of your work. Consider how you may continue developing a portfolio or career file throughout your CYC credential may assist your future self. Add to it as you go. Career files can include:

1. Courses: keep your course syllabi and assignments with feedback
2. Workshops/training: keep certificates or proof of attendance
3. Membership: keep record of association memberships
4. Community events: keep an item that represents these events—a flyer, a photo
5. Volunteer and practicum experiences: keep record of dates, supervisors, activities, and responsibilities
6. Awards and recognition: keep track of awards, scholarships, and formal and informal moments of recognition
7. References: keep any letters of recommendation or evaluations you receive or formal and informal evaluations on your performance—even a colleague or family saying something about your contribution
8. Special projects: keep materials of this work
9. Relationships: keep cards, notes, letters, correspondence, photos, and other significant items
10. Theoretical orientation: keep meaningful readings, powerful learning journal entries, etc.
11. Skills checklists: keep skills inventories and lists, job descriptions, and notes
12. Job application documents: keep past resumes and cover letters for reference
13. Dream jobs: keep job descriptions and job postings for dream jobs (or jobs you're curious about), even if this changes over time and even if you don't apply to them

Looking at the list above, what else would you include that would represent your learning, growth, development, and contributions over time? As you can see, this collection can become quite extensive. However, it will save you time, energy, and frustration when it comes time to prepare an application for your dream job down the line. Career files are the best source of information when it comes to applying to jobs in the field.

APPLYING TO JOBS IN THE FIELD

You may have years of experience applying for jobs in the CYC field, or you may be brand new to this experience. In either situation, an orientation to the job search process can help you put your best foot forward when applying for a new position.

Where do you search for jobs?

✓ General postings? Newspapers, job boards, bulletin boards on campus or in community centres, listserves, etc.

✓ Specific agencies or institutions? School districts, provincial or governments, park boards, social service agencies, etc.
✓ Generalist job-search websites? Indeed.com, Glassdoor, Simply Hired, LinkedIn, etc.
✓ Social service sector job-search websites? CharityVillage, etc.

Many job seekers will bookmark their favourite websites and check for new postings at regular intervals. If you follow them closely, you'll come to learn the day they post, so you can be updated as soon as their human resources department advertises positions. Where can you find job postings? Begin by searching the agencies represented in your seminar group, be they school districts, hospitals or health authorities, or social service agencies. Each website will have a "Career" or "Job Postings" section. You may have to first click their "About Us" page or look to the footer of the website to find job listings. Don't limit yourself by only looking at these pages and postings. You can learn a lot about the organization and their work by visiting other pages. This is valuable research to do, long before you apply for a job.

Job Application Preparation

When it comes time to apply for specific jobs in the field, the following items continue to be required: resumes, cover letters, interviews, and references. The following section will review how your most recent practicum experience can help you attend to these requirements.

Analyzing the Agency

Sometimes we can become focused on the job itself but disregard other information. Am I eligible to apply for this job? Do I have the required skills and knowledge? Does the job description—including tasks and responsibilities—look like something I want to perform and am able to perform? We can do this to the exclusion of other questions. Ask:

• Does this agency's mission and values align with your theoretical orientation to practice? Does this agency's mandate and programs spark curiosity in you?
• What else have you heard about this agency that draws you to want to explore more?
• Is this a place you think you'd want to devote your time and energy? Is there room for you to grow?

While you may not be able to answer all of these questions without meeting the people and spending time there, you can explore now.

When it comes time to apply for a particular position, all the preparatory work you've done—getting to know the agency, collecting data from your experiences in a career file, making an exhaustive list of your skills and knowledge—will make your life much easier.

Resume Building

As a part of your practicum placement process, you were likely required to develop a resume. Find that now. Is it up to date? Is it as thorough as it could be? See below for a very basic example of how a current CYC diploma student may represent their experience. Don't stop there; check out examples of resumes online for more creative use of font, space, size, formatting, and white space.

Sample CYC Resume

First and Last Name
Address
Address
Phone Number and Email Address

Statement: As an emerging CYC practitioner, gaining experience supporting young people in their life-space, I practise with a strengths-based and developmentally appropriate approach, and I am committed to advocating for young people's needs.

Summary of Skills, Knowledge, and Experience

- Develop, strengthen, and maintain relationships with youth and staff
- Provide developmentally-appropriate, life-skills activity programming
- Grounded in developmental understanding of young people's wellness and needs
- Effective oral and written communication skills, including information technology

Education

Child and Youth Care Diploma
Postsecondary Institution
2018–Present

- Completed courses in: interpersonal communication, lifespan development, professional issues, activity facilitation, and practicum
- Focused academic papers and group work assignments on: youth homelessness, mental health issues, and social-emotional activity facilitation

General Studies
Postsecondary Institution
September 2017–2018

- Completed courses in: academic writing, English literature, psychology, and sociology

Work Experience

Child and Youth Activities Program Assistant (practicum)
Youth Drop-in Centre, Recreation Centre
January–February 2019

- Facilitated activities that promoted life skills, social-emotional development, and wellness
- Developed relationships with diverse youth
- Contributed to writing incident reports and staff communication logs
- Assisted organizing the Youth in Care Week event

Barista, Coffee Shop, Location
Coffee Shop, Location
April 2017–Present

- Work within a fast-paced, team environment
- Provide excellent customer service and communication
- Responsible for the accuracy and prompt delivery of beverages
- Provided training, orientation, and mentorship to new staff

Volunteer Experience and Community Involvement

Boys and Girls Club Volunteer, Summer 2017
Walk for the Cure, 2015, 2016, 2018
Student CYC Association, 2018–Present

Awards and Recognitions

Employee of the Month, Coffee Shop, 2018
Student Bursary, Postsecondary Institution, 2017

Additional Training

- Food Safe, Current
- Driver's Licence Class 5, Current
- First Aid, Current
- Trauma-Informed Practice Workshop (3 hrs), 2019

Personal Interests and Leisure

Cooking, swimming, sport-fishing, comic book reading and writing, family gatherings, and attending cultural events in the community.

References available upon request.

As you read through the details of the sample resume, what do you notice that is similar or different than your resume? For students with minimal work experience, your main challenge will be how to communicate the meaningful skills and abilities you've gained in your experiences thus far. Ways you can accomplish this include identifying specific courses, training and related work outside the CYC field. Don't forget to include your personal side. There is no ideal sample resume that will fit your exact experience. However, learning how to articulate your experiences through this format will help you communicate to agencies where you'd like to work.

Laing (2016) says that students should focus on accomplishment descriptions, use action verbs, and state the associated task and its positive result. For example:

> Highlight the courses that you're taking so they know. Most people don't know.
> —Heather, CYC Student

> It wasn't until later on I realized some of these skills I had. I created a resource brochure. I can do event planning. I co-facilitated forums. Because we have a certain understanding of knowledge of communities, children, and youth, we can share that with others. Essentially, we're expert at people skills.
> —Jenn, CYC Student

"Planned and implemented six field trips for 25 clients ranging from neighbourhood nature walks to museum trips"
"Applied knowledge of child development to deliver programming"
"Updated team members on issues; collaborated on effective resolutions"

While on the topic of action verbs, McAleer (2009) lists a number of verbs that may be helpful to describe your experience and help your intended reader visualize your work in action:

authored	innovated	negotiated
controlled	invented	organized
counselled	led	planned
designed	liaised	reviewed
facilitated	mediated	supported
implemented	mentored	trained
initiated	motivated	

Most job descriptions, course outlines, and competencies will also include action verbs that you can use. Make note of them. You do not have to reinvent the wheel.

Finally, the following list of resume dos and don'ts can help you when completing your own resume and/or reviewing your classmates'. Getting feedback from someone in a similar situation as you can be helpful. They will notice things that you may miss.

Table 13.3: Resume Dos and Don'ts

	Resume Dos	**Resume Don'ts**
Aesthetics and Format	Use white space Keep formatting simple Keep fonts and page colour standard	Include photographs Include decoration Include clutter
Overall Format	Decide on a format Chronological, functional, or combination of the two	Go beyond two pages, even if not specified
Sub-sections	Consider all relevant sections that your experience can be represented: • education • work and volunteer experience • relevant training and certificates • awards, accomplishments, and recognitions • membership and group affiliations • additional relevant skills • personal interests relevant to the position	Forget to include all the contributions you've made to your community, even if they don't fit into standard formatting
Inclusion/Exclusion	Outline tasks, responsibilities, outcomes, and contributions	Include irrelevant details
Grammar and Language	Use active verbs Watch out for accurate verb tense (be consistent) Keep sentence structure consistent throughout	Use jargon, acronyms, or abbreviations
Accuracy	Be informative Include specific timelines Be succinct yet descriptive	Be humble Exaggerate

Cover Letter Building

As part of your practicum placement process, you may have been required to develop a cover letter to accompany your resume. If you have that, find it now. Meanwhile, pull out the job you'd like to apply for as you consider some of the following recommendations for creating cover letters.

Laing (2016) says an effective cover letter accomplishes four main goals, beyond the administrative specifics such as the posting number, addresses, and contact information:

1. Cover letters target specific jobs
2. Cover letters specifically demonstrate your suitability for the job
3. Cover letters indicate why you want to work for the agency and how you'll contribute
4. Cover letters focus on your most relevant qualifications and their key job requirements

McAleer (2009) has a number of recommendations for writing the body of a cover letter and a series of questions you can ask once you've completed writing a draft (see Table 13.4).

Review the sample cover letter below for a practicum student applying to a residential support worker position while she is completing her CYC diploma.

As you review this and other cover letter examples online, what do you notice? Practise preparing your own cover letter for the job posting you found. Then share it with your seminar group or community of practice to obtain feedback. Are you accurately and thoroughly describing your experience? What may you be leaving out? What could be considered a minor detail, more appropriate for a resume? Is your letter persuasive and engaging? Reflect on each other's letters to learn ways to improve them to reach your goal of getting to the interview stage. Remember, cover letters and resumes are designed to communicate with a selection committee, trying to convince them to want to meet you. Approach it this way, and your personality will shine through.

> When doing your job search, looking online, a lot of them say they want a diploma. But that's not always the case. So send out your resume saying you're almost done your diploma. I've gotten a couple of responses back.
> —Trina, CYC Student

Table 13.4: Cover Letters

Cover Letters Must...	Reviewing Your Cover Letter
✓ Engage, impress, and convince your reader ✓ Use specific vocabulary to describe your skills, strengths, experience, accomplishments, and unique attributes ✓ Use wording from the job advertisement ✓ Back up all claims with details ✓ Keep your letter to one page	• Is the letter well organized? • Is the letter persuasive? • Does the letter describe unique skills, accomplishments, or credentials? • Is the letter error free? • Would you ask this person for an interview?

Adapted from McAleer, D. (2009). *Report writing for the community services* (p. 146). Toronto, ON: Pearson Education.

Sample CYC Cover Letter

My First and Last Name

Address

Date

Selection Committee

Agency Name

Address

RE: Application for Job Posting # 1234—Residential Support Worker

Dear Selection Committee:

Please accept this letter and accompanying resume as my application for your Residential Support Worker position, as found on your agency website. Your posting indicates that you're looking for someone who can build relationships, facilitate life-skills activities, complete documentation, and work within a multidisciplinary team to support the needs of youth. The following experience demonstrates how I would be able to perform this position well.

In my first practicum as an activity support worker at a youth drop-in hub, I facilitated numerous activities, developed relationships with youth, and worked within a large team at the recreation centre. As a second-year student in a CYC diploma, I have been developing my knowledge and application of interpersonal communication, professional ethics and legislation, activity facilitation, and lifespan development, with a focus on at-risk youth. I've had the chance to contribute to incident reports and communication logs as well as numerous academic assignments, receiving excellent evaluations.

My approach to practice is a blend of strengths-based, developmental, relational, contextual, and socially just practice, all in the life-space of youth. I would consider it a great privilege to contribute my knowledge, skills, and experience to your agency in its support of youth in government care through its residential homes and support services.

Thank you for your time and consideration of my application. I look forward to the opportunity to discuss my suitability for the position. Please do not hesitate to contact me for any further information you may need.

Warm regards,

[My Signature]

First and Last Name

Phone Number

Email Address

Interview Preparation

When preparing for an interview, there is a lot to attend to. Whether you're applying for a job and successfully reached the interview stage, or you'd like to prepare for your next practicum placement interview, consider the following guidelines.

Szewello Allen and Robertson (2012) recommend several preparatory steps for an interview. See Table 13.5 for their summary. Treat this list as a checklist when it comes time to apply for a job.

The actual questions you'll be asked in an interview will typically fall into three categories: traditional, behavioural, or situational (McAleer, 2009). Traditional questions include: why are you applying for this position? How are you best suited for the position? What are your strengths and weaknesses? How do you deal with conflict or challenge? Behavioural questions focus on your behaviour in response to a challenge, such as "tell me about a time that you dealt with conflict." Here, you would relay a situation, your actions, and the outcome. Situational questions give you a scenario and ask you to explain how you would respond.

In all responses, it's helpful to remember to circle back to the actual job. For example, if asked what your strengths and weaknesses are, try to imagine how those strengths and weaknesses would show up in the position (and how you'd manage the challenge). Further, identifying strengths and weaknesses requires self-awareness. Tell the committee how you value self-awareness and how it helps you do your job well. If you're asked to respond to a scenario, remember to link back to the actual position. Tell them how you would apply

Table 13.5: Interview Preparation

Tips for Preparing for Your Interview	Tips for Interviewing Successfully
✓ Research the skill set required for the job ✓ Review an annual report from the organization ✓ Look up the organization online ✓ Find out who is on the board of directors: do you know someone you can speak to about the job? ✓ Talk to people who work in this area to find out what the job might be like ✓ Match your skill set and knowledge to the expected skill set and knowledge base of the job	✓ Dress modestly and professionally. Don't overdress or underdress ✓ Arrive with a notebook in hand ✓ Be prepared to be interviewed by a panel ✓ Don't babble, say *um* or *eh*, or use colloquial language ✓ Don't say you don't know something. Reframe the question and say what you do know or that you are willing to learn in an area you are less familiar with ✓ When sitting, lean forward with your hands on the table ✓ Don't fidget ✓ If you need to, practice with some friends ✓ Have your notebook open and write down questions during the interview

Adapted from Drolet, J., Clark, N., & Allen, H. (Eds.). (2012). *Shifting sites of practice: Field education in Canada* (pp. 272–273). Toronto, ON: Pearson.

these skills to the position, not just to the scenario you describe. While you won't know the ins and outs of the actual position, going this extra step convinces the committee that you're one step closer to performing the job well. Show them you're the best person for the job.

Don't forget that you're interviewing them too. An interview is a chance to get to know the agency and the people who work for it. Sometimes you'll be interviewed by one person, but in many cases, it will be a group of people. A selection committee typically has the direct supervisor of the position, their supervisor, and sometimes a human resources staff person. Sometimes the committee will have a peer or a person in a similar position. Some progressive organizations even include young people on their committees. If you take the perspective that you're also interviewing them, you can pay attention to the workplace culture that emerges in the discussion. You can ask them pointed questions to learn more. You can feel more at ease, re-balancing the power in the room. While you won't have time to ask all of them, one or two of the following detailed, thoughtful questions will help you 1) gain valuable information about the agency and 2) communicate to the selection committee that you're a serious, competent applicant.

1. What does a typical day-in-the-life of this position look like?
2. How would you describe the workplace culture of the agency?
3. How does this agency support the wellness of its staff?
4. How would you describe the agency's perspective and approach to practice?
5. What would you say are the main issues, struggles, and barriers your young people face?
6. When will applicants hear back about the position?

Finally, a follow-up email or note within 48 hours of your interview thanking the selection committee is always wise. Even if you're not successful in obtaining the position, you'll leave a lasting impression that will help for the next position you apply to at their agency.

References

References are the people in your professional life who can speak to the skills, knowledge, and ways of being you've developed, the professionalism you bring to your practice, and the contributions you've made to your community. A person who provides a reference can be someone who has supervised your work in a formal supervisory capacity. When you're seeking someone to comment on your practice, consider a wide scope of people. For example, for an entry-level position, it would be typical for an employer to see some combination of the following people listed as your references:

- Your practicum's primary supervisor
- Your practicum colleagues who supervised work that your supervisor did not

- Volunteer supervisor
- Your practicum faculty-instructor
- Your course instructors (especially for applied courses)
- Past or current work supervisor (especially for CYC positions or positions in other industries that have relevant skills: interpersonal communication, teamwork, problem-solving, etc.)
- A leader or mentor in the field who can speak to any community work that you've done

When you ask potential referees for a reference, try to give them as much advanced notice as possible. They may have many students they're supervising. It may have been some time since they've supervised you. In this case, it's helpful to remind them of your work with them. Consider the following notes.

Hello Sonia,

I hope this note finds you well.

As I near the end of my CYC diploma, I am embarking on a job search and I am hoping you'll consider being a reference for me.

You were my practicum faculty-instructor for CYC 1234 (fall 2018) and observed my contribution to seminar, reviewed my assignments, facilitated my performance evaluation meetings, and discussed CYC practice in office hours a number of occasions. I believe you could speak to my strengths in X, Y, and Z areas.

[or]

When you supervised my practicum placement between April and June 2019, we worked together to develop the social-emotional skills group activity for the kids in your program, liaised with a number of parents, and ran the community event. I believe this experience will be relevant to many of the positions I'm applying for. I believe you could speak to my strengths in X, Y, and Z areas.

Please let me know if you are able to be a reference and if so, your preferred contact information. If I am successful in obtaining interviews, I will let you know when you should expect contact from the selection committees.

Many thanks,

Your Name

You'll notice a few things in these notes. You are asking for a general reference (so that you don't have to ask them five times for specific references). You are reminding them of your relationship and time together (they'll remember you, but they'll also have many other students under their instruction and supervision. It helps to refresh their memory). You are also highlighting some of the strengths they identified in your practice. While they will identify many more strengths to the selection committee, reminding them of the strengths you think are relevant is a helpful strategy to focus their memory. You may also want to attach relevant material: your performance evaluation review, assignment feedback, your current resume, and so on. These notes also give them the chance to decline. They may be too busy or think someone else may be a more appropriate referee. But your encouraging, kind tone will go far in helping you obtain a reference for your search.

If you do know the position you're applying to, let the referee know. Provide a webpage link to the job posting in your correspondence and tell them why you're interested in applying for the position. Enthusiasm is contagious. Your past supervisor will like learning how you foresee yourself contributing to the field.

Agencies will likely want to contact your references after a successful interview, but sometimes they want this information included in your application package. When you're applying for many jobs at once—such as when you graduate from your credential—it's helpful to contact a handful of referees (three is recommended) to let them know that 1) you're applying for a number of positions, 2) you'd like their reference, and 3) you'll let them know when you expect someone will contact them. Selection committees typically call or email references. Alternatively, if the position requires you to include a reference letter in your application package, it's useful to have these prepared well in advance. When you complete a practicum, for example, it's helpful to ask your supervisor to complete a reference form, such as the one included in Appendix F. This way, you can use this form for multiple applications when needed.

While it's recommended you write "references available upon request" at the end of your resume, it's also recommended you bring a list of referees to your interview, including their first and last name; their current position, agency name, and contact information (phone and email); as well as a brief note as to the context in which they supervised you. That last item is important. The referee may currently be in a different position than when they were your supervisor. Including information as to when and in what capacity they supervised your practice will help the selection committee understand their role.

References are more than just someone who can speak to your practice so that you can obtain a job or volunteer position. They are your network in the field. Maintaining relationships with your colleagues, supervisors, communities of practice, and your seminar group classmates—who are your professional peers you will cross paths with in many capacities throughout your career—is important. You never know when you'll need to check in, seek support from, ask for a consultation, or debrief with them, and perhaps seek a reference.

PUTTING IT ALL TOGETHER

You'll have your entire credential to prepare and plan for how you'll enter into the CYC profession. Practicum offers up a window into CYC practice, for you to observe, experiment, learn, and be changed. Gather your learning and use it intentionally, listening to people's stories and wisdom along the way. You never know where the thing that will forever change you will be. Let the field mentor you. We conclude this section of this chapter with guidance from the field.

Listening to the Wisdom of Leaders in the CYC Field

On Gaining Experience

Boys and Girls Clubs are an ideal place for students to volunteer and build their experience. Our volunteers gain practical hands-on experience and confidence to try new things, develop a multitude of relationships, and access mentoring and leadership opportunities. Just as importantly, our volunteers make a huge impact in the lives of our young participants by being caring, attentive leaders and role models in our programs and services, and by contributing their great ideas and skills to our organization.

> —Avril Paice, Organizational Development, Boys and Girls Clubs

Every time one volunteers as a mentor, they open the door to long lasting friendships and expand their personal and professional networks. Who can be a mentor? Anyone who is looking to invest in the future of young people by donating a few hours of their time every month. This especially includes mentors who identify as LGBTQ+, Indigenous, Black, Racialized, Immigrants, or Refugees or part of other diverse community groups. Volunteers will tell you mentoring has been one of the most impactful experiences in their lives.

> —Aamer Esmail, National Director, Equity, Diversity and Youth Engagement, Big Brothers Big Sisters of Canada

On Specialized Competencies and Knowledge

We are specifically looking for staff who either understand or align with conducting their work within a Trauma Informed Framework, understanding that: behaviour is based in pain and trauma; clients' behaviours are not about us; children and youth do well when they can; emphasis is on safety and trust; choice, collaboration, and connection are key; focus on identifying strengths and skills; and individual approaches for all.

> —Jennifer Hanrahan, Director of Operations and Residential Services, St. Leonard's Youth and Family Services

On Job Applications

Customer service skills are an often overlooked but absolutely essential part of working at most non-profit organizations, and especially in social service agencies. Probably every interaction you have with clients will draw upon customer service skills learned elsewhere, including: preventing escalation, defusing situations, engaging with the public, identifying clients' needs, prioritizing, and multitasking.

—Marina Dawson, Manager, Community and Content, CharityVillage

I cannot emphasize the importance of not only a good resume, but a strong cover letter. I always read cover letters first. This is your opportunity to convince me of why I should interview you. This is not a time to be humble, rather it's a time to be honest and sincere. Show us that you know who we are, what we do, and why you want to work for us.

—Jennifer Hanrahan, Director of Operations and Residential Services,
St. Leonard's Youth and Family Services

Workers in our field have a difficult time talking about their strengths and what they can bring to our organization. I would really like to see new applicants to carefully consider what they believe or have been told their strengths are. Conversely, I'd like applicants to have an awareness and understanding of their areas of growth.

—Jennifer Hanrahan, Director of Operations and Residential Services,
St. Leonard's Youth and Family Services

On Our Certification

Set learning goals... attend additional training, volunteer, and employment opportunities... practice skills in each of the five domains... keep track of your hours and additional training... attend a webinar... hold on to certificates and course descriptions... join a provincial association... get actively involved... join working committees, focus groups or join the Board of Directors.

—Julia Margetiak, Chair, CYC Certification Process Committee

CYC Network

Don't forget the special resource available for you at www.cyc-net.org. Here you're able to join with like-minded (and otherwise minded) colleagues who will encourage, equip, and challenge you. Join the Facebook discussion group... Download and read *CYC-Online* each month... Write about your experience and submit it to the journal... Contribute your voice by writing about your experience or learning and share it with the world.

—James Freeman, Editor, *CYC-Online: E-journal of the International Child and Youth Care Network*

BACK TO THE CLASSROOM

So you've finished your practicum. You've submitted your remaining assignments. You've considered employment options in the field. You're likely heading back to class soon to keep pursuing your CYC credential. How will you take what you learned in practicum and bring it back to class? How will it inform your critical understanding of the theories and practices being introduced to you in classes to come?

> CYC is a life-long learning process. This is just the beginning to an open world of endless possibilities.
> —Saira, CYC Practicum Faculty-Instructor

Shaw and Trites (2013) ask us to consider not just how theory is applied to practice but how practice informs theory. They invite us to ensure our work builds on theory as well as challenges and questions practice norms. When you move forward in your classwork, continually ask yourself: does this theory reflect what young people experience? Does it help advance their needs and interests? What is missing? What is incorrect? What helps me support young people grow and develop? What doesn't?

At the end of practicum, we have the opportunity to take a philosophical position, without the pressure of performance or assignments. We can ask ourselves:

1. What did I learn about young people?

   _____

   _____

2. What did I learn about CYC practice?

   _____

   _____

3. What did I learn about myself?

   _____

   _____

Then, take this learning back to class to inform your (and our) future work.

While you continue on in your courses, you are also developing your sense of identity as a CYC practitioner. Take the time you need welcoming yourself into the group. Contribute yourself, your knowledge, and your skills. And don't forget: you came to this field to amplify the voices and needs of young people and their families across all of our communities. A course, a practicum, a training, a job, and even a theory—they're all the same. We learn and immerse ourselves in

> CYC lends its hand to innovative and creative practice and that's exciting. I don't like to work inside boxes and I think with the right conversations, the right proposals, and the right development you have the opportunity to do so much.
> —John, CYC Student

each of them not to demonstrate perfection, meet assessment criteria, or accumulate hours and years of experience. We complete them to support young people and to change the very conditions in which they are attempting to make a good life for themselves. Wherever you enter the field and wherever you end up, let's join young people in that dream.

LEARNING JOURNAL

Where are you heading? How will you take the skills, knowledge, and ways of being you've just immersed yourself in practicum back to the classroom? Your last learning journal entries may benefit from you scanning your learning journal in full. Look to your first few days. Focus on one particular question that you answered in each entry. Notice your development. Then write or reflect about that. How have you changed?

PRACTICE SCENARIOS

Take a look at the practice scenarios that conclude this chapter: "Kellie's Community" and "Back to Class." Use the content read in this chapter to inspire your thinking about the scenario. Notice how the scenario may relate to your own situation at your current practicum placement, even if it is not exactly what you are experiencing. Consider the questions posed at the end of each scenario to help you expand and apply the concepts presented in this chapter.

SEMINAR GROUP AND COMMUNITY OF PRACTICE DISCUSSION QUESTIONS

In your seminar or community of practice group, consider the following questions for discussion:

1. Select one of your original learning goals. Tell your group why you identified the goal, how you planned to achieve it, and how you did or did not achieve it. Share the materials or evidence that you could include in a portfolio that demonstrates this goal. Listen to others.
2. Bring a copy of your ideal job description (found on CharityVillage, for example), your resume, and a cover letter and review it with your group. (While you're at it, conduct a mock interview, rotating roles: interviewee, employer, and observer.)
3. How will you bring your learning back to the classroom?
4. What is one significant learning experience that taught you something important about young people? What impact do you think that learning will have on you moving forward?

IN CLOSING

This final chapter has covered a lot of territory. We've moved from reflecting on learning, to demonstrating that learning through portfolios, to preparing to apply for positions in the field, and to consider how we can take our learning back to the classroom in future courses. Over the course of your practicum placement, you oriented yourself to a new environment, actively observed practitioners in the field, experimented with the theories and approaches you've learned in class, learned from your peers across different contexts, and developed your theoretical orientation to practice. For some practicum students, practicum has been your first entry into the world of CYC practice. For others, practicum will have built upon your experience. For everyone, it is a time to intensely and intentionally focus on your learning and synthesis of theory with practice and contribute to young people's wellness.

Your practicum experience will stay with you. You'll remember the staff who impacted you, the young people who made a lasting impression, the challenges that you overcame, and the successes you experienced. As an emerging practitioner in the field, practicum is one of the most memorable experiences we carry forward in our careers into this diverse, challenging, and complex field we call Child and Youth Care.

Welcome. We are glad you are here.

PRACTICE SCENARIOS

Kellie's Community

Kellie wants to apply to a position at the youth centre but feels that because she's only halfway through her diploma, she may not be as "good" as the other applicants. She's considering not even applying. She decides to make an appointment with her practicum faculty-instructor, asking for some application advice. Kellie says that she has lots of work experience, but it's not directly with children and youth. At the retail shop she's worked at since she was 16, she's worked on a big team, planned events, dealt with conflict with customers, and oriented a few new staff. Meanwhile, when her faculty-instructor reminds her of all the community advocacy work she's mentioned in class, Kellie recalls quite a few cultural events, environmental protests, and memorial marches she's attended or helped organize. Her faculty-instructor also asks her about her hobbies and personal interests, and she shares that she cares for her family's kids, likes music from many genres, and occasionally fosters dogs from the local SPCA. Time stops them from brainstorming more.

Is there something in your life that you feel connects to Child and Youth Care practice that doesn't necessarily fit within the typical education, work, and volunteer sections of a resume? What creative way could you professionally represent that important personal, community, and related professional work within the constraints of a resume or other job application material?

_____

_____

_____

Back to Class

At practicum, Chandra was inspired when learning about restorative justice programs in schools. Heather was inspired by trauma-informed practices at the group home. Will was struck by the devastation caused by the opioid epidemic in the urban centre. Nicki was moved to see the kids be impacted by mindfulness practices. Zola was shocked at the lack of resources for youth aging out of care. Adair was witness to the strength of young people to get through difficult days.

Soon, you'll re-enter the classroom to review more perspectives, issues, and practice approaches in Child and Youth Care. What inspired you in your practicum placement—an issue, a population, a problem, a practice? What can you not stop thinking about? How will you bring purpose, critical thought, and enthusiasm back to your classroom, to question, explore, expand, and figure out the things that matter to you most?

_____

_____

_____

APPENDIX A

GUIDEBOOK CONSULTANTS

CYC Students

Adrian is a proud male member of the Tsleil-Waututh First Nations band, having recently received a diploma in CYC, Aboriginal Stream. His two practicum placements were within elementary schools. Dealing with a traumatic childhood himself, he feels it is important to support our youth with their trials as they transition through the years. He feels it is important to let our youth know they are not alone, they are seen, they are heard and respected.

Cody is a CYC student, who identifies as male, using the pronouns he/him/his. Cody's ancestors are settlers from the land now called the United Kingdom; however, he was raised in Surrey, British Columbia. Cody completed first- and second-year practicum placements at a recreational and community youth outreach team while also working in the field. Cody reflects that the inspiration to continue doing good work comes from a deep connection to community, and a responsibility to understand privilege, and how he can be a tool in empowering others through advocacy and action.

Heather is a recent CYC degree graduate. She had the opportunity to complete practica in a youth drop-in centre for street-entrenched youth, as well as a centre for parents to meet with their children who are currently in care. Heather is Canadian of French and Irish descent and grew up in and currently lives in Metro Vancouver. She is most inspired by the resiliency of young people and their ability to overcome traumatic experiences and hopes to continue her career in the health care sector.

Harman is a recent CYC degree graduate, having completed her practica at an Indigenous family services society, a secondary school program, and a community services centre supporting newcomers to Canada. She immigrated to Vancouver from India when she was 11 years old. Harman is passionate about providing support to young people and admires young people's resiliency through their adverse experiences.

Jasmine graduated with a BA and MA in CYC (along with a youth justice diploma). Her very first practica in the field were at an interagency alternative school for youth involved in the criminal justice system and at a drop-in service for street-entrenched youth, many of whom were challenged with addiction. She is of mixed African-American and British descent, and she grew up in Manitoba before moving to British Columbia as a child. She is passionate about her current clinical work supporting children, adolescents, and families and is inspired by the strength, resiliency, and recovery she sees in individuals she serves.

Jenn has her BA in CYC and spent her time as a student exploring diverse practicum experiences. Her practicum roles included a school-based youth and family worker, an outreach worker, and a community-focused role in an MLA's constituency office. She comes from Dutch and Norwegian descent and was born and raised in Greater Vancouver.

She is passionate about social justice and dismantling oppressive systems. She finds daily inspiration from the authenticity and strength of the young people she supports.

John is a graduate of a degree in CYC. He completed practicum placements in a school district and in child protection. He is an international human being of mixed European and Métis biological cultural heritage/ethnicity, and his CYC ideology inspires him to change and/or develop human service–related professions to better suit the needs of an ever-evolving society.

Margaret is a female student with Filipino ancestry, coming from a first-generation immigrant family, born in the Philippines and raised in Canada. She is a future graduate of the CYC degree program and has had practicum placements in a middle school, high school, and community youth centre. Margaret is inspired by the growth and knowledge gained from the relationships built with youth by their curiosity and personal stories.

Natalie is a graduate of the CYC degree program, where she completed a variety of practicum placements: an alternative secondary school, an all-girls youth residential home, and an inner-city elementary school. She was born and raised in Vancouver and has ancestors from the UK and France. What inspires her most about young people is their ability and resiliency to persist through personal adversity, and she hopes to be able to provide advocacy for growth and change.

Sam was born in England and has lived in Canada from the time she was eight years old. Her practicum placements were at an alternate school, elementary school, and middle school. She is drawn to working with young people who struggle behaviourally and who other staff have trouble building connections with. She loves what she does and loves looking back on the journey that led to where she is now.

Tamara is a recent graduate of the CYC degree program, having completed her practicum placements at a residential treatment facility for youth, as a school-based CYC worker, and as a child and youth mental health outreach worker with a government agency. She acknowledges that her place of birth, residency, and work are on the unceded traditional territories of the Coast Salish Peoples. Tamara is constantly humbled by the strength and perseverance that can be found with children and youth and hopes to foster these qualities through her practice.

Trina holds a diploma in CYC with a major in its Aboriginal Stream. She is the mother of three young girls, and she is from the Ahousaht First Nation. Her practicum placements were at an Indigenous alternative school and a family services program. She believes the story of what drove our ambition to join CYC is what we have to offer the youth we want to walk alongside, make connections, and build relationships with. She says there is no set template of an ideal CYC worker, just as there is no set template of the ideal youth in need of our support.

CYC Supervisors

Annie is an executive director of a community research organization. She moved to Canada from the UK in 2005, having worked with youth in the UK and the US. Annie has supervised CYC practicum students for over a decade. She always enjoys running into program graduates who are now working in the field or are continuing their studies, and hearing how they continue to apply what they learned during their practicum.

Chris is a recreation program coordinator who has worked out of two dynamic and fast-paced recreation centres in the youth services area. He is of American and Belgian descent and was born in Canada. Chris has been hosting and supervising CYC practicum students since 2011. His goal for all practicum students is to build on their passions, while developing their skills and interests, to support them in accomplishing goals and a legacy project.

Donna is a neighbourhood assistant at an enhanced services school. She is of Canadian-Chinese descent, born and raised in the unceded territories of the Coast Salish Peoples. As a new CYC mentor, she enjoys listening to and sharing students' ideals, perspectives, hopes, and goals. Donna looks forward to sharing her experiences with the new group of CYC professionals.

Farah is a case manager at non-profit organization that houses, supports, and provides services to children and youth in care in a family setting. She is of British and East African descent and a second-generation settler on Coast Salish territory. In her supervisory capacity, she loves the fresh ideas and passion that students bring to the organization. Her mantra is "you are never an expert in your field, but always a learner."

Mindi is a family-strengthening team leader at an Indigenous family services organization and a 2010 graduate of the CYC degree program with a specialization in child welfare (with practicum placements at a group home, elementary school, and in child welfare). She is Indigenous from Fond du Lac First Nation, Saskatchewan, and has worked solely with Indigenous families since graduating. Mindi is inspired by young people's passion and commitment to creating positive changes with respect to reconciliation and how we support families.

Rose is a recently retired manager and program coordinator of a trauma-informed, long-term residential home for female youth. She's supervised CYC, youth justice, and social work students for approximately 50 years. She identifies as female with French-Canadian heritage. Rose is inspired and enthused with teaching, supervising, and being taught by students about their own stories and sharing her stories and the stories of the amazing youth we care for each day.

Sonja is a school district behavioural specialist in a Metro Vancouver school and contract instructor in CYC. Her goal is to improve herself, while working toward improving the capacity of all educators to respond to children, youth, and families from a trauma-informed lens. Sonja's most demanding and rewarding job in CYC is being a mom to a teenage daughter and pre-teen son, often joking that she runs a teen drop-in program in her home. She locates herself as a white, cisgender female of European descent. Sonja considers it a privilege to support and work with the next generation of CYC counsellors who bring their innate drive for social equality to the field, fuelled by passion and creativity.

Tom is a recreation programmer at a community services centre in Vancouver's lower mainland, working with young people and supervising CYC practicum students for over 20 years. He is Japanese Canadian, born in Japan, moving to Canada and becoming a visitor on Coast Salish territory at a young age. As a supervisor of many practicum students, he enjoys sharing passion and knowledge about our field with the new generation of people coming into the field. The energy and excitement the students bring is invigorating. They provide opportunities to revisit and learn new theory, and reflect on how, what, and why we practice.

CYC Faculty-Instructors

Andrew is a faculty-instructor in CYC in Prince Edward Island. One of the aspects of student growth and development into a CYC practitioner that he finds very rewarding is the professional contact the local communities and cultures provide to students during practica. Practicum experiences are keystone opportunities students have to put their signature on their professional style.

Deb is faculty in CYC and began teaching practicum in 1991 (and hosted practicum students in the group home she managed at the same time). She is a fourth-generation visitor to the Sto:lo territory and her family comes from Norway, Scotland, and England. Deb is grateful to have had the opportunity to support students in practicum. She enjoys assisting students as they make the connection between what they learn in the classroom and what happens in the field, as well as watching them develop their own style of practice.

Kristy is a faculty member in CYC and has been teaching practicum since 2001. She is a second-generation white settler of Dutch, Irish, and Swedish descent living on Coast Salish territories. Kristy loves working with students in the field, supporting them to ask critical questions about how and why we practise the ways we do.

Mackenzie is a faculty-instructor in CYC and a queer, cisgendered, white settler of European descent who has been living and working on Coast Salish territories since 2007. Having a graduate degree in CYC herself, Mackenzie is passionate about teaching in the field of CYC. In particular, Mackenzie enjoys supervising students on practicum because of the concrete opportunities it presents for a critical reflection of one's practice and the context in which it occurs.

Rhonda is a faculty-instructor in CYC and works as a psychiatric social worker with youth, families, and communities. She is a third-generation settler on Coast Salish territory on her maternal side and a member of Eastern Woodland Métis Association on her paternal side. She enjoys mentoring students and the rich learning opportunities that come with the position, and she feels it is an honour to be a part of a student's learning journey.

Saira is an internship coordinator and faculty at a number of Ontario colleges in their CYC programs. Saira locates herself as a brown, Indo-Caribbean Canadian cisgender female of Indo-Caribbean/South Asian Indian descent and first-generation settler in Toronto, Ontario. Preparing students for the field is her favourite course to teach, as she is able to provide students with the necessary skills and tools that will support them throughout their journey in the CYC program.

Yvonne is faculty in CYC. She locates herself as a white female of European descent and first-generation settler on Turtle Island. Yvonne believes that practicum is a space where theory can truly come alive—students can grow deep roots and be tested by the elements, and it produces life-changing experiences. She considers it a gift to be a part of students' journeys, adding to and developing their practice knowledge and skills on practicum.

APPENDIX B

STUDENT PREFERENCES FORM

Practicum Course and Student Contact Information

Course title and academic term: _____

During the practicum placement process, I can be best reached by my preferred:

Phone number: _____

Email address: _____

Home address (home and city): _____

My mode of transportation (public transport, car, etc.): _____

Practicum Placement Preferences and Interests

Ages
Using a scale of 1 through 4 (where 1 is most preferred and 4 is least preferred), please indicate your preference/interest in a particular age group:

Childhood: _____ Middle childhood: _____

Early adolescence: _____ Older adolescence: _____

If you have a specific group of young people you'd like to work with, please indicate that information here (e.g., newcomers to Canada, specific cultural heritages, LGBTQ+ youth, homeless youth, mental health, developmental disabilities, criminal justice, etc.):

_____

Settings
If you have a particular agency where you'd like to complete your practicum, please indicate that here, as well as any contact information for that site, and whether or not you've been in touch with them:

_____

_____

Is there anywhere you do not want to be placed for practicum? Why?

_____

Using a scale of 1 through 3 (where 1 is most preferred and 3 is least preferred), please indicate your preference/interest in CYC practicum settings: school-based, community-based, or residential-based settings. Use a checkmark if you are interested in any of the sub-settings listed within each of the three categories, if desired.

School   Community   Residential

settings: _____   settings: _____   Settings: _____

- ☐ School—anywhere
- ☐ Elementary school
- ☐ Middle school
- ☐ Secondary school
- ☐ Alternate elementary school program
- ☐ Alternate middle school program
- ☐ Alternate secondary school program
- ☐ Other: _____

- ☐ Community—anywhere
- ☐ Recreation/leisure
- ☐ Family support
- ☐ Hospital-based—outpatient
- ☐ Policy and research
- ☐ Other: _____

- ☐ Residential—anywhere
- ☐ Residential group home
- ☐ Hospital-based (e.g., mental health inpatient, etc.)
- ☐ Correctional facility
- ☐ Other: _____

Student Availability

Please use the chart below to indicate your availability. Mark *X* where you are not available and indicate those time commitments (e.g., *X* and "12–3 p.m.").

Anticipated Availability for Practicum							
	Sunday	Monday	Tuesday	Wednesday	Thursday	Friday	Saturday
Morning							
Afternoon							
Evening							

Practicum Student Reflection

1. What ages and settings have you worked with in the past?

   _____

2. What do you consider your strengths?

   _____

3. What are some areas you'd like to develop?

   _____

4. What are your long-term career goals at this time? What is your dream job after you finish your credential? What roles are you drawn to?

   _____

5. Are there any specific considerations you would like to share that you think would be helpful for the placement process?

   _____

Student Requirements

Upon submission of this form, I acknowledge that:

☐ I have completed this form to the best of my knowledge, and it is as current as possible.

☐ Practicum placement decisions are based on a number of factors, including student preferences, but the decision is ultimately up to the CYC program.

☐ I will inform my program coordinator/assigned faculty-instructor of any changes.

☐ I will check my phone and email messages at least once per 48 hours during the placement process.

☐ I have submitted a current copy of my resume, attached to this form.

☐ I have kept a copy of this form for my own records.

☐ I understand that I must register for the course and complete institutional requirements as they become required (e.g., tuition payments) for my coordinator/instructor to pursue placement.

Practicum Student Name (printed): _____

Signature: _____

Date: _____

APPENDIX C

PLACEMENT INFORMATION FORM

Practicum Placement Contact Information

Practicum Placement Program Name: _____

Agency Phone Number: _____

Address: _____

Website: _____

Primary Supervisor Name and Title: _____

Phone—Office/Cell: _____

Email Address: _____

Student Name: _____

Phone: _____

Email Address: _____

Faculty-Instructor Name: _____

Phone—Office/Cell: _____

Email Address: _____

Practicum Placement Schedule

Placement Duration (Day/Month/Year–Day/Month/Year): _____

Proposed Schedule:

Proposed Practicum Student Schedule at Practicum Site							
	Sunday	Monday	Tuesday	Wednesday	Thursday	Friday	Saturday
Morning							
Afternoon							
Evening							

Postsecondary institution and agency procedures and requirements reviewed with student:

- ☐ Institutional-Agency Practicum Agreement in place
- ☐ Copy of criminal record check provided to site
- ☐ Liability, health, safety, and labour restrictions and liability reviewed with student
- ☐ Appendix D: Emergency Contact Form reviewed with student
- ☐ In case of illness, process reviewed with student
- ☐ Other requirement: _____

Copies of this form provided to:

- ☐ Practicum Student
- ☐ Practicum Supervisor
- ☐ Practicum CYC Faculty-Instructor

APPENDIX D

EMERGENCY CONTACT FORM

Contact Information

Practicum Student
Name: _____

Preferred phone number: _____

Email address: _____

Physical location(s) in placement: _____

Practicum Placement Primary Supervisor
Name: _____

Preferred phone number: _____

Email address: _____

Physical location(s) in placement: _____

Alternate Contact to Primary Supervisor
Name: _____

Preferred phone number: _____

Email address: _____

Physical location(s) in placement: _____

CYC Practicum Faculty-Instructor
Name: _____

Preferred phone number: _____

Email address: _____

Physical location(s) in placement: _____

Potential Emergencies

List the potential emergencies that may occur at this setting along with the steps the practicum student should take if such events were to occur.

(Note: to be completed by practicum supervisor with student present; emergencies could include: allergic reaction, physical injury, violence, threats, fire, risk to self/others, earthquake, etc.)

Scenario #1: _____

_____

_____

Scenario #2: _____

_____

_____

Scenario #3: _____

_____

_____

Scenario #4: _____

_____

_____

Scenario #5: _____

_____

_____

List the policies and procedures manual title where emergency response procedures exist:

_____

_____

List of emergency resources in community (e.g., hospital, RCMP/police emergency and non-emergency, shelter, crisis line, child welfare, etc.):

_____

_____

APPENDIX E

Sample Practicum Timesheet and Activities Form

Sample Practicum Timesheet & Activities Form			
Day/Month/Year	Brief Description of Activities	Time In/Time Out	Total Hours
29 April 2019	Gr.3 class (behaviour support); High5 lunch group; Playground; IEP meeting; after school Staff Mtg	8:00am – 4:00pm	8 hours
		Total Hours	
		Supervisor Initials	

APPENDIX F

Recommendation for Practice Form

PRACTICUM PLACEMENT INFORMATION

Practicum student name: _____

Practicum duration _____ and Total hours: _____

Practicum agency and program name: _____

Practicum supervisor name and position: _____

CYC program postsecondary institution name: _____

SUMMARY OF EVALUATION

Summary of practicum student activities, responsibilities, and accomplishments

_____

_____

_____

_____

_____

_____

_____

_____

_____

_____

Summary of practicum student strengths

_____

_____

_____

_____

_____

_____

Areas for further development

_____

_____

_____

CONTACT INFORMATION

Practicum supervisor preferred contact info	Signature	Date

Faculty-instructor preferred contact info	Signature	Date

Practicum student preferred contact info	Signature	Date

APPENDIX G

Child and Youth Care Practice Standards—Competencies for Professional Child and Youth Work Practitioners

The CYC Competencies are organized across five domains:

1. Professionalism
2. Cultural & human diversity
3. Applied human development
4. Relationship & communication
5. Developmental practice methods

I. PROFESSIONALISM

Professional practitioners are generative and flexible; they are self-directed and have a high degree of personal initiative. Their performance is consistently reliable. They function effectively both independently and as a team member. Professional practitioners are knowledgeable about what constitutes a profession and engage in professional and personal development and self-care. The professional practitioner is aware of the function of professional ethics and uses professional ethics to guide and enhance practice and advocates effectively for children, youth, families, and the profession.

    A. Foundational Knowledge
- History, structure, organization of Child and Youth Care Work
- Resources and activities of CYC
- Current and emergent trends in society, services, and in CYC
- Structure and function of Codes of Ethics applicable to practice which includes the Code of Ethics, Standards for Practice of North American Child and Youth Care Professionals (www.acycp.org)
- Accepted boundaries in professional practice
- Stress management and wellness practices
- Strategies to build a professional support network
- Significance of advocacy and an array of advocacy strategies
- Relevant laws, regulations, legal rights and licensing procedures governing practice

B. Professional Competencies
1. Awareness of the Profession
   a. access the professional literature
   b. access information about local and national professional activities
   c. stay informed about current professional issues, future trends and challenges in one's area of special interest
   d. contribute to the ongoing development of the field
2. Professional Development and Behavior
   a. Value orientation
      (1) state personal and professional values and their implications for practice including how personal and professional beliefs, values, and attitudes influence interactions
      (2) state a philosophy of practice that provides guiding principles for the design, delivery, and management of services
   b. Reflection on one's practice and performance
      (1) evaluate own performance to identify needs for professional growth
      (2) give and receive constructive feedback
   c. Performance of organizational duties
      (1) demonstrate productive work habits
         (a) know and conform to workplace expectations relating to attendance, punctuality, sick and vacation time, and workload management
         (b) personal appearance and behavior reflect an awareness of self as a professional as well as a representative of the organization
   d. Professional boundaries
      (1) recognize and assess own needs and feelings and keeps them in perspective when professionally engaged
      (2) model appropriate interpersonal boundaries
   e. Staying current
      (1) keep up-to-date with developments in foundational and specialized areas of expertise
      (2) identify and participate in education and training opportunities
3. Personal Development and Self Care
   a. Self awareness
      (1) recognize personal strengths and limitations, feelings and needs
      (2) separate personal from professional issues
   b. Self care
      (1) incorporate "wellness" practices into own lifestyle
      (2) practices stress management
      (3) build and use a support network
4. Professional Ethics
   a. describes the functions of professional ethics
   b. applies the process of ethical decision-making in a proactive manner

      c. integrates specific principles and standards from the relevant Code of Ethics to specific professional problems

      d. carries out work tasks in a way that conforms to professional ethical principles and standards

  5. Awareness of Law and Regulations

      a. access and apply relevant local, state/provincial and federal laws, licensing regulations and public policy

      b. describe the legal responsibility for reporting child abuse and neglect and the consequences of failure to report

      c. describe the meaning of informed consent and its application to a specific practice setting

      d. use the proper procedures for reporting and correcting non-compliance

  6. Advocacy

      a. demonstrate knowledge and skills in use of advocacy

      b. access information on the rights of children, youth and families including the United Nations Charter on the Rights of the Child

      c. describe the rights of children, youth, and families in relevant setting/s and systems advocate for the rights of children, youth, and families in relevant settings and systems

      d. describe and advocate for safeguards for protection from abuse including institutional abuse

      e. describe and advocate for safeguards for protection from abuse including organizational or workplace abuse

      f. advocate for protection of children from systemic abuse, mistreatment, and exploitation

II. CULTURAL AND HUMAN DIVERSITY

Professional practitioners actively promote respect for cultural and human diversity. The Professional Practitioner seeks self understanding and has the ability to access and evaluate information related to cultural and human diversity. Current and relevant knowledge is integrated in developing respectful and effective relationships and communication and developmental practice methods. Knowledge and skills are employed in planning, implementing and evaluating respectful programs and services, and workplaces.

  A. Foundational Knowledge

     The professional practitioner is well versed in current research and theory related to cultural and human diversity including the eight major factors which set groups apart from one another, and which give individuals and groups elements of identity: age, class, race, ethnicity, levels of ability, language, spiritual belief systems, educational achievement, and gender differences.

     • Cultural structures, theories of change, and values within culture variations

- Cross cultural communication
- History of political, social, and economic factors which contribute to racism, stereotyping, bias and discrimination
- Variations among families and communities of diverse backgrounds
- Cultural and human diversity issues in the professional environment

B. Professional Competencies

    1. Cultural and Human Diversity Awareness and Inquiry

        a. describe own biases

        b. describe interaction between own cultural values and the cultural values of others

        c. describe own limitation in understanding and responding to cultural and human differences and seeks assistance when needed

        d. recognize and prevent stereotyping while accessing and using cultural information

        e. access and critically evaluate resources that advance cultural understandings and appreciation of human diversity

        f. support children, youth, families and programs in developing cultural competence and appreciation of human diversity

        g. support children, youth, families and programs in overcoming culturally and diversity based barriers to services

    2. Relationship and Communication Sensitive to Cultural and Human Diversity

        a. adjust for the effects of age, cultural and human diversity, background, experience, and development on verbal and non-verbal communication

        b. describe the non-verbal and verbal communication between self and others (including supervisors, clients or peer professionals)

        c. describe the role of cultural and human diversity in the development of healthy and productive relationships

        d. employ displays of affection and physical contact that reflect sensitivity for individual development, cultural and human diversity as well as consideration of laws, regulations, policies and risk

        e. include consideration of cultural and human diversity in providing for the participation of families in the planning, implementation and evaluation of services impacting them

        f. give information in a manner sensitive to cultural and human diversity

        g. contribute to the maintenance of a professional environment sensitive to cultural and human diversity

        h. establish and maintain effective relationships within a team environment by:

           (1) promoting and maintaining professional conduct;

           (2) negotiating and resolving conflict;

           (3) acknowledging and respecting cultural and human diversity; and

           (4) supporting team members

3. Developmental Practice Methods Sensitive to Cultural and Human Diversity
   a. integrate cultural and human diversity understandings and sensitivities in a broad range of circumstances
   b. design and implement programs and planned environments, which integrate developmental, preventive, and/or therapeutic objectives into the life space, through the use of methodologies and techniques sensitive to cultural and human diversity
      (1) provide materials sensitive to multicultural and human diversity
      (2) provide an environment that celebrates the array of human diversity in the world through the arts, diversity of personnel, program materials, etc.
      (3) recognize and celebrate particular calendar events which are culturally specific
      (4) encourage the sharing of such culture specific events among members of the various cultural groups
   c. design and implement group work, counseling, and behavioral guidance with sensitivity to the client's individuality, age, development, and culture and human diversity
   d. demonstrate an understanding of sensitive cultural and human diversity practice in setting appropriate boundaries and limits on behavior, including risk management decisions

III. APPLIED HUMAN DEVELOPMENT

Professional practitioners promote the optimal development of children, youth, and their families in a variety of settings. The developmental-ecological perspective emphasizes the interaction between persons and their physical and social environments, including cultural and political settings. Special attention is given to the everyday lives of children and youth, including those at risk and with special needs, within the family, neighborhood, school and larger social-cultural context. Professional practitioners integrate current knowledge of human development with the skills, expertise, objectivity and self awareness essential for developing, implementing and evaluating effective programs and services.

A. Foundational Knowledge
   The professional practitioner is well versed in current research and theory in human development with an emphasis on a developmental-ecological perspective.
   • Life Span Human Development
   • Child/Adolescent Development (as appropriate for the arena of practice), including domains of
   • Cognitive Development
   • Social-emotional Development
   • Physiological Development

- Psycho-sexual Development
- Spiritual Development
- Exceptionality in Development including at-risk and special needs circumstances such as trauma, child abuse/neglect, developmental psychopathology, and developmental disorders
- Family Development, Systems and Dynamics

B. Professional Competencies

1. Contextual-Developmental Assessment
   a. assess different domains of development across various contexts
   b. evaluate the developmental appropriateness of environments with regard to the individual needs of clients
   c. assess client and family needs in relation to community opportunities, resources, and supports

2. Sensitivity to Contextual Development in Relationships and Communication
   a. adjust for the effects of age, culture, background, experience, and developmental status on verbal and non-verbal communication
   b. communicate with the client in a manner which is developmentally sensitive and that reflects the clients' developmental strengths and needs
      (1) recognize the influence of the child/youth's relationship history on the development of current relationships
      (2) employ displays of affection and physical contact that reflect sensitivity for individuality, age, development, cultural and human diversity as well as consideration of laws, regulations, policies, and risks
      (3) respond to behavior while encouraging and promoting several alternatives for the healthy expression of needs and feelings
   c. give accurate developmental information in a manner that facilitates growth
   d. partner with family in goal setting and designing developmental supports and interventions
   e. assist clients (to a level consistent with their development, abilities and receptiveness) to access relevant information about legislation/regulations, policies/standards, as well as additional supports and services

3. Practice Methods That Are Sensitive to Development and Context
   a. support development in a broad range of circumstances in different domains and contexts
   b. design and implement programs and planned environments including activities of daily living, which integrate developmental, preventive, and/or therapeutic objectives into the life space through the use of developmentally sensitive methodologies and techniques
   c. individualize plans to reflect differences in culture/human diversity, background, temperament, personality and differential rates of development across the domains of human development

d. design and implement group work, counseling, and behavioral guidance, with sensitivity to the client's individuality, age, development, and culture

e. employ developmentally sensitive expectations in setting appropriate boundaries and limits

f. create and maintain a safe and growth promoting environment

g. make risk management decisions that reflect sensitivity for individuality, age, development, culture and human diversity, while also insuring a safe and growth promoting environment

4. Access Resources That Support Healthy Development

a. locate and critically evaluate resources which support healthy development

b. empower clients, and programs in gaining resources which support healthy development

IV. RELATIONSHIP AND COMMUNICATION

Practitioners recognize the critical importance of relationships and communication in the practice of quality child and youth care. Ideally, the service provider and client work in a collaborative manner to achieve growth and change. "Quality first" practitioners develop genuine relationships based on empathy and positive regard. They are skilled at clear communication, both with clients and with other professionals. Observations and records are objective and respectful of their clients. Relationship and communication are considered in the context of the immediate environment and its conditions; the policy and legislative environment; and the historical and cultural environment of the child, youth or family with which the practitioner interacts.

A. Foundational Knowledge
   • Characteristics of helping relationships
   • Characteristics of healthy interpersonal relationships
   • Cultural differences in communication styles
   • Developmental differences in communication
   • Communication theory (verbal and non-verbal)
   • Group dynamics and teamwork theory
   • Family dynamics and communication patterns, including attachment theory as it relates to communication style

B. Professional Competencies
   1. Interpersonal Communication
      a. adjust for the effects of age, cultural and human diversity, background, experience, and development of verbal and non-verbal communication
      b. demonstrate a variety of effective verbal and non-verbal communication skills including
         (1) use of silence

          (2) appropriate non-verbal communication

          (3) active listening

          (4) empathy and reflection of feelings

          (5) questioning skills

          (6) use of door openers to invite communication, and paraphrasing and summarization to promote clear communication

          (7) awareness and avoidance of communication roadblocks

   c. recognize when a person may be experiencing problems in communication due to individual or cultural and human diversity history, and help clarify the meaning of that communication and to resolve misunderstandings

   d. assist clients (to a level consistent with their development, abilities and receptiveness) to receive relevant information about legislation/regulations, policies/standards, and supports pertinent to the focus of service

   e. provide for the participation of children/youth and families in the planning, implementation and evaluation of service impacting them

   f. set appropriate boundaries and limits on the behavior using clear and respectful communication

   g. verbally and non-verbally de-escalate crisis situations in a manner that protects dignity and integrity

2. Relationship Development

   a. assess the quality of relationships in an ongoing process of self reflection about the impact of the self in relationship in order to maintain a full presence and an involved, strong, and healthy relationship

   b. form relationships through contact, communication, appreciation, shared interests, attentiveness, mutual respect, and empathy

   c. demonstrate the personal characteristics that foster and support relationship development

   d. ensure that, from the beginning of the relationship, applicable procedures regarding confidentiality, consent for release of information, and record keeping are explained and clearly understood by the parent/caregiver and by the child, as appropriate to his/her developmental age. Follow those procedures in a caring and respectful manner

   e. develop relationships with children, youth and families that are caring, purposeful, goal-directed and rehabilitative in nature; limiting these relationships to the delivery of specific services

   f. set, maintain, and communicate appropriate personal and professional boundaries

   g. assist clients to identify personal issues and make choices about the delivery of service

   h. model appropriate interpersonal interactions while handling the activities and situation of the life-space

   i. use structure, routines, and activities to promote effective relationships

    j.   encourage children, youth and families to contribute to programs, services, and support movements that affect their lives by sharing authority and responsibility

    k.   develop and communicate an informed understanding of social trends, social change and social institutions. Demonstrate an understanding of how social issues affect relationships between individuals, groups, and societies

    l.   identify community standards and expectations for behavior that enable children, youth and families to maintain existing relationships in the community

3.   Family Communication

    a.   identify relevant systems/components and describe the relationships, rules and roles in the child/youth's social systems and develop connections among the people in various social systems

    b.   recognize the influence of the child's relationship history and help the child develop productive ways of relating to family and peers

    c.   encourage children and families to share folklore and traditions related to family and cultural background. Employ strategies to connect children to their life history and relationships

    d.   support parents to develop skills and attitudes which will help them to experience positive and healthy relationships with their children/youth

4.   Teamwork and Professional Communication Skills

    a.   establish and maintain effective relationships within a team environment by: promoting and maintaining professional conduct; negotiating and resolving conflict; acknowledging individual differences; and, supporting team members

    b.   explain and maintain appropriate boundaries with professional colleagues

    c.   assume responsibility for collective duties and decisions including responding to team member feedback

    d.   use appropriate professional language in communication with other team members, consult with other team members to reach consensus on major decisions regarding services for children and youth and families

    e.   build cohesion among team members through active participation in teambuilding initiatives

    f.   collect, analyze and present information in written and oral form by selecting and recording information according to identified needs, agency policies and guidelines. Accurately record relevant interactions and issues in the relationship

    g.   plan, organize, and evaluate interpersonal communications according to the identified need, context, goal of communication, laws/regulations, and ethics involved. Choose an appropriate format, material, language, and style suitable to the audience

      h.   acknowledge and respect other disciplines in program planning, communication and report writing using multidisciplinary and interdisciplinary perspectives. Communicate the expertise of the profession to the team

      i.   establish and maintain a connection, alliance, or association with other service providers for the exchange of information and to enhance the quality of service

      j.   deliver effective oral and written presentations to a professional audience

      k.   demonstrate proficiency in using information technology for communication, information access, and decision-making

V. DEVELOPMENTAL PRACTICE METHODS

Practitioners recognize the critical importance of developmental practice methods focused in CYC practice: Genuine Relationships, Health and Safety, Intervention Planning, Environmental Design and Maintenance, Program Planning and Activity Programming, Activities of Daily Living, Group Work, Counseling, Behavioral Guidance, Family (Caregiver) Engagement, Community Engagement. These are designed to promote optimal development for children, youth, and families including those at-risk and with special needs within the context of the family, community and the lifespan.

A.   Foundational Knowledge
- Health and safety
- Intervention theory and design
- Environmental design
- Program planning and Activity Programming including:
  - developmental rationales
  - basic strategies of program planning
  - specific developmental outcomes expected as a result of participating in activities
  - principles of activity programming, e.g. activity analysis, adaptation, strategies for involving youth in activities
  - relationship of developmental processes to the activities of daily living (eating, grooming, hygiene, sleeping and rest)
  - the significance of play activities
  - community resources for connecting children, youth and families with activity and recreational programs
- Behavioral Guidance methods including conflict resolution, crisis management, life space interviewing
- Behavior Management methods
- Counseling Skills
- Understanding and Working with Groups
- Understanding and Working with Families
- Understanding and Working with Communities

B. Professional Competencies
1. Genuine Relationships
   a. recognize the critical importance of genuine relationships based on empathy and positive regard in promoting optimal development for children, youth, and families (as fully described in Section III)
   b. forming, maintaining and building upon such relationships as a central change strategy
2. Health and Safety
   a. environmental safety
      (1) participate effectively in emergency procedures in a specific practice setting and carry them out in a developmentally appropriate manner
      (2) incorporate environmental safety into the arrangement of space, the storage of equipment and supplies and the design and implementation of activities
   b. health
      (1) access the health and safety regulations applicable to a specific practice setting, including laws/regulations related to disability
      (2) use current health, hygiene and nutrition practices to support health development and prevent illness
      (3) discuss health related information with children, youth and families as appropriate to a specific practice setting
   c. medications
      (1) access current information on medications taken by clients in a specific practice site
      (2) describe the medication effects relevant to practice
      (3) describe the rules and procedures for storage and administration of medication in a specific practice site, and participate as appropriate
   d. infectious diseases
      (1) access current information on infectious diseases of concern in a specific practice setting
      (2) describe the components relevant to practice
      (3) employ appropriate infection control practices
3. Intervention planning
   a. assess strengths and needs
   b. plan goals and activities which take agency mission and group objectives, individual histories and interests into account
   c. encourage child/youth and family participation in assessment and goal setting in intervention planning and the development of individual plans
   d. integrate client empowerment and support of strengths into conceptualizing and designing interventions
   e. develop and present a theoretical/empirical rationale for a particular intervention or approach

      f.   select and apply an appropriate planning model

      g. select appropriate goals or objectives from plans, and design activities, interactions, and management methods that support plans in an appropriate way

      h. work with client and team to assess and monitor progress and revise plan as needed

4. Environmental Design and Maintenance

      a. recognize the messages conveyed by environment

      b. design and maintain planned environments which integrate developmental, preventive, and interventive requirements into the living space, through the use of developmentally and culturally sensitive methodologies and techniques

      c. arrange space, equipment and activities in the environment to promote participation and prosocial behavior, and to meet program goals

      d. involve children, youth and families appropriately in space design, and maintenance

5. Program Planning and Activity Programming

      a. connect own childhood activity experiences and skills, and adult interests and skills, to current work

      b. teach skills in several different domains of leisure activity

      c. assist clients in identifying and developing their strengths through activities and other experiences

      d. design and implement programs and activities which integrate age, developmental, preventive, and/or interventive requirements and sensitivity to culture and diversity

      e. design and implement challenging age, developmentally, and cultural and human diversity appropriate activity programs

         (1) perform an activity analysis

         (2) assess client's interests, knowledge of and skill level in various activities

         (3) promotes client's participation in activity planning

         (4) select and obtain resources necessary to conduct a particular activity or activity program

         (5) perform ongoing (formative) and outcome (summative) evaluation of specific activities and activity programs

      f. adapts activities for particular individuals or groups

      g. locate and critically evaluate community resources for programs and activities and connect children, youth, and families to them

6. Activities of Daily Living

      a. integrate client's need for dignity, positive public image, nurturance, choice, self-management, and privacy into activities of daily living

      b. design and implement, and support family members and caregivers to implement, activities of daily living, which integrate age, developmental, preventive, and/or interventive requirements and sensitivity to culture and diversity

    (1) age and cultural and human diversity appropriate clothing

    (2) pleasant and inviting eating times that encourage positive social interaction

    (3) age and developmentally appropriate rest opportunities

    (4) clean and well maintained bathroom facilities that allow age and developmentally appropriate privacy and independence

    (5) personal space adequate for safe storage of personal belongings and for personal expression through decorations that do not exceed reasonable propriety

  c. design and maintain inviting, hygienic and well maintained physical environments and equipment and supplies which positively support daily activities

  d. encourage client development of skills in activities of daily living

    (1) personal hygiene and grooming skills

    (2) developing and maintaining of areas related to daily living, e.g. maintaining living space, preparing and serving meals, cleanup

    (3) socially appropriate behavior in activities of daily living: respecting other's privacy, expected grooming and dress for various occasions

7. Group Process

  a. assess the group development and dynamics of a specific group of children and youth

  b. use group process to promote program, group, and individual goals

  c. facilitate group sessions around specific topics/issues related to the needs of children/youth

  d. mediate in group process issues

8. Counseling

  a. recognize the importance of relationships as a foundation for counseling with children, youth and families (as fully described in Section III, Relationships and Communication)

  b. has self awareness and uses oneself appropriately in counseling activities

  c. able to assess a situation in the milieu or in individual interaction and select the appropriate medium and content for counseling

  d. able to make appropriate inquiry to determine meaning of a particular situation to a child

  e. assist other adults, staff, parents and caregivers in learning and implementing appropriate behavioral support and instruction

  f. employ effective problem solving and conflict resolution skills

9. Behavioral Guidance

  a. assess client behavior including its meaning to the client

  b. design behavioral guidance around level of client's understanding

    c.   assess the strengths and limitations of behavioral management methods

    d.   employ selected behavioral management methods, where deemed appropriate

    e.   assist other adults, staff, and parents and caregivers in learning and implementing appropriate behavioral guidance techniques and plans

    f.   give clear, coherent and consistent expectations; sets appropriate boundaries

    g.   evaluate and disengage from power struggles

    h.   employ genuine relationship to promote positive behavior

    i.   employ developmental and cultural/diversity understandings to promote positive behavior

    j.   employ planned environment and activities to promote positive behavior

    k.   employ at least one method of conflict resolution

    l.   employ principles of crisis management

        (1) describe personal response to crisis situations

        (2) describe personal strengths and limitations in responding to crisis situations

        (3) take self protective steps to avoid unnecessary risks and confrontations

        (4) dress appropriately to the practice setting

        (5) employ a variety of interpersonal and verbal skills to defuse a crisis

        (6) describe the principles of physical interventions appropriate to the setting

        (7) conduct a life space interview or alternative reflective debriefing

10. Family (Caregiver) Engagement

    a.   communicate effectively with family members

    b.   partner with family in goal setting and designing and implementing developmental supports and/or interventions

    c.   identify client and family needs for community resources and supports

    d.   support family members in accessing and utilizing community resources

    e.   advocate for and with family to secure and/or maintain proper services

11. Community Engagement

    a.   access up to date information about service systems, support and advocacy resources, and community resources, laws, regulations, and public policy

    b.   develop and sustain collaborative relationships with organizations and people

    c.   facilitate client contact with relevant community agencies

Association for Child & Youth Care Practice & Child and Youth Care Certification Board (2010). Retrieved from https://cyccb.org

APPENDIX H

Standards for Practice of North American Child and Youth Care Professionals: Principles and Standards (CYC Code of Ethics)

I. RESPONSIBILITY FOR SELF

- A. Demonstrates high standards of integrity and professional conduct
- B. Develops knowledge and skills necessary to benefit children, youth, and families
    1. Participates in education and training for ongoing professional development
    2. Engages in ongoing supervision and/or counsel as appropriate
- C. Maintains physical and emotional well-being
    1. Aware of personal values and their implication for practice
    2. Mindful of self as a growing and developing practitioner
    3. Understands the importance of self-care and the responsibility to seek guidance, counseling, and support

II. RESPONSIBILITY TO CHILDREN, YOUTH AND FAMILIES

- A. Does not cause harm
    1. Encourages safe and ethical practice
    2. Does not disrespect, exploit, or intimidate others
- B. Maintains privacy and confidentiality as appropriate to role
- C. Ensures services are culturally sensitive and non-discriminatory (regardless of race, color, ethnicity, national origin, national ancestry, age, gender, sexual orientation, marital status, religion, mental or physical capacity/ability, medical condition, political views, or socioeconomic status)
- D. Provides protection and advocacy
    1. Recognizes, respects, and advocates for the rights of the child, youth and family
    2. Supports individuals in advocating for their own rights and safety
- E. Fosters self-determination and personal agency
- F. Encourages a child or youth's participation within a family and community, and facilitates the development of social networks
- G. Recognizes the life space of young people involves physical, emotional, mental and virtual domains (including social media, messaging, gaming, etc.)
- H. Respects the diversity of life patterns and expectations
    1. Affirms that there are differences in individual and family needs and meets those needs on an individual basis

2. Ensures interactions reflect developmental age, status, understanding and capacity
3. Adapts to individual needs when designing and implementing plans and programs (including psychological, physical, social, cultural, and spiritual needs)

I. Values collaboration with colleagues and those from other disciplines
1. Makes referrals to other professionals as necessary and seeks assistance to ensure access to needed services
2. Observes, assesses, and evaluates services/treatments prescribed or designed by other professionals

J. Ensures appropriate boundaries between professional and personal relationships
1. Recognizes and adjusts for dynamics related to power, authority, and position
2. Does not engage in harassment or sexual misconduct with a child, youth, or family member

III. RESPONSIBILITY TO THE EMPLOYER AND/OR EMPLOYING ORGANIZATION

A. Responds to employer in a professional manner and seeks to resolve differences collaboratively
B. Treats colleagues with respect, courtesy, and equity
C. Models flexibility and inclusiveness in working with colleagues and family members
D. Respects the commitments made to the employer or employing organization

IV. RESPONSIBILITY TO THE PROFESSION

A. Acts in a professional manner toward colleagues
1. Seeks arbitration or mediation with colleagues as appropriate
2. Reports ethical violations to appropriate individuals or boards when informal resolution is not appropriate or sufficient

B. Encourages collaboration among professionals, children, youth, family and community to share responsibility for outcomes

C. Ensures professional practice in training and research activities
1. Ensures education and training programs are competently designed and delivered
2. Ensures research is of high quality and is designed, conducted, and reported in accordance with quality and ethical standards

D. Ensures that practitioners, supervisors and administrators lead programs according to high-quality and ethical practice

V. RESPONSIBILITY TO THE COMMUNITY

    A. Promotes awareness of the profession and the needs of children, youth, and families to the community

    B. Models ethical behavior in relationships and interactions with community members

    C. Promotes respect and appreciation of diversity, racial equality, social justice and cultural humility

    D. Encourages informed participation by the public in shaping social policy and decisions affecting children, youth, and families

Association for Child & Youth Care Practice (2017). Retrieved from www.acycp.org

REFERENCES

Ainsworth, K. (2016). *Reimagining practicum in twenty-first century child and youth care.* Master's thesis, University of Victoria, Victoria, BC, Canada. Retrieved from https://dspace.library.uvic.ca/handle/1828/7493

Anderson, L. W., & Krathwohl, D. R. (Eds.). (2001). *A taxonomy for learning, teaching, and assessing: A revision of Bloom's taxonomy of educational objectives.* New York, NY: Addison Wesley Longman.

Anderson-Nathe, B. (2010). *Youth workers, stuckness, and the myth of supercompetence: Not knowing what to do.* New York, NY: Routledge.

Anglin, J. P. (2000). What exactly is child and youth care work? *CYC-Online: E-journal of the International Child and Youth Care Network,* 14 (March). Retrieved from https://www.cyc-net.org/cyc-online/cycol-0300-anglin.html

Anglin, J. P. (2001). Child and youth care: A unique profession. *CYC-Online: E-journal of the International Child and Youth Care Network,* 35 (December). Retrieved from https://www.cyc-net.org/cyc-online/cycol-1201-anglin.html

Anglin, J. P. (2002). *Pain, normality, and the struggle for congruence: Reinterpreting residential care for children and youth.* London, UK: Routledge.

Anglin, J. P. (2014). Pain-based behaviour with children and adolescents in conflict. *Reclaiming Children and Youth, 22*(4), 53–55.

Association for Child and Youth Care Practice. (2017). *Standards for practice of North American child and youth care professionals.* Retrieved from https://www.acycp.org/images/pdfs/ethics_and_practices_ACYCP_v2-1.pdf

Association for Child and Youth Care Practice and Child and Youth Care Certification Board. (2010). *Competencies for professional child and youth work practitioners.* Retrieved from https://www.acycp.org/images/pdfs/2010_Competencies_for_Professional_CYW_Practitioners.pdf

Awai, S. (2018). *Practicum supervision in child and youth care: A guide for site supervisors.* Master's thesis, University of Victoria, Victoria, BC, Canada. https://dspace.library.uvic.ca/handle/1828/9273

Baldwin, C., Kelber, A., Pick, M., & Wilson, S. (2017). Transformative learning theory as a framework for child and youth care training. *Relational Child and Youth Care Practice, 30*(1), 23–34.

Barbezat, D. P., & Bush, M. (2014). *Contemplative practices in higher education: Powerful methods to transform teaching and learning.* San Francisco, CA: John Wiley & Sons.

Barford, S. W., & Whelton, W. J. (2010). Understanding burnout in child and youth care workers. *Child and Youth Care Forum, 39*(4), 271–287.

Barker, B., Goodman, A., & DeBeck, K. (2017). Reclaiming Indigenous identities: Culture as strength against suicide among Indigenous youth in Canada. *Canadian Journal of Public Health, 108*(2), e208–e210.

Batasar-Johnie, S. (2017). Reflections of supervision: The development of a growing CYC. *CYC-Online: E-journal of the International Child and Youth Care Network,* 223 (September), 33–40. Retrieved from https://www.cyc-net.org/cyc-online/sep2017.pdf

BC Association of Social Workers, Indigenous Working Group. (2016). *Towards a new relationship: Toolkit for reconciliation/decolonization of social work practice at the individual, workplace, and community level.* Retrieved from https://www.bcasw.org/wp-content/uploads/2011/06/Reconciliation-Toolkit-Final_May-11.pdf

Beneteau, C. (2002). My developmental stages as a child and youth care student. *CYC-Online: E-journal of the International Child and Youth Care Network,* 37 (February). Retrieved from https://www.cyc-net.org/cyc-online/cycol-0202-beneteau.html

Benshoff, J. M. (2001). Peer consultation as a form of supervision. *CYC-Online: E-journal of the International Child and Youth Care Network,* 31 (August). Retrieved from https://cyc-net.org/cyc-online/cycol-0801-supervision.html

Birkenmaier, J., & Berg-Weger, M. (2011). *The practicum companion for social work: Integrating class and field work* (3rd ed.). Boston, MA: Allyn & Bacon.

Bogo, M. (2012). Getting started: Preparing to learn in the field. In J. Drolet, N. Clark, & H. Allen (Eds.), *Shifting sites of practice: Field education in Canada* (pp. 19–38). Toronto, ON: Pearson.

Brendtro, L. K., Brokenleg, M., & Van Bockern, S. (2002). *Reclaiming youth at risk: Our hope for the future.* Bloomington, IN: National Education Service.

Brendtro, L. K., & Larson, S. J. (2006). *The resilience revolution: Discovering strengths in challenging kids.* Bloomington, IN: Solution Tree.

Brockett, S., & Anderson-Nathe, B. (2013). "If I'da thrown that chair at you, it woulda hit you": Seeing difficult behaviours through the lens of meaning and resilience. *Relational Child and Youth Care Practice, 26*(2), 6–11.

Bronfenbrenner, U. (1979). *The ecology of human development: Experiments by nature and design.* Cambridge, MA: Harvard University Press.

Burns, M. (2006). *Healing spaces: The therapeutic milieu in child and youth work.* Kingston, ON: Child Care Press.

Burns, M. (2012). *The self in child and youth care: A celebration.* Kingston, ON: Child Care Press.

Cambridge Dictionary. (2018). Reflexivity. Retrieved from https://dictionary.cambridge.org/dictionary/english/reflexivity

Canadian Institutes of Health Research. (2014). *Common cultural interventions* [research report]. Retrieved from http://www.addictionresearchchair.ca/

Catalano, R. F., Berglund, M. L., Ryan, J. A. M., Lonczak, H. S., & Hawkins, J. D. (1998). *Positive youth development in the United States: Research findings on evaluations of positive youth development programs* [research report]. Retrieved from https://aspe.hhs.gov/report/positive-youth-development-united-states-research-findings-evaluations-positive-youth-development-programs

Cech, M. (2010). *Interventions with children and youth in Canada.* Don Mills, ON: Oxford University Press.

Cech, M. (2015). *Interventions with children and youth in Canada* (2nd ed.). Don Mills, ON: Oxford University Press.

Centre of Excellence for Women's Health. (2013). *Trauma-informed practice guide* [research report]. Retrieved from http://bccewh.bc.ca/wp-content/uploads/2012/05/2013_TIP-Guide.pdf

Chalupa, M. (2015). The beginnings of documentation practices in child and youth care. *Relational Child and Youth Care Practice, 28*(2), 77–80.

CharityVillage. (2019). *Find a job.* Retrieved from https://charityvillage.com/app/job-listings

Charles, G. (2016). Connecting child and youth practice and supervision: Another piece of the puzzle. In G. Charles, J. Freeman, & T. Garfat (Eds.), *Supervision in child and youth care practice* (pp. 8–21). Cape Town, South Africa: CYC-Net Press.

Charles, G., & Alexander, C. (2016). The beginning of the journey: Supervising students. In G. Charles, J. Freeman, & T. Garfat (Eds.), *Supervision in child and youth care practice* (pp. 80–87). Cape Town, South Africa: CYC-Net Press.

Charles, G., Freeman, J., & Garfat, T. (2016). Introduction. In G. Charles, J. Freeman, & T. Garfat (Eds.), *Supervision in child and youth care practice* (pp. 5–7). Cape Town, South Africa: CYC-Net Press.

Charles, G., Freeman, J., & Garfat, T. (Eds.). (2016). *Supervision in child and youth care practice.* Cape Town, South Africa: CYC-Net Press.

Charles, G., & Garfat, T. (2009). Child and youth care practice in North America: Historical roots and current challenges. *Relational Child and Youth Care Practice, 22*(2), 17–28.

Charles, G., & Garfat, T. (2013). Exploring self to be with other: Relationship in action. In T. Garfat, L. C. Fulcher, & J. Digney (Eds.), *Making moments meaningful in child and youth care practice* (pp. 41–58). Cape Town, South Africa: CYC-Net Press.

Child and Youth Care Certification Board. (2017). *Professional level portfolio guidelines.* Retrieved from https://www.cyccb.org/images/pdf-forms/Professional-level-Portfolio-Guidelines-3-0-Dec-2017.pdf

Child and Youth Care Certification Board. (2019). *Certification process.* Retrieved from https://www.cyccb.org/get-certified/certification-process

Child and Youth Care Education Consortium of British Columbia. (2018). *A model for core curriculum and related outcomes to inform child and youth care education in British Columbia.*

Child and Youth Care Educational Accreditation Board of Canada Research Committee. (2016). *A preliminary investigation into field work models in Canadian child and youth care education* [research report]. Retrieved from http://www.cycaccreditation.ca/docs/FWM.pdf

Clark, N. (2012). Beyond the reflective practitioner. In J. Drolet, N. Clark, & H. Allen (Eds.), *Shifting sites of practice: Field education in Canada* (pp. 79–96). Toronto, ON: Pearson.

Council of Canadian Child and Youth Care Associations. (n.d.). *Child and youth care scope of practice.* Retrieved from http://www.garthgoodwin.info/Scope_of_Practice.pdf

Cross, T. L. (2012). Services to minority populations: What does it mean to be a culturally competent professional? *Journal of Child and Youth Care Work, 24,* 86–89.

Curry, D., Eckles, F., Stuart, C., & Qaqish, B. (2010). National child and youth care practitioner professional certification: Promoting competent care for children and youth. *Child Welfare, 89*(2), 57–77.

Curry, D., Schneider-Munoz, A. J., & Carpenter-Williams, J. (2012). Professional child and youth work practice—five domains of competence: A few lessons learned while highlighting the knowledge base. *Journal of Child and Youth Care Work, 24,* 6–15.

Damsgaard, D. (2011). *Activity-oriented approaches in child and youth care interventions.* Master's thesis, University of Victoria, Victoria, BC, Canada. Retrieved from https://dspace.library.uvic.ca:8443/handle/1828/3506

Danso, R. (2012). The practice of diversity in a multicultural society. In J. Drolet, N. Clark, & H. Allen (Eds.), *Shifting sites of practice: Field education in Canada* (pp. 161–182). Toronto, ON: Pearson.

Danso, R. (2018). Cultural competence and cultural humility: A critical reflection on key cultural diversity concepts. *Journal of Social Work, 18*(4), 410–430.

Davies, S. (2012). Embracing reflective practice. *Education for Primary Care, 23,* 9–12.

D'Cruz, H., Gillingham, P., & Melendez, S. (2007). Reflexivity: A concept and its meanings for practitioners working with children and families. *Critical Social Work, 8*(1), 1–18.

de Finney, S., Little, J. N. C., Skott-Myhre, H., & Gharabaghi, K. (2012). Roundtable: Conversations on conversing in child and youth care. *International Journal of Child, Youth and Family Studies, 3*(2–3), 128–145.

Delano, F. (2010). "If I could supervise my supervisor…": A model for child and youth care workers to own their own supervision. *CYC-Online: E-journal of the International Child and Youth Care Network, 138* (August). Retrieved from https://www.cyc-net.org/cyc-online/cyconline-aug2010-delano.html

Denholm, C. J. (1989). A synthesis of critical ingredients in the development of curriculum at the school of child and youth care. *Journal of Child and Youth Care, 4*(1), 1–16.

Deol, J. (2017). Supervision in child and youth care: A personal reflection on two experiences. *CYC-Online: E-journal of the International Child and Youth Care Network, 223* (September), 47–52. Retrieved from https://www.cyc-net.org/cyc-online/sep2017.pdf

Derksen, T. (2010). The influence of ecological theory in child and youth care: A review of the literature. *International Journal of Child, Youth and Family Studies, 1*(3/4), 326–338.

Dunn, D. S., Beins, B. C., McCarthy, M. A., & Hill, G. W. (2010). *Best practices for teaching beginnings and endings in the psychology major: Research, cases, and recommendations.* New York, NY: Oxford University Press.

First Nations Education Steering Committee. (2008). *First peoples principles of learning.* Retrieved from http://www.fnesc.ca/wp/wp-content/uploads/2015/09/PUB-LFP-POSTER-Principles-of-Learning-First-Peoples-poster-11x17.pdf

Foucault, M. (1965). *Madness and civilization: A history of insanity in the age of reason.* New York, NY: Random House.

Fraser, L. L. (2013). *A journey reconsidered: An autoethnographic exploration of a CYC international practicum placement.* Master's thesis, University of Victoria, Victoria, BC, Canada. Retrieved from https://dspace.library.uvic.ca:8443/handle/1828/5026

Freeman, J. (2013). Reflections on daily life events in child and youth care. *Relational Child and Youth Care Practice, 26*(2), 18–21.

Freeman, J., & Garfat, T. (2014). Being, interpreting, doing: A framework for organizing the characteristics of a relational child and youth care approach. *CYC-Online: E-journal of the International Child and Youth Care Network,* 179 (January), 23–27. Retrieved from https://www.cyc-net.org/cyc-online/jan2014.pdf

Garfat, T. (2005). Editorial: Reflective child and youth care practice. *CYC-Online: E-journal of the International Child and Youth Care Network,* 77 (June). Retrieved from https://www.cyc-net.org/cyc-online/cycol-0605-editor.html

Garfat, T. (2008). Editorial: What makes a person write an article? *Relational Child and Youth Care Practice, 21*(2), 3–4.

Garfat, T. (2012). The inter-personal in-between: An exploration of relational child and youth care practice. In G. Bellefeuille, D. Jamieson, & F. Ricks (Eds.), *Standing on the precipice: Inquiry into the creative potential of child and youth care practice* (pp. 7–34). Edmonton, AB: MacEwan Press.

Garfat, T., & Charles, G. (2007). How am I who I am? Self in child and youth care practice. *Relational Child and Youth Care Practice, 20*(3), 6–16.

Garfat, T., Freeman, J., Gharabaghi, K., & Fulcher, L. (2018). Characteristics of a relational child and youth care approach revisited. *CYC-Online: E-journal of the International Child and Youth Care Network,* 236 (October), 7–44.

Garfat, T., & Fulcher, L. C. (2012). Characteristics of a relational child and youth care approach. In T. Garfat & L. C. Fulcher (Eds.), *Child and youth care in practice* (pp. 7–28). Cape Town, South Africa: CYC-Net Press.

Garfat, T., Fulcher, L. C., & Freeman, J. (2016). A daily life events approach to child and youth care supervision. In G. Charles, J. Freeman, & T. Garfat (Eds.), *Supervision in child and youth care practice* (pp. 28–47). Cape Town, South Africa: CYC-Net Press.

Gharabaghi, K. (2008). Relationships within and outside of the discipline of child and youth care. *Child and Youth Services, 30*(3–4), 235–255.

Gharabaghi, K. (2010). *Professional issues in child and youth care practice.* London, UK: Routledge.

Gharabaghi, K. (2016). External models of supervision. In G. Charles, J. Freeman, & T. Garfat (Eds.), *Supervision in child and youth care practice* (pp. 95–104). Cape Town, South Africa: CYC-Net Press.

Gharabaghi, K. (2018). Self care and the imagination. *CYC-Online: E-journal of the International Child and Youth Care Network,* 236 (October), 59–64.

Gharabaghi, K., & Anderson-Nathe, B. (2015). Editorial: The voice of young people. *Child and Youth Services, 36*(2), 95–97. Retrieved from https://www.cyc-net.org/journals/cys/cys-36-2.html

Gharabaghi, K., & Phelan, J. (2011). Beyond control: Staff perceptions of accountability for children and youth in residential group care. *Residential Treatment for Children and Youth, 28*(1), 75–90.

Government of Canada. (2011). *National occupational classification: 4212 Community and social service workers.* Retrieved from http://noc.esdc.gc.ca/English/NOC/SearchIndex.aspx?ver=06

Government of Canada. (2015). Guide to essential skills profiles. Retrieved from https://www.canada.ca/en/employment-social-development/programs/essential-skills/profiles/guide.html

Gronlund, G., & James, M. (2005). *Focused observations: How to observe children for assessment and curriculum planning.* St. Paul, MN: Redleaf Press.

Hamlet, H. S. (2017). *School counseling practicum and internship: 30 essential lessons.* Los Angeles, CA: SAGE.

Hanley, J. H. (1999). Beyond the tip of the iceberg: Five stages toward cultural competence. *Reaching Today's Youth, 3*(2), 9–12. Retrieved from https://cyc-net.org/reference/refs-culturalcompetence.html

Hann, K. (2017). From kinder cubby to cubicle: A transition from frontline CYC to policy development. *Relational Child and Youth Care Practice, 30*(4), 30–34.

Hare, F. G. (2010). The logic of chronos: Age-based and other mandated transitions. *CYC-Online: E-journal of the International Child and Youth Care Network,* 138 (August). Retrieved from https://www.cyc-net.org/cyc-online/cyconline-august2010.html

Hartje, J., Evans, W., Killian, E., & Brown, R. (2008). Youth worker characteristics and self-reported competency as predictors of intent to continue working with youth. *Child and Youth Care Forum, 37*(1), 27–41.

Hasford, J., Amponsah, P., & Hylton, T. (2018). Anti-racist praxis with street-involved African Canadian youth. In S. Kidd, N. Slesnick, T. Frederick, J. Karabarow, & S. Gaetz (Eds.), *Mental health and addictions interventions for youth experiencing homelessness: Practice strategies for front-line practitioners* (pp. 125–137). Toronto, ON: Canadian Observatory on Homeless Press.

Healthy Kids Community Challenge. (2016). *Needs assessment and asset mapping of Danforth-East York* [research report]. Retrieved from http://healthykidstoronto.com

Heaney Dalton, K. (2018). Finding your resilient self. In P. Kostouros & M. Briegel (Eds.), *Child and youth care practice: Collected wisdom for new practitioners* (pp. 120–123). Cape Town, South Africa: CYC-Net Press.

Hillman, M. (2018). Reflections on CYC practicums. In P. Kostouros & M. Briegel (Eds.), *Child and youth care practice: Collected wisdom for new practitioners* (pp. 69–72). Cape Town, South Africa: CYC-Net Press.

Hills, M. D. (1989). The child and youth care student as an emerging professional practitioner. *Journal of Child and Youth Care, 4*(1), 17–32.

Hoffmann, M. (2013). Impact of training to strengthen child and youth care worker core competencies. *Relational Child and Youth Care Practice, 26*(3), 14–25.

Huebner, A. J. (2003). Positive youth development: The role of competence. In F. A. Villarruel, D. F. Perkins, L. M. Borden, & J. G. Keith (Eds.), *Community youth development: Programs, policies, and practices* (pp. 341–357). Thousand Oaks, CA: SAGE.

Iwasaki, Y. (2014). Reflection on learnings from engaging and working with high-risk, marginalized youth. *Relational Child and Youth Care Practice, 27*(4), 24–35.

Kalau, D. (2018). Before your practicum begins. In P. Kostouros & M. Briegel (Eds.), *Child and youth care practice: Collected wisdom for new practitioners* (pp. 21–32). Cape Town, South Africa: CYC-Net Press.

Kavanagh, H. (2017). Being a subject in supervision matters. *CYC-Online: E-journal of the International Child and Youth Care Network,* 223 (September), 59–66. Retrieved from https://www.cyc-net.org/cyc-online/sep2017.pdf

Keller, T. E. (2005). The stages and development of mentoring relationships. In D. L. DuBois & M. J. Karcher (Eds.), *Handbook of youth mentoring* (pp. 82–99). Thousand Oaks, CA: SAGE.

Keough, M. (2016). Sailing through the fog: Practicums in Canadian child and youth care education. *Relational Child and Youth Care Practice, 29*(3), 123–136.

Kolb, D. A. (1984). *Experiential learning: Experience as the source of learning and development.* Englewood Cliffs, NJ: Prentice Hall.

Kostouros, P. (2018). Preparing for trauma triggers and self-care. In P. Kostouros & M. Briegel (Eds.), *Child and youth care practice: Collected wisdom for new practitioners* (pp. 40–44). Cape Town, South Africa: CYC-Net Press.

Kostouros, P., & Briegel, M. (Eds.). (2018). *Child and youth care practice: Collected wisdom for new practitioners.* Cape Town, South Africa: CYC-Net Press.

Kouri, S. (2015). The canonical self and politicized praxis: A tracing of two concepts. *International Journal of Child, Youth and Family Studies, 6*(4), 595–621.

Laing, S. (2016, April). *Mobilize your job search: CYCC 2440* [PowerPoint slides]. Coquitlam, BC: Douglas College.

Lawrence-Lightfoot, S. (2012). *Exit: The endings that set us free.* New York, NY: Farrar, Straus, and Giroux.

Lawson, S., & Whitehouse, K. (2018). Challenging the competent trainee: Taking risks in the classroom. In T. Wright (Ed.), *How to be a brilliant mentor: Developing outstanding teachers* (2nd ed., pp. 92–107). New York, NY: Routledge.

Lee, E., & Bhuyan, R. (2013). Negotiating within whiteness in cross-cultural clinical encounters. *Social Service Review, 87*(1), 98-130.

Leon, A. M., & Pepe, J. (2010). Utilizing a required documentation course to improve the recording skills of undergraduate social work students. *Journal of Social Service Research, 36*(4), 362–376.

Liptak, S. (2009). Practica experiences. *CYC-Online: E-journal of the International Child and Youth Care Network,* 130 (December). Retrieved from https://www.cyc-net.org/cyc-online/cyconline-dec2009-liptak.html

Little, J. N. (2011). Articulating child and youth care philosophy: Beyond binary constructs. In A. Pence & J. White (Eds.), *Child and youth care: Critical perspectives on pedagogy, practice, and policy* (pp. 3–18). Vancouver, BC: UBC Press.

Loiselle, E., de Finney, S., Khanna, N., & Corcoran, R. (2012). "We need to talk about it!": Doing CYC as politicized praxis. *Child and Youth Services, 33*(3–4), 178–205.

Loiselle, M., & McKenzie, L. (2006, May). *The wellness wheel: An Aboriginal contribution to social work.* Paper presented at the meeting of the First North-American Conference on Spirituality and Social Work, Waterloo, Ontario, Canada. Retrieved from http://www.spiritualityandsocialwork.ca/uploads/2/5/8/0/25806130/loiselle.pdf

Lutsky, N. (2010). Teaching psychology's endings: The simple gifts of a reflective close. In D. S. Dunn, B. C. Beins, M. A. McCarthy, & G. W. Hill (Eds.), *Best practices for teaching beginnings and endings in the psychology major* (pp. 331–345). New York, NY: Oxford University Press.

Martin, D., & Tennant, G. (2008). Child and youth care in the community centre. *Relational Child and Youth Care Practice, 21*(2), 20–26.

Martin, S. (2014). *Take a look: Observation and portfolio assessment in early childhood* (6th ed.). Don Mills, ON: Pearson.

McAleer, D. (2009). *Report writing for the community services.* Toronto, ON: Pearson Education.

McGrath, J. (2018). Attitude is everything. In P. Kostouros & M. Briegel (Eds.), *Child and youth care practice: Collected wisdom for new practitioners* (pp. 124–127). Cape Town, South Africa: CYC-Net Press.

McManus, N. (2009). Reflections on a successful practicum experience in child and youth care. *CYC-Online: E-journal of the International Child and Youth Care Network,* 125 (July). Retrieved from https://www.cyc-net.org/cyc-online/cyconline-july2009-mcmanus.html

Merriam, S. B., Caffarella, R. S., & Baumgartner, L. M. (2007). *Learning in adulthood: A comprehensive guide* (3rd ed.). San Francisco, CA: John Wiley & Sons.

Milne, D. (2018). Suggestions for a successful practicum experience. In P. Kostouros & M. Briegel (Eds.), *Child and youth care practice: Collected wisdom for new practitioners* (pp. 28–32). Cape Town, South Africa: CYC-Net Press.

Modlin, H., & Newbury, J. (2016). Thinking and doing together "as a field." *Relational Child and Youth Care Practice, 29*(1), 6–35.

Moleiro, C., Marques, S., & Pacheco, P. (2011). Cultural diversity competencies in child and youth care services in Portugal: Development of two measures and a brief training program. *Child and Youth Services Review, 33*(5), 767–773.

Moore, C. (2019). The role of supervision. *CYC-Online: E-journal of the International Child and Youth Care Network,* 239 (January), 30–40.

Morris, J. (2010). In-between, across, and within difference: An examination of "cultural competence." *International Journal of Child, Youth and Family Studies, 1*(3/4), 315–325.

Moscrip, S., & Brown, A. (1989). Child and youth care: The transition from student to practitioner. *Journal of Child and Youth Care, 4*(1), 71–80.

Myers-Kiser, P. (2016). *The human services internship: Getting the most from your experience* (4th ed.). Boston, MA: Cengage Learning.

The National Mentoring Partnerships. (2015). *"They always come and they never say goodbye:" Understanding healthy closure in youth mentoring.* Retrieved from www.mentoring.org

Newbury, J. (2007). Reflexivity in practice: Reflections on an overseas practicum. *Relational Child and Youth Care Practice, 20*(2), 50–56.

Oates, R. (2016). Exploring child and youth care internships. *Relational Child and Youth Care Practice, 29*(3), 46–58.

O'Hara, A., Weber, Z., & Levine, K. (2010). *Skills for human service practice: Working with individuals, groups, and communities.* Don Mills, ON: Oxford University Press.

Ostinelli, P. (2015). The essential first CYC practicum. *Relational Child and Youth Care Practice, 28*(3), 36–40.

Oxford Dictionary. (2018). Reflection. Retrieved from https://en.oxforddictionaries.com/definition/reflect

Pacini-Ketchabaw, V. (2011). Rethinking developmental theories in child and youth care. In A. Pence & J. White (Eds.), *Child and youth care: Critical perspectives on pedagogy, practice, and policy* (pp. 19–32). Vancouver, BC: UBC Press.

Peterson, A. M. (2011). *Mentor perceptions of closure in formal youth mentoring relationships.* Master's thesis, Eastern Illinois University, Charleston, Illinois, USA. Retrieved from https://thekeep.eiu.edu/cgi/viewcontent.cgi?article=1695&context=theses

Phelan, J. (2005). Child and youth care education: The creation of articulate practitioners. *Child and Youth Care Forum, 34*(5), 347–355.

Phelan, J. (2012). Building relationships: A developmentally responsive approach to child and youth care intervention. In G. Bellefeuille, D. Jamieson, & F. Ricks (Eds.), *Standing on the precipice: Inquiry into the creative potential of child and youth care practice* (pp. 73–106). Edmonton, AB: MacEwan Press.

Ramey, H. L., Lawford, H. L., & Vachon, W. (2017). Youth-adult partnerships in work with youth: An overview. *Journal of Youth Development, 12*(4), 38–60.

Reynolds, V. (n.d.). "Zone of fabulousness": Q&A with Vikki Reynolds. Retrieved from https://fsw.ucalgary.ca/news/zone-fabulousness-q-vikki-reynolds

Richardson, C., & Reynolds, V. (2012). "Here we are, amazingly alive": Holding ourselves together with an ethic of social justice in community work. *International Journal of Child, Youth and Family Studies, 1*, 1–19.

Richmond, A., Braughton, J., & Borden, L. M. (2018). Training youth program staff on the importance of cultural responsiveness and humility: Current status and future directions in professional development. *Children and Youth Services Review, 93*, 501–507.

Ricks, F. (1989). Self-awareness model for training and application in child and youth care. *Journal of Child and Youth Care, 4*(1), 33–41.

Ricks, F. (2011). Self-awareness model for training and application in child and youth care. *CYC-Online: E-journal of the International Child and Youth Care Network, 147*, 5–11.

Ricks, F., & Griffin, S. (1995). *Best choice: Ethical decision making in human services practice.* Victoria, BC: Ministry of Skills, Training and Labour.

Ruth-Sahd, L. A. (2003). Reflective practice: A critical analysis of data-based studies and implications for nursing education. *Journal of Nursing Education, 42*(11), 488–497.

Ryerson University, School of Child and Youth Care. (n.d.). *Pre-internship handbook.* Toronto, ON: Author. Retrieved December 31, 2018, from https://www.ryerson.ca/content/dam/cyc/Documents/student-resources/internships/pre-internship-handbook.pdf

Ryerson University, School of Child and Youth Care. (n.d.). *Student internship manual: CYC 30 a/b.* Toronto, ON: Author. Retrieved December 31, 2018, from https://www.ryerson.ca/content/dam/cyc/Documents/student-resources/internships/internship-manual-cyc-30-ab.pdf

Sapin, K. (2009). *Essential skills for youth work practice.* London, UK: SAGE.

Saraceno, J. (2012). Mapping whiteness and coloniality in the human service field: Possibilities for a praxis of social justice in child and youth care. *International Journal of Child, Youth and Family Studies, 3*(2–3), 248–271.

Sauvé-Griffin, J. (2009). When we stop to ask why: Reflective practice in action. *Relational Child and Youth Care Practice, 22*(3), 44–45.

Schon, D. A. (1983). *The reflective practitioner: How professionals think in action.* New York, NY: Basic Books.

Sensoy, Ö., & DiAngelo, R. (2017). *Is everyone really equal? An introduction to key concepts in social justice education* (2nd ed.). New York, NY: Teachers College Press.

Sercombe, H. (2010). *Youth work ethics*. London, UK: SAGE.

Shaw, K., Reid, J., & Trites, J. (2013). Using daily life events in the context of a child and youth care diploma program. *Relational Child and Youth Care Practice, 26*(2), 47–52.

Shaw, K., & Trites, J. (2013). Child and youth care education is child and youth care practice: Connecting with the characteristics of practice. *Relational Child and Youth Care Practice, 26*(4), 11–15.

Shebib, B. (2013). *Choices: Interviewing and counselling skills for Canadians* (5th ed.). Toronto, ON: Pearson.

Simpson, J. (2009). *Everyone belongs: A toolkit for applying intersectionality*. Retrieved March 31, 2019, from https://www.criaw-icref.ca/sites/criaw/files/Everyone_Belongs_e.pdf

Skott-Myhre, H. A. (2005). Radical youthwork: Creating a politics of mutual liberation for youth and adults. *CYC-Online: E-journal of the International Child and Youth Care Network, 75* (April). Retrieved from https://www.cyc-net.org/cyc-online/cycol-0405-radical.html

Skott-Myhre, H. A. (2008). *Youth and subculture as creative force: Creating new spaces for radical youth work*. Toronto, ON: University of Toronto Press.

Snell, H. (2015). Editorial: Watch yourself! *Relational Child and Youth Care Practice, 28*(3), 3–5.

Snell, H., Magnuson, D., McGrath, J., & Pauls, M. (2018, May). Outstanding in the field? Starting a conversation about field practicum in CYC postsecondary education. In Child and Youth Care Association of British Columbia (Chair), *Transitions and transformations: Influencing change through relational practice*. Symposium conducted at the meeting of the 20th and 12th Triennial International Child and Youth Care Conference, Richmond, BC, Canada.

Snell, H., McGrath, J., Pauls, M., & Magnuson, D. (Forthcoming). *What is the purpose of fieldwork in higher education? The example of Canadian child and youth care.*

Spencer, R., & Basualdo-Delmonico, A. (2014). Termination and closure of mentoring relationships. In D. L. DuBois & M. J. Karcher (Eds.), *Handbook of youth mentoring* (2nd ed., pp. 469–479). Thousand Oaks, CA: SAGE.

Staudt, M. M., Dulmus, C., & Bennett, G. A. (2003). Facilitating writing by practitioners: Survey of practitioners who have published. *Social Work, 48*(1), 75–83.

Stenbeck, Z. (2018). Building child and youth care relationships. In P. Kostouros & M. Briegel (Eds.), *Child and youth care practice: Collected wisdom for new practitioners* (pp. 54–64). Cape Town, South Africa: CYC-Net Press.

Stuart, C. (2013). *Foundations of child and youth care* (2nd ed.). Dubuque, IA: Kendall Hunt.

Szewello Allen, H. (2012). Getting started: Preparing to learn in the field. In J. Drolet, N. Clark, & H. Allen (Eds.), *Shifting sites of practice: Field education in Canada* (pp. 19–38). Toronto, ON: Pearson.

Szewello Allen, H., & Robertson, J. (2012). Transitioning from student to practitioner: Launching your career. In J. Drolet, N. Clark, & H. Allen (Eds.), *Shifting sites of practice: Field education in Canada* (pp. 267–283). Toronto, ON: Pearson.

Testa, D., & Egan, R. (2015). How useful are discussion boards and written critical reflections in helping social work students critically reflect on their field education placements? *Qualitative Social Work, 15*(2), 263–280.

Thompson, J. (2018). Always be prepared. In P. Kostouros & M. Briegel (Eds.), *Child and youth care practice: Collected wisdom for new practitioners* (pp. 45–47). Cape Town, South Africa: CYC-Net Press.

Tilsen, J. (2013). *Therapeutic conversations with queer youth: Transcending homonormativity and constructing preferred identities*. Lanham, MD: Rowman & Littlefield.

Tilsen, J. (2018). *Narrative approaches to youth work: Conversational skills for a critical practice*. New York, NY: Routledge.

Truth and Reconciliation Commission of Canada. (2015). *Truth and Reconciliation Commission of Canada: Calls to action*. Retrieved from http://trc.ca/assets/pdf/Calls_to_Action_English2.pdf

Ungar, M. (2004). A constructionist discourse on resilience: Multiple contexts, multiple realities among at-risk children and youth. *Youth and Society, 35*(3), 341–365.

Ungar, M. (2008). Putting resilience theory into action: Five principles for intervention. In L. Liebenberg & M. Ungar (Eds.), *Resilience in action* (pp. 17–38). Toronto, ON: University of Toronto Press.

University of the Fraser Valley. (2017). *CYC 410: Comprehensive field guide for students and field supervisors.* Retrieved from https://www.ufv.ca/media/assets/cyfs/practicum-centre/CYC-410-Field-Guide-201902.pdf

VanderVen, K. (2012). You are what you do and become what you've done: The role of activity in development of self—a non-linear dynamic systems relational approach. *Journal of Child and Youth Care Work, 24,* 205–219.

Verniest, L. (2006). Allying with the medicine wheel: Social work practice with Aboriginal peoples. *Critical Social Work, 7*(1). Retrieved February 7, 2020, from https://ojs.uwindsor.ca/index.php/csw/article/download/5778/4717?inline=1

Vradenburg, K. (2007). *Building bridges and blurring lines: The value of reflexivity in CYC-based humanitarian practice.* Master's thesis, University of Victoria, Victoria, BC, Canada.

Walker, J. A. (2003). The essential youth worker: Supports and opportunities for professional success. In F. A. Villarruel, D. F. Perkins, L. M. Borden, & J. G. Keith (Eds.), *Community youth development: Programs, policies, and practices* (pp. 373–393). Thousand Oaks, CA: SAGE.

Weston, A. (2006). *Creative problem-solving in ethics.* New York, NY: Oxford University Press.

White, J. (2007). Knowing, doing and being in context: A praxis-oriented approach to child and youth care. *Child and Youth Care Forum, 36*(5), 225–244.

White, J. (2011). Re-stor(y)ing professional ethics in child and youth care: Toward more contextualized, reflexive and generative practices. In A. R. Pence & J. White (Eds.), *Child and youth care: Critical perspectives on pedagogy, practice, and policy* (pp. 33–52). Vancouver, BC: UBC Press.

Wiedow, J. S. (2014). Redefining supervision in the field of youth work. In *Moving youth work practice forward: Reflections on autonomy and authority* (pp. 107–119). Retrieved from http://web.augsburg.edu/sabo/NorthStarWorkingpapers2013-2014.pdf

Winfield, J. (2009). An exploration of reflection and reflective practice. *CYC-Online: E-journal of the International Child and Youth Care Network,* 119 (January). Retrieved from http://www.cyc-net.org/cyc-online/cyconline-jan2009-winfield.html

Winnipeg Outreach Network. (2018). *Winnipeg street guide.* Retrieved from https://www.mys.ca/news/read,article/188/winnipeg-outreach-network-launches-new-guide-for-street-involved-youth-and-adults

Yoon, J. (2012). Courageous conversations in child and youth care: Nothing lost in the telling. *International Journal of Child, Youth and Family Studies, 3*(2–3), 164–186.

Zak, J. (2015). Mindfulness in CYC practice: A look within to prevent professional burnout. *Relational Child and Youth Care Practice, 28*(3), 92–97.

Zinga, D. (2012). Journeying with youth: Re-centering Indigeneity in child and youth care. *Child and Youth Services Review, 33*(3–4), 258–280.

Zubizarreta, J. (2009). *The learning portfolio: Reflective practice for improving student learning* (2nd ed.). San Francisco, CA: Jossey-Bass.

YOUR LEARNING JOURNAL

This week's date: _____

Summary of this week's activities, tasks, and responsibilities:

_____

_____

This week, I attended to relationship development by:

_____

This week, I was challenged by or struggled when:

_____

Something I learned about myself or young people this week was:

_____

Based on my reflections, something I need to focus on improving is:

_____

Briefly describe one intervention—who, what, where, when, and how. What informed and influenced my approach to this encounter? What was the outcome? What is one alternative way of responding to the encounter?

_____

_____

_____

_____

_____

_____

What theories, coursework, readings, or other sources of knowledge did I draw upon this week that influenced my approach to the situation(s) I encountered?

_____

A question or situation I'd like to explore with my supervisor the next time we meet is:

_____

_____

This Week's Date: _____

Summary of this week's activities, tasks, and responsibilities:

_____

This week at practicum, I noticed…

_____

_____

_____

_____

_____

_____

_____

_____

_____

_____

_____

_____

_____

_____

_____

_____

_____

_____

_____

_____

_____

YOUR LEARNING JOURNAL

This week's date: _____

Summary of this week's activities, tasks, and responsibilities:

_____

_____

This week, I attended to relationship development by:

_____

This week, I was challenged by or struggled when:

_____

Something I learned about myself or young people this week was:

_____

Based on my reflections, something I need to focus on improving is:

_____

Briefly describe one intervention—who, what, where, when, and how. What informed and influenced my approach to this encounter? What was the outcome? What is one alternative way of responding to the encounter?

_____

_____

_____

_____

_____

What theories, coursework, readings, or other sources of knowledge did I draw upon this week that influenced my approach to the situation(s) I encountered?

_____

A question or situation I'd like to explore with my supervisor the next time we meet is:

_____

_____

This Week's Date: _____

Summary of this week's activities, tasks, and responsibilities:

_____

This week at practicum, I noticed...

_____

_____

_____

_____

_____

_____

_____

_____

_____

_____

_____

_____

_____

_____

_____

_____

_____

_____

_____

_____

_____

YOUR LEARNING JOURNAL

This week's date: _____

Summary of this week's activities, tasks, and responsibilities:

_____

_____

This week, I attended to relationship development by:

_____

This week, I was challenged by or struggled when:

_____

Something I learned about myself or young people this week was:

_____

Based on my reflections, something I need to focus on improving is:

_____

Briefly describe one intervention—who, what, where, when, and how. What informed and influenced my approach to this encounter? What was the outcome? What is one alternative way of responding to the encounter?

_____

_____

_____

_____

_____

_____

What theories, coursework, readings, or other sources of knowledge did I draw upon this week that influenced my approach to the situation(s) I encountered?

_____

A question or situation I'd like to explore with my supervisor the next time we meet is:

_____

_____

This Week's Date: _____

Summary of this week's activities, tasks, and responsibilities:

_____

This week at practicum, I noticed…

_____

_____

_____

_____

_____

_____

_____

_____

_____

_____

_____

_____

_____

_____

_____

_____

_____

_____

_____

_____

_____

_____

YOUR LEARNING JOURNAL

This week's date: _____

Summary of this week's activities, tasks, and responsibilities:

_____

_____

This week, I attended to relationship development by:

_____

This week, I was challenged by or struggled when:

_____

Something I learned about myself or young people this week was:

_____

Based on my reflections, something I need to focus on improving is:

_____

Briefly describe one intervention—who, what, where, when, and how. What informed and influenced my approach to this encounter? What was the outcome? What is one alternative way of responding to the encounter?

_____

_____

_____

_____

_____

_____

What theories, coursework, readings, or other sources of knowledge did I draw upon this week that influenced my approach to the situation(s) I encountered?

_____

A question or situation I'd like to explore with my supervisor the next time we meet is:

_____

_____

This Week's Date: _____

Summary of this week's activities, tasks, and responsibilities:

_____

This week at practicum, I noticed…

_____

_____

_____

_____

_____

_____

_____

_____

_____

_____

_____

_____

_____

_____

_____

_____

_____

_____

_____

_____

_____

_____

YOUR LEARNING JOURNAL

This week's date: _____

Summary of this week's activities, tasks, and responsibilities:

_____

_____

This week, I attended to relationship development by:

_____

This week, I was challenged by or struggled when:

_____

Something I learned about myself or young people this week was:

_____

Based on my reflections, something I need to focus on improving is:

_____

Briefly describe one intervention—who, what, where, when, and how. What informed and influenced my approach to this encounter? What was the outcome? What is one alternative way of responding to the encounter?

_____

_____

_____

_____

_____

_____

What theories, coursework, readings, or other sources of knowledge did I draw upon this week that influenced my approach to the situation(s) I encountered?

_____

A question or situation I'd like to explore with my supervisor the next time we meet is:

_____

_____

This Week's Date: _____

Summary of this week's activities, tasks, and responsibilities:

_____

This week at practicum, I noticed…

_____

_____

_____

_____

_____

_____

_____

_____

_____

_____

_____

_____

_____

_____

_____

_____

_____

_____

_____

_____

_____

_____

YOUR LEARNING JOURNAL

This week's date: _____

Summary of this week's activities, tasks, and responsibilities:

_____

_____

This week, I attended to relationship development by:

_____

This week, I was challenged by or struggled when:

_____

Something I learned about myself or young people this week was:

_____

Based on my reflections, something I need to focus on improving is:

_____

Briefly describe one intervention—who, what, where, when, and how. What informed and influenced my approach to this encounter? What was the outcome? What is one alternative way of responding to the encounter?

_____

_____

_____

_____

_____

What theories, coursework, readings, or other sources of knowledge did I draw upon this week that influenced my approach to the situation(s) I encountered?

_____

A question or situation I'd like to explore with my supervisor the next time we meet is:

_____

_____

This Week's Date: _____

Summary of this week's activities, tasks, and responsibilities:

_____

This week at practicum, I noticed…

_____

_____

_____

_____

_____

_____

_____

_____

_____

_____

_____

_____

_____

_____

_____

_____

_____

_____

_____

_____

_____

YOUR LEARNING JOURNAL

This week's date: _____

Summary of this week's activities, tasks, and responsibilities:

_____

_____

This week, I attended to relationship development by:

_____

This week, I was challenged by or struggled when:

_____

Something I learned about myself or young people this week was:

_____

Based on my reflections, something I need to focus on improving is:

_____

Briefly describe one intervention—who, what, where, when, and how. What informed and influenced my approach to this encounter? What was the outcome? What is one alternative way of responding to the encounter?

_____

_____

_____

_____

_____

What theories, coursework, readings, or other sources of knowledge did I draw upon this week that influenced my approach to the situation(s) I encountered?

_____

A question or situation I'd like to explore with my supervisor the next time we meet is:

_____

_____

This Week's Date: _____

Summary of this week's activities, tasks, and responsibilities:

_____

This week at practicum, I noticed…

_____

_____

_____

_____

_____

_____

_____

_____

_____

_____

_____

_____

_____

_____

_____

_____

_____

_____

_____

_____

_____

YOUR LEARNING JOURNAL

This week's date: _____

Summary of this week's activities, tasks, and responsibilities:

_____

_____

This week, I attended to relationship development by:

_____

This week, I was challenged by or struggled when:

_____

Something I learned about myself or young people this week was:

_____

Based on my reflections, something I need to focus on improving is:

_____

Briefly describe one intervention—who, what, where, when, and how. What informed and influenced my approach to this encounter? What was the outcome? What is one alternative way of responding to the encounter?

_____

_____

_____

_____

_____

What theories, coursework, readings, or other sources of knowledge did I draw upon this week that influenced my approach to the situation(s) I encountered?

_____

A question or situation I'd like to explore with my supervisor the next time we meet is:

_____

_____

This Week's Date: _____

Summary of this week's activities, tasks, and responsibilities:

_____

This week at practicum, I noticed…

_____

_____

_____

_____

_____

_____

_____

_____

_____

_____

_____

_____

_____

_____

_____

_____

_____

_____

_____

_____

_____

_____

YOUR LEARNING JOURNAL

This week's date: _____

Summary of this week's activities, tasks, and responsibilities:

_____

_____

This week, I attended to relationship development by:

_____

This week, I was challenged by or struggled when:

_____

Something I learned about myself or young people this week was:

_____

Based on my reflections, something I need to focus on improving is:

_____

Briefly describe one intervention—who, what, where, when, and how. What informed and influenced my approach to this encounter? What was the outcome? What is one alternative way of responding to the encounter?

_____

_____

_____

_____

_____

What theories, coursework, readings, or other sources of knowledge did I draw upon this week that influenced my approach to the situation(s) I encountered?

_____

A question or situation I'd like to explore with my supervisor the next time we meet is:

_____

_____

This Week's Date: _____

Summary of this week's activities, tasks, and responsibilities:

_____

This week at practicum, I noticed...

_____

_____

_____

_____

_____

_____

_____

_____

_____

_____

_____

_____

_____

_____

_____

_____

_____

_____

_____

_____

_____

_____

YOUR LEARNING JOURNAL

This week's date: _____

Summary of this week's activities, tasks, and responsibilities:

_____

_____

This week, I attended to relationship development by:

_____

This week, I was challenged by or struggled when:

_____

Something I learned about myself or young people this week was:

_____

Based on my reflections, something I need to focus on improving is:

_____

Briefly describe one intervention—who, what, where, when, and how. What informed and influenced my approach to this encounter? What was the outcome? What is one alternative way of responding to the encounter?

_____

_____

_____

_____

_____

What theories, coursework, readings, or other sources of knowledge did I draw upon this week that influenced my approach to the situation(s) I encountered?

_____

A question or situation I'd like to explore with my supervisor the next time we meet is:

_____

_____

This Week's Date: _____

Summary of this week's activities, tasks, and responsibilities:

_____

This week at practicum, I noticed...

_____

_____

_____

_____

_____

_____

_____

_____

_____

_____

_____

_____

_____

_____

_____

_____

_____

_____

_____

_____

_____

_____

_____

YOUR LEARNING JOURNAL

This week's date: _____

Summary of this week's activities, tasks, and responsibilities:

_____

_____

This week, I attended to relationship development by:

_____

This week, I was challenged by or struggled when:

_____

Something I learned about myself or young people this week was:

_____

Based on my reflections, something I need to focus on improving is:

_____

Briefly describe one intervention—who, what, where, when, and how. What informed and influenced my approach to this encounter? What was the outcome? What is one alternative way of responding to the encounter?

_____

_____

_____

_____

_____

What theories, coursework, readings, or other sources of knowledge did I draw upon this week that influenced my approach to the situation(s) I encountered?

_____

A question or situation I'd like to explore with my supervisor the next time we meet is:

_____

_____

This Week's Date: _____

Summary of this week's activities, tasks, and responsibilities:

_____

This week at practicum, I noticed…

_____

_____

_____

_____

_____

_____

_____

_____

_____

_____

_____

_____

_____

_____

_____

_____

_____

_____

_____

_____

_____

YOUR LEARNING JOURNAL

This week's date: _____

Summary of this week's activities, tasks, and responsibilities:

_____

_____

This week, I attended to relationship development by:

_____

This week, I was challenged by or struggled when:

_____

Something I learned about myself or young people this week was:

_____

Based on my reflections, something I need to focus on improving is:

_____

Briefly describe one intervention—who, what, where, when, and how. What informed and influenced my approach to this encounter? What was the outcome? What is one alternative way of responding to the encounter?

_____

_____

_____

_____

_____

What theories, coursework, readings, or other sources of knowledge did I draw upon this week that influenced my approach to the situation(s) I encountered?

_____

A question or situation I'd like to explore with my supervisor the next time we meet is:

_____

_____

This Week's Date: _____

Summary of this week's activities, tasks, and responsibilities:

_____

This week at practicum, I noticed…

_____

_____

_____

_____

_____

_____

_____

_____

_____

_____

_____

_____

_____

_____

_____

_____

_____

_____

_____

_____

_____

_____

_____

_____

YOUR LEARNING JOURNAL

This week's date: _____

Summary of this week's activities, tasks, and responsibilities:

_____

_____

This week, I attended to relationship development by:

_____

This week, I was challenged by or struggled when:

_____

Something I learned about myself or young people this week was:

_____

Based on my reflections, something I need to focus on improving is:

_____

Briefly describe one intervention—who, what, where, when, and how. What informed and influenced my approach to this encounter? What was the outcome? What is one alternative way of responding to the encounter?

_____

_____

_____

_____

_____

What theories, coursework, readings, or other sources of knowledge did I draw upon this week that influenced my approach to the situation(s) I encountered?

_____

A question or situation I'd like to explore with my supervisor the next time we meet is:

_____

_____

This Week's Date: _____

Summary of this week's activities, tasks, and responsibilities:

_____

This week at practicum, I noticed...

_____

_____

_____

_____

_____

_____

_____

_____

_____

_____

_____

_____

_____

_____

_____

_____

_____

_____

_____

_____